Starting

Congregations

Second Edition

By Daniel R. Sanchez, D.Min., Ph.D.
Ebbie C. Smith, Ph.D.

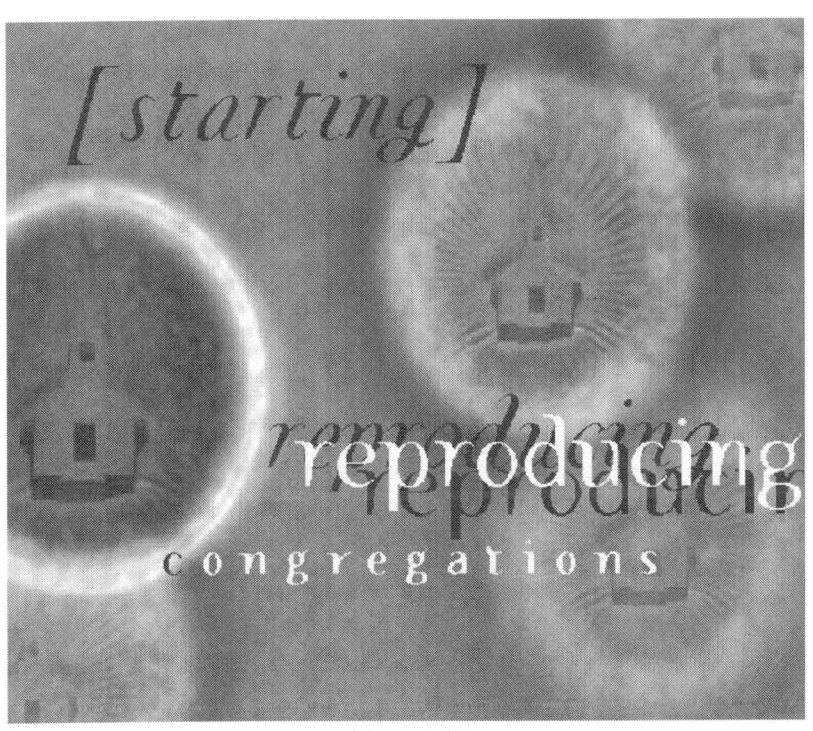

ChurchStarting.net

STARTING REPRODUCING CONGREGATIONS
Second Edition
Copyright © 2011 by
Daniel R. Sánchez and Ebbie C. Smith

All Rights Reserved

www.ChurchStarting.net

Cover Design by

Daniel E. Sánchez
daniel@mayaadvertisingdesign.com
Dallas, Texas

Library of Congress Cataloging-in-Publication Data

Sánchez, Daniel R 1936 –
Ebbie C. Smith 1932 –
Includes bibliographical references

ISBN   978-0-9846207-6-0
0-9846207-6-1

Printed and bound in the United States of America

DEDICATION

To our spouses

Carmen B. Sánchez
Donna R. Smith

TABLE OF CONTENTS

PART 2: Formulate Ministry Plans

PART 3 Cultivate Community

PART 4 Implement New Congregation

PART 5 Develop New Congregations

PART 6: Reproduce New Congregations

CONCLUSION
ABOUT THE AUTHORS
Daniel R. Sanchez, D. Min. Ph. D.
Ebbie C. Smith, Ph. D.

INTRODUCTION

The 21st Century Church is poised to make the greatest church starting impact in Christian history. This promise rests primarily on two factors: a worldwide profound sense of spiritual hunger and an unprecedented commitment to church starting.

A convergence of religious and socio-political transitions in the dusk of the 20th Century has contributed toward a deep sense of spiritual hunger in the dawn of the 21st Century in both the western and non-western areas. The astonishing collapse of communism, the dramatic decline of atheism, and the significant transition from a secular to a postmodern worldview have led key church leaders to conclude that a "new Apostolic Age" has emerged.[1] George Hunter[2] explains that the God-centered Christendom Paradigm[3] of the Middle Ages, followed by the secularism of the 20th century, has been superseded by a postmodern worldview.[4]

The Postmodern Challenge

Diogenes Allen describes this postmodern worldview as one in which there is "widespread disillusionment with the technological society produced by scientific rationalism, a disquieting feeling of alienation, and a profound desire for supernatural empowerment."[5] Leith Anderson observes that: "After decades of advancing secularism and declining spiritual interest, a spiritual awakening is sweeping the World."[6]

Spiritual interest, however, does not necessarily mean an interest in Christianity or the church. Many are searching for an experience with God and are joining vibrant congregations while others are seeking to quench their spiritual thirst in such activities as the New Age movement, introspection, astrology, and supernatural powers through human mediums (palm readers, fortune tellers, and spiritual gurus.[7]

This intense spiritual hunger is good news for the Church for Christianity faces an unprecedented opportunity to reach millions with the gospel of Jesus Christ and to disciple them in congregations that cultivate a genuine sense of spirituality. However, due to their secularist background, large segments of today's Western society, even in America's "Bible Belt," know little about the basic truths of Christianity.[8] Twenty-first century church starters in Western societies, therefore, face the urgent challenge of understanding, reaching, and discipling people who are spiritually hungry, yet may be resistant to, indifferent toward, or ignorant about Christianity.

The Apostolic 21st Century

There is a sense in which the non-Western world has always resembled the socio-religious context of the early church. The modern involvement of people in folk religions is very similar to the animism that people practiced in the first century.[9] For years, missionaries have encountered the animistic practices of spiritism, demonology, witchcraft, and divination in non-Western societies.[10] In these contexts church starters today encounter the challenge of reaching and discipling people groups who have a predisposition for that which is spiritual yet are steeped in the superstition, fear, and the oppression of animistic practices.

Other church starters face the challenge of reaching people groups who are Buddhists, Hindus, Muslims, nominal Christians, or syncretistic Christians and have not come to a saving knowledge of Jesus Christ. In addition to the challenge of reaching people groups with different religious and ideological backgrounds, many contemporary church starters encounter the hurdles of seeking to reach people in culturally pluralistic urban societies.

To meet this "new Apostolic Age" the 21st century Church urgently needs to return to the "Apostolic Paradigm" of the first century Church. This Apostolic Paradigm as described by Loren Mead is one in which "the early church was conscious of itself as a faithful people surrounded by a hostile environment to which each member was called to witness to God's love in Christ."[11] He explains:

> The central reality of this church was a local community, a congregation "called out" (ecclesia) of the world. It was a community that lived by the power and the values of Jesus. That power and those val-

ues were preserved and shared within the intimate community through apostolic teaching and preaching, through fellowship itself, and through ritual acts, preeminently the sharing of the bread and wine of the Eucharist. You gained entrance into this community only when the community was convinced that you also held those values and had been born into that power. The community was intense and personal. Belonging to it was an experience of being in immediate touch with God's Spirit... The other side of this community image was an image of a world environment that was hostile to what the church stood for. The world was not neutral; it was opposed to the community... The community was to "Go into the world.." To be "in the world but not of it." Much of the congregation's life was defined by its sense of being on the mission frontier to a hostile world. But it also perceived that the meaning of its life was to build up its members with the courage, strength, and skill to communicate God's good news within the hostile world. Its internal task was to order its life, to establish roles and relationships that matured the members of the congregation in the mission that involved each member. Members perceived that the power to engage in that mission—the crossing of the missionary boundary—came from the Holy Spirit.[12]

To be effective, the 21st century church needs to have the power and values of Jesus evidenced by the 1st century church. The 21st century Church also needs to have the wisdom that the 1st century church demonstrated in communicating the gospel. Hunter explains the four objectives that the early apostolic church had in the communication of Christianity: "1) Facing a population with no knowledge of the gospel, the Christian movement had to *inform* people of the story of Jesus, the good news, its claims, and its offer. 2) Facing hostile populations and the persecution of the state, the Church had to "win friends and *influence people*." 3) Facing an Empire with several entrenched religions, the Christians had to *convince* people of Christianity's truth, or at least its plausibility. 4) Since entry into the faith is by an act of the will, Christians had to *invite* people to adopt this faith and join the messianic community and follow Jesus as Lord. These were the components of persuasion in the ancient apostolic setting."[13]

Responding to the Challenge

Many 21st-century church starters also face a population with no knowledge of the gospel, hostile attitudes, and numerous entrenched religions. Good news, however, remains as church starters strive to inform, influence, convince, and invite people to commit to Jesus Christ and join a community of fellow believers. Today, more church starting strategies are being designed and implemented than ever before in the history of Christianity. Today more innovative and culturally appropriate church starting models are being developed. More church starting organizations exist today than ever before. More International Mission Agencies are establishing church starting as their top priority than previously was the case. More two-thirds world church starters are being commissioned and sent than ever before in missionary history. Today more church starting movements are sweeping entire areas of the world. Today, more men and women are responding to the call, receiving specialized training, and positioning themselves in strategic areas to start vibrant, reproducing churches. Today, more local churches are promoting and sponsoring church starting efforts. Today, numerous theological seminaries are not only offering church starting courses but also entire degrees in Church Planting. Some of these seminaries have linked with domestic and international mission agencies to make it possible for students to complete their final year's academic work while doing a church starting assignment on the field under supervision.[14] Today, more technological tools are being placed at the disposal of church starters. Of even greater significance is the fact that today more people are involved in concerted efforts to pray for the establishment of vibrant, reproducing churches at home and around the world.

In his book, *Evangelism in the Early Church*,[15] Michael Green points out that a convergence of factors (or pathways) contributed toward the breath-taking expansion of the gospel in the first Century. He states that the *pax Romana* made it possible for Christians (e.g., Paul) to move safely and rapidly (through the road systems of the Empire) in order to communicate the gospel. The Greek culture, with a widely used language, highly respected thought patterns, and even the methods of the Greek philosophers, contributed to a *preparatio evangelica* upon which Christians could build in order to evangelize people.

In addition to this, the Jewish religion with its monotheistic emphasis, ethical values, synagogue worship, Scripture reading, and zeal to gain adherents, paved the way for the rapid expansion of the gospel in Jerusalem, Judea, Samaria, and to the ends of the earth. The convergence of factors in our new Apostolic Age are not a coincidence but a providential ordering of pathways through which millions of people can be evangelized, and an unprecedented number of churches can be started for the glory of God.

In response to the marvelous challenge of this new Apostolic Age, this book, *Starting Reproducing Congregations,* presents biblically sound principles, logically developed procedures, and innovative, practical methodologies that will enable church starters to design contemporary, culturally contextualized strategies to start and multiply churches at home and around the world.

To accomplish **this vision**, the book outlines a church starting process consisting of the phases: 1) Prepare, 2) Formulate, 3) Cultivate, 4) Implement, 5) Develop, and 6) Reproduce.

Some books focus on principles and others on methods. This book's intends to provide church starters with principles, processes, and practical methodologies for contextualized, 21st-century church starting.

PART 1

Prepare Ministry Foundations

Church starting, like starting any other new endeavor, requires and demands adequate preparation. In fact, preparation marks the first and vital stage in the pilgrimage to any effort at starting new congregations. Prior to beginning a new church, the church starter needs to have a strong motivational, biblical, spiritual, evangelistic, strategic, philosophical, leadership, and financial foundation. In this section, we focus on the concepts that contribute to the establishment of a solid, balanced and challenging foundation for 21st Century church starting.

CHAPTER 1

MOTIVATIONAL FOUNDATION

Church members often ask, "Why do we need to start new churches?" Some believe that we have enough churches already. Others feel that there are better ways to win the lost than to make the investment of people, time, and money to start new churches. Others contend that starting new churches weakens the leadership and financial resources of existing churches. Still others think that only strong churches should start new congregations.

Such misconceptions and lack of vision prevent many Christians and churches from committing themselves to the task of starting churches. Biblical, as well as experiential reasons indicate why all Christians and churches should be involved in church starting. Armed with these motivations, church starters need to be prepared to effectively answer typical objections as well.

Biblical Reasons for Church Starting

The Bible presents at least five reasons for starting new churches that give a solid foundation for church starting.

New Churches Extend the Kingdom of God

The first biblical reason for starting new churches is based upon the message that Jesus Christ proclaimed. Mark summarizes this message: *"The time has come... The Kingdom of God is near. Repent and believe the good news"* (1:15). Jesus proclaimed the rule, reign, or sovereignty of God over all creation. He proclaimed the kingdom of God by both word and deed. However, while the incarnation of Jesus fulfilled Old Testament prophecy (and in this sense the kingdom is "already" fulfilled), yet the consummation of the kingdom of God is still waiting to be fulfilled at the end of the age (and in this sense it is "not yet").[16] During this age, believers live out the kingdom of God as they display their submission to the Lordship of Christ.

The Kingdom of God is not to be confused with the institutional church. The church is a community of persons drawn together under the Lordship of Christ. Thus, the kingdom actually creates the church. "The church is but the result of the coming of God's Kingdom into the world by the mission of Jesus Christ."[17] However, the church should be a witness to that kingdom by its words and its deeds.

So, how do new churches relate to the kingdom of God? New churches are created by the dynamic rule of God that has been actualized in the coming of Jesus Christ, and new churches participate in the mission of God (the *missio dei*) to announce, by word and deed, the sovereignty of God over all.

New churches have the opportunity to demonstrate the kingdom of God, even though imperfectly as a genuine counter culture to a pagan culture around them. New churches are needed today because many existing congregations no longer incarnate the kingdom of God by their words and deeds. Instead they have lost their true nature and identity. Chuck Colson indicts the North American church writing:

> The hard truth is that we have substituted an institutionalized religion for the life-giving dynamic of a living faith. For most of us the church is the building where we assemble to worship; its ministries are the programs that we get involved in; its mission is to meet the needs of its parishioners; and its servants are the professional clergy we hire to shepherd us. Church growth has come to refer more to such things as location, marketing, architecture, programs, and head counts than to the maturity of the body of Christ.[18]

We maintain that new churches have an opportunity to begin anew and afresh. Although 21st century church starts will need to make decisions regarding locations, buildings, and programs, these new churches have an opportunity to work towards a more biblical approach to "church." As **Inagrace** Dietterich so concisely stated:

> It is the active rule and the eschatological [future] mission of God—the kingdom of God—rather than institutional survival or efficiency or even societal service that provides the criteria for church management.[19]

We trust that these new communities of believers may once again develop a God-centered congregation that bears witness to the message of Jesus regarding the "nearness" of the kingdom of God.

New Churches Enlarge the Kingdom of God

The second biblical reason for starting new churches is that new churches enlarge the people of God. As churches are started among the various people groups in a given locale, additional categories of people are enfolded into congregations. The Bible underscores the equality of all persons who are part of the people of God. "*Whether Jew or Greek, slave or free*" is an expression of the new reality that all people groups may find unity in their diversity through acknowledging their common place in God's family through redemption that comes only by faith through Jesus Christ.

Believers from all walks of life stand together in the church as the people of God. Often the Greek term, *ekklesia*, in the New Testament is translated as "church." This word was used in the first century to refer to the local "assembly" that met to tend to the affairs of the city. However, it became the common designation for the community of believers. Stanley Grenz underscores the significance of the term.

> The choice of *ekklesia* as the designation of the Christian community suggests that the New Testament believers viewed the church as neither an edifice nor an organization. They were a people—a people brought together by the Holy Spirit—a people bound to each other through Christ—hence, a people standing in covenant with God. Above all, they were God's people (2 Cor. 6:16).[20]

New churches often enlarge the people of God by creating new communities of believers among population segments that have not previously been reached. As a community, the new church provides both corporate fellowship and also reciprocal relationships between believers. Grounded in their common bond of loyalty to God through Christ, the congregation stands in sharp relief to secular forms of societal relationships and provides an alternative form of community to a 21st century society that yearns for relationship.

New Churches Can Reproduce Themselves

A third biblical reason for starting new churches may be seen in the Apostle Paul's example who started new churches in the cities makes it clear that he "fully preached the gospel" from Jerusalem to Illyricum (Rom 15:19). These two points mark the ends of an arc that extends from Jerusalem around the northern coast of the Mediterranean almost to Spain. Paul's missionary journeys took him into the major administrative centers of each of the Roman provinces along this route. These cities were the centers for political, commercial and religious life in their province. As places with large populations (several over 100,000 people in the first century), the cities along the northern Mediterranean served as sources of communication for the whole surrounding region.

But how could Paul assert that he had "fully preached the gospel" across that geographical expanse? The answer to this question lies in understanding Paul's view of church starting. It appears that Paul adhered to a "radiating principle" that viewed the church starts that he began in each city as a central hub from which additional churches would be started throughout the surrounding areas. Romans 15:19-23 seems to indicate that for Paul, once he established these initial congregations, natural multiplication would occur.

Historically evangelical churches in North America have viewed themselves as "sending" churches. As a church with a missions program, millions of dollars have been given and thousands of people have gone from evangelical churches in the support of missions around the world. However, the biblical paradigm appears to be more of a missionary congregation that lives out the mission of God than merely a church with a missions "program."[21]

New churches can more easily engage our postmodern Western culture in missionary terms than established churches. We invite you to view North America *as a mission field* in its own right. A proper missional response requires that new churches address North American cultures and seek to embody the gospel within those cultures while simultaneously challenging sinful cultural norms and practices. Lesslie Newbigin summarized this sentiment well.

[Ours is not,] as we once imagined, a secular society.

4

It is a pagan society, and its paganism, having been born out of the rejection of Christianity, is far more resistant to the gospel than the pre-Christian paganism with which cross-cultural missions have been familiar. Here, surely, is the most challenging missionary frontier of our time.[22]

New Churches Can Proclaim a Contextualized Gospel

A fourth biblical reason for starting new churches is the Apostle Paul's example as he shared the gospel with various groups as he traveled on his missionary journeys. As he shared the gospel, Paul's evangelistic strategy needed to account for the great diversity of cultural, ethnic, philosophical, and religious backgrounds. He declared that *"though I am free from all men, I have made myself a slave to all, so that I may win more"* (1 Cor 9:19).

Making himself a slave refers to "his willingness to accommodate himself to whatever social setting he found himself in..."[23] In 1 Cor 9:20f, Paul outlines some of the social settings in which he practiced evangelism. The range of social settings comes in four categories: to the Ethnic Jews (the Jews), the Religious Jews (those under the law), the Non-Jews (those without the law), and the Pseudo-Christians (those who are weak).

The Paul obviously reached the various people groups throughout Euro-Asia through a contextualizing methodology. On his missionary journeys, he varied the way in which he shared the gospel. "It may be said that he has only one subject of conversation—the crucified and exalted Lord—but the presentation of that one subject is always suited to the audience."[24]

Today we call this process of accommodation to audience "contextualization." Like the Apostle Paul, church starters encounter a great diversity of cultural, ethnic, philosophical, and religious backgrounds as they attempt to proclaim the gospel to the neo-pagan society of western culture. New churches in the 21st century have the unprecedented opportunity to develop ways to express the truth of the gospel in terms that a postmodern, post-Christian society can understand.

New Churches Can Effectively Make Disciples

A fifth biblical reason for starting new churches rests on the fact that this method represents the best way to implement Jesus' imperative to *"make disciples."* Jesus commanded his followers to make disciples of all people groups. Church starting constitutes the best methodology for reaching, winning, discipling, and mobilizing people with the gospel of Jesus Christ. We will detail as we look at the Biblical foundations for church starting.

The Bible obviously calls for church starting. Experience also underlines this necessary ministry. These experiential reasons for starting new churches hold a vital place in the motivation of church starters.

Experiential Reasons for Church Starting

Nine other reasons stem from discoveries in the experiences of church starters.

Expanding Populations Need New Congregations

The first practical reason for starting churches is that expanding populations continue to demand new congregations. The need for new churches based on population growth continues even in areas where a good number of congregations already exist. This need for new churches rests on the fact that if we do not start new churches, we will soon have fewer churches in proportion to the population. The witness in our communities, therefore, will be weaker rather than stronger as time goes by.

Established Churches Tend To Plateau

A second practical reason why we should start new churches is that established churches generally tend to plateau by the time they are ten old years.[25] This tendency results partly from the fact that as they grow, churches focus more of their activities within their buildings, and therefore, the members are less devoted to the task of winning the lost with the same fervor they had when they were a younger congregation. Churches ten years of age and over tend also to concentrate on their own development rather than on the unchurched community.

New Churches are Flexible and Adaptable

A third practical reason for starting new churches is that new congregations are more flexible and can adapt more readily to the needs of the communities they serve. Established churches generally become satisfied with their styles of worship, education, evangelism, and leadership. This sense of satisfaction results in an unwillingness to change in order to attract new people.

No One Church Can Reach Everyone

A fourth practical reason for starting new churches relates closely to the first reason. No one church can reach and retain all the people in its city. In most cities, church starters find differing groups of people from varying socio-economic levels that have different preferences with regard to the language, music, worship styles, and fellowship patterns that are utilized in churches. Lyle Schaller affirms that: "there is not a congregation that possesses the abilities and the financial resources to attract, reach, serve, and respond to the needs of all the residents of a community."[26]

This fact indicates that there is a need for different churches for the different tastes and styles of the people in the city. This is not to say that a church should reject people who do not have the same tastes but it does mean that people have the tendency to attend the type of worship service in which they feel at home.

New Churches Win More People

A fifth practical reason for starting new churches is that, in general, these congregations win and baptize more unchurched people, proportionately, than do established churches. Studies by several denominations indicate that a significant portion of the conversions and baptisms grow out of the efforts of the new churches.[27] C. Peter Wagner affirms this declaration by stating, "Without exception, the denominations that are growing are the ones that emphasize the establishment of new churches."[28]

New Churches Develop New Leadership

A sixth practical reason for starting new churches is that these congregations develop new leadership.[29] Generally, established churches utilize only a small number of their members in positions of leadership. This situation means that there are numbers of members in the church for whom there are no positions of leadership. In some cases these people simply become accustomed to the situation and consequently do not develop their leadership capacities. When these same people have the opportunity to participate in the ministry of a new congregation, in many cases their leadership abilities come to the front and blossom. As a result, these people contribute to the Kingdom and the church, and the number of responsible leaders increases also.

New Churches Encourage Established Churches

A seventh practical reason why we should establish new churches is that this method often stimulates the established churches to greater efforts. Many churches that have begun new congregations have experienced a revival. After seeing their daughter congregation grow, established churches have gained a new enthusiasm and have enlarged their vision of fulfilling the Great Commission. The ministries of the daughter churches have stimulated these established churches to evangelize with more zeal and have reminded them of their priorities regarding discipleship.

New Churches Reach Needy Areas

An eighth practical reason for starting new churches rests on the truth that it is easier to win people if congregations locate near where they live. Many communities (sometimes whole towns) do not have churches. In other situations, the kinds of churches most likely to reach particular groups cannot be found in the immediate neighborhoods where these particular groups reside. The closer the congregations are to the people, the easier it will be for these churches to reach the people with the gospel and disciple them.

Proximity Enhances Discipleship

A ninth practical reason for starting new churches is that

members participate more fully in the activities of the church when they live close to their churches. In other words, proximity to the church's place of meeting enhances the discipleship of the members. Usually, people who are a far distance from the church's meeting place attend only one weekly service—either Sunday morning or Sunday night.

Often, members who live far from the church facility do not participate in the activities that help them to grow spiritually, such as prayer meetings, fellowship meetings, and the ministries of the church. Persons who live closer to the church engage in greater participation in its activities.

Answering Objections to Church Starting

Church starters face numerous objections to starting new congregations from a variety of persons. Gene Getz and Joe Wall[30] list several of these objections in their book, *Effective Church Growth Strategies*. Other experienced church starters can relate to still other objections that are often projected. Church starters who challenge churches and organizations to enter the task of church starting will face many of these reasons for remaining out of church starting efforts. Wise church starters prepare adequate answers to these and other objections to church starting.

Hurts the Home Church

"It will hurt the home church."[31] Of course this is a natural concern to many people. One pastor refers to the needs of the home church in relationship to its missions outreach when he states, "Keep Daddy Healthy." The idea is that the home base must remain strong spiritually, financially, and provide healthy leadership. While this is true, the benefits of a reproductive DNA in the home church that produces new church starts have been overlooked. Sponsoring churches that emphasize church starting reap internal blessings and eternal rewards of an outward and evangelistic focus. This viewpoint also misunderstands the many varied ways in which churches are started. Most of church starting approaches do not require an excessive expenditure of finances or a severe loss of leadership. The usually improve the home church's conditions.

Costs Too Much

"The cost is too high; we can't afford it now." Surely the cost factor in church starting appears to be prohibitive for many churches. However, again, this objection misunderstands the many ways in which churches are started and new churches are financed. While it is true that finances are a critical issue that must be addressed in the strategy planning of a new church, several different sponsorship methods are available to help any church to become part of starting new churches.

Loses Too Many People

"We will lose too many of our people and too much of our talent and leadership." Many pastors have spent years reaching and discipling people. To "give them" to a new church start may seem counterproductive. However, not all methods of church starting require an infusion of people and talent from the sponsoring church. In many cases when people do leave the home church to become part of a new church, the sponsoring church pastor will find that they are replaced by others in the congregation whose spiritual gifts may have lain dormant for many years.

Too Many Needs Already

"Our own ministry still has too many needs that should occupy the pastor's time and energy." Some may object to church starting because they view the time and energy needed to start a new church as excessive. They point to the many needs that cannot always be filled in the existing church. The existence of this objection to starting new congregations may indicate a need for a biblical, Great Commission mindset. However, there are some practical concerns as well. The relationship between the church starter and the sponsors needs to be defined, including the role of the pastor of a sponsoring church.

Shouldn't Force a New Church

"We shouldn't force a church on an area. We should wait until interested people approach us from a specific area." While it is always important to study the sociocultural and demographical dimensions of any area under consideration, church starting fol-

lows the biblical mandate to "Go" and tell others the good news of Jesus Christ. The principal objective of church starting is to bear witness to the gospel to those who have previously not been reached. Most unreached people are not knocking on the church's door waiting to hear the gospel. We should not wait until interested Christians approach us about starting a new church in an area that is not being reached.

Impedes Home Church's Growth

"Another church nearby will impede the growth of our church." This objection arises from a faulty view of church growth. Ministry is in the "business" of living out the kingdom of God through spiritual maturation and seeing the people of God grow as new believers come to faith. When Jesus said, "I will build my church," he was not referring to the numerical growth of a particular congregation. Instead he referred to extending the rule and reign of God through the reproduction of congregations who follow him.

Actually, a new church, even if it is near the sponsoring congregation, in most cases will not slow the growth of the mother church. The two congregations will most likely reach different groups. The increased visibility of the two congregations may stimulate the progress of both.

It is also true that, ideally, church starters, like the Apostle Paul, would not build on another's foundation. However, two churches may be geographically side-by-side and not work against each other; they simply may each be reaching different socio-cultural groups from within the larger community. New churches should not be seen as competition, but rather as fulfillment of kingdom growth.

Cannot Protect Sound Doctrine

"We cannot be certain that the doctrine and practices of many new churches will remain sound and correct." Starting many new churches, especially if this plan calls for many house churches under the leadership of lay pastors, frightens many church leaders. Most often the established leaders surface two main fears. First, these leaders fear that many congregations and local leaders may develop heretical, or at least unacceptable, teachings and practices. So many new

11

congregations and leaders cannot be adequately supervised, the leaders contend.

Secondly, some denominational groups or independent fellowships fear that if many congregations are started some of these new groups might develop tendencies that would lead them to affiliate with other groups. This fear often leads to apprehension that the new congregations may leave their denominational group. As a matter of fact, either or both of the fears might become reality.

Actually, however, wrong doctrinal teachings seldom arise in churches. Slight deviations from the stated norms and practices are not always crucial—in fact these alterations might even become helpful both to the new congregation and the more established churches.

Some of the new congregations may well move away from the doctrine and practices of the denomination, fellowship, or the mother church. Should this alteration come to pass, the starting group should thank God for the new congregation, support the group in the path they take, and move on to begin other congregations. A Kingdom view helps alleviate this problem and its results.

Sound doctrine and correct practice are important. The church starter or church starting group, even celebrates, some alternatives to their beliefs and practices. The alternatives that arise might be more culturally appropriate than those of the sponsoring group. Should serious doctrinal errors or harmful practices arise, the church starter may need to attempt to influence the direction of the movement.

Creates Intradenominational Competition

Some people are opposed to the idea of church starting for fear that it will create intradenominational or intrafellowship competition. Some present the argument that starting another church of the same denomination in a given community will be divisive and will weaken the existing church. Others state that better stewardship of resources can be practiced if churches are started in areas where the denomination is not represented. It is obvious that churches that are located in close proximity and are seeking to reach the same target group utilizing similar methods can find themselves in a competitive situation.

A counter argument, however, can be presented from the standpoint of effectiveness and church health. Lyle E. Schaller explains:

> Contrary to conventional wisdom, congregations usually benefit from intradenominational competition. While it is impossible to isolate one factor as being decisive, the presence of two or more congregations with the same denominational affiliation usually results in a higher level of congregational health and vitality than if one congregation has a denominational monopoly in that community. One obvious advantage of intentional redundancy is that disoriented members of one congregation can seek a new church home without leaving the denomination.[32]

One Church in One City is New Testament Pattern

A similar objection is based on the argument that there should only be one church per city. This argument is heard most often abroad and asserts that the New Testament mentions only one church in each city. Typically the proponents of this argument are pastors of churches that were the first to be established in their city and feel that new congregations will only weaken their church.

This argument is flawed for at least two reasons. First, there is no clear teaching in the New Testament that there should be only one church per city. The truth of the matter is that the epistles were written when churches were in their initial stages of development. In other words, there had not been sufficient time for numerous churches to be started in each city. Also, the churches that are mentioned were not the typical institutions that are common today with their spacious buildings, fully supported professional staffs, and ample financial resources for a large variety of programs. To a large extent, the house church was the most prevalent congregational model of that day.

Will Not Enhance My Career Path

While it is not voiced openly, some pastors of growing congregations feel that starting new congregations will not enhance their image in the eyes of their denomination or fellowship. They feel that it is mainly the pastors of large congregations that get invited as speakers and get elected to prominent positions in the national organizations of their denomination.

Even in cases where this is so the pastors who hold such views are nearsighted in that their ultimate goal should be to please God and not their peers. In addition to this, they should be aware of the fact that they could be the pastors of large churches that, in turn, start many new congregations at home and abroad.

Conclusion

Undoubtedly, other reasons for starting new churches exist and other objections may need to be addressed. These fourteen powerful reasons, nevertheless, should motivate all Christians and churches to fulfill the Great Commission by starting new churches. Being prepared to answer these ten common objections may help church starters to motivate others to be involved in church starting. C. Peter Wagner says, "The single most effective evangelistic method under heaven is church planting."[33]

CHAPTER 2

BIBLICAL FOUNDATION

Every church starting effort must be solidly based on a strong biblical foundation. Starting reproducing churches in the 21st century is such an awesome and demanding task that all who prepare for the effort must rest their efforts squarely on the Word of God. Ed Stetzer declares point-blank that although some oppose the idea of church planting, we must do it anyway because it is biblical. He continues saying, "Without church plating, we will not fulfill the Great Commission."[34] The biblical foundation for church starting grows out of obedience not only to the Great Commission of Christ but also to faithfulness to the church starting models that we find in the Bible.

The Great Commission

The injunction to evangelize the entire world is most clearly stated in the Great Commission Jesus gave His disciples as recorded in Matt. 28:16-20. The Commission is expressed in other biblical passages (Mark16:15; Luke 24:46-49; John 20:19-23; Acts 1:8) but finds its most clear and compelling form in the Matthean passage. The Great Commission provides vital guidance as to the authority, the imperative, the scope, and the promise of the imperative.

The Authority

Often people start the Great Commission with the words "go and make disciples." It is extremely important that we start at the beginning, where Christ speaks about His authority. *"All authority has been given unto me in heaven and on earth"* (Matt 28:16). This means that no area, no people, or culture lies outside the domain of his power, authority, or desire. Having arisen, he now has exalted authority over the whole world. It is important to note that authority precedes mandate. We must keep in mind that the mandate does not come from someone who wishfully hopes that somehow we might be able to fulfill it. It comes from the resurrected, exalted, empowered

Christ who is capable of providing every resource needed to fulfill his command.

The Imperative

After making it clear that he has all authority, Jesus gave the missionary mandate, "As you are going, make disciples, of all nations, baptizing them in the name of the Father and of the Son and of the Holy Ghost: teaching them to observe all things whatsoever I commanded you: and lo I am with you always, even unto the end of the world." In the Greek, the words "going, baptizing, and teaching" are all participles, helping verbs. The imperative, the command, ("matheteusate") is make disciples.

If we diagram the commission it looks like the illustration below. The imperative involves making persons from every people group disciples of Jesus Christ. This command of Christ involves more than getting decisions (which is the starting point). Making disciples involves leading people to receive Jesus as Savior and Lord, to become an integral part of His church as life-long followers, learners, and ministers working toward the spread of His kingdom. The helping words of going, teaching, and baptizing, suggest some of the procedures that followers of Jesus will use in the primary task of making disciples.

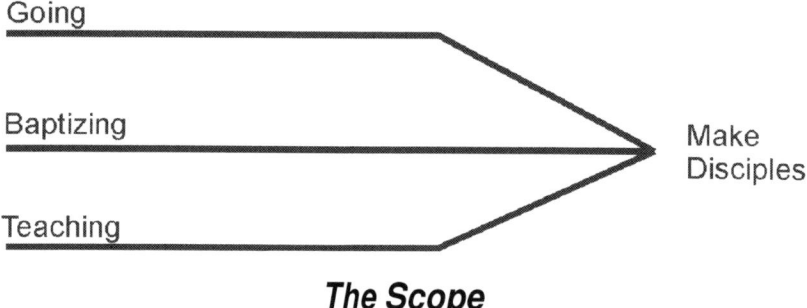

Going

Baptizing — Make Disciples

Teaching

The Scope

Jesus enjoined His followers *"make disciples of all nations."* The Greek word for *"all nations"* is *"ta ethne"* from which we get the word "ethnic." This means that the scope of the commission includes all people groups in the entire world. Every people group needs to be reached with the gospel and discipled. In order to implement the command, the followers of Christ will of necessity cross linguistic, sociological, racial, cultural, religious, ideological, generational, and geographical boundaries. Another way of stating this is that churches need to be started among all of the segments of the societies of the world. Christian ministry must bridge every barrier to the gospel by establishing churches that are near to the un-churched, not only geographically but also socially.

The Promise

As we look at chapters 16 and 28 of Matthew, we find two powerful and reassuring promises. First, Jesus promises to build His church. In Matthew 16:18 Jesus stated: *"I will build my church and the gates of hell will not prevail against it."* It is clear from this passage that the establishment and expansion of the Church is first and foremost a divine endeavor.

Jesus has promised to build His church, and He never made a promise that He could not keep. It is also very important to note that the picture that Jesus gives of His church is not one that defensively survives the onslaught of the enemy but one that aggressively tears down the strongholds of the enemy and rescues people with the gospel of salvation. Jesus promised to build His church.

Second, Jesus promises to be with His followers as they obey His command: *"Lo I am with you even to the end of the age"* (Matt.28:20). Jesus promises to be with His disciples and with His church until he brings human history to His intended and determined end. This promise holds true for all time. There will not be a time when He will not be with His followers who are doing His will and obeying His command. He will not only be present but He will be there to guide His followers in the task that He has commanded them.

The expression *"to the end of the age"* assures us that Jesus will not rescind His command until He has accomplished His purpose. It also assures us that there will not be a time when He will not be with His disciples. His church has gone through many trying times throughout her long and arduous history but his true followers have never been and will never be without His presence.

Let's look for a moment at the ways in which the word "**all**" is used in the Great Commission: **All** power, **all** peoples, **all** the commands, and **all** of the time. In other words, the one who has **all** the power sends us to make disciples of **all** people groups, teaching them **all** of the things He has commanded us, and He will be with us **all** of the time.

How did the disciples make disciples? They did so by establishing churches. The disciples, without a doubt, thought of the way in which Jesus had discipled them. He had shared with them the message of the kingdom, invited them to follow him, spent time instructing them, prayed with them, fellow-shipped with them, drew them into a community of believers, and then sent them out to make disciples. When the disciples, therefore, dedicated themselves to the task of implementing the command of Jesus, they thought not only about communicating the message but also about gathering the people so that they would form a fellowship in which the believers could continue to grow spiritually.

Biblical Church Starting Models

The Bible itself provides the most significant models for church starters. Two of these models, which establish important principles for church starting, grow out of the accounts of the church in Jerusalem and the church in Antioch. The study of these two churches establishes and clarifies biblical models for church starting.

The Church in Jerusalem

The Jerusalem fellowship demonstrated some of the most important and effective church starting principles. No study of church starting in the Bible can be complete without consideration of this church.

Birth of the Church in Jerusalem

The Jerusalem church was born during a prayer meeting in the upper room of a private house in the ancient and historic city of Jerusalem. Christ had commanded his disciples to return to the city and await the coming of the Holy Spirit. Out of that group of humble disciples, waiting in faith and obedience, God brought the Church into being. From its inception, the Church, endowed with the Holy Spirit, was given the spiritual gifts it needed to carry out its functions as a local expression of the body of Christ.

Functions of the Jerusalem Church

In this infant church we perceive the functions it needed to carry out not only to survive but also to thrive. Acts 2:40-47 provides a description of these functions. There was:

- **Proclamation**. This was done through testimony and preaching (v.40).
- **Incorporation.** Those who believed were baptized and added to the Church (v. 41).
- **Discipleship.** They persevered in the Apostles' doctrines (v. 42).
- **Fellowship.** This was evident in the agape meal, the Lord's Supper (v.42), and their unity (v.44)
- **Prayer.** They continued in prayers (v. 42).
- **Ministry.** They voluntarily sold of their possessions and shared their resources with those who were in need (v. 45).
- **Worship.** This included a sense of awe (v. 43), joy (46), and praise (v. 47).
- **Cultural Identification.** "They found favor with the people" (v. 47).
- **Propagation.** The Lord added daily those who were being saved (v. 47).

As we note the functions of this church, it is imperative that we understand that even though the methods may change, the functions remain vital to the life and ministry of every church. For example, we may use a wide variety of methods to proclaim the Gospel; however, the proclamation itself may not be ignored if the church is to be what the Lord intended her to be. Every function of the church will be in evidence in churches in all places and times.

Founding of the Church in Jerusalem

As we consider the miraculous manner in which the Jerusalem church came into existence, two questions come to mind: (1) Who authorized the establishment of this congregation; (2) When was the church established?

The answer to the first question is that Jesus authorized it when He said: "I will build my church." The Holy Spirit confirmed the establishment of the Church at Pentecost.

The answer to the second question as to when the church was actually established is that this took place when the gospel was preached and the people responded and were incorporated into the body of Christ. Another way of stating this is that *the establishment of the Church was the birthright of those who heard the gospel and decided to become disciples of Jesus Christ.*

Form of the Church in Jerusalem

The founding of the Jerusalem church was a spontaneous action, which resulted from the proclamation of the Gospel in the power of the Holy Spirit. We perceive in the New Testament that this new congregation and the others, which were established subsequently, developed forms through which their functions could be carried out. In fact, these congregations were not all the same. Variations existed and these variations often resulted in varying patterns.

In light of this we ask:

What is it that we do not find *in the early church?*

We do not find an apostolic hierarchy. This was evident in the fact that the Holy Spirit utilized different persons to address the challenges that the church faced. In Acts 5, the Holy Spirit utilizes Peter to confront the deception of Ananias. In Acts 6, the twelve summoned the congregation to select seven men who would address the problem of the neglect of the Hellenistic widows (Hebrew widows who had assimilated into the Greek culture) in the distribution of the bread. It is interesting to note that most of the deacons who were selected had Hellenistic names. Could it be that the Holy Spirit guided the church to select those who had the best understanding and the greatest cultural sensitivity to the widows who felt they were being neglected? In Acts 15, it was James who presided over the meeting that decided not to impose Jewish cultural and ceremonial practices upon the Gentile converts. Had they not freed the church from the Jewish cultural trappings, **the movement** would have remained a sect of Judaism.

The picture we see is one of the Holy Spirit as the agent of the birth of the church in Jerusalem and the guide of the church as she faced those difficult issues which could have altered her nature and derailed her mission. We do not find, therefore, in the Jerusalem church an Apostolic Hierarchy that made the decisions for the church.

What is it that we do find in the church in Jerusalem?

We do find that there was sensitivity to the Holy Spirit. At every juncture the church sought the guidance of the Holy Spirit. "The church in Jerusalem continued to be a church at prayer, obeying Christ's commands and seeking the power of the Holy Spirit at every step."[35]

There was also a strong commitment to lay a solid doctrinal foundation. Aware of the fact that the Lord had commanded them to "make disciples" and to "teach them whatsoever I have commanded unto you" (Matt 28:19, 20), the Apostles took great care to establish the Jerusalem church upon the teachings of Christ. We see evidence of this when the new church "persevered in the apostles' doctrines" (Acts 2:42). These doctrines were not their own teachings but those that they had received from Christ. There was great care to carry out the functions of the church (Acts 2:40-47) based upon the foundation that had been established.

The church in Jerusalem, therefore, was a church that came into being by the will and power of the Holy Spirit. As people heard the proclamation of the gospel of the risen Savior and responded to it by deciding to become active members of the local expression of the body of Christ, a community came into being which had the task of implementing the great commission. The Apostles were the instruments of the Holy Spirit in the establishment of this church. The establishment of the church, however, was the birthright of those who had heard and responded to the gospel.

The Church in Antioch

Equally important with the church in Jerusalem, at least in regard to church starting principles, is the church in Antioch. Studying this church provides even further insight into the process of a church that starts other churches.

The Antioch stands as an inspiring model for its time and the ages to follow of a congregation that gained an understanding of its responsibility to contribute toward fulfilling the Great Commission. Ken Hemphill provides a comprehensive account of the Antioch and presents this congregation a guide and example for Christian fellowships everywhere.[36]

As we study this church we discover that it was a refugee church, a witnessing church, a compassionate church, a culturally receptive church, a training church, a missionary church, and a cooperating church. The Antioch Church provides a guide for congregations everywhere. The example this church gives of sending missionaries continues as one of its most significant contributions.

Establishment of the Church in Antioch

It is instructive to note that it took Acts 8:1 to fulfill Acts 1:8. Actually Acts 1:8 was given by Jesus in response to a very ethnocentric question. The apostles asked Jesus: "Lord, are you going at this time going to restore the kingdom of Israel? Jesus responded: "You shall receive power after that the Holy Spirit has come upon you and you shall be my witnesses both in Jerusalem and in all Judea and in Samaria, and the remotest part of the earth." It was not, however, until a great persecution against the church broke out in Jerusalem that the believers were "scattered abroad through all the regions of Judea and Samaria."

Acts 8:4 adds: "Therefore, they that were scattered abroad went everywhere preaching the word." Acts 11:19 picks up the narrative that "They therefore that were scattered abroad upon the persecution that arose about Stephen, travelled as far as Phoenicia, and Cyprus, and Antioch..." In all three of these verses the word "*diesparesan*" is used. John Polhill points out that: "They were scattered like one scatters seed. But scattered seeds grow, and the irony is that persecution and scattering of the Christians only led to further increase. With the dispersal of the Hellenist Christians, the second phase of Jesus' commission began."[37]

This leads us to ask two questions: What will it take for Christian individuals and churches to take the Great Commission seriously? How are we to see martyrdom, persecution and dispersion in light of the Great Commission? History bears witness to the fact that the very means utilized by Satan to destroy the Christian witness results in the precise instrument for the dispersion of the gospel.

Some of the scattered believers went to Antioch, the third largest city in the Empire next only to Rome and Alexandria. It happened that there were around 50,000 Jews in Antioch. Was this a coincidence or was this the work of the Holy Spirit? Once there, they did what was natural to them. They shared the gospel with those who spoke their language and understood their culture. They are to be commended. They had fled for their lives leaving everything behind. They were in the process of adjusting to a new and different area. It is great to know that they shared the good news of salvation in the midst of those circumstances. However, we must ask the questions: "What if that is all they had done?" "Would they have been obedient to the command of the Great Commission? Is it possible that we have too many churches" in our day? (Acts 11: 19).

Thank the Lord for Acts 11:20 "But some of them, men from Cyprus and Cyrene came to Antioch and spoke to the Greeks too and told them the good news of the Lord Jesus." The men from Cyprus and Cyrene were Hellenistic Jews who could speak both languages and understood both cultures. It is obvious that they had caught the vision of sharing the Gospel with Gentiles. They even contextualized the presentation of the Gospel because they did not preach about Jesus as the "Messiah" but as "Lord" which was a term that was better understood in the Gentile world.

Characteristics of the Church in Antioch

A Spirit-filled Church

Acts 11:21, 22 and 24 state: "And the Lord's hand was with them; and a great number believed and turned to the Lord... News of what they were doing came to the ears of the church in Jerusalem. So they sent Barnabas out as far as Antioch. When he came and saw the grace of God he was glad and he exhorted them all to make it the purpose of their hearts to cleave to the Lord..."

The power of the risen Christ was upon them. The presence of the one who said: "Lo, I am with you always" was evident among them. The more believers are involved in fulfilling the Great Commission, the closer Christ is to them. Paul said to the Thessalonians: "Our gospel came not unto you in word only, but also in power, and in the Holy Spirit, and in much assurance... (1 Thess. 1:5).

Additional evidence that this was a Spirit-filled church is found in the congregation's prayer life. They were fasting and worshipping when the Holy Spirit instructed them to set aside Barnabas and Saul. Then they fasted and prayed before laying hands on them and sending them (13:2-3).

A Training Church

Acts 11:25, 26 states that Barnabas "went away to Tarsus to look for Saul and when he found him he brought him to Antioch. For a whole year they were with the Church and they instructed a large number of people." Ten years had gone by since Barnabas had vouched for Saul in Jerusalem. Barnabas knew that Saul could be a great blessing to the Antioch church. It is evident that Barnabas was aware of the fact that Saul possessed spiritual gifts which could complement his own gifts and enable both of them to work as a team for the advance of the Kingdom of God in Antioch and beyond. It could well be that "a Theologian with Paul's competence in the scriptures, capacity to argue strongly, resolution and capacity for organization was urgently needed."[38] Barnabas and Saul ministered very effectively and learned important lessons while serving in church that had a variety of cultures in its membership. "Likely they particularly continued the witness to Gentiles. This experience prepared them in their first mission together in Cyprus and southern Turkey (13:4- 14:26)."[39] We need more of these types of churches that serve as training bases for missionary service as we hope for expansion such as was experienced in the New Testament period.

A Compassionate Church

Acts 11: 27-30 describes the prophecy of impending hunger in Jerusalem and the offering that was taken up by the Antioch congregation and sent by Barnabas and Saul. Here we have for the first time Gentiles and Jews contributing to an offering for their Jewish brothers and sisters. This demonstrates the tearing down of barriers that the Gospel can accomplish in the lives of the believers. It is also inspiring to note that the members of this church responded in faith even in advance of the actual occurrence of the catastrophe.

A Culturally Inclusive Church

Acts 13:1 states: "In the church at Antioch there were prophets and teachers: Barnabas, Simeon called Niger, Lucius of Cyrene, Manaen (who was brought up with Herod the tetrarch) and Saul." The universal appeal of the Gospel is reflected in the leaders of this church. Barnabas was a Jew from Cyprus. Lucius came from Cyrene in North Africa. Simeon called "Niger" was very likely of African ancestry. Polhill affirms this idea when he states: "Simon called Niger perhaps indicates that he was a black person, since *niger* is the Latin word for black. Some suggest that he might have come from Cyrene, like Lucius, or from elsewhere in North Africa."[40] Some scholars wonder if he was the one who carried the cross of Jesus. Manaen was a person of significant social standing. Saul was a Jew from Tarsus who had grown up bilingually and biculturally. William Barclay observes: "In this little band there is exemplified the unifying influence of Christianity. Men from many lands and many backgrounds had discovered the secret of togetherness because they had discovered the secret of Christ."[41] The culturally inclusive environment of the Antioch church was, no doubt, ideal as a training ground for these cross-cultural missionaries.

A Missionary Church

Acts 13: 2, 3 states: "While they were worshiping the Lord and fasting, the Holy Spirit said: 'Set apart for me Barnabas and Saul for the work to which I have called them.' So after they had fasted and prayed, they placed their hands on them and sent them off."

It is important to take note of the fact that it was the Holy Spirit who was leading in this missionary effort. The expressions "set apart for me" and "to the work to which I have called them" make it clear who calls and who directs.

The Antioch church became a genuine missionary congregation. This was the first congregation to witness to Gentiles in its own city. Then it became the first congregation to send forth missionaries into the larger world. This church's understanding of the Great Commission was evident in that they did not see witnessing at home and abroad as mutually exclusive activities. This church followed the leadership of the Holy Spirit and gave evidence that it was willing to obey the Great Commission. Commitment to the Great Commission should be in the DNA of every church we start anywhere in the world.

A Cooperating Church

The Antioch congregation was a cooperating congregation. The Book of Acts records that:

> "Some men came down from Judea to Antioch and were teaching the brothers: 'Unless you are circumcised, according to the custom taught by Moses, you cannot be saved.' This brought Paul and Barnabas into sharp dispute and debate with them. So Paul and Barnabas were appointed, along with other believers, to go to Jerusalem to see the apostles and elders about this question. The church sent them on their way, and as they traveled through Phoenicia and Samaria, they told how the Gentiles had been converted. This news made all the brothers very glad. When they came to Jerusalem, they were welcomed by the church and the apostles and elders to whom they reported everything God had done through them. Then some of the believers who belonged to the party of Pharisees stood and said, 'The Gentiles must be circumcised and required to obey the Law of Moses'" (Acts 15:1-5).

The Church at Antioch demonstrated the characteristics of cooperation. They had sent an offering to the Jerusalem church, now they send messengers to participate in the Jerusalem Council. This crucial issue needed the attention of the whole church. Paul and Barnabas "reported everything God had done through them." The Judaizers (converted Pharisees) insisted not only on the moral law but also on the ritual observances (circumcision, food laws, scrupulous ritual purity). These were a part of their oral traditions. To have required these things would have made them into Jews and cut them off from the rest of the Gentiles. This would have severely restricted, perhaps even killed, any Gentile mission. What oral traditions (extra-biblical requirements) must we be on guard against so these will not restrict the flow of the Gospel?

A Christian Church

Acts 11:26 "And it was at Antioch that the disciples were called Christians." The believers at Antioch did not come up with the term "Christian" to refer to themselves. This term is of Gentile origin Jews would not have called them "followers of the Messiah." "Christianoi" which meant "belonging to or of the party of Christ." The term "followers of the Messiah" is used three times in the NT and it us used by outsiders to designate followers of Christ (in this verse, by Agrippa in Acts 26:28; and in Peter's reference to the term used by persecutors 1 Pet 4:16). This perhaps indicates the growth of the Gospel among Gentiles. It also is indicative that Gentiles saw in them certain characteristics that distinguished them from typical Jews and others. What would people call us if they used a name to describe us by what they observe in us? We are followers of whom?

The example of the Antioch church is indeed one that we need to emulate as we start new congregations. G. Campbell Morgan's description of the Antioch church is an excellent summary of the characteristics of a congregation committed to implementing the Great commission:

> Certain men of Cyprus and Cyrene had preached in Antioch to these Greek men the Gospel of the Lord Christ; and these men hearing the Gospel of the Lord Christ had believed and been baptized by the Holy Ghost, constituted the Church. There had been no consecration of a building. There had been no apostolic visitation. The Church was not the result of official action, but of proclamation of the Lord and belief in Him and baptism into His life, by the overruling God... Presently they cooperated with the church in Jerusalem; but Antioch was independent of Jerusalem; and the Holy Spirit could speak to the church in Antioch. In that church in Antioch were gifts bestowed by the Spirit: prophets and teachers. Whence came these gifts? From the Lord himself. How? By the bestowment of the Holy Spirit.[42]

May the Lord enable us to be instrumental in the starting of more congregations like the Antioch Church!

Pattern of the Church in Antioch

A question that we must address is: was the model of the Jerusalem church followed in the establishment of the Antioch church?

There was an identical doctrinal pattern. Throughout the book of Acts and in the Epistles we see an uncompromising commitment on the part of the Apostles to build upon the foundation of Jesus Christ. This could very well have been the motivation of the Jerusalem church in sending Peter and John to Samaria in connection with the glorious response to the Gospel as a result of Philip's evangelistic activity. Barnabas's presence in Antioch could well have had the same purpose. We must keep in mind, however, that while doctrinal purity was a primary concern, we see no evidence of the Jerusalem church functioning as the sole guardian of the "faith once delivered to the saints." The Apostle Paul felt so strongly about the importance of building upon Christ's foundation that he made visits, wrote letters, and engaged in personal confrontations with those who were departing from these doctrines. The Antioch church sent Paul and Barnabas to the Jerusalem Council. These were not summoned to appear by the Jerusalem church. There was, therefore, a deep commitment to build upon the foundation of Christ, but this was the responsibility of every local church and not just the church in Jerusalem.

There was an identical pattern with regard to function. The functions of the Jerusalem church, which we described earlier, were reflected in all of the other churches. In other words, all of them had to be involved in proclamation, incorporation, worship, etc., if they were to be true local expressions of the body of Christ.

Different patterns, however, related to the manner by which these functions were, however, clearly practiced in other congregations. There was variation in the methodologies that were used in the exercise of the functions mentioned above. The Antioch church, for instance, by virtue of the fact that it had reached many Gentiles, had a different worship style (music, etc.,) and utilized a different language (Greek, in addition to Aramaic). Such variations also became apparent in the church in Corinth and many others.

Examination of the birth of the Jerusalem church and the establishment of the Antioch church presents several important lessons that we must heed today as we design church starting strategies. First, it was the Holy Spirit who gave birth to the Jerusalem church. The church in Antioch was also started through the initiative of the Holy Spirit. Second, the Apostles and later others who were converted (e.g., Barnabas) were instrumental in establishing a sound doctrinal foundation (*teaching that which the Lord had commanded*). Third, the Jerusalem church became an "enabler" in the establishment of the church in Antioch. Although the church in Antioch was never referred to as a "daughter congregation," it can be stated that the Jerusalem church was an enabler in that out of it came some of those who started and later contributed to the development of the Antioch church.

The Antioch church, in turn, served a similar function in relation to the churches that Paul and Barnabas started. Fourth, the Jerusalem church and the Antioch church became sister churches with the latter contributing financially when the former was in need. Fifth, the Jerusalem church and the Antioch church along with other churches participated in the deliberations of the Jerusalem Council (Acts 15) thus giving evidence of the fact that they were cooperating churches.

These congregations in Jerusalem and Antioch provide excellent examples of what Christian churches should be. They incorporate the fellowship and ministry that are needed in churches in every day and area.

Nature of Church Starting in the New Testament

We have noted the establishment of the Jerusalem church and the Antioch church. In each case, we stated that the initiative was taken by the Holy Spirit. We also stressed the importance of human instrumentality in starting churches and ensuring that these remain built upon the solid doctrinal foundation that Jesus gave the Apostles. A crucial question arises, "How can we become instruments of the Holy Spirit in initiating and developing churches without hindering their development either through our methodology or terminology?" That question remains as we examine, first of all, the methodology that Paul used in the starting and establishment of the church at Ephesus.[43]

Paul's Methodology at Ephesus

As we initiate the discussion about the methodology employed by Paul, we need to remind ourselves that the Holy Spirit led Paul to Ephesus. Also, the Holy Spirit prepared the hearts of the hearers, furnished the assistants who would work with Paul, and in due time *"gave the increase."* The procedure that Paul used in starting the church in Ephesus followed a definite pattern as outlined in the book of Acts.

Initiation of Relationships (Acts 18)

On his way back from Corinth to Antioch of Syria, Paul made his initial visit to Ephesus. As he had done in other cities, Paul visited the synagogue where he was permitted to speak. Through his message Paul planted the seed of the Gospel among the local Jews. Due to the fact that some of them were receptive, Paul promised to return, *"if God wills"* (v. 21). This shows that Paul was quite aware that the Holy Spirit could well alter his plans, even though at the time this seemed like a very logical thing to do.

Emergence of a Nucleus of Believers

Paul was not able to remain in Ephesus after making the initial contact but he did leave Priscilla and Aquila there to establish a beachhead (Acts 18:18). While in Ephesus, Priscilla and Aquila met Apollos, an eloquent preacher who was a follower of the teachings of John the Baptist. Noticing that he was deficient in his understanding of the Scriptures, especially regarding the Messiah, Priscilla and Aquila discipled him (18:26). Apollos then went to Achaia (v. 27). Apparently there was a nucleus of believers at Ephesus by this time because verse 28 states that *"the believers decided to help him."* Through the work of Priscilla and Aquila, a nucleus was established in Ephesus.

Establishment of a Church

Paul returned to Ephesus with the purpose of evangelizing and establishing a church (Acts 19). He did this in several ways. First, he spent time correcting the faith of those who had been baptized with the baptism of John but had not had a personal experience of salvation in Jesus Christ (vv. 1-7).

Second, Paul went into the synagogue and communicated the gospel, presenting Christ as the Messiah. There were some who were stubborn and refused to believe (v. 9). Those who believed, however, followed Paul as he obtained entrance into the hall of Tyrannus where he held discussions every day (v. 9). This hall became his pulpit to the city and to the entire province for two years (v. 10).

Paul's ministry gained so many converts and caused such an impact on the commercial ventures related to the goddess Artemis that a riot ensued. Local business leaders, feeling the impact of the religious change, led an uprising against Paul. The impact of the Gospel became so great that people were burning their magic books and otherwise avoiding the local religious customs. Because of these events and the riot, Paul had to leave the city of Ephesus (20:1).

Development of the Church

The Apostle Paul assisted the development of the church through follow-up visits, training, and writing. The Apostle returned and continued to train and encourage the new believers in Ephesus. Paul also assisted the church in its development by sending his assistants, Timothy, Titus, and Tychicus. These workers cooperated in the task of instructing the believers, correcting the false doctrines, organizing the church, and nurturing the believers. Paul also assisted the church in its development by writing letters, for example the Epistle to the Ephesians.

In this epistle Paul deals with doctrine, Christian piety, and ethical matters. In the epistle, as well as his visits, Paul reveals his concern for the spiritual and doctrinal soundness of this new congregation. When he bids the Ephesian elders farewell he reveals his confidence in the work of the Holy Spirit to encourage and sustain this new congregation: *"And now I commend you to the care of God and to the message of his grace, which is able to build you up and give you the blessings God has for all his people"* (Acts 20:32). The Apostle was obviously deeply involved in the development of the church in Ephesus.

Paul's Overall Methodology

The methodology that Paul employed at Ephesus was a part of his overall methodology that he employed in the establishment of the other churches. In his book, *Planting Churches Cross- Culturally,* David Hesselgrave outlines what he calls the "Pauline Cycle" of church starting.[444]. He suggests the following steps.

Missionaries Commissioned (Acts 13:1-4)

At Antioch, while the church fasted and prayed, the Holy Spirit instructed them to *"Set apart for me Barnabas and Saul, to do the work to which I have called them."* It is important to note that it was not the church that called them nor was it the church that motivated them to go. The church merely recognized the fact that the Holy Spirit had already called them for missionary service. The task of the church was merely to release them to do the task to which they had been assigned.

We understand, once again, that the Holy Spirit initiated the church starting endeavor. In one sense, we can say that the Antioch church "enabled the church starting team." They did so by providing the training ground in which the church starters could sharpen their skills for cross-cultural church starting. The church also enabled them by providing on-going prayer and moral support for the church starters while they were starting churches in distant places. The Antioch congregation, therefore, was more of a "sending church" or an "enabling church" than a "mother church" to the new churches that were springing up all over Asia Minor.

Audience Contacted (13:14-16; 14:1)

During the early part of his church starting ministry Paul customarily went first to the Jewish Synagogue in the target city. There he generally found three types of people: (1) Jews, (2) Proselytes, and (3) God-fearers. In most instances the bulk of those who received the message were from the latter two categories. When the Jews shut the doors of the synagogue, Paul simply looked for other places in which to meet (e.g. the hall of Tyrannus) and kept right on with the task of finding those who would listen to the gospel.

Gospel Communicated (13:17ff.; 16:31)

It is important to note that Paul employed a wide variety of methods to communicate the Gospel. He preached in the synagogues, taught in rented halls, proclaimed in palaces (during his trial), witnessed by the riverside, evangelized in homes, led people to Christ in jails, shared Christ in the marketplace, communicated the gospel in stadiums, used his contacts as a tentmaker to reach people with the gospel (Priscilla and Aquila) and even used the experiences of being mobbed and going through a shipwreck to let people know the good news of the Gospel. If Paul were alive today he would undoubtedly use all the means at his disposal (including fax, e-mail, and teleconferencing) to proclaim the message of Jesus Christ. He proclaimed the gospel to those who were previously excluded from the family of God (Gentiles and outcasts) and he made it known that these new believers would be first class citizens in the Kingdom of God (Ephesians 2).

Hearers Converted (13:48; 16:14-15)

Paul took the Great Commission seriously. His goal was not merely the proclamation of the Gospel but the conversion of the hearers in order that they might begin to live a life of Christian discipleship. His greatest desire for all people, Jew and Gentile alike, was that they might be saved (Rom. 10:11-12). The mission was not completed until the unbelievers had become followers of Jesus Christ.

Believers Congregated (13:43)

Paul was aware that in order to disciple the converts adequately he needed to gather them together in congregations. These congregations met in rented halls, homes, and wherever else space was available. The important thing was not the place but the congregation of believers. We find no instance in which Paul took into consideration the place in which the congregation was meeting in order to determine if this group could be considered a church. As a matter of fact, he uses the expression "the church that is in your house" repeatedly in his writings (Rom. 16:5).

Faith Confirmed (14:21-22; 15:41)

As Paul and his missionary team saw people come to a saving

knowledge of Christ, they immediately proceeded to make plans to disciple them. *"Paul and Barnabas preached the Good News in Derbe and won many disciples. Then they went back to Lystra, to Iconium, and on to Antioch in Pisidia. They strengthened the believers and encouraged then to remain true to the faith"* (14:21-22). We see that often in his ministry as well as in the ministry of the other Apostles: a strong commitment to provide a strong foundation (the teachings of Christ) for the emerging churches.

Leaders Consecrated (14:23)

"In each church they appointed elders..." (14:23a). It is significant to take notice of the fact that they called each of these congregations "a church." The appointment of elders in each of these young struggling churches points to the fact that Paul and his fellow church starters fully expected these congregations to become strong, responsible, reproducing churches. Their appointment of elders was a statement of faith as well as a practical step to ensure that these churches have the leadership they needed to attain their full potential.

Believers Commended (14:23; 16:40)

"And with prayer and fasting they commended them to the Lord, in whom they had put their trust" (14:23b). The believers were placed in the hands of the Lord and not of the "sending church." While it would be important for them to know that other fellow Christians cared for them, the new congregations were put in a direct line with their maker "the Lord," to whom they were to go in times of need and persecution.

This method implies trust in the Holy Spirit as well as in the new believers and their newly appointed leaders. Is it possible that if we show paternalism toward new Christians and new congregations we are also showing paternalism toward the Holy Spirit? Could this type of attitude imply that the Holy Spirit is not able to lead and undergird these churches in their early stages of development? Paul and his fellow church starters saw themselves as enablers (midwives) in the process of allowing the life of Christ to flow to the new believers, thus, giving birth to these new churches.

Relationships Continued (15:36; 18:23)

"Some time later Paul said to Barnabas, Let us go back and visit our brothers in every town where we preached the word of the Lord, and let us find out how they are getting along" (15:36). It is important to note that Paul and Barnabas had a deep and abiding concern for the welfare of those whom they had led to the Lord. It is also significant to note that they do not call them "children" but "brothers." We see here a concern that seeks to enable the continued spiritual growth of new Christians but also a respect for them knowing that in the ultimate analysis they belong to the Lord and not to them.

Sending Churches Convened

The question of whether Gentiles needed to become Jews culturally and ceremonially in order to be considered fully Christian was of crucial importance to the Church. To impose the practices of the Judaizers upon the Gentiles would have caused Christianity to remain a sect of Judaism. One local congregation could not settle questions regarding this practice alone. The Jerusalem church did not summon the other churches as though she had a higher status. The fact that the Antioch church sent Paul and Barnabas (a former member of the Jerusalem church) indicates that there was a degree of autonomy which each of these churches enjoyed yet a sense of colleagueship as sister churches. Acts 15:2 appears to indicate that it was the Antioch church that took the initiative in this matter.

Significance of Paul's Methodology

What are some things that we can conclude from our study of Paul's methodology at Ephesus and his overall methodology in starting and developing the other churches? First, we see that Paul and his fellow church starters acknowledged time and again that the Holy Spirit was the Divine Director in all of their efforts. A question for us today is: How can we keep our structures, methodologies, and terminology sensitive so that they will enable the work of the Holy Spirit to bring new churches to their complete fruition rather than obstructing His work?

Second, it is evident that prayer undergirded every evangelistic and church starting effort. The church in Jerusalem was born in a prayer meeting. The missionary careers of Barnabas and Saul started in a prayer meeting. When the church starting teams encountered opposition and persecution, they did not contact the denominational headquarters but went directly to God in earnest and fervent prayer. The enabling churches, undoubtedly, bathed every effort in prayer. What is our church starting prayer strategy?

Third, the goal of the apostles was the establishment of responsible, reproducing churches built upon the foundation of Jesus Christ.[45]

Fourth, the terminology that the church starters employed was one that was conducive to maturity and responsibility. They used such words as "believers, brethren, disciples, and churches (even the ones in homes)." There is absolutely no difference between the terminology used to refer to young Christians and young Churches and that employed to refer to more mature Christians and Churches. In other words, it was a terminology of empowerment, enablement, and encouragement and not one that created an attitude of inferiority and dependence. The new congregations were treated as though maturity was expected.

Conclusion

We end with this question: What church starting philosophies, strategies, methodologies, and terminologies do we need to employ to ensure that we respond to the Holy Spirit's initiative and guidance as we seek to encourage and accelerate the establishment of the largest number of New Testament, self-reliant churches throughout the world today? The answer to this important question lies in understanding and remaining faithful to the clear biblical foundation for church starting. No step in the preparation phase of church starting is more important than adherence to the biblical foundation.

CHAPTER 3

SPIRITUAL FOUNDATION

The spread of the gospel in the first century has to be the most amazing accomplishment in the history of the world. Have you ever stopped to consider how the Great Commission, *Go and make disciples of all nations,* must have sounded to the apostles? Lord, are you talking to us? We have never left Palestine. We only know one language and even those within our own land make fun of our accent. Aside from that, we have little or no formal education. Add to all that the fact that we have no financial resources. How then do you expect us to fulfill your command?

In addition to all these factors, the first disciples did not have the printing press, radio, television, fax machines, e-mail, automobiles, airplanes, church buildings, photo copiers, any central organization, financial resources, or influential friends. How then can we account for the fact that during the lifetime of the apostles the Gospel reached Rome, the capital of the then known world, and to the ends of the Empire? Arrayed against them were the ecclesiastical power of the Jewish religion with the Sanhedrin court and the political and military might of the Roman Empire. These early Christians were able to transform the Roman Empire only because of spiritual power brought into reality by the presence and power of the Holy Spirit in them and with them.

In the preparation phase of church starting, no part of the foundation holds a place more important than the spiritual. We turn now to the methods by which we can allow God to work within us the spiritual realities that make a solid spiritual foundation for church starting. Gaining this spiritual foundation begins with depending on the Holy Spirit.

Depending upon the Holy Spirit

As we consider the awesome task of church starting we must focus on the essential, vital, crucial role that the Holy Spirit played (and continues to play) in the spreading of the Gospel and the establishment of the church. When the Holy Spirit came upon the New Testament believers, the Lord gave them everything that they needed to accomplish the task. Church starters need to be thoroughly familiar with the role that the Holy Spirit plays in starting new congregations and completely dependent on his guidance, presence, and power as they seek to accomplish this awesome task.[46]

Neil Cole acknowledges the value of utilizing correct methods but points out that there are merely tools in the accomplishment of the main objective. He explains:

> Hear me when I say that it is not the methodology that transforms lives. It is only the power of the gospel of Jesus Christ applied to a needy soul by the Holy Spirit. The methodology is only helpful in that it brings the desperate sinner into prolonged contact with God and His Word in the context of community with others who are also pursuing the Lord.[47]

Craig Van Gelder echoes this when he observes that "the church's focus must be primarily that of discerning and responding to the leading of the Spirit."[48] Clearly, the church starter must depend solidly on the Holy Spirit.

The Holy Spirit Empowers for Mission

The last thing Jesus said to his followers before being taken up into heaven was: "You shall receive power when the Holy Spirit has come upon you and you shall be My witnesses both in Jerusalem, and in all Judea and Samaria, and even to the remotest part of the earth" (Acts 1:6-8). His disciples had enquired about political power to overthrow the Roman oppression, "Wilt thou at this time restore the kingdom to Israel?" But Jesus promised and promises a different kind of power: "dunamis." The term dunamis relates to the complete and adequate equipment of mind and spirit necessary for the gigantic task of world evangelization.

Commenting on the implications of Pentecost for the work of the Church, missionary historian Albert von Ostertag states: "The church received from Christ not merely the command but also the inner, mighty, irresistible drive of life and love to transmit to her environment the life she had received."[49] [50]

How did the Holy Spirit empower the early Christians and how does he empower us today?

First, the Holy Spirit empowered and empowers by giving a spirit of courage. This is seen most dramatically in Simon Peter who denied the Master before a domestic servant but later proclaims Christ before a bewildered multitude (Acts 2). We see this also in Acts 4 and 5. In face of the threats and warnings of the Jewish leaders, threats which included imprisonment and even death, the Apostles with the entire body of believers prayed: *"Now, Lord, consider their threats and enable your servants to speak your word with great boldness"* (Acts 4: 29).

The same phenomenon is reported in Acts chapter 5. The authorities had threatened Peter and the Apostles against teaching in the name of Jesus. But they responded fearlessly: *"We must obey God rather than men."* Then they proceeded to witness even to those who were threatening them: *"The God of our fathers raised up Jesus whom you put to death by hanging him on the cross. He is the one whom God exalted to His right hand as a Prince and Savior to grant repentance to Israel and forgiveness of sins. And we are witnesses of these things; and so is the Holy Spirit, whom God has given to those who obey Him"* (Acts 5: 30-32). Without question the Holy Spirit empowered and emboldened both the Apostles and the entire body of believers.

Second, the Holy Spirit empowers by giving a spirit of love. Evangelistic zeal does not grow out of intellectual beliefs nor out of theological arguments but out of love. Knowledge of Christ is so rich a treasure that the spirit of love necessarily produces desire to share and impart it. Rom 5:5 says: *"And hope maketh not ashamed because the love of God is shed abroad in our hearts by the Holy Spirit which is given to us."*

Third, the Holy Spirit empowers by inspiring the words of the witness. When Peter shared the Gospel at Pentecost his words were so inspired by the Holy Spirit that his hearers were *"cut to the heart"* (Acts 2:37). When Stephen addressed the elders in the Synagogue, they were *"unable to withstand the wisdom and the Spirit with which he spoke."* One of the main fears of potential witnesses is that they might not know what to say. They need to be assured that the Holy Spirit will be there to inspire their words.

Nate Krupp sums up the biblical truth relating to the work of the Holy Spirit in equipping God's people for the task. He points out that the Spirit equips the body to function. He teaches that the Church is not to operate using the talents and strengths of natural men. Rather, he says, "The Church functions as God designed when the Holy Spirit is allowed to freely and completely fill, anoint, gift, and move in and through all of the believers who are assembled together."[51]

The Holy Spirit Provides Strategy for Mission

In addition to empowering God's servants for ministry, including church starting, the Holy Spirit also provides the strategy for mission. First, the Holy Spirit provides the overall strategy. I have not ceased to be amazed at the manner in which the Holy Spirit led the early church. In Acts 1:8, Jesus gives the outline of the strategy that the Holy Spirit would furnish. *"And you shall be my witnesses in Jerusalem, and in all Judea and Samaria and even to the remotest part of the earth."* This declaration provides the outline; the rest of the book of Acts shows how the mission actually took place.

Second, the Holy Spirit leads individuals at strategic moments. The Holy Spirit did certainly provide the overall strategy for the spread of the Gospel. He also, however, led individuals: (1) Philip to the Ethiopian (Acts 8:29); (2) Peter to Cornelius (Acts 10:19); (3) Paul to Macedonia (Acts 16:6, 7). In his book *Missionary Methods: Saint Paul's or Ours*, Roland Allen spends a great deal of time describing the marvelous missionary strategy employed by Paul. Allen shows that Paul concentrated in population centers of Roman Administration, Greek civilization, Jewish influence, and world commerce.[52]

Allen continues reminding that the Holy Spirit led Paul. There were many centers like these. But as the Holy Spirit opened the door Paul seized upon that place and made it a strategic center of evangelistic activity. In essence, Allen is saying that it was the Holy Spirit's strategy and Paul simply followed. Does the Holy Spirit have a plan for the evangelization of your state, city, or community?

Third, the Holy Spirit leads the Church at strategic moments. The Holy Spirit helped the apostles to solve the crisis related to the Grecian Widows as reported in Acts 6. He led the Apostles to leave Jerusalem and begin spreading the Message in Samaria and other regions (Acts 8). He commissioned the missionary team (Acts 13). At the Jerusalem Council (Acts 15) He helped the church leaders to make the right decision concerning Gentile converts.

Missionary strategy is never a human creation. Missionary strategy is ever a divine matter. An important part of the spiritual foundation for all ministries, including church starting, relates to seeking the guidance of the Holy Spirit in forming the strategy to be followed. Without this spiritual foundation, church starting will not reach God's ideal.

The Holy Spirit Produces Results

As God's workers must look to the Spirit for power and strategy, so must they look to the Spirit for the results of the mission. In the ultimate analysis, it is not by might, nor by power, but by my Spirit says the Lord of hosts (Zech 4:6). How does the Spirit assure the results of a mission?

First, the Holy Spirit convicts of the truth of the gospel. We live in a world in which people have changed the truth of God for a lie and worship the creature rather than the creator. How can we convince people who have their own saints, prophets, shrines, pagodas, books, beads, and astrologers that Jesus is the Son of God? It is only through the power of the Holy Spirit that people can come to knowledge of Jesus Christ. "No man can say Jesus is Lord except by the Holy Spirit" (1 Cor 12:3).

Second, the Holy Spirit convicts of sin. Many people with whom we deal have little or no sense of sin. Some people are so steeped in sin that they are past feeling. Some have come to love darkness rather than light. Mahatma Gandhi admired Jesus Christ and was very fond of the Sermon on the Mount. But he did not take kindly to the notion that man is a sinner. He thought that the Indians were an ancient and noble race and did not like for outsiders to come and tell them they were sinners.

Where no human can convince others of their sinfulness, the Holy Spirit has conviction of sin as a major part of His task. John 16:8 clearly states: "And when he is come, he will reprove the world of sin and of righteousness and of judgment."

Third, the Holy Spirit converts the sinner. While human instruments are called upon by God to proclaim the good news of salvation, it is ultimately the work of the Holy Spirit to bring about the transformation in the life of the sinner. The Spirit of God makes real the salvation experience within the lives of believers.

Joe Hernandez provides an excellent summary of the work of the Holy Spirit's role in church planting. He includes the following:

- Empowers and emboldens for evangelization
- Enables cross-cultural communication of the gospel
- Provides the power which brings spiritual awakening
- Works through willing vessels (believers)
- Qualifies, equips, and empowers Kingdom service
- Enablement to endure persecution for the gospel
- Guidance for divine appointments
- Encouragement
- Kingdom expansion
- Conviction of the lost
- Consecration and commissioning
- Guidance in and to the harvest
- Speaks through believers[53]

The preparation phase of church starting seeks to establish, by God's power and leading, the necessary spiritual foundation. This spiritual foundation comes by and through the Holy Spirit. Another factor in the spiritual foundation for church starting is discovering and using spiritual gifts.

Discovering and Using Spiritual Gifts

Church starters must discover and use their spiritual gifts in the ministry of starting new congregations. The Holy Spirit provides all the gifts that are necessary for this ministry. The Apostle Paul enumerates spiritual gifts in 1 Corinthians 12, Romans 12, and Ephesians 4. These lists are most likely not exhaustive, but still, in these lists one can find the gifts that are essential for church starting. Among these gifts are evangelism, preaching, teaching, faith, leadership, administration, and ministry.

As a preliminary step, prospective church starters should seek to discover the spiritual gifts that God has given them. Three activities can help them to discover and utilize their spiritual gifts for church starting. First, study what the Bible says. Second, utilize the gifts to find confirmation from God and from spiritual people around them. Third, exercise the spiritual gifts that have been confirmed in their lives as they engage in church starting. Some biblically based, carefully prepared spiritual gift inventories can help in gaining understanding regarding the gifts that God has given them.

Those who start reproducing congregations should recognized that no one Christian will receive all the spiritual gifts and no one of the gifts is intended for every believer. This fact impacts working together to start these congregations. The group can seek out people with differing gifts so that the task of the congregation can be most effectively carried out.

As the reader will understand from the material in this book, the overall task of starting reproducing churches demands various types of church starters. Different groups of spiritual gifts provide the needs of persons to start different kinds of churches or to employ different methods of church starting. Church starters must, therefore, discover and use their spirit-given abilities.

Evaluating Your Spiritual Disciplines

In addition to discovering their spiritual gifts, church starters need to evaluate their spiritual disciplines. Several vital spiritual disciplines can enable the church starter to be an effective instrument in God's hands. If, however, a church starter is weak in these disciplines, his/her work will not reach its highest potential.

In his book *The Spirit Of The Disciplines*, Dallas Willard discusses "disciplines of abstinence" as well as "disciplines of engagement."[54] Both of these types of spiritual disciplines are important and we will list the ones that relate more directly to church starting.

Disciplines of Abstinence

Some of the needs for ministry can be termed disciplines of abstinence—that is, the discipline to abstain from certain activities for the sake of the ministry. Among these disciplines of abstinence are:

- **Solitude/Silence** - To be alone and remain quiet before God (Psa 46:10)

- **Fasting** - To abstain from eating in order to focus on God (Acts 13:2)

- **Frugality** - To adopt a simpler lifestyle (Mic 6:8; Jam 5:1-5)

- **Moral Purity** - To possess one's vessel in sanctification and honor (1 Thess 4:4; 1 Cor 7:5)

- **Sacrifice** - To abandon oneself and one's possessions to God in faith (Luke 21:2-4)

Disciplines of Engagement

Other disciplines might be called disciplines of engagement since they represent actions and attitudes actually attempted by believers. These disciplines include:

- **Study** - To read, hear, inquire, and meditate on God's Word and his Work (2 Tim 3:16)

- **Worship/Celebration/Fellowship** - To express the beauty, greatness, and goodness of God in common activities of worship, study, prayer, celebration, and service with other believers (Rev 4:11; 6:1-3)

- **Service** - To serve the Lord by ministering to others (Matt 20:25-28; Col 3:22-24)

- **Prayer** - Talking with and listening to God (1 Thess 5:17)

- **Submission** - To accept humbly the authority of those whom God has set over us (Heb 13:7; Eph. 5:21)

Obviously, some of the disciplines listed above (e.g. fasting) may be engaged in during specific periods of time. Others, however, are essential, ongoing disciplines. It is difficult to imagine that church starters can be effective either in their personal lives or in their ministries without such disciplines as the study of God's Word, prayer, worship, and service. At the outset of a church starting effort, therefore, it is very helpful for church starters to stop and analyze their walk with the Lord from the standpoint of these spiritual disciplines.

Spiritual disciplines can be listed under the following categories: Personal Devotions, Corporate Worship, Christian Service, Gospel Witness, Christian Character, and Christian Stewardship. For a survey on these spiritual disciplines, see chapter 2 in the Starting Reproducing Congregations Workbook.[55]

Church starters should strive to incorporate into their lives such disciplines as daily witnessing, scheduled meetings with a mentor, worship, etc. An analysis of these disciplines in the lives of church starters would lead them to ask for the Lord's guidance as they establish action plans to be more diligent in specific areas. The Spiritual Disciplines Inventory provided in the workbook for this chapter can help church starters address this area of their preparation.

Because church starting is a spiritual task, setting a spiritual foundation is absolutely essential. Church starters should engage in the task with a full knowledge of and dependence upon the work of the Holy Spirit. They should never forget that the same risen Lord who said: "I will build my church" also made provision for the coming of the Holy Spirit to guide in the accomplishment of this divine goal. While church starters have the assurance that the Holy Spirit will be present to guide and empower their efforts, they must be mindful of the spiritual warfare that they will encounter. This will manifest itself as direct warfare, indirect warfare, and warfare in the lives of the non-Christian prospects. This warfare can only be countered with a personal prayer life and the active involvement of an intercessory prayer team. Additional spiritual disciplines such as worship, Bible study, and service will contribute toward establishing a solid foundation for church starting.

Engaging in Spiritual Warfare

Satan fears new congregations. Some of the most serious threats to Satan and his designs are congregations reproducing by starting new congregations, Christians living lives consistent with the Scriptures, and believers sharing their God-given faith with unbelievers. Satan and his demon co-workers tremble at the sight of any of these three "threats" to the satanic efforts. Because new congregations constitute some of the most direct threats to satanic plans, the Devil will resist all efforts to start new churches. These new congregations and the efforts that bring them into being are the most effective evangelistic avenues we have.

Because of the importance of new churches, Church starters will inevitably face satanic efforts to nullify their efforts and bring failures to their ministries. Because of the spiritual power that is involved in starting these congregations, Satan must seek to disrupt. Clinton Arnold writes that Christians (and Church starters) can no more evade spiritual warfare than a gardener can evade weeds.[56] Church starters must prepare for the inevitable warfare they will face with Satan.

The Meaning of Spiritual Warfare

What do we mean by the term spiritual warfare? Spiritual warfare is the direct effort by Christians to confront the inevitable conflict with Satan and his minions as they attempt to bring suffering and distress to this world. Spiritual warfare takes place when Christians use the powers available from God to overthrow Satan and his plans. Spiritual warfare is the efforts to move toward the goal of deliverance from this power and influence. Believers accept the certainty of the conflict but also the definite promise of power for the victory. A full definition of spiritual warfare can be stated:

> Spiritual Warfare, the process of working in God's supernatural power, involves the ministries of combating the living, personal, evil, demonic powers of Satan and his demons on the societal, territorial, and individual levels for the purposes of resisting and curbing their evil efforts and influences and reaching freedom from satanic bondage through such power encounters as cleansing, healing, knowledge, exorcism, and social reconciliation for the purposes of gospel proclamation, evangelism, cleansing, assuring, and restoring men and women and churches to spiritual health and maintaining them in that state.[57]

The Bible definitely and directly asserts that Christians will engage in a struggle against rulers, authorities, powers, and the spiritual forces of evil.

> [10]Finally, be strong in the Lord and in his mighty power. [11]Put on the full armor of God so that you can take your stand against the devil's schemes. [12]For **our struggle** is not against flesh and blood, but **against the rulers, against the authorities, against the powers of this dark world and against the spiritual forces of evil in the heavenly realms.** [13]Therefore put on the full armor of God, so that when the day of after you have evil comes, you may be able to stand your ground, and done everything, to stand (Eph 6:10-13).

Scripture likewise assures believers that they already, in Christ, possess sufficient power and strength for this struggle. We need no magic formulae or rituals. God supplies His servants with adequate and sufficient resources for this cosmic effort. While remaining certain of Satan's reality and presence and the evil efforts of demons, 21st-Century Christians remain confident that Christ defeated Satan when the Savior died on the Cross and this victory remains certain until the end. Again the Apostle affirms:

> [9]For in Christ all the fullness of the Deity lives in bodily form, [10]and you have been given fullness in **Christ, who is the head over every power and authority**. [11]In him you were also circumcised, in the putting off of the sinful nature, not with a circumcision done by the hands of men but with the circumcision done by Christ, [12]having been buried with him in baptism and raised with him through your faith in the power of God, who raised him from the dead (Col 2:9-12).

Deliverance of people, churches, and societies from the corroding power of Satan is the goal of spiritual warfare. Bondage is Satan's plan. Deliverance from this bondage is the direction that the Spirit intends for all people and groups. Satan's bondage power will be broken as sincere believers accept God's great power to break the Devil's power. Christians should remember, however, that spiritual warfare rages on the individual and personal level every day as Satan seeks to move believers from the path of consistent Christian living to the destructiveness of unbiblical attitudes and acts. The Bible stresses:

> [1]As for you, you were dead in your transgressions and sins, [2]in which you used to live when you followed the ways of this world and of the ruler of the kingdom of the air, **the spirit who is now at work in those who are disobedient**. [3]All of us also lived among them at onetime, gratifying the cravings of our sinful nature and following its desires and thoughts. Like the rest, we were by nature objects of wrath. [4]But because of his great love for us, God, who is rich in mercy, **[5]made us alive with Christ** even when we were dead in transgressions—it is by grace you have been saved (Eph 2:1-5).

The concept of deliverance is clearly expressed in the Book of Acts:

> [5] Then I [The Apostle Paul] asked, 'Who are you, Lord?' 'I am Jesus, whom you are persecuting,' the Lord replied. [16]'Now get up and stand on your feet. I have appeared to you to appoint you as a servant and as a witness of what you have seen of me and what I will show you. [17]I will rescue you from your own people and from the Gentiles. **I am sending you to them [18]to open their eyes and turn them from darkness to light, and from the power of Satan to God, so that they may receive forgiveness of sins and a place among those who are sanctified by faith in me'** (Acts 26:15-18).

Spiritual warfare is, then, the effort of trusting Christians to operate in the power of Christ to resist and overcome the efforts of Satan and his demons by guiding people everywhere to experience the deliverance that resides only in Christ. The method is by the power of God though the Holy Spirit.

The purpose is deliverance from the bondage in which Satan delights in holding believers and congregations. Never should efforts in spiritual warfare be used or considered in matters of personal notoriety. The ultimate goal is the glory of God in his wondrous works. Christians who participate directly in spiritual warfare must, however, hold basic convictions concerning spiritual warfare and the ways it is engaged if they hope to be effective in their ministries.

Convictions Regarding Spiritual Warfare

Church starters must live by biblical convictions in every aspect of their ministries and service. The need for biblical convictions is nowhere more important than in the area of spiritual warfare. In considering spiritual warfare, one encounters many ideas and concepts. Some of these concepts are not fully biblical. The following biblical convictions about spiritual warfare are necessary for church planters:

- The reality of Satan and demons who are living and acting today fully as much as they did in New Testament days

- The evil designs that Satan and his demons have toward humankind, the churches, societies, institutions, and God's Kingdom in general

- The inevitability of conflict with Satan and his demons in carrying out the efforts to start new and reproducing congregations

- The belief that Satan's power, though significant, is limited and that the conclusion to the struggle is already certain having been settled on the Cross

- The truth that adequate power for this conflict is available to Christians in Christ

- The truth than human magic, ritual, or strength is unnecessary in spiritual warfare. In fact, attempting to find and use any magic or human effort could negate God's power to provide in the struggle

- The understanding that Satan will do all in his power to disturb and defeat the efforts to win more people, plant more congregations, and guide the believers into new life

Church starters cannot evade or escape spiritual warfare. God's Word assures that those who will start reproducing congregations that they will face satanic forces and yet can have full assurance that they serve with all that is needed to defeat Satan and reach the full intention of God. The servants of the Lord rest in the absolute faith that God's plan will be achieved.

The struggle on this plane will be won and the eventual struggle over the evil powers will be conclusive. These four imperative assurances, then, form the foundations for 21st century church starters:

- Because of Satan's reality and obvious intentions, church starters will of necessity engage in spiritual warfare with Satan and his co-workers.

- Church starters will enter this struggle with full assurance of adequate power for winning this spiritual engagement

- Christians need nothing more than God's power through the Holy Spirit to accomplish the ultimate goals of spiritual warfare

- Due to the assurance of God's adequate powers, church starters have full confidence in the realization of their present ministries and the certain, eventual victory of God through the destruction of Satan and his demons.

The Directions for Spiritual Warfare

The methods that church starters will use in spiritual warfare are the same methods any other believer or group of believers will use. Those striving to start reproducing congregations should expect to receive special attention from Satan and the demons. This fact demands that church starters consider what methods and means they should church starters use in this inevitable spiritual warfare against Satan and his demons?

Recent years have seen the publication of reams of literature relating to spiritual warfare and ways Christians can and should participate in the struggle. Most of this material has great value. Some may overemphasize certain aspects of the effort. Looking at spiritual warfare in church planting, we would suggest the following simplified pattern for church starters and their engagement in spiritual warfare. Each church starter will find the exact types of efforts that will equip him/her for engagement in spiritual warfare in this day.

Prepare

As with most endeavors, success begins with preparation.

Obviously, church planters will expect resistance from Satan and must prepare for the struggle. The first reality of this preparation consists of accepting the reality and presence of satanic activity in this world in general and the planter's service in particular.

As part of the preparation for spiritual warfare, the church planter should reach the point of acceptance of the reality and certainty of satanic attack. The Church starter should move away from what C. S. Lewis calls the materialistic position. By the term, "materialistic position" Lewis means the refusal or failure to believe in and accept the reality of Satan and demons. This mistaken conviction, says Lewis, is one of the two most dangerous ideas connected with spiritual welfare.

The second dangerous and mistaken concept relating to spiritual warfare, according to Lewis, is that of magician, by which he means one who gives too much attention to demons, spends too much time seeking them, and thinking that demons and Satan can be controlled by magic means such as rituals or sayings. Lewis writes,

> There are to equal and opposite errors into which our race can fall about the devils. One is to disbelieve in their existence. The other is to believe, and to feel an excessive and unhealthy interest in them.[58]

Later in the same book, Lewis has Screwtape tell Wormwood that if humans can be made either materialists (disbelieving in devils) or magicians (having excessive interest in the devils or believing they can be controlled by ritual or magic) the "end of the war would be in sight."[59] Thus, a biblical understanding of Satan, demons, and spiritual warfare is a starting point for the way to prepare for spiritual warfare.

A second effort in preparing for spiritual is the practice of developing spiritual armor for the battle. The spiritual armor of course comes from God through the ministry of the Holy Spirit. As parts of this spiritual armor the church planter should ask for biblical understanding of Satan and his means of attack. The Apostle Paul counsels the Christian to accept and put on the "full" armor of God because our struggle is not against flesh and blood (that is human foes) but the dark powers that are superhuman (Eph 6:10-13).

Constant watchfulness is a third aspect of preparing for spiritual warfare. Knowing that Satan is always on the job and seeking disruption and destruction of God's plans, guides the Christian to constant vigilance in spiritual matters. The Christians prays for the Holy Spirit to make him aware of direct stacks by satanic powers on either individuals or groups such as churches.

A fourth and most important aspect of preparing for spiritual warfare is simply living the consistent Christian life. The spiritual discipline of consistent living develops strength for the struggle for Satan that may take many forms. Living in relationship to the Father through the Son and the aid of the Holy Spirit makes one able to participate fully and successfully in the struggles with satanic forces.

Spiritual warfare will arise in the church starters life and ministry. Adequate preparation is essential. After the preparation, the church planter will engage in spiritual warfare as needed in his life and work.

Engage

Having prepared for spiritual warfare, the church starter should be ready and willing to engage directly in the struggle. Spiritual warfare is far more than a few open and spectacular events of opposing Satan. Every day the church starter will strive to practice those Christian virtues of love, mercy, kindness, purity, and servanthood. Satan makes every effort to move Christians to hate, vengeance, selfishness, impurity, and unkindness. Allowing God's Spirit to deliver us from such unbiblical practices is as much spiritual warfare as participating in an exorcism. Church starters engage in spiritual warfare on the personal level.

In the process of engaging in spiritual warfare, Christians should be careful never to becoming excessively concerned about these encounters. Spirits do not lurk behind every bush. Every evil happening is not the direct action of a demon. We do not practice our ministry looking for evidences of satanic efforts that we can resist. These evil efforts will arise without our seeking. The church planter will, however, remain on guard and watchful for evidences that events are indeed the work of the Evil One.

When evidence of Satan's work and opposition do arise, the church starter should be prepared, ready, and willing to engage the satanic powers. Without resorting to magic or ritual, the Christian will allow the Holy Spirit to guide him/her in the effort to face the evil power. If exorcism (the ministry of delivering a person from the domination of Satan or demons) is called for, the Christian should be willing to perform the ministry. The fact that some might questions such activity should not deter Christians form direct activity in spiritual warfare.

The church starter will be willing to engage directly in spiritual warfare when the need arises. Due to the available power for the effort and the inevitability of the struggle, church planters bravely face the confrontation with Satan. This effort to directly face Satan and his efforts is not, however, the primary task of the church planter. Wining people to Christ, developing them in the Christian disciplines, and gathering them into reproducing congregations constitutes the task of the church planter. Over concern about certain aspects of spiritual warfare can at times distract church starters from their main tasks.

Trust

As already indicated, the church planter does not provide the power or ability either to start the new congregation nor to resist and defeat the designs of the Evil One. These powers come only from God. Christians in their own strength never have the abilities to accomplish either task. Christians can but trust to the Holy Spirit for needed power.

Also as already indicated, the church starter will not depend on any man-made methods, objects, rituals, or approaches. Any hint of magic in spiritual warfare constitutes a major danger and flaw. Using any form of magic is actually a sign of not fully trusting in God. Magic is both unnecessary and dangerous and has no place in the lives of dedicated and believing Chritians.

As Jesus gave the Great Commission, he proclaimed that all authority in heaven and earth was his. On the basis of this authority, Jesus sent his people (including contemporary church starters) to make disciples from among all nations. In this promise, church starters can rest and trust God for guidance, power, and success in spiritual warfare. The Great Commission is the marching order for God's people but it is also assurance for their victory.

Glorify God

A recurring problem attaches itself to efforts in spiritual warfare—the problem of seeking personal advance from the process. Christians today should enter spiritual warfare only to glorify God and participate in His great program for winning this world. Personal fame or profit must ever be avoided in spiritual warfare. To God be the glory and to His cause be the advance. Every activity and every victory in spiritual warfare should result in glory to God and His greatness. All the church starter strives to do must be directly in the effort to glorify God.

Because of the importance of their work in God's Kingdom, church starters can expect to be assaulted by the efforts of Satan and his demons. Christians engaged in starting new congregations will face spiritual opposition from satanic forces. Christians should, therefore, rely on God's power, through God's Spirit to defeat the evil forces of Satan and have a part in God's great and ultimate victory. God's people participate in spiritual warfare for His glory and no other reason.

Establishing a Prayer Foundation

Prayer is an indispensable part of the spiritual foundation for church starting. Jesus said: *"I will build my church and the gates of hell shall not prevail against it"* (Mt. 16:18). Two powerful implications emerge in this statement.[60] First, it is Jesus who builds his church and not the church starter. Since Jesus is the architect, it is very important for the church starter to cultivate the habit of spending time in prayer seeking instruction and guidance from the Lord regarding the church that is being started.

Second, church starting is a spiritual endeavor. The statement, *"the gates of hell shall not prevail against it,"* reveals the fact that the church is involved in a spiritual battle. In this battle, Jesus gives the picture of the Church as advancing even to the strongholds of Satan and liberating people with the power of the gospel. The apostle Paul reminds us that we wrestle not against flesh and blood, but against powers—both human and supernatural (Eph 6:12). The person who believes that church starting is simply a matter of utilizing appropriate strategies and methods is as ill equipped for the battle as persons using bows and arrows against an army with automatic weapons. The church starter, therefore, must have a well-defined prayer strategy personally as well as for the intercessors.

Personal Prayer Strategy

The prayer foundation for church starting begins with personal prayer strategy. Thomas Wade Akins, a missionary who has been instrumental in starting hundreds of churches in Brazil and throughout the world makes the following suggestions concerning a personal prayer strategy.[61]

- **Praise** -begin your prayer with praise. Sing hymns to God, sing or read praise choruses, and read passages of prayers in the Bible and personalize each verse. When you praise God you thank him for who he is.

- **Thanksgiving** - gratefulness is thanking God for what he has done.

- **Confession** - during our time alone with God, the Holy Spirit may bring to mind recent unconfessed sins. We should confess all the sins in our hearts.

- **Hearing God's voice** - God uses primarily two means to speak to His believers on a daily basis: the Holy Spirit and His Word. It is necessary, therefore, to read and apply the lessons from Scripture continually.

- **Paraphrasing the Word of God** - the church starter can use a verse to pray to God. Utilizing Eph 1:1, for example, you can pray: "I thank you God because you called me to be a disciple of Jesus Christ." Then proceed to the second verse, etc.

- **Intercession** - this means praying for other people (Eph. 6:18). Make a list of the days of the week and under each place the name of the people for whom you will pray. For example: Sunday - pray for the pastor and church leaders; Monday - pray for family members and friends; Tuesday - pray for people you know who are lost; Wednesday - pray for missionaries and convention leaders; Thursday - pray for the leaders of your country (1 Tim 2:1,2); Friday - pray for people who have fallen away from the church; Saturday - pray for fellow church members and special projects in which you are involved.

- **Meditation and Scripture memory** - God's purpose is to make the church starter conform to the image of Christ (Rom 8:29). Choose a verse in the Bible each week. Read the verse in its context. Ask God to show you the spiritual truths in this verse. Personalize the verse in a prayer. Write the verse on a card including the reference. During the day, read the verse several times. Read the verse before you go to bed to embed it in your subconscious.

- **Supplication** - this means simply presenting to God our own needs. "Let us then approach the throne of grace with confidence, so that we may receive mercy and find grace to help us in the time of need" (Heb 4:16).

Additional guidance for prayer is found in the Master Life program.[7] In this discipleship training guide, Avery Willis gives the following steps for praying in faith: (1) Abide in Christ (John 15:7); (2) Abide in the Word (John 15:7); (3) Allow the Holy Spirit to lead (John 16:13-15; 14:26); (4) Ask according to God's will (John 15:7; Matt 7:7-11); (5) Accept God's will in faith (1 John 5:14-15); and (6) Act on the basis of God's Word for you (John 9:7; Luke 17:14).

In this guide, Willis also stresses the importance of putting on God's spiritual armor for spiritual battles. He states: "The spiritual warrior begins every battle on his knees." It is through prayer that he/she clothes himself/herself with all the other articles of spiritual armor before going out to meet the foe.[62] Willis then suggests how a Christian can put on this armor:

- **The Helmet of Salvation** - Picture the helmet of salvation that you received when Christ saved you.

- **The Breastplate of Righteousness** - Picture the breastplate that was given you by Christ and has produced righteous living in you.

- **The Belt of Truth** - Picture the belt of truth that holds the rest of the armor in place. Truth in this passage means integrity and moral uprightness.

- **Feet Shod with the Preparation of the Gospel of Peace** - Picture the studded sandals of a soldier on your feet. The preparation of the gospel of peace means that you are prepared and ready for battle.

- **Sword of the Spirit** - Picture the sword of the Spirit, the Word of God, in your right hand. The Word means "God's utterance" and refers to God's speaking to you about specific situations.

- **Shield of Faith** - Above all, picture yourself holding the shield of faith in your other hand. Let the shield of faith remind you to claim victory, advance in faith, and quench all the fiery darts of the wicked.

It is essential that the church starter put on the spiritual armor before engaging in the battle of starting churches. Just as experienced pilot checks out all of the equipment in the airplane before initiating the flight, the church starter should pray every day for the spiritual armor that God has promised His soldiers. The personal prayer life of the church starter needs to provide a strong foundation for the church starting task.

Intercessory Team Prayer Strategy

In order to be effective, the church starter also needs to be supported by the fervent, constant, and focused prayers of an intercessory team. Every church starter should seek a group of dedicated Christians to bond with him/her for prayer for the mission. These prayer partners will be fully committed to and engaged in the project. Those who are chosen as prayer partners need to have the following characteristics:

- Passion for the lost and church planting
- A consistent prayer life
- An interest in your ministry
- Faithfulness to their prayer commitments
- The ability to keep confidence63

The Heavenly Prayer Partners

When church starters think about the concept of prayer partners, they are prone to focus only on earthly prayer partners. Dan Crawford reminds us that we have heavenly prayer partners. He quotes Wesley Duewel: "God the Son is your enthroned prayer partner and God the Holy Spirit is your indwelling prayer partner." Crawford adds:

> As our prayer partner, Jesus prays for us just as He did for His own disciples (Luke 22:23; John 17; Heb 7:25). As a prayer partner, Jesus affects our prayer life in at least three ways: we learn to pray in agreement with Him, in confidence with Him, and in persistence with Him. The Holy Spirit also acts as a prayer partner. According to Rom 8:26-27, the Holy Spirit *"helps our weaknesses," "guides us in how to pray as we should," "intercedes for us," "searches our hearts,"* and helps us to discern *"the will of God."* In addition to Jesus and the Holy Spirit serving as our prayer partners, there is a partnership entered into with the angels. Angels are assigned by God "to render service for the sake of those who will inherit salvation (Heb 1:14).[64]

It is reassuring to know that the church starter can count on the heavenly prayer partners whom God provided. Other prayer help is also available to church planters.

The Earthly Prayer Partners

In addition to the heavenly prayer partners, earthly prayer partners also contribute in significant ways to the effectiveness of the church starter. Jesus encouraged his followers to pray together when He said: *"If two of you agree on earth about anything they may ask, it shall be done for them by my Father who is in heaven* (Matt 18:19). Prayer partners can play a key role when they join the church starter in seeking God's will and asking for His power and guidance in a church starting effort.

Prospective church starters often and properly ask the crucial question, "Where can I find effective prayer partners?" Robert Logan has excellent suggestions for those seeking to find an answer to this question. He advises: "Make a list of any people who: (1) have said they will pray for you; (2) call and ask for prayer requests; (3) ask if you have had answers to their prayers; (4) you know to be people of prayer; (5) have received ministry from you where you felt a 'chemistry,' that is, you liked them and they liked you."[65]

In addition to these prayer partners, prospective church starters may enlist additional intercessors that the church starter has trained to pray. Some church starters conduct prayer seminars and in the process get to know people who are gifted in the area of prayer but have never developed the gift. From such persons, the church starter can find prayer partners.

Once the intercessors have been found, the church starter should seek to help them to understand their roles. It is also very important to share prayer requests with the partners on a regular basis. These requests need to be specific so that both the intercessors and the church starter can know when prayers have been answered. Asking God to "bless a community" or to bless efforts to "reach a target group" is too vague. Specific prayers, on the other hand, will give the intercessors the opportunity to rejoice when God answers their prayers.

It is very helpful also to share information about prayer (e.g. books, articles) with intercessors. This shared information helps the intercessors continue to grow in their ministry. Encouraging the intercessors to pray for one another as well as for the church starter can also contribute toward their spiritual growth.

A prayer foundation is absolutely essential for church starting. The church starter needs to have a disciplined prayer life. Recognizing that Jesus, the Holy Spirit, and God's angels are a part of the prayer team can give the church starter a deep sense of confidence and power. The ministry of an intercessory prayer team is also vital to the success of a church starting effort. Throughout the epistles of Paul we find examples of the prayers that he prayed for his co- workers as well as of his requests for prayer. Paul knew that the spiritual battle inherent in church starting could not be won without the continued fervent prayer of the faithful. The church starter should have the same commitment to prayer.

Conclusion

A strong spiritual foundation remains an absolute essential in starting reproducing congregations. This foundation involves depending fully on the Holy Spirit's power and working solely through the Spirit's ever sufficient empowering. This spiritual foundation also involves discovering, developing, and working within the church starter's spiritual gifts and disciplines.

The church starter also will recognize that starting new congregations that envision continuing reproduction challenge Satan's kingdom. Satan will answer this challenge with his evil opposition. The church starter will anticipate, engage in, but not fear engaging in spiritual warfare. The church starter moves in the assurance that adequate power for this struggle exists and will be available.

The spiritual preparation of the church starter must include the establishing of a vital and growing prayer foundation. The prayer foundation for the spiritual task of starting reproducing congregations involves both personal prayer and that of persons recruited to join the church starter in prayer for the endeavor.

Church planting is a spiritual undertaking and must, therefore, have a vital, living, and adequate spiritual foundation.

CHAPTER 4

EVANGELISTIC FOUNDATION

Of all the factors in the preparation phase of church starting none is more important that the evangelistic foundation. ***Evangelism is an absolutely essential part of church starting***. Church starters need to contact unchurched people, develop friendships with them, establish with them a level of trust, communicate the basic truths of the Gospel, lead them to a personal faith in Jesus Christ, baptize them into the fellowship of the church, and guide them in ongoing discipleship. Dependence upon the guidance and work of the Holy Spirit, as has been emphasized in the previous chapter, is the first step in the evangelization task.

Many people have the tendency to think that there is only one method of evangelism. Too often this method either intimidates the evangelist or those to whom they witness. All effective church starting requires an evangelistic foundation that consists of a variety of evangelistic methods.

Methods of Evangelism

A study of the New Testament reveals that the Holy Spirit guided the early church to utilize a wide variety of evangelistic methods. Among these methods one detects references to mass evangelism, cell-group evangelism, personal evangelism, subtle evangelism, and literary evangelism.[66]

Mass Evangelism

The early church utilized a variety of mass evangelism methods. As long as they had the opportunity they preached the Gospel in the temple in Jerusalem (Acts 5:42). As they scattered to other regions they preached in the synagogues. The strategy of Paul and his co-workers was to go first to the synagogue of each city and present Christ as the fulfillment of Old Testament prophecies. When the doors of the synagogue closed to them, the early Christians found other public places.

Paul, for example, utilized the school of Tyrannus (Acts 19:9). The Christians also preached in open-air gatherings (Acts 3), in the market place (Acts 17:17), and in stadiums (Acts 17:19).[67]

In each case we see an adaptation in the methodology of the early church to the circumstances that they encountered. They were not confined to one method of mass evangelism. When they encountered obstacles while utilizing one method, they simply found other ways and other places in which to preach Christ.

Cell-Group Evangelism

The early church also utilized cell-group evangelism as another method. In the book of Acts, we find that the family was the basic social unit. This is indicated in the concept of the Greek word "*oikos*," which basically involved the family, intimate friends, and, at times, the domestic help. In the book of Acts, mention is made of the "*oikos*," or home cell group, engaging in prayer (12:12), fellowship (21:7), the Lord's Supper (2:46), worship (20:7), witnessing (10:22, 24; 16:32), instruction (5:42), and discipleship (18:26). The New Testament mentions the homes of such people as: Jason (Acts 17:5), Justus (Acts 18:7), Lydia (Acts 16:15), Stephanas (I Cor. 1:16; 16:15), and the mother of John Mark (Acts 12:12).[68]

The home-cell group took into account and built on the fundamental unit of the society in that day. One of the most effective channels of communication was the family network. In addition to this, as Donald McGavran asserts, cell-group evangelism involved the members of the family as leaders.[69] This method contributed automatically to the presentation of the message in ways that were relevant to the local culture and made it possible for many home cell-groups to be established since they were not dependent on the availability of large buildings or outside resources to carry out their evangelistic strategy.

Personal Evangelism

A study of the New Testament indicates that the Christians in the early church used a wide variety of personal evangelism methods. For example, Philip's experience of sharing the gospel with the man from Ethiopia (Acts 8:26-40) reveals several aspects of personal evangelism. Other New Testament sources indicate the Christians employed various forms of personal evangelism including visitation evangelism, extemporaneous evangelism, and friendship evangelism.

Visitation Evangelism

Visitation evangelism consisted of consistent efforts to witness to people at specific times and in specific places. It was said of the early Christians that *"every day, in the temple and from house to house, they kept right on teaching and preaching Jesus as the Christ" (Acts 5:42).* Again, Philip's experience with the Ethiopian shows the principle of going to the unchurched person rather than waiting for the unchurched to approach the believer or the congregation. Biblical evangelism involves going to the unchurched rather than the witness promoting a "come to" invitation.

Extemporaneous Evangelism

Another method of personal evangelism that was utilized by the early church was extemporaneous evangelism. They took advantage of unexpected opportunities to witness. Paul, for example, spoke to some women who had met by the riverside, and Lydia was converted (Acts 16:14).

Also, after his shipwreck, Paul utilized the opportunity to witness to the ruler of the island (Acts 28). Early Christians shared the gospel extemporaneously in the normal course of their daily lives. Many opportunities for extemporaneous evangelism arise today and Christians should seize these opportunities.

Friendship Evangelism

The New Testament records several examples in which early Christians practiced friendship evangelism. Andrew brought his brother Simon Peter to the Lord so that Simon could hear Him, *"He found first his own brother Simon, and said him: We have found the Messiah"* (John 1:41). Philip did the same with his friend Nathaniel (John 1:45). Cornelius followed the same type of network of relationships and friendships when he "called together his relatives and close friends" in order that they might hear the gospel (Acts 10:24).

This type of evangelism overcame the barriers of suspicion

and unbelief because the person that invited them was a person they trusted. Nathaniel, for example, had doubts about Jesus when he asked: *"Can any good thing come out of Nazareth?"* (John 1:46). Philip simply answered: "Come and see." Because Nathanael trusted Philip, he went and he found salvation in Jesus.

Subtle Evangelism

In addition to employing direct methods of evangelism, the early church utilized subtle methods. In his book, *Evangelism In the Early Church*, Michael Green introduces the possibility that first century Christians may have utilized the decorations in their homes as a way of capturing the interest of their visitors in order to speak to them about Christ.[70] Some of these decorations were mosaics depicting scenes of the Lord's Supper, the symbol of the fish, and of people in an attitude of prayer. Without a doubt these had great meaning for the believers, but, at the same time, they prompted unbelievers to ask questions or at least begin to think about their meaning. In this sense they were utilizing a form of subtle evangelism. Christians should be alert to opportunities for subtle evangelism today but never allow this form of evangelism to replace other means of winning people.

Literary Evangelism

The Gospel of Luke is an example of literary evangelism that the early church practiced. Luke writes to Theophilus *"that you might know the exact truth of the things that you have been taught"* (Luke 1:4). These *"things"* were *"what Jesus began to do and to teach"* (Acts 1:1-2). The book of Acts is another letter from Luke to Theophilus to instruct him more in the faith. The other Gospels also are efforts to present the life, the ministry, and the message of Jesus Christ to different target audiences, as we mentioned in the introduction of this book. John, for example, explains his purpose for writing when he says: *"But these have been written so that you may believe that Jesus is the Christ, the Son of God, and, that believing, you may have life in his name"* (John 20:31). Literary evangelism, therefore, was an effective method for the propagation of the gospel.

Summary

We see, therefore, in this brief review of the New Testament that the early church utilized a great variety of methods in order to communicate the gospel: mass evangelism, cell-group evangelism, personal evangelism, subtle evangelism, and literary evangelism. Although they did not have the technological tools that we have today (radio, television, telephones, computers, fax machines, airplanes, etc.) they utilized all the means at their disposal to evangelize. When some doors closed, they looked for others in order to continue their task of fulfilling the great commission.

It is important to note that they did not limit themselves to one method. Conscious of the great diversity of cultures, religions, and socioeconomic levels, the early church did not limit the presentation of the message to one method. Relying on the fact that the Holy Spirit would guide them, as Christ promised, they felt the freedom to present the message in a way that would be relevant to people in each socio-cultural context. Contemporary church starters should adopt the policy of seeking a variety of evangelistic methods in keeping with the needs of the peoples they serve.

Contextualizing Evangelistic Methods

One of the most demanding, yet exciting, tasks that 21st century church starters face is that of contextualizing evangelistic methodology so that it will be relevant to the enormous variety of groups that make up today's society. The early Christians were firm in their convictions and principles with regard to the content of the Gospel. They were very creative and flexible, however, when it came to the methodologies that they employed in communicating the good news of salvation. Incorporating such flexibility and creativity remains an imperative task that modern church starters face today.

Daniel Sanchez in his book, *Hispanic Realities Impacting America*, calls for Evangelical Christians to accept the challenges of developing contextualized evangelistic and church starting methods for reaching the expanding Hispanic population in the United States. Sanchez notes that this challenge includes equipping Hispanic evangelists to share their faith in a more effective way with those from a Roman Catholic background who have not experienced a personal relationship with Jesus Christ. In this important book, Sanchez urges Evangelicals to seize the opportunities presented by the current Hispanic response to the gospel.[71]

How can contemporary church starters communicate the venerable truth of the Gospel in such a way that people cannot only understand it but also respond in a positive way? Someone has said that often people are not opposed to the gospel; they are simply repelled by the methods we use to approach them. How can we, therefore, contextualize our evangelistic methodologies? The following suggestions are meant to help church starters think in creative ways and to develop viable methods for communicating the pure gospel in the setting of today's culture.

Contextualizing Mass Evangelism

Many Christians still have vivid memories of the Billy Graham crusades. Who can forget the inspiring scenes while this consecrated evangelist preached those soul-gripping sermons, and, as he gave the invitation, thousands went forward as the song "Just As I Am" was being sung by the choir. Others have similar memories of evangelistic campaigns conducted by such effective evangelists as Luis Palau. It is highly interesting to know that both of these evangelists have utilized their campaigns in connection with church starting efforts. In Rosario, Argentina, Luis Palau was the evangelist for a citywide evangelistic campaign that resulted in forty-two new congregations.[72] In Orlando, Florida, over 30 congregations were started in connection with a Billy Graham Crusade.[73]

In Latin America, Evangelism-in-Depth eventuated in thousands of professions of faith but the churches showed only meager increase. When the situation was studied carefully, the conclusion was that the problem was that Evangelism-in-Depth lacked the element of starting new churches. When church starting was added to the methods of Evangelism-in-Depth, the results proved more effective. [74]

In these instances of mass evangelistic events, church starting strategy was incorporated into the plan. In the Florida effort, for instance, a significant amount of time was spent training the church starters, cultivating the people in the target communities, initiating home cell group Bible studies, developing the core groups, and doing all of the other necessary things that contribute to the starting of a church. Others have used a tent or a rented building where they have had mass evangelism meetings for months or even years as they reached and discipled people and formed the core group around which the congregation would develop. These are but a few examples of the utilization of mass evangelistic activities with the express purpose of starting churches.

Contextualizing Visitation Evangelism

Visitation evangelism is vital to church starting. This makes it possible for church starting teams to find people that do not have contact with the church or with evangelical Christians. Sometimes as church starting team members go out to visit they meet people with whom the Lord is already working through some circumstance in their life and who are hungry to hear the Gospel. In many cases, people who accept Christ when they are first visited are those who have been cultivated. As a result of something that has happened in their lives, of someone who has shared the message with them previously, or of some disappointment with their own religious tradition, these people are searching for something that will satisfy their spiritual needs.

In such cases, the person who visits helps the people understand the gospel and make a decision that perhaps they had contemplated making for some time. In many cases, however, these are the exceptions and not the rule.[75] Therefore, the question that should be answered is: What should we do when the people that we visit do not show an interest in hearing the gospel or do not understand what we are saying?

Obviously when we visit unresponsive people we should try to understand their attitude toward the gospel and toward evangelicals. We should then incorporate this understanding into our strategies of presenting the gospel. If we discover that they are afraid or resistant to the idea of hearing the gospel, we should try to find ways of cultivating their friendship and of earning their trust so that at a later time we will be able to lead them to Christ. Our methodology for visitation evangelism, therefore, should be adapted to the level of receptivity in the community where we work.

Too many Christians have arrived at the conclusion that visitation evangelism should not be utilized under any circumstances. Perhaps this reluctance stems from the fact that they have experienced rejection while attempting to visit. This feeling does not mean, however, that visitation evangelism itself is a method that should be discarded. There are different types of visitation—that is, visitation of persons with whom the evangelist is not yet acquainted, of well-known people, and of family and or friends. Also, there are different purposes for visitation. Some visitors try to elicit a decision; some gain acquaintance with the people and leave the door open for future visits; some offer a ministry of the church that relates to a need; and some deepen the friendship of a person that they already know with the purpose of sharing the message at an opportune time.

If the community is generally resistant to the Gospel, an evangelistic methodology that has as its object getting a decision on the first visit likely will not be very successful. In the discussion that follows, we will share ideas on how to cultivate people that at first may not be very receptive to the Gospel. It is important to note here, however, that we should not discard the concept of visitation simply because one of the ways in which it has been utilized in the past has not produced good results in resistant communities. What we should do is continue to look for the type of visitation that best fits the local context.

Contextualizing Extemporaneous Evangelism

The importance of practicing extemporaneous evangelism is that it reaches people that may have been put in our path by divine appointment. The experience of Philip with the Ethiopian eunuch is an example of this type of evangelism (Acts 8:16-40). As we witness extemporaneously, it is important to have an idea of how much people know about the gospel and what their attitude is toward the gospel. In this way, we can present the Gospel in a manner that allows them to understand. Remember that the first question that Philip asked the eunuch was not, "will you accept Christ?" but "do you understand what you are reading?" In the case of Philip, the Eunuch already had some knowledge of the Scriptures and was spiritually hungry. He only needed someone to explain the Scriptures to him. It is important, therefore, to recognize that in some cases the only thing we can do is sow the seed and pray for them. Extemporaneous evangelism reaches persons whom the witness may not know very well.

Contextualizing Cell-Group Evangelism

Many Christians today are using their homes for evangelism in a wide variety of ways. Christians use their homes by: (1) inviting people for a meal, (2) having small groups over for fellowship during which a brief word of testimony is shared, followed by informal conversation, (3) holding Bible Study Fellowships,[76] (4) offering special classes (sewing, cooking, piano, nutrition, money management, art, hand crafts, dieting, drama, etc.), (5) forming special clubs (reading clubs which include good Christian books), (6) contacting new arrivals in the neighborhood, (7) being available to advise if counseling is needed, (8) watching Christian movies with non-Christians and dialoguing with these unbelievers, (9) serving as tutors. Certainly, many other methods of using the home and starting cell groups are available to Christians.

Such activities as mentioned above could lead to a group that can continue to function as an evangelistic outreach method. The concept here is that even cell groups need to be adjusted to the needs and characteristics of the peoples served. Every cell group will not follow the same pattern. Contextualization remains as much an imperative in cell group methods as in any other facet of missionary service.

Contextualizing Servanthood Evangelism

One of the debates regarding evangelism relates to three different emphases: presence, proclamation, and persuasion.[77] The objective of presence evangelism is that of establishing a Christian presence in a community by means of a good testimony and the manifestation of compassion and care in responding to the needs of the people. Proclamation evangelism focuses on the communication of the Gospel in a way that people will hear and understand it. Persuasion evangelism has the objective of convincing people to receive Jesus Christ as their Savior.

There are those who emphasize only presence evangelism, others only proclamation evangelism, and still others only persuasion evangelism. It is interesting that in the New Testament one finds all of these methods and other types of evangelism as well. In Acts 2, for example, we find that the Christians went from house to house proclaiming the word (v.46); they persuaded the people by means of the preaching (v.40); but they also established a Christian presence in the way in which they helped the needy (v.45). For this reason the people had a favorable impression of them (v.47).

Many situations demand the establishment of a Christian presence in a community in order to erase the negative impressions and erroneous concepts that people have about the gospel and about evangelicals. Many people, for a variety of reasons, close their minds immediately if the first thing that they hear from us is that we want them to make a decision pertaining to their religious life. This attitude often changes if they have the opportunity to see us as compassionate people that are interested in helping them in any way that we can.

The first step toward this contextualizing servanthood evangelism is discovering the needs and attitudes of the people in the target community. The evangelist can discover these needs and attitudes in several ways. First, the evangelist can interview people and ask them about the needs and attitudes in their community and then listen compassionately and carefully to their answers. Another way to understand community needs involves observation. Reading the newspapers, listening to comments about the problems that the people face in that community, and simply noting the obvious community needs contribute to the evangelist's understanding of the community. Talking to community leaders also reveals needs and attitudes the evangelist must recognize.

After finding out what these needs are, it is necessary to find believers who are willing to serve the Lord in one of these need-meeting ministries. In many cases it will be necessary to train the people so that they will know how to perform these ministries. It is obvious that most churches do not have the human and financial resources to provide all of the ministries that are needed in each community. The church, however, can choose the ministries it can provide in light of its resources.

Some of these ministries will be directed toward individuals, others toward families, and others toward needy groups. Some of these groups can be people who come from other countries and need to learn the local language and customs. Other groups may be drug addicts, alcoholics, people who have lost a loved one, parents of adolescents who exhibit serious problems, couples who need to know how to improve their marriages, parents of mentally retarded children, people who are unemployed and need to develop their skills in order to secure adequate employment, families of inmates, elderly people who need help and companionship, young mothers who need to learn how to look after their children, new people in the community who need to know how to function in a new environment, children who need activities during weekends and vacation time, women who are at home alone all day, families that need to learn how to manage their finances, widowers or widows that need to adapt to life after they have lost their spouse. In short, there are untold numbers of needs that provide opportunities for church members to serve in the name of the Lord and at the same time cultivate the field so that the seed of the Gospel can be sown.

One of the potential limitations of servanthood evangelism is that one can spend all the time serving people without making an effort to share the message of salvation with them. In some cases these activities could be considered pre-evangelistic which, as we have already mentioned, are extremely important factors. It is necessary, however, to seek the Lord's leadership to know how to give a word of testimony, when to begin a Bible study, and when to guide the people to accept Jesus Christ as their Savior. This type of evangelism is essential especially in contexts where we have to overcome barriers so that the people will listen to the Gospel.

Contextualizing Friendship Evangelism

Friendship evangelism is indispensable in order to reach certain types of people. Friendship evangelism is necessary when, due to the lack knowledge of the Gospel on the part of the prospect, a certain amount of cultivation is needed. In these cases an evangelistic strategy that utilizes a series of Bible studies can help the prospect gradually to understand the implications of the Gospel.

Friendship evangelism is also necessary when the prospects have negative attitudes toward the Gospel. These negative attitudes toward the Gospel often spring from what they have learned in their religious traditions. In these cases, in addition to cultivating a friendship it is necessary to explain patiently and gradually the basic element of the gospel and to pray that the Holy Spirit continues to work in them so that they can conquer their doubts and accept Jesus Christ as Savior. Friendship evangelism is necessary to reach people who will only listen to the message from the lips of someone they can trust. Experts in personal communication say that the listener has to trust the messenger in order to accept the message.

When the Gospel is communicated through friendship and kinship ties, the prospect already has a high level of trust in the witness; consequently, the possibility of receiving the message is greatly increased. A survey that was done to ascertain why people joined Christian churches revealed that 10 percent joined the church on their own initiative, 20 percent joined the church as a result of the ministry of the pastor, and 70 percent (in some churches 90 percent) joined the church as a result of the influence and the work of family and friends.[78] These figures undoubtedly will be different in every country and in every community. Obviously, the ministry of family and friends is absolutely necessary to reach the people that will only listen to someone they trust.

The evangelistic strategy of a church should sensitize and equip its members not only to share the gospel with those they already know but also to enlarge their circles of friendship in order to be in position to share the Gospel with others. Studies have demonstrated that the longer people have been members of evangelical churches, the fewer friends they have outside of the church.[79] On the positive side, this change in friendship patterns indicates that the new believers enjoy the fellowship of the church and may have broken relationships with persons who had a negative influence on them. On the other hand, however, the new friendship patterns result in a reduced evangelistic potential of the church due to the smaller friendship circles of the members with unchurched people.

The church should, therefore, encourage and cultivate a strategy that guides members to form friendship ties with their neighbors, colleagues, and acquaintances to be in a better position to share the message in a way that has relevance to the life of the prospects. A relational evangelism strategy should include an analysis of the persons in our spheres of influence, an analysis of where persons are in terms of their knowledge of the Gospel, and a specific plan to deepen friendship ties in order to lead them to a personal experience with Jesus Christ.

The first question should be, therefore, who are the people in my sphere of influence?

Relatives

In your world you have close relationships with many different people. Some of these close ties are with family members. In your Jerusalem, there are also persons that form a part of your extended family such as your parents, brothers and sisters, grandparents, aunts and uncles, and cousins. These are the persons that are closest to you. You know them, are aware of their needs, and have their trust. You, therefore, are in the best position to share the gospel with them in such a way that it will be relevant to their lives.

These are the persons whom God has placed in your sphere of influence for a purpose. Sometimes we have the tendency to focus our evangelistic efforts on total strangers while overlooking those that are closest to us.[80] Generally in these instances you do not need to spend time studying their worldview and religious beliefs. You are personally acquainted with them and are in a position to design the best strategy to share the gospel message with them. Those that are closest to you and with whom you have the most in common are the persons in your Jerusalem with whom you can start sharing the gospel message.

Friends

Aside from those with whom you have kinship ties, there are those with whom you have dealings on a daily basis. These are the persons with whom you have common interests (your friends) and common community (your neighbors). You may not have as strong ties as those with your family, but you can deepen your communication level to the extent that they will listen to you when you speak to them about the Lord.

Neighbors

There are others in your neighborhood with whom you do not have a close friendship but who have needs that can serve as channels through which to communicate the gospel. Even though you do not consider them close friends, you can take time to get to know them better, to cultivate a friendship, so that you can know the best way to witness to them.

Persons with Whom the Evangelist Is Not Acquainted

Every evangelist should become aware of people who live in their own community but with whom he/she has not had an opportunity to get personally acquainted. These could be people who either have a similar religious background to yours or who identify with one of the major religions of the world (Muslims, Hindus, Buddhists, Animists, Syncretists) or even with some of the current groups of unchurched people (Secularists, Post-Modernists).

While there is no significant geographical distance between these unreached persons and you, there is a wide religious and/ or philosophical gap that needs to be bridged. An effort to reach these target groups requires a study of their world-view, religious beliefs, attitudes toward Christianity, and methodologies suggested by those who have had sig-nificant experience in evangelizing these groups. Genuine friendship can be the best bridge through which the gospel is communicated.

A most helpful source for studying methods of sharing the gospel with persons from another religious background is the book, *Sharing the Good News with Your Roman Catholic Friends* written by Daniel R. Sánchez and Rudolph D. Gon-zález.[81] In this helpful work, Sánchez guides Christians to a most effective way to help persons of a Roman Catholic back-ground who have not trusted Jesus as Savior to understand the full meaning of the biblical message.

The first step in friendship evangelism, therefore, is an analy-sis of the persons that are in your world. These are the per-sons whose friendship you can cultivate in order to communicate the message of salvation.

Conclusion

The early church obviously utilized a wide variety of evan-gelistic methods under the guidance of the Holy Spirit. The task of contextualizing evangelistic methods is one of the greatest challenges for today's church starters. A very important principle to keep in mind is that somehow (utilizing whatever methods might be more relevant) church starters must establish meaningful contact with large numbers of persons who are unchurched.

Various church starters may be more comfortable with particular evangelistic methods. The important factor here is which method will be the most effective method for my target group? If the church starter learns that his most comfortable method is not that which is most effective in the community, he/she must be willing to learn new methods in order to be more effective.

In addition to ascertaining the type of community in which the church starters are working, it is imperative that they understand the attitude of the community toward the Gospel message and the process it uses in making decisions. This understanding of decision-making processes in the community will help the witnessing person provide ways for the people to make decisions for Christ.

CHAPTER 5

STRATEGIC FOUNDATION

Part A
Parenting, Pioneering,
& Partnering Models

The strategic foundation holds an imperative place in the preparation phase of church starting. In fact, one of the most important decisions for any church starting effort is that of determining the model that the ministry will utilize. Highly successful church starters have designed, developed, and implemented numerous excellent models for starting new congregations.82

In this study, we are going to divide these models into five major categories: (1) Parenting, (2) Pioneering, (3) Partnering, (4) Propagating, and (5) People Group Models. Each model has advantages and each has disadvantages. Understanding these models and the advantages and disadvantages of each helps the church starter select the appropriate model and maximize its advantages while minimizing its disadvantages or weaknesses.

Parenting Models

Parenting models utilize the method in which a mother (or sponsoring) church assumes the responsibility of starting a daughter congregation. In this model, the sponsoring church makes available to the new congregation at least some of the resources of members, finances, guidance, and facilities. This model of parenting for starting new congregations is one of the more often employed methods. The presence of a mother church is not totally necessary but is highly effective and often needed.

Several variations of the parenting model exist.

Mother Church - Daughter Congregation

The "Mother church - Daughter Congregation" variation of the parenting model is the most frequently used pattern. The sponsoring church assumes extensive responsibility for a new congregation. In essence, the mother church accepts responsibility for looking after the establishment and development of the daughter congregation. This model fits the ecclesiology of some denominations that hold the conviction that established churches should be the primary agents for starting new churches. A mother church can establish a mother-daughter relationship in several ways.

Colonizing

In this variation of the model, the mother church sends a core group to the new community to start a new congregation. This pattern has several advantages. First, the new congregation has leaders for its ministries from the very beginning. Second, the new congregation has a financial base from which to work. As this core group tithes, it provides the financial resources that are needed to start the congregation. Third, the leaders of the new congregation have a solid doctrinal foundation from the start. Fourth, the core group has a strong connection with the mother church and there is continuing support for the new congregation. Fifth, and certainly not least, the new congregation has members and attendees from the beginning.

Several disadvantages accompany this model. First, the core group may be committed to reproducing a replica of the mother church. The values and style of the mother church may be very commendable but if the community and ministry focus groups are different, the new congregation may be totally out of touch with its new community.

Second, the members of the core group may be so comfortable with each other that they may lean more toward maintenance ministry than evangelistic outreach. Third, the members of the core group may be resistant to new leaders who emerge from the community. The new leaders may be seen as greenhorns who know little about the church and the denomination. This attitude hinders the new church's identification with and understanding of the community.

Fourth, another possible disadvantage relates to the possibility of the mother church exercising too much control by not allowing opportunity for the daughter congregation to develop into an autonomous, indigenous church. Fifth, this model can only be implemented in keeping with the distance that the members of the core group are willing to travel. Sixth, the core group can develop a proprietary attitude toward the new congregation, feeling that the church belongs to them or that they should have a special place in the life and ministry of the church.

These are significant disadvantages. Forethought and advance planning can, however, minimize the errors of these disadvantages so that they do not overshadow the great advantages that this model offers.

Task Force

The Task Force variation of the parenting model has many similarities to the colonization approach. The major difference in the two approaches is that the core group does not have the intention of remaining with the newly formed congregation. From the beginning, they plan to return to the mother church after the new congregation has been established.

When the church start uses the Task Force pattern, the wise church starter will work out agreements that will minimize the impact related to the departure of the temporary task force (core group). First, the church starter may encourage the leaders of the core group to reproduce themselves by training the members of the new congregation before they return to their mother church.

Second, the members of the core group may stagger their departure so that all of them do not depart at the same time. This procedure allows the new leaders to emerge, be trained, and accept the responsibilities of the new work. The task force members must adopt the attitude of John the Baptist who said of Christ, "He must become greater; I must become less" (John 3:30).

Third, the members of the task force may recruit additional members from the mother church to join the new congregation and bring with them their talents, commitments, and support. Such recruitment will of necessity be with the knowledge and agreement of leaders in the mother church. Experience has indicated that churches that give up members to new congregations most often receive new people to take the place of those who have left to serve elsewhere.

Mother Church – Satellite Congregations[83]

In the mother church-satellite congregation variation of the parenting model, a sponsoring church may start and support several daughter congregations in different communities. This model has several advantages. First, the daughter congregations benefit from the support of the mother church. Since these congregations are considered extensions of the ministry of the mother church, they receive strong support in the areas of finances and personnel.

Second, the satellite congregations benefit from the image of the mother church. If the mother church is well known and respected in the city, the new congregations will not have to start from scratch in terms of developing a positive image in their communities.

Third, this pattern allows the mother church to have ministries among the different cultural and socioeconomic groups in the city. Each satellite congregation may target a different group and reach persons who might feel uncomfortable in the mother church. The pattern also allows for persons who desire a different type of worship/fellowship pattern.

A fourth advantage of the mother church-satellite congregation approach lies in the fact that buildings and other equipment are not required because these groups can meet in apartments, clubhouses, etc.

Fifth, this model holds the advantage that some churches see this approach as one which leads to increase in their membership rather than a decrease. This viewpoint allows some congregations to participate in church starting where they might resist new congregations if they conceived that the effort was decreasing the size of their church.

Along with these advantages, the mother church-satellite congregation model has some potential disadvantages. Perhaps the greatest of these is that the mother church may view these as "permanent extensions" and may not want to give the new congregations the freedom to exercise their potential of developing into autonomous churches. Church starting effort can overcome this disadvantage by leading the mother church to implement a flexible methodology which encourages the congregations that have the potential to become established churches in due time The mother church can use a revolving door approach in that it can turn right around and start new satellite congregations among other groups in the city.

Other satellite congregations, due to their financial and personnel limitations (such as communities where there is a high turnover rate), may remain as on-going ministries of the mother church. Retaining responsibility for the satellite congregations over long periods of time, however, should result from needs in the satellite group not from resistance to "letting go." Certainly, continuing control over the satellite should never be prompted by desires to count their numbers in the mother church's statistics. Possibilities for negative motivations for retaining the satellite congregation actually constitute a major disadvantage to the model.

An additional disadvantage of this model lies in the possibility that new congregations that have the potential of becoming established churches may fail to do so because they have developed an attitude of dependency on the mother church. The mother church should watch for any tendency toward dependency that would interfere with the satellite becoming independent. The goal, even in the mother church-satellite congregation pattern, is an independent, reproducing church.

Both the mother church and the satellite congregation in this model should address these potential disadvantages prior to the implementation of this model. The intention would be to minimize the effect of the negative features of the model. Actually, the advantages of the model far outweigh the negative aspects. By utilizing what they call "an indigenous satellite strategy," Tim Ahlen and J.V. Thomas provide helpful solutions to these potential limitations.[84]

Sponsoring Church - Revitalization Project

Another variation of the parenting model of church starting, the sponsoring church-revitalization project, involves an existing church seeking to aid in the revitalization of a declining or dying churches.85 The mother church relates to the declining or dying church with help in leadership, planning, finances, and attitude to rebuild the vision and effectiveness of the hurting congregation. The intention is that of helping the church come back to life.

Implementation of this model involves the development of a contract between the two congregations. Generally this contract includes the following: (1) reversion of the dying church to daughter congregation status; (2) the appointment of a transition committee made up of members of the sponsoring church and the daughter congregation; (3) empowering the transition committee to make the necessary decisions relating to finances and facilities; (4) training the members of the daughter congregation; (5) studying the community; (6) designing outreach strategies; (7) employing new pastoral leadership; and (8) launching the revitalizing congregation. While it is true that this pattern in essence seeks the revitalization of an existing congregation, for all practical purposes, it can achieve the same result as a church starting effort as it preserves a congregation that might cease to exist.

Sponsoring Church - Reclamation Project

The sixth variation of the parenting model of church starting, the sponsoring church-reclamation project, has many characteristics in common with the revitalizing project. The difference lies in the fact that in the reclamation process the church that had existed previously is officially declared out of existence. Generally in these cases some time is allotted to shut down all operations of the congregation and to communicate to the community that the congregation has been disbanded.

Under this plan, the property and all other assets are placed in the hands of the sponsoring church. Often, the members, including the leadership, of the disbanded congregation will become members of the sponsoring church. At the appointed time, a new church is started under new management.

Often the ministry focus of the new congregation is different from that of the disbanded congregation. Since the new ministry focus group reflects the composition of the community in which the new congregation is launched, a new sense of excitement, vitality, and purpose often arises. For all practical purposes, therefore, this is a new church start.

This pattern has several advantages. First, there are resources present (e.g. a building) that many new congregations do not have. Second, generally the sponsoring church has personnel with expertise in exegeting the community, determining the needs, designing appropriate strategies, obtaining appropriate personnel, and supporting the effort with personnel and monetary resources.

One possible disadvantage is that the building may require so much money for upkeep that the new congregation may not have funds for anything else. This disadvantage, however, may be overcome by renting portions of the building or using them for ministries that generate income that in turn is invested in ministry. The sponsoring church also can help with these necessary repairs by financial aid and by providing persons to work on the repairs.

A third disadvantage relates to any lingering attitude problems in the community directed to the disbanded congregation. The effort can minimize this disadvantage by closing the old congregation for a time and communicating to the community that an entirely new and different church is emerging.

Pioneering Models

The main feature of Pioneering Models for church starting, the second group of models, is that the church starter has to start from scratch without a core group from a sponsoring church. Because this model does not involve a sponsoring church, the church starter cannot count on a church starting team, financial resources, or hands-on guidance. This means that the church starter does not inherit a core group but has to recruit one. By the same token, the church starter does not have a ready-made church starting team but has to develop one mainly from the new field in which the new church is being started.

Other potential difficulties in this approach relate to the fact that local leadership may develop slowly and that the understanding of denominational distinctives may be limited. These limitations can become intense if the new church suffers from untrained and perhaps under-motivated leadership. Also, if the new group has limited understanding of and appreciation for the distinctive doctrines of the denomination with which the church starter desires to affiliate, some tensions will result.

Some of the potential disadvantages, however, may actually become advantages. First, the new congregation can be fashioned in a way that reflects the biblical priorities of the church starter over against traditional approaches that perhaps were effective in the past. Second, the new congregation will almost automatically be contextualized in its community because that is where the members have come from. Thirdly, the new congregation can develop in such a way that it will have as a part of its genetic makeup to reproduce itself. Fourth, this model provides unlimited opportunities for church starters who have excellent self-starting capabilities. A variety of church starters can be involved in pioneering church starting efforts.

Church Starter – Developer

The church starter-developer variation of the Pioneering Model involves a church starter who intends from the beginning to remain with the new congregation and lead it to develop as a church. This variation demands that the church starter feel called to and committed to a given community. The church starter-developer commits to do everything that it takes to start a church in that community, to stay there to develop the church, and to guide the church to start other churches. This type of person must have church starting as well as pastoral skills and be able to utilize these gifts to start a church and to lead it to develop its full potential.

The church vision does not, however, end with the starting and establishing of the church in the given community. The church- developer will strive to guide the new congregation to accept the responsibility for starting other the new churches.[86] In this way, an ongoing church starting movement may be established.

Church Starter – Initiator

The church starter-initiator variation of the Pioneering Model involves a church starter who starts a new congregation, turns its development over to another leader, and moves to another region to repeat the church starting process. The church starter initiator is primarily gifted in the area of church starting. Generally this person neither has the vision, desire, nor the skills to develop a congregation once it has been started. This type of worker may become bored once the exciting initial phase is over and much time has to be dedicated to maintenance and administrative matters. The uniqueness of this type of church starter lies in the fact that he/she possesses primarily the gifts that are needed to start new churches. Instead of fretting over the fact that this type of person does not possesses church development gifts, the strategy should be one that maximizes the church starting gifts and then enables the person to go to another field and repeat the process.

Due to the fact that many people do not possess church-starting gifts, specialized strategies and support systems should be developed for church starter-initiator types. These workers possess the advantages of mobility and adjustability. Church starting movements should be on the lookout for and ready to develop workers who show evidences of the skills and attitudes needed for church starter initiators.

Partnering Models

A third major type of model for church starting, the Partnering Models, consists of pooling the resources of existing churches or groups to start new congregations. This cooperative effort between churches or between churches and denominational agencies can result in the starting of many new congregations. Several variations expand the way this partnering can be accomplished.

Multiple Sponsorship Model

The multiple sponsorship variation consists of several churches participating together to start a new congregation. Certain advantages derive from the utilization of this model. First, the group approach involves resources so the sponsoring entity can provide the financial resources, the personnel, the materials, the publicity, the transportation, the facilities, and the resources the church starting effort and the new congregation needs. The cooperation of the partnering churches gives a great guarantee that sufficient resources will be available for the church starting effort.

Second, this model facilitates the starting of new congregations in places where otherwise this would be difficult, if not impossible. Existing churches in many areas are so weak and limited that they do not have the resources to support starting new congregations. Pooling resources from several limited churches provides the needed support without over extending any one congregation.

As usual, several potential disadvantages exist in the utilization of this model. First, this can lead to a situation in which "everybody's business is nobody's business." In other words, each sponsoring church may be depending on the others to provide the necessary resources and the church starter might not receive the aid that is needed.

Second, the church starter may have too many "bosses." These first two disadvantages can be overcome if a coordinating council with representatives from each sponsoring church is established. This council can receive reports from the church starter, enlist the resources from the sponsoring churches, and keep them informed regarding the needs and the progress of the new congregation. Another way to overcome this disadvantage is to designate one church as the primary sponsor with the other churches helping this sponsor with the needs of the new congregation.

There is yet another potential disadvantage in the utilization of this model. Robert Logan observes, "A coalition collapses the vision of the sponsoring churches and reduces the number of new church starts."[87] This observation is certainly valid. Churches that have the potential to start new congregations on their own may settle for joining a partnership which is less demanding on their resources.

One potential way of averting this disadvantage is to enlist in the partnership only the churches that are not able to sponsor new congregations on their own. Another potential solution may be to enlist churches in the partnership with the understanding that the first year will be a learning experience for them and that after that they will explore the possibility of sponsoring a new congregation on their own.

Multi-Congregational Model

A second variation of the Partnering Model, the multi-congregational pattern, is especially suited for culturally pluralistic metropolitan areas. In many cities, churches share their buildings and resources with other congregations that conduct their worship services in other languages or in different ways. Those who utilize this model view themselves as one church which is made up of several congregations.

One of the advantages of this model is that the church can reach the various cultural groups in the community by having congregations that speak their language and understand their culture. Another advantage of the multi-congregational pattern is that, in cities in which the cost of the buildings is excessively high, several congregations can pool their resources and have a building that they can share. By using different parts of the building at the same time or the entire building at different times these congregations satisfy their own needs and the needs of others. For example, there are congregations that have their Sunday school while the other congregations are using the sanctuary for the worship service and vice versa. Some congregations have their services on Sunday afternoons or on Saturday evening in order to maximize the utilization of the building available to them. Yet another advantage of this model is that it makes it possible for people at the various stages of assimilation into the predominant culture to worship in the language and culture with which they are comfortable. For example, the children (or grandchildren) of immigrant parents (in the United States) may feel more comfortable attending a Sunday School class taught in English and a worship service conducted in English while their parents worship in another part of the building in their own language.

As always, this model also has some potential disadvantages. One disadvantage is that one congregation may view itself as the dominant congregation thus making other groups feel a lack of or a lessening of worth or significance. Another potential disadvantage is that the various congregations may not have the freedom to express their congregational life (e.g. leadership, worship styles) in ways that are consistent with their culture. In other words, some may confuse unity with uniformity. A third potential disadvantage is that a congregation that is in this partnership may call a pastor who does not have the vision or skills for this type of church. Multi-congregational churches demand cross-cultural abilities and strong organizational skills. The leader or leaders of multi-congregational churches must be carefully selected and trained. A fourth potential disadvantage is conflict between the congregations. Members of the congregation that was in the location first may resent the new comers. The larger or earlier group may be inclined to hold back a congregation that has grown rapidly and is able to branch out on its own. The differing lifestyles of the cultural groups in the congregation may lead to misunderstandings and conflict.

Church leaders can address these disadvantages in several ways. First, the congregations can enter into a formal agreement that articulates clearly what is expected of each congregation. Second, an executive council with representatives from each congregation can be established to make significant decisions relating to finances, building utilization, and cooperative ventures. Third, each congregation can agree that it will not call a pastor who is not willing to work in keeping with this agreement. By having laypersons in the executive council, the congregations can ensure that there will be continuity even when pastoral leadership changes occur. Fourth, the cooperating congregations can come to an agreement that when a congregation is ready to branch out on its own arrangements will be made to enable this to take place and the remaining congregations will then seek to start a church with a new unreached group in their community.

An important feature of a multi-congregational church is the possibility for inter-congregational relationships. Various activities, meals, services, fellowships, and special events can be planned and carried with all congregations participating. In this way, the congregations meet the needs of their particular group while contributing to the ministry of the other congregations.

Multi-Cell/Celebration Model

Yet another variation of the multi-congregational model is a church that reaches people of different cultures and languages in small groups (homes, office buildings, apartments, etc.) and then brings them together for worship (celebration) in a central location. One such church is the International Community Church in Richmond, Virginia. This church focuses on reaching refugees, first generation immigrants, second generation immigrants, interracial families, international workers, and international students and scholars. Currently this church has small group meetings made up of Burmese, Chinese, Cambodians,

Colombians, Nepalese, and Vietnamese. Meeting in various locations throughout the city as house/small/cell groups; gathering together once a month for worship celebration and fellowship. Meeting in various locations throughout the city as house/small/cell groups, they gather together once a month for worship celebration and fellowship. The worship service is conducted in simple English. This provides a common language for all of the groups and gives them an opportunity to continue practice English which they are learning in classes provided by the church.

The leaders of this church view their approach as one that provides: "A foretaste of heaven (Rev. 5:9; 7:9); A ministry of reconciliation (Gal. 3:28); A hub of many terminals so many can connect with God (1 Cor. 9:22, 23); and an incubator for future ethnic churches."[88] The activities of the church involve finding persons of peace (people, families, students, and children), establishing life-long relationships, gathering them into small groups, building worshiping communities among all peoples, and transforming lives for eternity.[89] Their "Life Infinity Initiative" consists of two tracks: The International Community Church and Life Training Center which has a variety of ministries.

One ministry is the Life Forum which consists of: Annual events (3-4 times per year) and bringing together seasoned business owners, financial/legal experts and ethnic minority entrepreneurs for the purpose of experience/resources sharing and networking. A Second focuses on Life Skills which includes: Business seminars: 10-week program on business management and development; ESL classes: 10-week program on English language and culture; Computer seminars: 10-week program on technical skills to run a business. The third ministry is EthnicRichmond.com. This includes: Complete online guide to Richmond's faces, places, and cultures, directory of local services & businesses owned by ethnic minorities, and Wikipedia of all ethnic groups living in Metropolitan Richmond.[90] Minh Ha Nguyen summarizes what they have learned as they have implemented this model:

- Go to people... equip new believers to impact their community

- Life-long relationships are key to success starting with the person of peace

- Keep it simple... tell stories...

- Partnership with local churches is another key to success. They provide resources, volunteers, and prayers

- Each group has something to offer. No one group is only a receiver

- Leadership is also multi-ethnic... we are all equal and equally valued

- House groups are often indigenous and it's where discipleship and evangelism take place

- Needs are met within house groups whether they are social, emotional, or spiritual

- House groups are often sponsored by a local church that has a heart for internationals

- ICC is more than an international church. It is becoming a movement: the internationalization of the church.[91]

This model combines a number of very important features which enable a church planting team to address issues related to group identity and language utilization on the one hand and reconciliation cooperative ministries on the other.

The obstacle posed by the fact that initially many of the immigrant groups have very limited financial resources is overcome through the utilization of available facilities for the small group meetings (in homes) and for the celebration meetings in existing church buildings. The perception on the part of the Church Planting leader, who is Vietnamese, that "immigrant groups who have in the past been the recipients of the gospel and much needed ministries, now have the opportunity to minister to other immigrant groups" is truly inspiring."[92]

Multi-Site Model

A variation of the multi-congregational model is the multi-site church. In their book entitled The Multi-Site Church Revolution Geoff Surratt, Greg Ligon, and Warren Bird define a multi-site church as "one church meeting in multiple locations – different rooms in the same campus, different locations in the same region, or in some instances different cities, states, or nations. A multi-site church shares a common vision, budget, leadership, and board."[93] The multi-site concept of church is generally predicated on the ministry of a teaching pastor (or pastors), campus pastors for the people who worship in venues that on their original campus (for different generational, cultural, and linguistic groups) or in sites that are away from the original campus, and the use of technology to get the sermons or lessons to the various congregations.[94]

In some instances the campuses are close enough that the teaching pastor can get to them and present the message in person. In other instances the messages are presented through CDs, DVDs, or simulcast formats. The Leadership Network Survey indicates that 46% use almost all in-person teaching/pasturing methods, 34% use a combination of in person and video methods, and 20% use almost all video methods.[95] While some of the campuses (in schools, storefronts, YMCAs, movie theaters, community recreation centers, auditoriums, church buildings are in relatively close proximity of the original campus others (generally called "international churches") may be in other countries.[96]

In some of these multisite churches the praise time is led by local worship leaders utilizing the music and instruments that are relevant in their contexts. At an agreed upon time, the sermon is presented by the teaching pastor through a simulcast or video presentations on large screens. The concluding activities (e.g., offering, announcements, and decisions) take place after the presentation of the sermon or teaching lesson. Other versions of this model have the entire service on video formats. In some instances there is capability for interactive segments during the worship service.

Some of the meeting places that are not associated with a church are called "third place." Roy Oldenburg believes that third places are central to developing a vital community.[97] Oldenburg lists characteristics of third places:

- They are located on neutral ground
- They are "levelers" where rank and status don't matter

- Conversation is a main activity
- They are easy to access and accommodating
- They have a core group of influential regulars
- They have a low profile instead of being showy
- The mood is playful
- They feel like a home away from home[98]

Proponents of the multi-site model cite several advantages in the utilization of the multi-site model.

- One advantage is that it helps overcome limitations related to the scarcity of available land and the exorbitant costs of buildings, especially in metropolitan areas.

- Another advantage mentioned by the proponents of this model is that it enables people to have the same quality of preaching, teaching, and singing that churches with abundant financial resources have.

- Another advantage cited is diversification. "Certain types of locations attract certain types of people. A church may choose to operate in a rehabbed downtown warehouse space to attract the young professionals living in a gentrified urban neighborhood. The same church may choose a campus in a public school located in a suburban area of their community, to attract young families who have children attending the school."[99]

- Yet another advantage mentioned by those who favor this model is that it gives a church an opportunity to have an extensive ministry, even internationally, without having to utilize significant amounts of money supporting missionaries and traveling to distant lands.

- In addition to this, supporters of this model state that it facilitates the training and utilization of lay people in the central campus as well as in the other campuses. A Leadership Network survey states that most of the persons interviewed "reported that leadership skills have grown as volunteers and lay leaders have stepped into new roles."[100]

- Others cite church multiplication as a reason for employing this model. The Leadership Network authors state: "A respectable number of multisite campuses are in turning birthing campuses of their own. At the same time, multi-sites are planting other churches. This means that multisite and church planting seem to go hand in hand."[101]

- Some cite stewardship as a reason for having multisite churches. John Piper states: "Our first sanctuary, which lasted about 110 years, held 400. The current one holds 1,000. Is it better theology to build a bigger sanctuary, hope that an adequate amount of parking appears and risk an empty albatross in the coming years, or to develop multiple campuses, built of about 1,000 each, maybe 5 of them, covering perhaps 10,000 people total?"[102]

- Another reason for utilizing the multisite model is evangelism. John Piper states: "There are thousands of people who are within driving distance of us and who, in not treasuring Christ, are not heading for heaven... It's not an option for us to avoid thinking about these people."[103]

Those who question the effectiveness of this approach give several reasons. Surratt, Ligon, and Bird give a summary of objections they hear from people who disagree with the use of this model: [104]

- Preachers don't know people personally

- Churches are just following the latest fads and trends

- Multi-Sites make church into a show

- There are going to be negative outcomes

    o The multi-site approach will hurt existing smaller churches in the community[105]

    o Multi-sites cater too much to American consumerism and might create an even more consumer attitude.

o Multi-sites elevate one leader too promi-
  nently, and if that leader falls, the ripple
  effects will be multiplied across all campuses.

o Multi-sites appear to people in a society
  that likes name-brand recognitions, but
  when the culture shifts to preferring bou-
  tique-style stores, multi-sites will begin to
  flounder.

• Multi-Sites fail to make disciples

There is a sense in which some of these objections could apply to almost any church of any size. This however, does not
mean that careful thought should not be given to these objections and proper steps should not be taken to address them
from a biblical perspective. A pastor responding to the negative
evaluations of multi-site churches stated: "The bottom line is
that if the sending church is lacking in any of these areas, the
satellites will be lacking also. But if the sending church is
strong, outward focused, and developing healthy networks of
care and community, then the satellites will do well in these
areas. After all we are not out to replicate a church service,
we're out to replicate the entire life of the church. That includes
healthy vertical and horizontal relationships."[106]

In light of the fact that the current expression of the multi-
site church is relatively new, additional on-going studies are
needed to evaluate their contributions as well as limitations.
One example for the need for on-going research is the establishment of sites in other countries and ethnic groups in this
country.[107] While the proponents of this model are careful to
point out that there is significant contextualization in the international sites that are formed, it will be helpful to study what
segments of the population are being reached. It is obvious
that a number of persons who are proficient in English or want
to learn it would be in interested in being a part of a congregation where a least part of the service is in English. As a matter
of fact, this interest can be a positive factor in reaching people
who otherwise would not be reached. At the same time, it must
be acknowledged that other segments of the population in these countries will only be reached with ministries in their own
language. Also, long term studies would be needed to assess
the discipleship of persons who continually hear messages pre-

pared primarily for people who live in a different cultural and geographical context. To what extent are the sermon themes that are selected for the people in the original campus in the United States relevant to the daily lives of listeners in other countries or cultures? There is also the matter of the local people assuming total responsibility for the ministry of their church. Can the multi-site model contribute to the development of an on-going dependence on outside sources?

The multi-site model is currently being instrumental in the establishment of many sites where the gospel is being preached to many unchurched people. There is evidence to substantiate the assertion that the new sites are growing faster than the original (sponsoring) ones. The Leadership Network study indicates that 45% of the newer campuses grow faster than the original ones, 28% were even in growth, and 27% of the original campuses grew faster.[108] While this is true the concerns mentioned above must be given attention if the quality of discipleship and ministry is going to be solidly biblical and culturally relevant.

Adoption Model

Another partnership-type model, the adoption variation, involves the newly established congregation seeking affiliation with a particular denomination. There are several reasons why a new congregation may want to do so. One reason is that it may simply want to establish its identity by affiliating with an existing denomination. Another reason may be that the church needs help in financial matters, in selecting a pastor, or in organizational matters. Yet another reason may be that the new congregation feels that it has an affinity with the doctrinal distinctives of a particular denomination and wants to be a part of it.

Some potential disadvantages may be that the new congregation, and/or its leaders, may be interested only in physical aid—financial, equipment, and materials. This materialism might lead to weakness in the congregation. It also could cause the new congregation to accept only physical help and eschew other types of aid such as leadership, advice, and warnings.

Another disadvantage may be that their core group may be dysfunctional with relation to the denomination with which it might desire to affiliate. This dysfunction might result from the fact that the new church has been established in a fashion or form isolated either from the area or peoples the church intends to serve or from the denominational group desired. This isolation might stem from the fact that the leaders of the new group simply did not know how to formally relate to a denominational entity. On the other hand, if the leadership of the new group has the characteristic of non-conformity, relating to any denominational group may prove problematic. The new church should engage in careful planning for forming the denominational relationship.

While the denomination to which the church seeks affiliation may be in an excellent position to help this new congregation, the relationship should be formed with caution. The church should be certain it understands the position and possibilities of the denomination. The denomination should make certain it allows sufficient time to get to know the group and determine how best to help it. Given these cautions, the adoption variation of the partnering model can provide excellent help to the new congregation.

Key Church Model

The Key Church Model is another version of the Partnering Model. This pattern calls for well-established churches and state organizations (such as conventions or conferences) to join their resources to start new congregations. The strategy requires the Key Church to do the following: (1) make a long term commitment to make missions outreach a top priority, (2) prioritize missions to the level of the church's religious education and music programs, (3) establish a Missions Development Council, (4) elect a full-time Minister of Missions to lead missions expansion, (5) begin a specified number of new mission congregations a year, (6) begin a comparable number of ministries each year; and (7) sponsor at least six Mission/Churches on a continuous basis.[109]

The state organization, in turn, will provide some of the needed finances and the necessary training for the Minister of Missions, who will involve the members of the Key Church (led by a Church Development Council) in starting several ministry points, many of which will result in new congregations. Many of these new congregations minister in multi-housing communities and among numerous ethnic groups.

This approach has some features in common with the Satellite Model. The ultimate goal of the Key Church approach is, however, that the congregations become autonomous churches and the established churches become more missional in vision and action. This model is fully described in One Church, Many Congregations: the Key Church Strategy.[110]

Part B
Propagating & People Group Models
Propagating Models

In a sense, Propagating Models have much in common with Pioneering Models. The distinctive feature of Propagating Models, however, is that these efforts envision maximum church multiplication and reach toward this vision. Two of the better-known Propagating Models are Multiplication through Leadership Training and Multiplication through Church Starting Movements.

Multiplication through Leadership Training

One variation of the Propagating Model of church starting, multiplication through leadership training, accomplishes its goal by multiplying a network of cell groups through theological education and evangelism by extension. Designed by Honduran missionary George Patterson, this pattern strives for "the voluntary multiplication of a church of any size, by God's power, in daughter churches of cells that in turn start granddaughters and so forth."[111] This program integrates church starting with discipleship. From the start, an effort is made to teach converts the full meaning of discipleship.

This discipling approach, according to Patterson, involves commitment to obey the specific commands of Jesus before and above all else. These commands are to: 1) Repent, believe, and receive the Holy Spirit; 2) Be baptized; 3) Love God and neighbor; 4) Break bread; 5) Pray; 6) Give; and 7) Disciple others.[112] By setting up a large number of theological extension centers and a leadership structure that oversees and encourages church starting efforts, Patterson has seen more than a hundred churches started in the part of the country where he works.

Claylan Coursey in Malindi, Kenya developed another example of church multiplication through leadership training.[113] After concluding that "the primary responsibility for church starting belongs to individual believers banded together as a local church," Coursey designed a plan to help pastors train their church members to start churches. The training involves eight simple steps: "1) Select a New Work Committee for the church; 2) Select the area for the new work; 3) Prepare the sponsoring church; 4) Prepare the selected area; 5) Begin the infant church; 6) Teach the new church about finances; 7) Plan the facilities with the new church; 8) Dedicate the new church."[114] By training the pastors and having ongoing follow-up sessions, Coursey was able to see over ninety new congregations started in Malindi in three years.

Several distinctive features adhere to the Multiplication through Leadership Training Model. First, in this model every Christian is seen as a potential church starter. Second, training is tied in with implementation. Patterson, for example, added "direct evangelism" to Theological Education by Extension. He did not feel that simply educating leaders without involving them in church starting ministries was enough. Third, in this model, a leadership structure was established to ensure the continuity of the church starting efforts. Fourth, this model is based on simple obedience to the commands of Christ. Patterson states: "Basically, church multiplication comes from our love for Christ and the resulting desire to obey his commands to disciple all peoples or ethnic groups."[115]

It is evident that this model works well in rural areas among people in the lower socio-economic levels. Leaders, like Richard Scoggins, Patterson's colleague, have found it also effective among urban, educated, affluent, middle-class Americans in the shadow of the oldest Baptist church and the oldest synagogue in the United States (in Providence and Newport, Rhode Island).[116] This method of obedience-based training deserves much more attention than it has received. Every effort at theological training or leadership training should include a strong church starting module. The evangelism and church starting aspects of the training should purposely include direct experience in witnessing and starting new churches.

Multiplication through Church Starting Movements

A second variation in the Propagating Model of church starting, multiplication through church starting movement, involves what David Garrison describes as "a rapid and exponential increase of indigenous churches planting churches within a given people group or population segment."[117] Garrison gives examples of church planting movements occurring in many parts of the world:

Southeast Asia -When a strategy coordinator began his assignment in 1993, there were only three churches and 85 believers among a population of more than 7 million lost souls. Four years later there were more than 550 churches and nearly 55,000 believers.

City in China [is this another heading or how should it be written?]-Over a four-year period (1993-1997), more than 20,000 people came to faith in Christ, resulting in more than 500 new churches.

Latin America - Two Baptist unions overcame significant government persecution   to grow from 235 churches in 1990 to more than 3,200 in 1998.

Central Asia - A strategy coordinator reports: "Around the end of 1996, we called around to the various churches in the area and got their count on how many had come to faith in that one year. When they were all added up, it came to 15,000 conversions to Christ in one year. The previous year we estimated only 200 believers altogether."

Ethiopia - A missionary strategist commented, "It took us 30 years to plant four churches in this country. We've started 65 cell churches in the last nine months."

Every region of the world now pulsates with some kind of Church Planting Movement. Sometimes we see only the numbers, but often they are accompanied by lively descriptions such as this recently received e-mail message: "All of our cell churches have lay pastors/leaders because we turn over the work so fast that the missionary seldom leads as many as two or three Bible studies before God raises at least one leader. The new leader seems to be both saved and called to lead at the same time, so we baptize him and give him a Bible. After the new believers/leaders are baptized, they are so on fire that we simply cannot hold them back. They fan out all over the country starting Bible studies, and a few weeks later we begin to get word back how many have started. It's the craziest thing we ever saw! We did not start it, and we couldn't stop it if we tried."[118]

There are ten characteristics, or "universal elements" that have been compiled from the study of church planting movements around the world:

1. *Prayer* - Prayer has been fundamental to every Church Planting Movement we have observed. Prayer typically provides the first pillar in a strategy coordinator's master plan for reaching his or her people group.

2. *Abundant gospel sowing* - We have yet to see a Church Planting Movement emerge where evangelism is rare or absent. Every Church Planting Movement is accompanied by abundant sowing of the gospel. The law of the harvest applies well: "If you sow abundantly you will also reap abundantly."

3. *Intentional church planting* - In every Church Planting Movement, someone implemented a strategy of deliberate church planting before the movement got under way.

4. *Scriptural authority* - Even among nonliterate people groups, the Bible has been the guiding source for doctrine, church polity and life itself. While Church Planting Movements have occurred among peoples without the Bible translated into their own language, the majority had the Bible either orally or in written form in their heart language. In every instance, Scripture provided the rudder for the church's life, and its authority was unquestioned.

5. *Local leadership* - Missionaries involved in Church Planting Movements often speak of the self-discipline required to mentor church planters rather than do the job of church planting themselves. This is not to say that missionaries have no role in church planting. On the contrary, local church planters receive their best training by watching how the missionary models participative Bible studies with non-Christian seekers. Walking alongside local church planters is the first step in cultivating and establishing local leadership.

6. *Lay leadership* - Church Planting Movements are driven by lay leaders. These lay leaders are typically

bivocational and come from the general profile of the people group being reached. As the movement unfolds, paid clergy often emerge. However, the majority—and growth edge of the movement—continue to be led by lay or bi-vocational leaders. This reliance upon lay leadership ensures the largest possible pool of potential church planters and cell church leaders.

7. *Cell or house churches* - Church buildings do appear in Church Planting Movements. However, the vast majority of the churches continue to be small, reproducible cell churches of 10-30 members meeting in homes or storefronts.

8. *Churches planting churches* - In most Church Planting Movements, the first churches were planted by missionaries or by missionary-trained church planters. At some point, however, as the movements entered a multiplicative phase of reproduction, the churches themselves began planting new churches. In order for this to occur, church members have to believe that reproduction is natural and that no external aids are needed to start a new church. In Church Planting Movements, nothing deters the local believers from winning the lost and planting new cell churches themselves.

9. *Rapid reproduction* - Most church planters involved in these movements contend that rapid reproduction is vital to the movement itself. They report that when reproduction rates slow down, the Church Planting Movement falters. Rapid reproduction communicates the urgency and importance of coming to faith in Christ. When rapid reproduction is taking place, you can be assured that the churches are unencumbered by nonessential elements and the laity are fully empowered to participate in this work of God.

10. *Healthy churches* - Church growth experts have written extensively in recent years about the marks of a church. Most agree that healthy churches should carry out the following five purposes: 1) worship, 2) evangelistic and missionary outreach, 3) education and discipleship, 4) ministry and 5) fellowship. In

each of the Church Planting Movements we studied, these five core functions were evident.[119]

In the history of Christianity perhaps two of the most effective developers of church starting movements have been the Apostle Paul and John Wesley. Through their leadership, they sparked multitudes of new congregations. Contemporary church starters should carefully study the church starting efforts of these pioneering workers.

Reviewing the Apostle Paul's leadership reveals that he followed several principles in his church starting efforts.

- First, it is quite evident that Paul was sensitive to the leadership of the Holy Spirit who instructed him where not to go as well as where to go (Acts 16:9).

- Second, Paul was willing to pay the price to go where God wanted him to go even if it meant suffering for Christ (2 Cor 6:5).

- Third, Paul was willing to adapt himself to the target group to whom the Lord sent him (1 Cor 9:19-23).

- Fourth, Paul was willing to adapt the presentation of the gospel to each target group (compare Acts 13 with Acts 17).

- Fifth, Paul saw himself primarily as a church starter. He did not stay long in any of the places where he started churches.

- Sixth, Paul did not tie his strategy to the availability of buildings. When he was no longer welcome in the synagogues he moved to whatever was available such as schools (Acts 19:9), homes (Col 4:15), the marketplace (Acts 17:17).

- Seventh, Paul was willing to trust the leaders that emerged in each church start (Acts 14:23).

- Eighth, Paul was committed to training and trusting the leaders (Acts 14:21; 15:35);

- Ninth, Paul did everything he could to encourage the leaders (Acts 14:22). In so doing he was instrumental in spawning a church starting movement that impacted the world.

Apostolic type persons are currently being recruited by mission organizations to serve as church starters who can facilitate church starting movements.

The International Mission Board of the Southern Baptist Convention, for instance, is utilizing "Strategy Coordinators" to start church starting movements. David Watson defines a Strategy Coordinator as "the person given responsibility and held accountable for designing and implementing strategies that initiate and nurture a Church Planting Movement among a specific ethno linguistic people group, segment of that group, or homogeneous unit.[120]

Some of the most important characteristics of Strategy Coordinators are articulated by Myers and Slack. These include:

- Unquestioned commitment to an all out assault against lostness

- Singular eye for this people group – a magnificent obsessions

- Posses entrepreneurial skills

- Spiritual leader reflecting a growing renewal lifestyle

- Gifted in group dynamics – strong people skills

- Visionary – nurtures and shares the vision well

- Commitment to working in the heart language of the target group

- Plays to the strengths of the team members

- Able to coordinate the varied responsibilities of the team

- Has adequate computer skills[121]

Scott Holstee explains that:

> A Strategy Coordinator uses multiple, culturally appropriate methods and works globally with increasing numbers of compatible people to realize multiple, indigenous, new church starts among a singular target people. A Strategy Coordinators constant prayer is the ability to cooperate with the Holy Spirit in experiencing a church planting movement." Watson adds that "the Strategy Coordinator's task

is to find out why things aren't happening among a people group. Sometimes the pieces are there, mission agencies and personnel are there, but nothing is happening. Maybe the radio broadcasters don't have anyone or know anyone on the ground to do follow-up. OMF is on the ground but doesn't have any leads. The Strategy Coordinator identifies and supplies what's missing and makes things happen."[122]

The North American Mission Board is employing a similar category of leaders that they call "Strategic Catalyzers." Joe Hernandez defines a Strategic Catalyzer as "person responsible for building and leading teams in the design and implementation of strategies that initiate and nurture a rapid church multiplication among a specific people group."[123] He proceeds to describe the role of a Strategic Catalyzer:

A Strategic Catalyzer uses multiple, culturally appropriate methods and scriptural sound principles while working globally with increasing numbers of compatible people to realize multiple, indigenous, new church starts among a singular target people. A Strategic Catalyzer's constant prayer is the ability to cooperate with the Holy Spirit in experiencing a rapid church multiplication. The Strategic Catalyzer does not go to an area exclusively to preach, or minister, or teach, or start individual churches, though all of those things may be done. Rather, he approaches an entire people group with one big-picture goal: to see an unstoppable rapid church multiplication begun, a movement that will empower local believers to worship God, evangelize their own people, reach out to others and continue as church planting churches. He identifies the needs of the unreached, acts as their advocate to Christians and mobilizes effective responses (prayer, workers, Scripture distribution, media, leader training, whatever it takes)—all the while keeping his eyes on the prize of a rapid church multiplication[124]

Hernandez goes on to describe the specific of a Strategic Catalyzer:

As an SC you will be involved in and involve others in: networking, strategizing, interceding, evangelizing, discipling, forming groups, casting vision, ministering, implementing, ensuring doctrinal integrity, advocating, leading/team building, and training, as well as developing a personal, hands on ministry.[125]

According to Hernandez a number of people can serve in the role of a Strategic Catalyzer. These include: Associational Missionaries, Church Planting Missionaries, Ministers of Missions, Church and Community Workers, Campus Ministry Workers, Church Ministry Leaders, Lay Leaders, and Seminary Students.[126]

Today, the Holy Spirit is utilizing these types of apostolic leaders to spark church starting movements in many parts of the world. The elements in a church starting movement are well documented in David Garrison's book, Church Planting Movements.[127] Here again is a method that deserves close attention.

Slack makes several observations regarding church starting movements:[128]

- First, these movements generally develop along the lines of people groups instead of simple geographical configurations. This means that these movements quite often cross national and political boundaries.

- Second, if a church starting movement is going to succeed, lay people need to play an active role in starting new congregations.

- Third, even though church starting movements appear to be totally extemporaneous, a structure is needed to continue to inspire and to train locally those who will start new units.

- Fourth, many church starting movements are taking place in societies that are basically pre-literate. Outreach methodologies, therefore, need to be in narrative formats (e.g. Bible Storying) rather than literate formats.[129]

- Fifth, church starting movements only take place when indigenous leaders experientially know the heart language and customs of the people do church starting. Commenting about the church in China, Raymond Fung states:

- Perhaps the single most obvious conclusion about Christianity in China today is that it is Chinese. People in the streets and in the communes no longer see Christianity in China as a foreign religion. Now after some 25 years of isolation, and eight years of acute suffering, with zero visibility, the church is seen to have survived and grown. For the first time in its history, the church has won its right to exist in China as a Chinese church. For the first time in its existence, it has its roots in Chinese soil.[130]

In addition to these observations, others need to be made to provide as realistic a picture as possible of church planting movements.

One observation refers to the rapidity with which growth takes place. While the definition of church planting movements indicates that there is "rapid multiplication," it needs to be pointed out that this does not mean "instantaneous multiplication." In some settings it took many years of seed sowing and the laying of an indigenous foundation before rapid multiplication began to take place. In his article entitled, "The Left Side Of The Graph," Clyde Meador points out that often while charting church planting movements, people tend to see only the portion of the chart that indicates dramatic growth but fail to take into account the extensive seed sowing that took place prior to the explosive growth. He explains:

> Most church planting movements have a "left side of the graph" lasting 20 or 30 or even 100 years or more. The ignored left side of the graph represents many years of faithful labor by often un-heralded servants of the Lord... Our experience is that most CPMs take a long period of cultivation, of relationship development, and credibility building before the harvest time for that people group comes... I have had the privilege of witnessing a few great movements in recent decades. One of the most dramatic movements in Asia has grown to a reported 900,000 believers, with the number of house churches possibly moving toward 100,000. This movement began in the early 90's with a major focal point being a group of 28 or 29 churches. The graph of that CPM is thrilling. Yet, it is essential that we realize that those 28 or 29 churches were the result of almost one hundred years of faithful ser-

vice by a small group of missionaries from a Euro-
pean Baptist sending agency. The left side of the
chart was long for that people group and founda-
tional for what was to come. This kind of history is
typical of many church planting movements.[131]

In addition to the faithful seed sowing that was done by early
missionaries, it can be pointed out that the practice of indigenous principles has laid a foundation for church planting
movements. This was certainly the case among the Kekchi in
Guatemala. An International Mission Board study led by Dr.
James Slack confirmed the fact that the early missionaries had
laid an indigenous foundation. Slack explains:

> The Kekchi Baptist CPM emerged out of a long his-
> tory of indigenous ministry that emphasized the use
> of heart-language as well as sound and consistent
> missiological modeling and mentoring. Southern
> Baptist work among the Kekchi began in 1964 and
> increased positively and incrementally from then
> until 1993.[132]

The early missionaries among the Kekchi lived among the
people, trained local converts, encouraged the people to provide their own meeting places, enabled them to utilize evangelism and church planting methods that were natural to their culture, encouraged their churches to govern themselves, and encouraged their congregations to reproduce themselves. When
the climate was right for a church planting movement to take
place, there was already a solid foundation.

Another observation has to do with the presence of the universal elements in church planting movements. These elements are not necessarily present in to same degree in all of
the church planting movements. Due to the fact that a number
of the church planting movements emerged prior to the articulation of the universal elements, there were varying degrees of
attention given to each of the elements.[133] The fact that the
studies of these movements revealed that these elements were
present confirms their significance.[134]

Few methods show more promise in multiplying the numbers
of congregations and winning the lost to salvation than the
church starting movements approach. All workers interested
and engaged in evangelizing the peoples of the world should

carefully consider this methodology. While only God can produce such movements, church starters should seek to realize these blessings and do nothing neither to hinder nor discourage their development. We will expect to experience continuing growth and effective church starting as God's servants learn better way to employ the methods of church starting movements in various parts of the world.

People Group Models

People Group (Ethnic) church starting models have much in common with the other models already discussed. Due to the fact, however, that significant cultural and linguistic factors need to be taken into account, it is helpful to establish a separate category for the discussion of these models. An ethnic group typically is seen as a minority group living in the context of a predominant society. Factors such as a common origin, language, culture, history, and social interaction patterns combine to provide a sense of identity for an ethnic group.

This sense of identity, however, is modified when segments of an ethnic group begin to experience varying degrees of assimilation into the predominant society. This variation in assimilation significantly impacts church starting. Prior to determining the model of church starting that will be employed, it is important to understand several things about an ethnic group.

Vital Information about People Groups

One important piece of information on people groups answers the question of how they became residents of their adopted country. There are significant differences between the predominant society and the ethnic groups in a given country.[135] Aside from what may be obvious linguistic[136] and phenotypic characteristics, factors such as mode of entry, socio-economic level at the point of entry, and cultural congruity (vis-à-vis the predominant society) account for significant differences between ethnic groups.

The mode of entry has a great deal to do with the mind-set of the ethnic group as well as with the attitude of the predominant society. Some of the modes of entry are: (1) Annexation[137]; (2) Forced Migration[138]; (3) Voluntary Migration (Political Refugees, Documented Immigration, and Undocumented Immigration).[139] Each of these types carries with it a cluster of historical, social, political, and economic factors which affect the ethnic group's self-perception as well as the predominant society's attitude toward it.

A second question deals with the group's level of assimilation? In addition to inter-group variations there are intra-groups variations. In other words, ethnic groups are not always homogeneous entities. The analyses of such social researchers as R. A. Schermerhorn,[140] Andrew Greeley,[141] Malcolm McFee[142] and Milton Gordon[143] show that within ethnic groups there are segments that are at different stages of assimilation in relation to the predominant society. To facilitate this discussion we will place these segments under five categories: (1) Total Ethnic, (2) Median Ethnic, (3) Marginal Ethnic, (4) Assimilated Ethnic, and (5) Revitalized Ethnic.[144]

Assimilation Stages

The fact that ethnic peoples have arrived at differing stages of assimilation requires that different types of congregations be established. Total Ethnics are persons whose identity and social contacts are entirely within their own social/linguistic group. Median Ethnics have more of a tendency to be bilingual and to have social contacts outside their own group. Marginal Ethnics are more fluent in the language of the predominant society and have more social contacts outside their cultural group than within it. Alienated Ethnics generally have virtually no social contacts with their group of origin and do not speak the language of their ancestors. Revitalized Ethnic denotes persons who are seeking to move away from cultural assimilation and toward their cultural roots.[145]

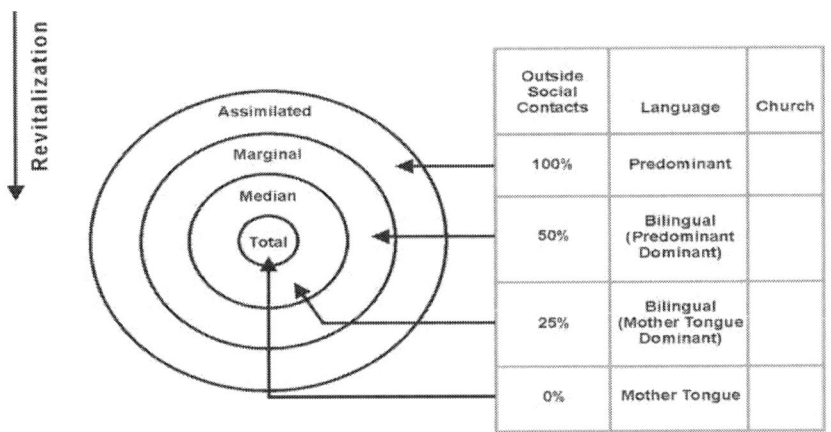

Variety of Congregational Models Needed

The fact that ethnic groups in many countries have experienced varying degrees of assimilation into the predominant society means that a variety of congregational models are imperative. First, the language that a congregation employs will need to be determined wisely. Total Ethnics will need congregations that speak their mother tongue. Median and Marginal Ethnics will need bilingual congregations. Assimilated Ethnics will perhaps be better prospects for congregations that speak the language of the predominant society.

Secondly, different pastoral leadership is needed for the various groups. A newly arrived immigrant minister may have difficulty reaching a community that is made up of Marginal Ethnics who were born in the adopted country. Conversely, a highly acculturated (into the predominant society) pastor may have difficulty communicating with new immigrants even if they have the same cultural heritage.

Thirdly, the fact that an ethnic group speaks the language of the predominant society does not necessarily mean that an ethnic congregation is not needed in that community. Unless they have experienced significant structural assimilation into the predominant society, ethnic persons will not generally come in large numbers to existing churches that speak the language of the predominant society.[146]

Congregational Models Currently Employed

Several heterogeneous models are now being utilized to address the diverse needs of ethnic groups. In one such model, the Multi-Cultural Model, the congregations are made up of individuals who have different sociocultural backgrounds. Often the individuals in these congregations are at a similar stage of assimilation and, therefore, have quite a bit in common with each other. Where this is not the case, an extra, ongoing effort is needed to ensure that those who are different culturally and socioeconomically are a part of the leadership as well as the membership of the church.

A second model, the Congregational Consortium Model, differs from the multi-cultural model, in that in this model there are ethnic groups instead of just individuals. There are at least two variations of this model. In one instance the various ethnic and majority culture congregations utilize the same building and resources but (for the most part) worship separately in different parts of the building or at different times.[147] Yet another variation of this model is when the groups meet separately for Sunday school but worship together.

A third model, the Sponsorship Model, takes various forms. Some of the following are examples of sponsorship models. The ethnic congregation resides within a majority culture church. In some instances this arrangement is a temporary phase until the ethnic congregation is ready to become an autonomous church. In other cases, a majority culture church starts ethnic congregations outside its own building. Most likely, the sponsoring church will provide the building for which the daughter congregation will assume future responsibility.

Still another model, the joint-sponsorship model, calls for the majority culture and ethnic churches jointly to sponsor an ethnic mission. The right combination of resources and expertise can go a long way toward helping a daughter congregation to get a good start.

One other method calls for an ethnic church to sponsor an ethnic mission of the same culture. This method is currently being more used now than previously. The ethnic sponsoring church has the built-in advantage of knowing the culture of the daughter congregation.

This variety of congregational models, based on solid sociocultural analysis, therefore, holds vast significance for effective ethnic church starting.[148] All groups working in areas characterized by ethnic diversity should be aware of the variation within ethnic peoples and devise strategies that avoid the "same for all" approach and find various means to reach the differing groups of ethnic peoples. The day of one type of "mission" for one ethnic group has long passed.

Criteria for Selecting the Appropriate Model

In light of the fact that a wide variety of models is needed and is being utilized effectively today, a valid question remains. What model should I be using? Equally valid is the question as to how we can select the appropriate model for the group among whom we plan to start a new church. Obviously, one cannot give a simple answer. Church starters must consider several factors in making this decision.

First, what is the giftedness of the church starter? Some church starters are uniquely gifted for Pioneer Models. They have the vision, the personality, the leadership style, and the calling to go to new areas and start a congregation or a series of congregations from scratch. They have the willingness to enlist, train, and empower local leaders to assume responsibility for the churches that are started. These persons are comfortable in the pioneering pattern.

Others, on the other hand, do well only if they have a ready-made group of people with which to start and a clearly defined support structure (including finances). These church starters, obviously, can fit better in Parenting or Partnering models. Aside from the general characteristics of church starters, matters such as cultural background, cross-cultural skills, personality, leadership style, followership style, work style, philosophy of ministry, skills, and gifts need to be taken into account in selecting the appropriate church starting model. A good exercise is for the church starter to evaluate him/her on a scale of 1 to 5 on each of the models that are being considered in light of the characteristics discussed above.

Second, who is the target group? An understanding of the target group is absolutely essential in selecting an appropriate church model. Factors such as the worldview, religious background, cultural background, socio-economic level, lifestyles, patterns of social interaction, and decision-making patterns need to be taken into account in selecting the church starting model. Some church starters have made serious mistakes seeking to implement a model that has been used very successfully elsewhere without taking into account the cultural context of the target group. It is in this area that ethnographic and psychographic studies of the target group can be very helpful.

Third, what resources are available? It is useless to try to implement a Parenting Model if the area in which the church starter is working does not have any sponsoring churches. Admittedly, some sponsors who are a distance away from the new congregations can be enlisted, but their involvement will be very limited. The financial and human resources available, therefore, inform the process of selecting a model.

Fourth, what is the ultimate objective of this model? The objectives of Church Starting Movement Models are very different from those of Satellite Units Models. If the goal is to spark rapidly growing, reproducing congregations, Propagation Models are absolutely essential. The secret is to adjust the model to the objectives of the effort.

Fifth, what amount of freedom is available? In some of the restricted countries the missionary involved in church starting may not have the freedom to set foot in the place where the new congregation is meeting. To do so would endanger the lives of the new Christians. In this case, obviously, only certain types of models would be available for the church starter.

Sixth, what are the characteristics of the model that is being considered? To help with this evaluation Steffen offers the following questions: "What is the model's historical context? What key features does it offer? What basic assumptions drive the model? What are the strengths and weaknesses? In what type of community is it most likely to succeed?"[149]

The selection of the appropriate model is of crucial importance. Church starters must keep in mind that often the resulting congregation reflects the personality and gifts of the church starter who started it. A pertinent question is if that type of church would fit in the culture in which it is being started. The characteristics of the cultural context of the target group must be taken into account. It is in this area that ethnographic and psychographic studies of the target group can be very helpful.

CHAPTER 6

PHILOSOPHICAL FOUNDATION

One of the most significant questions that every church starter must answer is: what is my philosophy of and strategy for church starting? To answer this vital question, the church starter will have to consider the following matters: What is my goal for the new congregation? Is it to remain a daughter forever or will it become an autonomous, reproducing church? In short, the church starter seeks to formulate his/her philosophical foundation for church starting.

In answering these questions, church starters and church starting groups must respond to four realities that constitute a basic foundation for church starting. Every church starter must come to grips with these four realities: (1) the Reproducibility Foundation, (2) the Indigenous Foundation, (3) the Contextualization Foundation, and (4) the Phase-out Foundation. A viable church starting effort cannot be built unless the church starters and those who support him/her have clear understandings of and commitment to these four realities that compose the philosophical foundation for church starting.

Reproducibility Foundation

The philosophical foundation for church starting begins with the reality of reproducibility. Church **reproduction** calls for congregations to engage in the task of starting other churches very soon after their beginning. The ultimate goal of 21st century church starting is to begin reproducing congregations that will reproduce themselves in order to reach the awaiting multitudes of the world.

Donald McGavran said in 1965 that "what the fantastically mounting population of this world needs is fantastically multiplying churches..."[150] This drive to multiply churches in order to reach the entire world rests at the heart of 21st century church starting.

The Inclusiveness of Reproducibility

Church planting efforts that provide for reproducibility insist on and maintain the quality of inclusiveness—that is, the characteristic of inclusiveness—purposely targeting all peoples and people groups. Church starting in the 21st century will only reach its goals as it incorporates this ultimate purpose. In other words, the characteristic of reproducibility envisions the inclusion of every population segment. 21st century church movements refuse to be shackled by an exclusive commitment to one target group when other needy groups exist. Inclusiveness demands an outward focus.

Too many church starting efforts, especially those that follow the colonization method or constitute the efforts of denominational entities, result in a new congregation that reaches only the same types of people as served by the sponsoring church or denomination. Such reproduction certainly is not in error. Twenty-first century church starting, however, contends that these efforts must move beyond the cloning stage of starting new congregations that simply mirror the characteristics of the starting church or group. 21st century church starting includes all people.

The new congregations in the 21st century church starting movement will usually reflect the doctrinal and church polity characteristics of the starting group. Those responsible for the church starting movements should, however, make certain that these efforts not be restricted to just one type of congregation or group of people. 21st century church starting movements will provide for the myriad of other peoples who spring from groups different from the starting entity.

A 21st century church starting movement refuses to accept its work as complete until the effort includes the vision and mechanism to reproduce churches that can and will reach both the entire local context as well as the entire population of the world. These churches seek not only to reach the same kind of people as the sponsoring church or church starting entity but also by their very natures reach out to other groups of people.

Reproducible churches focus both on the people of the world and also the people of people groups. Twenty-first century church starting movements are born with eyes open to see new groups of people who also need the gospel and hearts ready to achieve the necessary diversity of congregations that will accomplish the harvest. The reproducibility foundation insists that while every church remains faithful to the entire biblical teaching, these biblically faithful churches can and should exist in a remarkable and beautiful diversity of methods, worship styles, meeting places, polities, and other factors as they seek to reach the diverse peoples of the world.

These church starting movements may center and focus on one particular people group in the beginning period but will refuse to be limited permanently to just one type of congregation. Acceptable church starting movements will, both in the new congregations and in the overall goals of the movement, incorporate the vision for reaching the broadest range of peoples and assuring the proper diversity to reach all the people.

The ultimate goal should be "*panta ta ethne*" (all peoples). Inclusiveness of the entire community remains an important factor in reproducible church starting. For example, a church serving basically middle-class people may start a new church for middle- class people, perhaps in a new neighborhood. This church should, on the basis of the principle of inclusiveness, also be alert to needs of churches for the lower-socioeconomic people groups, for ethnic peoples in the area, and also for upper-class people who would not feel comfortable in the middle-class environment.

This concept helps explain the often-misunderstood strategy of the homogeneous unit church in church-growth thinking. While a local church may remain relatively homogeneous, serving one group of people, a denomination or group of churches should be as heterogeneous as the community served. Churches for every segment of the population should be started and cultivated. The church starting effort should move beyond the cloning mentality and start many different and diverse kinds of churches.

Characteristics that Contribute to Reproducibility

The concept of reproducibility requires that 21st century church starting movements seek to insure the presence of at least four key characteristics that contribute to reproducibility:

- the insistence on reproducibility,
- viewing non-reproduction as incomplete,
- building reproduction into the genetic code of new congregations,
- keeping congregations free to reproduce.

Without these key characteristics, little chance exists for beginning an ongoing, ever expanding church starting movement.

Insistence on Reproducibility

A first key characteristic of a church starting effort that contributes to reproducibility relates to the insistence that the congregations be both reproducible and reproducing. In 21st century church starting, the quality of reproducibility is a must! To be biblically sound, methodologically effective, and continuously healthy, every congregation and movement must constantly reside in the mode of reproduction.

Twenty-first century church starters insist that this quality of reproducibility remain paramount in all their efforts to begin new churches and new church starting movements. This insistence on reproducibility drives 21st century church starters to emphasize in the new churches those qualities that allow and encourage unlimited reproducibility. Twenty-first century church starting insists on reproducibility and refuses to incorporate into the new churches any factors that will discourage, hinder, or prevent the reproduction of these congregations.

Viewing Non-Reproduction as Incomplete

The second key characteristic that contributes to reproducibility views non-reproducing patterns as incomplete. Twenty-first century church starting considers its task incomplete (or even defective) until the new congregations themselves become reproducing entities, that is, these churches produce, by the Holy Spirit's leading and power, new congregations. David Garrison says, "Exponential multiplication is only possible when new churches are being started by the churches themselves—rather than by professional church starters or missionaries."[151]

When a group approaches the task of starting a new

congregation, that group should be thinking "reproduce." The plan will incorporate this characteristic from the beginning. The effort remains incomplete if it does not infuse the new congregation with the spirit and the means for reproducing itself. *Any church starting movement that does not incorporate the characteristic of reproducibility remains both incomplete and defective*.

Building Reproduction into the Genetic Code

The third key characteristic that contributes to reproducibility demands that the concept of reproducibility be written into the very genetic code of the new churches. This vision of reproduction marks the essence of the church and extends this church's vision from the local scene to the entire population of the world. In the words of Peter Wagner, "Aggressive outreach is part of the new 21st century DNA."[152]

From their conception, 21st century churches maintain this vision of reaching out to all the peoples of the world. They see the task as reaching the entire world rather than restricting their ministries to only one region or to one group of people. They are patterned to reproduce.

Church starting experts assert that if, by the third year of its existence, a church has not given birth to a new congregation, it is very unlikely that it ever will. That is why from the very beginning, the church starting team and the core group need to hear that their church will envision itself as a reproducing church. This concept becomes a part of the very nature of the new congregation; the DNA of the new church contains the trait of reproducibility.

Keeping Congregations Free to Reproduce

Protecting the new congregations from anything that might hinder or prevent the new churches from reproducing constitutes the fourth key characteristic that contributes to reproducibility. Twenty-first century church starting insists on keeping the new congregations free of and guarded from any hindrance for continuing reproduction. Anything that might hinder this continuing reproducibility should not be allowed or tolerated in 21st century church starting movements.

This characteristic of total and unhindered reproducibility in

the congregations that grow out of 21st century church starting is imperative and inclusive. Wise church starters insist that
every new church be free from entangling characteristics that
would handicap or prevent that congregation from reproducing. For example, methods that by subsidizing provide buildings,
equipment, or other implements that the new church can
never give to a daughter congregation limit the reproducibility of the church. Subsidized congregations most often never
gain the strength to give to new churches what they received.

Regulations that set forth unbiblical or unnecessary
requirements for churches, or church leaders, can prevent the
unhindered spread of the gospel and the diversity of congregations needed. Some groups have required that a congregation
have property before it can be considered a church. Others
have certain membership numbers as requirements. Still others
insist on church organization in the sense of constitutions or bylaws for a group to be considered a church. Such regulations
can hinder a new congregation from seeing itself as a church
and from accepting its responsibilities as a church.

Other unbiblical and unnecessary regulations relate to restrictions on the geographical proximity of new congregations
to older churches. Such restrictions may consider an area
"churched" if one congregation exists in the region. In modern
cities, in a three-mile circle, many different people groups may
exist. These diverse groups may call for a diversity of congregations. Considering an area reached because one type of work
is in place overlooks the many other needs. These types of regulations may stifle proper church growth through new congregations.

Unbiblical requirements for church leaders likewise can be a
barrier to 21st century reproducibility. To require a church leader to have a certain educational level or experience may keep
leaders from serving. Requirements for church leaders
might keep churches from reproducing because leaders
with certain qualifications are unavailable. The only
indispensable qualifications for church leaders are salvation
experience, divine call, and willingness to serve. Without these
qualities no person, no matter how qualified otherwise, can
hope to serve.

Parents seek to guard their children from disease and dangers that would prevent their reaching productive adulthood. Twenty- first century church starters guard the movements and congregations from those factors that could become barriers to constant and continuing reproduction. These church starters refuse to allow any limiting factors in their church starting designs. *The ultimate goal of 21st century church starting consists of continuously reproducing churches of such natures that these congregations can evangelize and disciple all of the differing peoples of the world.*

Indigenous Foundation

The second reality in the foundation of a church starting effort relates to the concept of the indigenous foundation. To what degree does the church starter desire and intend for the new church to become indigenous to the local culture? In order to achieve the objective of indigeneity, the church starter will need to become thoroughly acquainted with and committed to the indigenous church starting philosophy.

To be indigenous, something (plant, animal) needs to be native to a particular environment. For example, the banana plant is indigenous to a tropical climate. To keep a banana plant alive in colder climates one has to build and maintain a greenhouse. This costly and artificial process does not lead to healthy life for the banana tree. Even if kept alive by artificial means, however, the banana tree in the colder climate will not reproduce. The same truth relates to a church. A foreign church that does not fit the culture of the people for whom it is developed may exist in an artificial environment of subsidy but will not be able to reproduce.

Keith Eitel observes that the agricultural term "indigenous" describes a plant that thrives in a particular type of soil, in a particular location, and in a particular climate. The goal and purpose of missionary effort should be to start churches that conform to this model. Eitel states, "As missionaries cross cultural borders, the aim or goal ought to be to plant viable churches that are able to cultivate a natural appearance and form culturally relevant growth patterns."[153] The advice of Keith Eitel must be heeded by church starters around the world if the most effective advance of churches is to be achieved.

Understanding the Indigenous Approach

Joe Hernandez points out that some of the early missionaries articulated what have come to be known as the indigenous approach. He explains:

> Mid 18th century missionary leaders Henry Venn (British Anglican) and Rufus Anderson (American Congregationalist) were the first to use the term indigenous to address the challenges of missionaries starting churches among cultures and peoples foreign to themselves. In the late 1800's a Presbyterian missionary to China, John Nevius, built on these principles (3 Self). Nevius' principles focus upon cross-cultural missionaries and the methodology required for planting an indigenous church. Roland Allen was an Anglican missionary to China who developed a philosophy of indigenous missions. Allen's philosophy builds upon the three-self formula and Nevius' principles but significantly expands the theological rationale demanding indigenous practices by cross-cultural missionaries. Melvin Hodges, an Assemblies of God missionary popularized the indigenous church concept in America with his book, The Indigenous Church, written in 1957. He defined an indigenous church as one "which shares the life of the country in which it is planted and finds itself ready to govern itself, support itself, and reproduce itself." In Southern Baptist circles, Charles Brock was one of the earliest proponents of indigenous churches and indigenous church planting. Increasing use of sociology and anthropology by cross-cultural missionaries during the last fifty years has greatly impacted the current usage of the term indigenous among Evangelicals. In addition to the influences of sociology and anthropology, the introduction of the term "contextualization" in the 1970's accelerated the shift to new perspectives and meanings for the term indigenous church.[154]

Missiologist Allen Tippet projects several characteristics[155] that churches should reach before they can claim to be indigenous: (1) self-image; (2) self-function; (3) self-government; (4) self-support; (5) self-propagation; (6) self-ministry. Self-image means that the new church arrives at the stage of maturity in which it sees itself as the church of the Lord Jesus

Christ in that community. It is not merely an extension of another church from another region and among a different people but the church that the Lord has placed in the particular culture with a specific mission. The church does not depend on outside help in meeting its own needs or the needs of those within its ministry circle.

The term "Self-function" means that the congregation carries out all the activities of a church (e.g. worship, instruction, ordinances). Acts 2:40-47 reports a church that evangelized, discipled, worshiped, prayed, had fellowship, and ministered to others. A self-functioning church is one that carries out these activities under the leadership of the Lord and not from outside influence or by outside provision.

Self-government means that the new church arrives at the stage of maturity in which it makes its own decisions and plans its own future. These decisions relate to their meetings (time, place, length), their leadership (pastor, staff), their facilities (rented, purchased, built), their finances (budget, procedures), etc. No outside power or influence overrules the decision of the church itself. This church reaches these decisions in biblically and culturally relevant ways.

Self-support means that the church shoulders its own financial responsibilities through the contributions (tithes, offerings, gifts) of its members. This church does not develop dependence on outside sources but looks to itself, with the help of the Lord, to provide the resources needed for personnel, materials, buildings, programs, etc. The self-supporting congregation cares for the social needs of its community without resorting to outside help.

Self-propagation means that the church takes the Great Commission seriously and is devoted to the task of fulfilling it by winning souls and establishing churches. The self-propagating church seeks no outside aid in its missionary endeavors. This church assumes responsibilities for its own world.

Self-ministry means that the church utilizes its own resources of money and persons to serve the people in need in its community. Tippet labels this characteristic as self-giving. This church actively cares for the sick, the needy, and the lonely in the community.

Applying the Indigenous Principle

These characteristics of indigenous churches may seem to be very simple. A great variety of ways exist by which they can be applied to the different socio-cultural contexts. In order to develop contextualized 21st century churches it is necessary to give attention to the way that these characteristics are applied.

The term "self-government" does not just mean that the church makes its own decisions but also that the church utilizes its own style of decision making. Different cultural and socioeconomic groups have different decision-making styles. There should be flexibility so that the church utilizes its own way of making decisions, provided these are in agreement with the Scriptures. The outsider will move firmly away from exerting pressure on the local congregation to make certain decisions.

Self-support means that the church supports itself. This may be done in different ways. The model of a full-time pastor and a full-time staff serving a congregation that owns its own building is not applicable in all settings. Many churches do not have the financial base for this. In many places where churches are growing rapidly, there are a significant number of pastors who are leading several congregations or who are bi-vocational, supporting their families while continuing to serve their congregations.

To allow for the achievement of self-support, the missionary should avoid any subsidy that either makes the church dependent or that creates the feeling that material things are necessary for the life of the church. Anything given that the church cannot reasonably expect to provide for itself constitutes a mistake in attempting to apply the indigenous principle. Providing anything the church can never hope to supply to a daughter church is likewise a mistake.

Self-propagation does not only mean that the churches establish other churches but rather that they establish the type of churches that reflect the culture that surrounds them and not a foreign culture.[156] The church seeks out the unchurched for evangelism and the unreached areas for new church starts. The indigenous church does not wait for the denomination or the mission to start new congregations. An indigenous church propagates itself. This church is both reproducible and reproducing.

The indigenous church is self-giving in that it meets the needs of its community. The founders of the church should never assume the function of meeting the social needs in the community. From the beginning, the church should be taught that social ministries are the responsibility of the church itself.

The indigenous philosophy is imperative for every church starting effort. Centuries of missionary effort have taught us that a foreign church, doing things in foreign ways, under foreign leadership, and emphasizing foreign goals will never penetrate the culture and produce a growing, reproducing church. The church starter must embrace the philosophical foundation of the indigenous church.

Hernandez points out some very practical implications related to the application of indigenous principles:

- Believers, living under the Lordship of Jesus Christ and led by the Holy Spirit, shape the discipleship and discipline.

- Local congregations decide whether or not to have paid leadership.

- Local congregations determine which type of meeting place and building is best for growth.

- Leaders who emerge from the local group are recognized by the scriptural basis for leadership and learn from doing ministry according to their spiritual gifts.

- Believers are more likely to engage in reproducing themselves through church planting and church growth through discipling ministries.

- Natural witness by the whole membership is more likely.

- Witness and growth follow natural social networks of families and relationships within the surrounding community.

- Since these churches demonstrate easily reproducible patterns church growth and church planting are common outcomes.[157]

The Contextualization Foundation

A third reality in the philosophical foundation for church starting is the contextualization foundation. In one significant sense, the missiological discussion on indigenization has been challenged and enriched by the debate on contextualization. If indigenization is viewed largely as that which the missionary does for the national group, contextualization is viewed as that which the national group does for itself. In that light, it can be stated that indigenization can be a solid foundation for contextualization. This makes it possible to talk about some of the marks of contextualization that include contextualized vision, evangelistic strategy, worship service, and doctrinal reflection.

As a group moves toward contextualization it develops its own God-given vision. This vision motivates the church to implement the Great Commission at home and abroad. The group also develops its own contextualized evangelistic strategy. Instead of simply transplanting evangelistic methods that have been proven successful in other countries, this group seeks to understand the characteristics and needs of the society that surrounds it and engages in the task of developing approaches that will reach the people in that context.

The worship style of contextualized congregations also differs from that of churches elsewhere. This difference involves using the music, instruments, patterns of relationships, and communication styles of the local culture. If an American visits a church abroad and the only thing that is different is the language, there is a strong possibility that that congregation is not contextualized. On the other hand, if a national visits that church and feels at home culturally and linguistically, it is most likely a contextualized congregation.

Finally, contextualized congregations engage in theological reflection that focuses on the issues that are vital and urgent in its setting. There are general doctrines that all Christians must adhere to if, in fact, they are Christian. At the same time, much of the theological reflection that takes place in Western societies totally ignores the burning issues with which other societies are struggling. A contextualized church addresses the vital issues of its society through its preaching, teaching, and ministry. In summary, a contextualized church is in a position to make the same type of impact in its society that the early church made in the society of the first century.

The church starting team led by the apostle Paul utilized a contextualized strategy. When they left Antioch they did not try to clone the socio-cultural characteristics of that wonderful church. Instead, they sought to understand the local culture, to communicate the gospel in terms that they could understand, to gather believers in ways that were natural to them, to discover and train leaders on whom they would entrust the new congregations, to utilize the financial resources that were available locally, to encourage them to reproduce themselves along kinship and friendship ties, and to help them to see themselves as Christians who were under the mandate of Christ to make disciples of all people groups.

A contextualized church starting philosophy is needed at home and abroad. This is the only way that churches will be able to multiply and impact their communities and other groups around the world. While there is a tendency to believe that contextualized church strategies are needed only in the "exotic, primitive" cultures abroad, the success of new congregations anywhere depends upon the way in which they are viewed by the local community. Does the new congregation feel like it is "our church" or an extension of "somebody else's church?" Southern styled "y'all churches" sound as out of place to Northerners as Western style churches sound to non-Western societies.

Traditional (program-based) churches are also out of place in areas where innovative (friendship-based) churches are needed. Conversely, in communities where traditional churches are viable, innovative congregations may be perceived as "cults" and not churches. Contextualized churches, therefore, are needed to reach the various generational groups (e.g. Baby Boomer communities, Baby Busters, Generation X) as well as among the various linguistic cultural groups in our communities.

Church starters need to embrace the contextual foundation and strive to start churches that can and will fit into the cultures in which they are living. The tendency to copy one's own experiences and reproduce the church with which one is familiar projects a strong influence. Only as the church starter and the church starting group commits to the contextual principle will contextualized churches result.

The Phase-out Foundation

The final and all-important reality in the philosophical foundation that allows and enhances an unlimited and continuous movement is the trait of proper exiting of the missionaries, or what Tom A. Steffen calls "phase out."[158] David Garrison declares that only when the missionary (church starter) has actually stepped away from the work is the cycle of indigenous church starting competed and assured.[159]

A church group will become reproducing only to the extent that the founders of the church or movement move from evangelists to teachers, to resident advisors, to itinerant advisors, and to absent advisors.[160] The goal in every phase-out effort of the missionary or church starter is a clean exchange in which continued expansion of the Christian faith is uninterrupted. This fact leads Tom Steffen to declare that "knowing when to leave a church start is just as important as knowing when to begin it."[161]

The wise church starter realizes that the congregation or movement can never be either truly indigenous or totally reproducible until the leadership is solidly in local hands. Placing the leadership in local hands in most cases demands the church starter depart or at least minimize his/her leadership role. Leaving the church or movement often becomes the most creative and important phase of beginning a reproducing church.

Conclusion

Church starters must live and serve under the direction of a clear and impelling philosophy. This philosophical foundation determines the type of church, reproducible or limited to one congregation, indigenous or foreign, contextualized or unadjusted, phased-out or controlled. The differences are profound. A good philosophical foundation can help produce an effective church start. Until the approach to be used is clarified and the church starter is committed to a particular philosophy of church starting and development, the work will suffer. Every church starter should earnestly strive to build this philosophical foundation.

CHAPTER 7

LEADERSHIP FOUNDATION

Leadership factors assume significant place in the preparation phase of a church starting effort. Church starting, like every other human endeavor, demands and depends on adequate leadership. Church starters will of necessity be leaders; they must become "apostolic leaders" if the advances in evangelism and church births are to be reached.

Church starters accept the truth that apostolic ministry relies on the in-filling and empowering strength of God. This **apostolic** ministry directs its energy towards finding and winning the unchurched, incorporating them into living, growing, discipling congregations, and maturing these "found" sheep in the faith and outreach of the Lord. This section takes up the important subject of leadership for church starting.

This two-part chapter considers: A: The marks of those who, under the Spirit's guidance and filling, can become apostolic church starters; and B: Ways to assess persons for the various approaches to church starting.

PART A

Marks of Church Starters

Church Starter Characteristics

The Bible is the logical and most precise place to seek these models or characteristics of apostolic leaders. Among the many marks of Christian leaders, we suggest those of call, character, convictions, and commitment to be of special significance and importance.

A Clear Call

A primary mark of church starting leaders is the clear realization that this effort is God's plan and not just human desire. Abram (Abraham) went out, not knowing where he was going. He left his home because he knew that God was leading him to the new place and because of his faith in the absorbing promise (Gen. 12:1-3). Paul explained his experience of "call" to God's ministry (Acts 9:1-31) as he testified before Agrippa, *"So then, King Agrippa, I was not disobedient to the vision from heaven"* (Acts 26:19-20).

Church starters, like other Christian workers, of necessity, need the reassuring conviction that their lives are following God's design. Dave Page distinguishes between God's call to full-time Christian ministry in general and a specific call to church starting. Page considers church starting a "call within a call" and advises all who feel this leadership to be obedient to it.[162]

Aubrey Malphurs guides prospective church starters in finding this special leading or call to church starting. He teaches that the Word (Scripture) provides a positive source for help in finding God's will. Recognizing in ourselves God-given gifts for leadership, faith, evangelism, an entrepreneurial spirit, and love for ministry in the local church may well signal His intention that we become church starters.[163]

No person should undertake any effort toward starting a new church without the firm conviction that God has directed him/her to this ministry. The realization of this call of God to start a new church should relate not only to the worker's belief in God's intention for him/her to be a church starter but also to the place where the new church will be started. The divine call alone can sustain the church starter in this God-intended effort to start a new congregation.

A first mark for every biblical leader is a *clear call from God*.

A Clean Character

No amount of ability, drive, personality, or training can substitute for character in Christian leaders. This principle holds especially true for apostolic church starters. People whom God has used have invariably been men and women of respectable character. David Fisher underlines the need for integrity and character in leaders citing the "power of pastoral integrity."[164]

Joseph demonstrated the mark of character and integrity in all his actions of leading the people of Israel in their experiences in Egypt (Genesis 37-50). Paul writes to Timothy outlining the qualifications for leaders and begins with the mark, "*above reproach*" (1 Tim 3:2). The young pastor Titus heard the same message in that elders, whom he was to establish, were to be "*blameless*" (Titus 1:5-7).

To be "above reproach" demands that the leader be a man or woman of blameless character—one who is of such obvious integrity that no one can properly bring a charge of incorrect behavior. Thomas Lea suggests that "above reproach" might well be a general, covering term for the following list of virtues that must distinguish an acceptable Christian leader.[165]

The same emphasis on character is recorded in 1 Tim 4:12. Timothy is advised to set an example to the believers in speech, conduct (life), love, faith, and purity. These characteristics relate to living with integrity.[166]

Accepting the interpretation that "above reproach" is a covering concept to the other biblical virtues for leaders, we find that the leaders should be faithful to their spouses, "temperate," or in control of tendencies toward excesses, "self-controlled," or a sensible person who is trustworthy and balanced in judgment, "respectable," or one who demonstrates in outward behavior the inward presence of God in their life.

The character of the acceptable Christian leader will also be marked by "hospitality," or the willingness to share with others, the ability to teach or share truth and correction, the power to refrain from excesses, especially alcohol, and one who treats others with dignity, consideration, and care. The leader is not "violent," that is, does not "browbeat" others with threats of violence or anger or by intentionally manipulating them. The acceptable leader is never "quarrelsome" in the sense of contentious, grasping, or of a fighting disposition (see 1 Tim 6:4-5). Rather, the acceptable Christian leader is "gentile," that is kind, flexible, considerate, and loving rather than harsh and driving.

The character of the Christian leader includes a loving family leadership and a proper attitude toward material things. The Christian leader, if married and a parent, will manage (discipline) his household well with seriousness, keeping his children under proper guidance (control). Further, the acceptable leader has a proper attitude toward material things. Any hint of greed, dishonesty, or desire for money torpedoes spiritual leadership.

Paul concludes his list of necessities in the character of Christian leaders by mentioning good reputation with outsiders. Church starters must seek this quality. Leaders dedicated to starting new churches should strenuously avoid any action or tendency that would harm the church starter's reputation with the unchurched. Few things enhance the possibility that one will be able to start a new church in a new community more than the recognition on the community's part of the total integrity in the life of the church starter.

The effective leader and church starter must also develop the characteristic of contentment. The lives and ministries of many prospective church starters are damaged by their dissatisfaction with their lifestyles and statuses. This problem results either in their giving up on the church starting endeavor or allowing their lack of peace to limit their joy and satisfaction. To the degree that joy and satisfaction disappear from the church starter's life, effectiveness is greatly compromised.

The Apostle Paul underlined the necessity for contentment for all Christian leaders. He warned against ungodly persons who hold unbiblical teachings, who are conceited, and who promote discord due to their quarrelsome and controversial natures. Such people, says the Apostle, think that "godliness" is a means to "financial gain" (1 Tim 6:3-5 NIV).

"*Godliness with contentment is great gain*" according to the Apostle (1 Tim 6:6). Contentment is the quality of being independent of external circumstances or of being master of the situation. In Phil 4:10-11, Paul expressed that he had "*learned*" in whatever circumstances to be *content,* or master of the circumstances. One who is content avoids the spiritual ruin that accompanies the trap of greed or concern for security and comfort.

Church starters profit from the freedom from excessive desire for material things—ease, position, and fame—which the quality of contentment can bring. The ability to remain in a ministry little seen and perhaps unnoticed typifies most church starters because this lack of notoriety characterizes most efforts at church starting. Effective church starters can remain at the task because they do not see present worldly rewards as primary but rather only aim at the glory of God and His kingdom.

The character of an effective leader must demonstrate the quality of maturity in decision-making and action. Paul listed qualifications for leadership including that of an experienced Christian character (1 Tim 3:6) and one who has proven worth (1 Tim 3:10). Maturity is more a matter of spirit than chronological age. Paul advises against promoting a newly converted person to a place of leadership lest the person grow conceited due to the new position.

The opposite of maturity in Paul's teaching in 1 Tim 3:6-10 seems to be pride. This vice can occur in leaders either newly converted or long-time. Paul declares that such pride can lead to one's falling into the spiritual trap prepared by Satan. Satan blinds proud leaders to his traps and leads them to defeat, trouble, and ruin. Paul described the progression as falling, entanglement, and drowning (1 Tim 6:9). The Devil inflicts this damage on insensitive leaders who allow arrogance and conceit to separate them from the will of God.[167]

An effective church starter must have the spiritual maturity to realize that whatever success **results** comes only from God. While maturity in general also holds great value, the biblical teachings seem to point to this aspect of maturity as most important. Church starters who have genuine fruit will be those who by the virtue of maturity maintain the grace of humility.

Church starters need the quality of a growing Christian life and a willingness to change. No person possesses all of the qualities that are needed in church starters. The absence or weakness in some of these areas does not mean that one should discard the call to church starting. The call would be, by the help of God's Holy Spirit, to develop those characteristics that may be weak in the candidate's life.

The character of an effective church starter should include matters such as the ability to be a self-starter, not easily discouraged, abilities to be a team-player yet the capacity to work independently, a willingness to work out of the public view, and evangelistic abilities. The ability to grow and the willingness to change allows prospective church starters to discover their limits and strengthen their abilities in such areas. The quality of growth and willingness to change occupy a distinctive place in the character of the church starter.

Character, demonstrated by honesty, purity, considerateness, integrity, respect, maturity, and the ability to grow, assumes a vital and central place in church starting leadership. Joseph M. Stowell well says, "In the despairing darkness of the encroaching century the light of character-centered leadership will blaze like a torch that will lead many to Christ and the joy of a Christ-like life."[168] Church Starters must allow God's Spirit to build in them this godly character.

A Continuing Commitment

The effective leader (church starter) commits to the task and will not be turned aside. Disappointment, discouragement, opposition, or persecution cannot dissuade the committed church starter. A directing commitment allows apostolic church starters to persist in the face of whatever Satan might place in the way.

Moses chose to lead God's people without consideration of the "pleasures of sin" due to his commitment to the plan God had revealed. Nehemiah led in the rebuilding of Jerusalem and called the people to participate in the construction because he saw the task as God's direction for him and was committed to the task (Neh 1-7). Jesus refused to succumb to the temptations of Satan that He use His powers for personal ease because he remained committed to the Father's plan (Luke 4:1-13). In the face of threats they continued witnessing in the name of Jesus, and the Jerusalem Christian community prayed, not for relief or protection, but for boldness to preach the Word (Acts 4 :13-31).

Commitment to the new church effort rests solidly on the dual foundations of certain vision and persistent faith. Vision is the quality of what "can be." Every Christian worker needs vision. Church starters, however, need a particular brand and measure of vision.

Church starters have the God-given capacity to see unbelieving, unchurched, sometimes hostile peoples, being gathered into Christian, worshipping communities. Based on this kind of vision, apostolic church starters will not be deterred by threat, difficulty, discouragement, or obstacles. Church starters dream of new congregations, often among barren people, and hold the assurance that these dreams will become reality because of their certainty that the dreams came from God.

A second imperative foundation on which commitment to the church starting effort rests is that of a persistent faith that produces continuing and consistent courage. Joseph Stowell correctly observes that faith is *an unshaken confidence that what we believe about God and His Word is true*. It shows itself in actions lived out in light of that belief. Persistent faith is the actualization—the application—of what we say we believe. Faith in God manages and controls all that we are and do.[169]

Hebrews 11 chronicles the tremendous accomplishments God's people, empowered by faith in Him, have been able to accomplish. This great chapter in the Bible tells us more of what God's people can do if they believe God than it defines faith.

The emphasis is, however, on faith as that which enables the Christian leader to see the certain victory of God on the other side of the raging river of obstacles and discouragements and disappointments. Only men and women of faith will have the courage to push beyond their protective comfort zones, accept the risks of new work, and attempt big and great things for God.[170] It is persistent faith that allows the church starter to take risks that the church starting effort demands.

Church leaders face the temptation to place their faith in things other than the Lord of the Harvest. Some leaders focus their faith on people, others on plans, and still others on prosperity. To focus on people results in the leader often being manipulated and controlled by people. To focus on their own plans results in leaders managing and manipulating people to accomplish the leader's dreams. To focus on prosperity, either, financial gain, position, or notoriety, causes the leader to minister from motives of self- realization. These misplaced examples of faith result in the distortion of service. In this regard, Joseph Stowell well says:

> It is tempting to manage ministry from the perspective of our own safety and security and do those

things that are without risk to guarantee a lack of conflict or opposition. A shepherd whose primary linkage is to a safe and un-threatened environment will not only be unable to do the tough and risky tasks that are often required in a ministry that advances the glory and gain of Christ, but will ultimately create the very insecurity his focus has tried to avoid. When security and safety are self-manufactured, they are always at risk.[171]

Church starters face rivers of obstacles and mountains of barriers to beginning a new church. Resistance from friend and foe alike blur and endanger the way. Apathy on the part of the unchurched leave many church starters seeking the easier way of searching out those who already believe and trying to build the new congregation on transfer growth. Persistent faith empowers church starters to have the courage to step out, believing God, reaching the unbelieving, unchurched world and bringing them into the fellowship of new congregations. These church starters, in a word, become apostolic leaders who are willing to take the risk of targeting people who hold differing beliefs, practices, and worldviews.[172]

Commitment to the goal of starting new churches keeps church starters centered on and directed to the task. God-given vision and faith form the foundation for the commitment demanded of those who will start and complete apostolic church starting efforts. The committed church starter will never give up until the Lord indicates the task is completed.

Conducive Convictions

Productivity in church starting exists in direct relationship to the faithfulness of the church starter to biblical convictions that the Holy Spirit builds into them. Biblically informed church starters seek to allow the Spirit to build into their own lives and into the lives of the churches they start the biblical convictions that lead to reproducing churches. Church agencies that promote church starting should strive to build on a foundation that includes, encourages, and allows infinite reproducibility.

The Conviction of Purpose

One necessary conviction for 21- century church starting relates to the certainty that churches must have the goal or purpose of reproducing. The concept has been called purpose-driven strategy (Rick Warren's term) and end-vision (David Garrison's words). This conviction places the goal of reproducibility foremost and evaluates every possible method from the standpoint of its contribution to this goal. Should a method fail to contribute to the goal of reproducing churches, effective church starters will become ruthless in discarding the strategy.[173]

The purpose or end-vision of this conviction is a church starting movement with the goal of starting churches that can and will reproduce by starting other churches. An unending expansion thus becomes a reality. Churches and movements guided by the "reproduction principle" will employ only those elements that contribute to the purpose and will avoid those elements that detract there from.

Guided by the purpose of reproducible churches, the church starter will use the means that contribute and discard the means that detract from reaching the goal.

Conviction Regarding the Nature of Churches

Church starters who begin congregations and movements that continue to expand hold definite convictions as to the basic nature of churches. They also commit to the principle of considering necessary only *biblical characteristics* as to the nature of churches. Reproducible churches and movements only become possible when these churches eschew limiting requirements such as buildings, ordained leaders who require advanced education, and extensive constitutions and bylaws.

While affiliation with a local body (association or convention) may be helpful and even advisable, this membership should not be required of a group before they are recognized as a church. Buildings, ordained leaders, constitutions, and relationships in associations, while good and helpful for churches, are not theologically necessary for every congregation.

Churches should be free from regulations that might lower or prevent their abilities of reproduction. Such requirements can become "millstones" around the neck of the churches and make their reproduction almost impossible. The wise church starter avoids the extra-biblical regulations on congregations that sometimes hinder them from being accepted as churches.

The proper and biblical convictions as to the nature of churches allow for different models of congregations as they are needed to reach the population segments in the community. Church starters who desire to see a reproducing church or movement allow for and even encourage cell churches and home churches. At any rate, these leaders of reproducing churches refuse to allow unbiblical regulations to deny the use of methods that have proved efficient in starting true churches even if these congregations are somewhat different from existing "churches."

Conviction Concerning Church Reproduction

Church starters involved in starting reproducible and reproducing churches and movements work from a conviction that God intends churches to start other churches. This model has already been presented as the biblical foundation, the historical pattern, and the contemporary reality. Claylan Coursey, church starter among the Giryama peoples in the region of Malindi, Kenya, declares that God's plan for local churches is that these congregations give birth to new churches. He says the primary responsibility for church starting "belongs to individual believers banded together as the local church."[174]

Twenty-first century church starters hold the conviction that starting a church that remains one church only does not fulfill the intention of the Lord of the Harvest. They believe that the most efficient means for reaching the lost of the world is through the method of churches that start churches in a continuously expanding network. This conviction drives them to build into the congregations the truth that such reproduction is natural, possible, and expected.

Robert Logan, commenting on John 17:20-23, notes that even the fellowship within a church relates to the purpose of letting unbelievers know that God sent Jesus for them and loves them. Logan points out that fellowship that does not contribute to this evangelistic purpose is fellowship destined to wither—or be withered—like the fruitless fig tree cursed by Christ.[175] Mark Terry agrees, saying, "When churches start daughter churches, they follow the early church's example, obey the Great Commission, and enhance their growth potential."[176] One might also say these congregations live up to the very nature that God intends a church to have.

The church starter's conviction as to churches being reproducing and reproducible includes the understanding that this reproduction becomes most effective when it is rapid. A mistaken strategy declares that churches must first become large or strong and then they can consider starting other churches. The fact is that a rapid extension often provides for the widest extension of the Christian movement.

The churches, if they are to be biblically relevant, will strive to reach the unchurched by starting other churches. The aspect of starting new churches obviously constitutes part of the very nature of churches. Leaders who start churches that birth congregations know that reproduction constitutes a vital part of what a church is!

Conviction Regarding Biblical Methods

To reach the largest number of people possible, twenty-first century church starting, should employ only those methods that enhance reproducing church growth. Wise church starters eschew any method that will impede or hinder the starting of churches that will by their own use of the Holy Spirit's power and resources be able to and will actually start other churches. Charles Brock declares that anything other than the basics of Sower (church starter), Seed (the Word), Spirit (Holy Spirit), and Soil (the target population) may be, not simply superfluous, but actually a deterrent to effective church starting. Brock, therefore, advises and urges church starters to avoid "excess baggage."[177]

The biblical message cannot be altered. The methods by which this unalterable message is proclaimed are not only open to change but in many cases methodological change becomes imperative. In adjusting methods to cultural realities, the church starter maintains the conviction that biblical teachings and biblical ideals never be compromised. No method that contradicts biblical teachings can be valid. No method that produces unbiblical results (for example, an anti-missions church) should be tolerated. Methods used in church starting must in their natures and results conform to biblical standards. This principle, however, allows latitude in the exact nature of the methods employed.

This book has already outlined and will present many strategies and methods that lead to effective church starting. This section seeks to underline that the methods in church starting must be biblical and must result in biblical results. Methods should contribute to church starting that eventuates in reproducing churches.

Conviction Concerning Local Leaders & Resources

Reproducing churches find a firm foundation on certain convictions regarding local leaders and local resources. Methods that produce dependency either on outside leaders or outside resources detract from reproducibility in the experiences of the congregations.

Method of Local Leaders

No church or church starting movement that depends on outside leadership can or will reach unlimited reproducibility. The longer the sponsoring entity (mission, church, church starter) clings to authority, holds to leadership, or demands control the less likely is a reproducible church starting movement to result. For this reason, Tom Steffen calls for "passing the baton," that is, changing from foreign to local leadership.178 Only methods that incorporate trust and empower local leaders will produce reproducible church starting!

Charles Brock, calling upon his extensive experience in successful church starting, advises the church starter to use a reproducible style of leadership. He says that from day one the church starter should not do anything that the new converts cannot do soon after they are saved. Even the teaching methods and ways of leading public prayer must be those that the newest converts can easily employ.[179] Methods of preaching and teaching that demand highly trained and gifted leaders stifle the unlimited reproducibility in the movements.

Local leadership must, therefore, be incorporated and encouraged into the movement from the beginning. Tom Steffen mentions an axiom of church starting, saying:

> The more church starters become involved in the day-to-day activities of evangelism, church development, and church multiplication, the less delegation that will take place. Indeed, such an approach

to ministry usually impedes the spiritual development of nationals, and ultimately slows or halts the
phase-out process.[180]

Steffen continues teaching that one of the easiest ways to
ensure ongoing church starting is to incorporate local leaders
into all church activities from the beginning. He concludes:

> If church starters enter with an expanded world vi-
> sion, help that vision take root, and then release it,
> their contribution will be the creation of mature na-
> tional believers ready for phase-out.[181]

Methods that encourage and allow continuous reproduction
require the full and total incorporation of local leadership.

Refusing any imposition of extra-biblical, unnecessary requirements for church leadership can enhance the incorporation of local leadership. In the teachings of Jesus and the requirements for leaders in Paul, the characteristics of moral
character and willingness to follow Christ assume much larger
dimensions than theological training, academic degrees, or
extensive resumes. Those attempting to begin reproducing
churches and movements should guard against such unnecessary requirements for church leaders.

Requirements for extensive training, which often can be
obtained only in places far from their homes, can obstruct
local leaders from assuming their rightful places at the head
of the movements among their peoples. These requirements
sometimes take leadership from the real leaders of the
churches and give it to younger, more educated persons who
actually have less influence and respect of the local Christians. David Garrison writes, "Whenever well-intentioned
missionaries, churches or denominational leaders impose
requirements for church leaders that exceed those stipulated
by the New Testament, a Church Starting Movement is impeded."[182]

The methods of leadership selection and training must never
place restrictions on the continuous reproducibility of the
movement. Only as the local leaders, serving where they live,
can be empowered to guide the churches can churches reproduce. If every new church demands a highly trained leader
from without, the possibility of reproducible church starting

evaporates.

The effective church starter will, therefore, provide for leadership training on the local level that will equip local Christians to guide the churches. In this way, adequate leadership is available and unlimited. Any method that fails to provide for this leadership reality will not sustain reproducibility.

Method of Local Resources

Church starters who desire to start churches that can and will reproduce by giving birthing to new congregations must eschew reliance on material things that are not readily available to the local Christians. Church buildings, musical instruments, public address systems, and such items that the locals can never supply will seriously impede, if not totally deny, the possibility of the church that receives such "benefits" from starting and equipping another church in the future.

One mission began work in a certain country in 1954 and soon experienced the birth of several churches that became strong, gospel-proclaiming congregations. The missionaries insisted on providing each church with a piano, which in the context at the time was expensive, both to purchase and to maintain. The resulting problem was, however, not the piano in the churches equipped by the missionaries but the fact that these congregations never became strong enough to provide any new churches they might start with a piano. Some churches felt they could not start new churches because they could not **provide** the new congregations with equipment such as a piano.

The method that employs only what the local Christian groups can supply, i.e. local resources, allows for reproducible church starting. Charles Brock correctly observes:

> When the starter is dependent on material aids imported from without, he is teaching lessons that cannot easily be unlearned. When the new church thinks of starting another church, there may be frustration and a tendency to give up if it cannot afford to do it the way the church starter modeled. The material "crutches" used by the missionary appeared to be a blessing, but stymied, stunted, irreproducible growth becomes a tragedy. There is wisdom in being sensitive to the reproductive capabilities of the local

economy.[183]

Money, when wisely used, often can enhance church growth. David Garrison points out that funding can play a vital role in the support of missionaries and the promotion of things that lead to new churches. Introducing the Gospel to a new people group often requires some external support. The external funds can enhance outreach, the development of Christian literature, mass media outlets such as broadcasts and the *Jesus* film, Bible translation, and other helps.

External help, however, becomes problematic when the outside funding creates dependency, stifles initiative, and prevents a bonfire church starting movement.[184] When help becomes support, this creates dependency and dependency produces problems for reproducibility. Subsidy can be a critical enemy of reproducing church movements.

Problems related to subsidy are intensified in that it can limit outreach to the amount of subsidy that is available. In almost every case, the use of subsidy patterns places a ceiling on how fast the church starting effort can expand. Using subsidy for buildings, equipment, and pastors' salaries most often exerts an unwholesome effect on reproducible church starting. Again, Garrison says, "When well-intentioned outsiders prop up growth by purchasing buildings or subsidizing pastor's salaries, they limit the capacity of the movement to reproduce itself spontaneously and indigenously."[185]

The infinitely reproducible pattern turns away from dependence on material things—both in the ministry of the church starters and in the resulting churches. Nothing should be introduced that the local Christians cannot replace or maintain. Brock sums up this principle saying:

> From day one, the church starter should think reproducible. Do not provide any material as a crutch that the people cannot provide for themselves. Is this stingy? No, it is responsible stewardship with the long-term-best in mind for the people.[186]

The methods of the church starter who desires to begin a congregation or a movement that will and can reproduce must employ methods that rely on local resources. Many churches and movements fail to reach reproducible levels because of the unwise use of subsidy and material aids. The wise church start-er avoids such a trap.

Having noted these marks or qualities needed in the lives of church starters and the convictions that are imperative in their lives, we turn to the ways of discovering those who should become church starters. While the selection of church starters must always be a divine task, certain assessment tools are available to indicate that a person possesses the skills and characteristics that predict effectiveness as a church starter. These assessment tools guide the candidate for church start-ing and the agency that may be sending the church starter to understand the starter's qualifications. The assessment program will help answer these two questions: (1) should this person attempt to be a church starter? and (2) what type of church starting effort should this person attempt?

PART B

Assessment of Church Starters

The Need for Assessment

The critical nature of the process of finding appropriate leadership makes the assessment process one of the most significant aspects of the effort. Many churches have been started because the leaders had the qualifications that were imperative for that particular setting. Conversely, many sincere and dedicated people have experienced the frustration and a sense of failure that result from attempting to start a church while not having the requisite calling, gifts, skills, and temperaments for the church starting task. Thomas Graham points out that having unqualified personnel results in attrition in at least six ways in church starting: 1) lost souls are not reached, 2) churches go unplanned, 3) "windows of opportunity" are lost, 4) missionaries experience a sense of failure, 5) marriages and families experience stress, and 6) stewardship of resources is poor.[187]

Joel Comiskey shares his regret of not utilizing an assessment process to enlist a pastor for a church he had started. He explains what took place when the person that was enlisted was not being effective:

> This person felt "called" to join us and everything seemed to fall into place. It soon became apparent, however, that he was not a gatherer. He was an excellent pastor and worship leader, but he didn't have the catalytic mix to gather people together – and that's what was needed in those initial stages of our church plant... At the end of two years he left to find a role as a pastor of discipleship and worship – a role that fit his calling and gifting. As I look back, an assessment would have given me a better understanding of his gifts and abilities, and a realistic view of what I could expect from his ministry.[188]

These facts underscore the importance of finding and using qualified and trained church starters. Church starting leaders are considered so important in the church starting process that entire systems have been developed and assessment centers have been established to evaluate their spiritual, personal, social, and ministerial qualifications for the church starting task.

Benefits of an Assessment Process

Numerous benefits result from having an effective assessment process. First, an assessment process gives church starters an opportunity to evaluate themselves in terms of their church starting qualifications. This self-assessment (including carefully selected testing instruments) allows church starters to get a realistic picture of themselves and their fitness for the church starting task.

Second, the process allows potential church starters an opportunity to involve trained persons in the assessment of their church starting skills. Skilled assessors can point out strengths and limitations of which a potential church starter may not be aware.

Third, if taken early, the assessment process may enable a potential church starter to have the opportunity to design an entire ministry training plan focused on the church-starting task.

Fourth, church starting candidates may discover areas in which they can improve their abilities and correct their limitations. Further, the prospective church starter can ascertain the precise type of church starting effort for which he/she is best suited.

Fifth, people who do not have a church starting call and giftedness may discover this and focus on the type of ministry for which they are called instead of having to experience stress or failure before exploring other possibilities. The assessment process, therefore, has numerous benefits.

Assessment Methods

To date, a number of effective methods have been developed for the assessment process. Some of these include a self-assessment process, a church starter assessment interview, an assessment connected with an internship, and a combination of these methods.

Self-assessment Process

A self-assessment process has several advantages. One advantage is that it can be done quickly without having to take time and resources to involve others in the process. A variety of self-administered spiritual gift, personality trait, and leadership style inventories are helpful for this purpose. A second advantage is that potential church starters can spend time in self-analysis and reflection. The prospective church starters know better than anyone what their attitudes, capabilities, and perceptions are regarding church starting. Thirdly, the self-assessment approach can help potential church starters who spot their weaknesses and be motivated to seek help in specific areas.

There are some disadvantages, however, in utilizing this approach exclusively. First, potential church starters may focus on what they would like to be, or what they think they are, instead of what they really are. Second, potential church starters who use only a self-administered test approach miss out on the objective input that assessors may be able to give. Third, those who use this approach may not be in a position to compare themselves with others who have taken similar tests. This, therefore, takes away the possibility of rating themselves to see how they measure up in comparison with others. Fourth, those who use this approach may focus on irrelevant behavioral dimensions. A person, for instance, may have very high marks with regard to certain skills, but these are not necessarily essential in a church starting setting. Fifth, a potential church starter may not focus on sufficient areas to make an informed decision. Having found one area of proficiency, the person may ignore other areas that are very crucial for the church starting test. A sixth disadvantage is that this approach does not carry as much weight if potential church starters recommend themselves for this task over against having the recommendation of others. While there is some advantage to the self-administered church starting assessment approach, there are sufficient limitations to the method to encourage the potential church starter to enlist the help of those who are proficient in this area.

Assessment Interview

The method of a church starter assessment interview commends itself on many features. First, this type of interview generally involves people who have been trained. They know what to look for and how to help the person being interviewed to relax and focus on the areas of principal interest. They are trained to distinguish between typical and atypical behavior, to obtain sufficient examples and illustrations of behavior, and to focus on past behavior rather than future predictions about behavior. Second, this type of assessment interview has the advantage of utilizing several assessors, thus providing the opportunity for a comparison of observations and the reaching of a consensus regarding the assessment.

Third, this type of assessment is generally very thorough. Some assessors insist on a minimum of four hours for the interview itself, thus providing the opportunity of delving to get specific answers on which to build a profile. While potential church starters may be apprehensive about behavioral interviews, they should rest assured that if the interviewers have been trained, they will define the purpose of the interview, explain the process, clarify expectations, set a time schedule, and assure the confidentiality of the interview.

Assessment Connected with Internship

One of the best ways to assess a potential church starter is in connection with a church starting internship. In these types of assignments, a person who has had significant experience in church starting is selected to serve as a mentor. If this person does not have training in mentoring, it will be provided so that the intern will get the best possible care and guidance. As the process proceeds, the mentor and the intern design a covenant so that the mentor as well as the intern will thoroughly understand the expectations and procedures.

One of the provisions of the internship method calls for regular meetings and regular reporting periods. The reports should cover the areas that a typical interview would cover. As time goes on, the mentor has an opportunity to get to know the intern better both in terms of skills as well as behavioral patterns. At the end of the internship period, the mentor can meet with the intern, review the entire experience and write a final evaluation.

This evaluation can help the intern as well as those who

might be interested in selecting a person who has participated in a church starting effort under the guidance of a mentor. If the process is done correctly, the evaluation should have even more weight than a typical church starting interview due to the fact that it is based on observation of skills and behavioral patterns.

Combination of Assessment Approaches

Many times a combination of assessment approaches provides help in the assessment process. In some situations, for instance, self-administered tests are taken before a person is interviewed. At other times, especially in assessment centers, potential church starters take series of tests, are interviewed, and participate in group activities. This approach benefits from the strength of the numerous methods used. The combination method of assessment maximizes the opportunity for the potential church starter to participate in a wide variety of activities, thus providing more ways in which the assessment can be done.

Options in Assessment Process

Some potential church starters have a negative attitude toward assessment efforts because they fear that they will simply be rejected without any further recourse. To be sure, there have been those in the past who have based their assessment on a limited number of qualifying factors and have made dogmatic decisions regarding the suitability of the potential church starters. The assessment process faces the dual error of rejecting some who will become effective church starters and approving others who will not.

Assessment processes must guard against both of these errors. Obviously, assessment methods must avoid rejecting people who may have some of the necessary qualifications for church starting, yet lack others. It must, however, be clear that some people have neither the calling nor the qualifications for church starting. It will benefit them as well as possible church starting colleagues to discover this possibility before they are assigned to an area where they will only experience frustration and a sense of defeat.

One option in the assessment process may conclude that the

potential church starter has the necessary qualifications and is ready to start starting a church at the earliest possible opportunity. This option, obviously, is predicated on the assumption that the person has the necessary giftedness and training to assume this responsibility at once. Accepting qualified church starters marks the primary purpose of the assessment process. This option, however, obviously faces the dangers of placing persons in church starting who would be better suited to some other type of ministry. A second option in the assessment process allows potential church starters to discover that they do not possess the qualities that are needed for church starting. Perhaps further assessment in other areas will enable these persons to discover the most suitable area of ministry. This procedure, however, may result in difficult experiences for the church starter and harmful results in the work.

A third option in the assessment process calls for the person to gain additional experience, maturity, and or training. Many persons have some of the necessary qualifications, but have not sufficiently developed these skills. The recommendation may be, therefore, to postpone full-time church starting ministry and strengthen the specified qualifications.

A fourth option, which is related to the third one, may be for the potential church starter to serve in a church starting internship under a trained mentor with intensions to focus on specific qualifications that need to be developed. This internship allows the intern to gain additional confidence in the areas of strength and develop the areas of limitation so that a sense of balance will be attained.

The options for potential church starters who participate in an assessment process, therefore, are "yes," "no," "not yet," or "yes, but." The process may communicate to the prospective church starter that he/she needs to continue to develop or to strengthen certain areas. Assessment is an indispensable factor in every church starting effort.

Proper assessment methods allow placing the greatest number of church starters on the field as quickly as possible. At the same time, assessment increase the probably that persons will gain those needed characteristics and skills before undertaking that awesome task. Those are encouraged to pursue other areas of ministry will, in the long term, be grateful for this advice as will those who might have been their colleagues in church starting. These workers will begin the church starting ministry with greater confidence.

Areas of Assessment

Numerous experts have compiled valuable lists of church starting qualifications. Charles Ridley provides focused work in his manual, *How to Select Church Planters*. Ridley suggests a "Church Planter Profile" with the characteristics: visionizing capacity, intrinsically motivated, creates ownership of ministry, relates to the unchurched, spousal cooperation, effectively builds relationships, committed to church growth, responsive to the community, utilizes giftedness of others, flexible and adaptable, builds group cohesiveness, demonstrates resilience, and exercises faith.[189]

C. Peter Wagner's, *Church Planting For A Greater Harvest*, projected the following list of qualifications for church starters: a committed Christian worker, a self-starter, willingness to endure loneliness, adaptable, a high level of faith, supportive spouse and family, willing and able to lead, a friendly personality, clearly called by God to plant a church.[190]

In his book, *Passing the Baton: Church Planting that Empowers*, Tom Steffen lists the following characteristics as being essential for church starters: commitment to God's call, spiritual maturity, managed household/ singleness, psychological maturity, evangelistic experience, discipleship experience, international political awareness, emphatic contextual skills, servant leader/ follower, effective action planner, flexibility and adaptability, physical vitality, basic medical skills, financial support maintenance expansion.[191]

Bill Fudge, missionary Area Director in Asia for the Southern Baptist International Mission Board, lists the following criteria for the leaders of church starting movements: initiators (self- initiative), risk takers, innovative (not tied to U.S. methodologies), willing to develop their own models, must have courage, facilitator, networker, must have computer skills, team leader, willing to adapt the presentation of the Gospel (e.g. storying vs. inductive or deductive Bible studies).[192]

In discussing the qualifications of "Strategy Coordinators" who direct church starting efforts in large and often restricted areas of the world, Fudge states that they must be willing and able to do the following: answer the call to follow Christ across today's world, work within the Christian world mission as a missionary, cross political frontiers as an alien or foreigner, minister cross-culturally, from own culture to a different group, evangelize among unevangelized populations as primary role, search with a global orientation for other great commission cooperators, serve as a professional missionary, focus on target segment as overarching vocation, not hobby or part-time interest, obey national laws concerning overt evangelism, remain apolitical and secure from state hostility, evictions, or banning, become non-traditional as traditional residential missions is impossible, become non- residential, as necessary, for reaching target population, and remain mobile and flexible while resident with family 70 percent of the time.[193]

The International Center for Excellence in Leadership has developed a self-assessment approach which focuses on seven dimensions: 1) Discipleship; 2) Servant Leader; 3) Team Player; 4) Cross-Cultural Witness; 5) CPM Facilitator; 6) Mobilizer; and 7) Family member.[194] In each of these areas potential church planters have an opportunity to evaluate themselves utilizing the following categories: Nearly Always, Often, Sometimes, Rarely, and Never. In this assessment tool, potential church planters are instructed to tabulate the results and begin to formulate a strategy to address the dimensions that need the greatest amount of development. The designers of this assessment tool believe that this is the place for interested persons to begin to explore the possibility of being a church planting missionary. The dimensions that are addressed in this assessment tool are closely connected with the attitudes, tasks, and abilities that are necessary for effective missionary service.

In his book, *Planting Growing Churches For The 21st Century*, Aubrey Malphurs suggests primary as well as secondary areas for assessment.[195] The primary areas are: spiritual gifts, passion, temperament, leadership, and ministry lifecycle. The secondary areas: natural gifts, talents and abilities, unique styles of thinking, learning, decision making, and evangelism.

It is obvious that there are some qualifications that all of the authors quoted above have listed as being important in the church starting task. These could well be considered "generic" qualifications that all church starters should possess. It is also clear that there are some qualifications that some authors (e.g. Steffen, Fudge) list with specific church starting models in mind. These qualities, therefore, can be considered "specialized" qualifications that assessors must take into account in specialized church starting situations.

It will be helpful, therefore, to compile a list of generic qualifications and then a list of model specific qualifications. A listing of these generic qualifications under several categories (spiritual, personal, and administrative) could be helpful in ascertaining which qualifications are of most crucial importance as well as in prescribing the areas in which potential church starters need to concentrate in their efforts to improve their personalities and skills.

Generic Qualifications

The generic qualifications for church starters begin with the spiritual category. The spiritual category includes: a committed Christian, clearly called by God to start a church, a high level of faith, spiritual maturity, and spiritual giftedness. The personal category includes: intrinsically motivated, a friendly personality, psychological maturity, supportive spouse and family, managed household/ singleness, flexibility and adaptability, physical vitality, relates to the unchurched, committed to church growth, responsive to the community, values others.

The administrative category includes: willing and able to lead, servant leader/follower, effective action planner, financial support maintenance / expansion, visionizing capacity, creates ownership of ministry, utilizes giftedness of others, builds group cohesiveness, evangelistic experience, and discipleship experience. There is a sense in which the generic qualifications listed above are generally more congruous with Parenting and Partnering models of church starting. The reason for this is that these models are generally implemented within the cultural group of the church starter and have a greater possibility of obtaining resources (financial and personnel) from the sponsoring entities.

A self-assessment of generic qualifications would include the items mentioned above. Self-assessment can be done in several ways. One consists of listing the items mentioned above and then utilizing a scale of 1 to 5 to seek to determine the strong and weak points. Another way is to list these items and then to write a brief paragraph describing how the potential church starter has demonstrated an understanding of and proficiency in each of these areas.

Specialized Qualifications

In addition to the generic qualifications, there are some specialized qualifications that are generally more closely related to the pioneering and propagating church starting models. These specialized qualifications can also be placed under the spiritual, personal, and administrative categories. The spiritual category includes: willing to follow Christ across today's world and work within the Christian world mission. The personal category includes: willingness to endure loneliness, capacity for social adaptability, a self-starter, remaining mobile and flexible while resident with family 70% of the time, and demonstrating resilience. The administrative category includes: serving either as a bivocational or professional missionary, focusing on a target segment as a vocation, global geopolitical awareness, empathetic contextual skills, ability to cross social and political frontiers (as an alien or foreigner), ministering cross-culturally, using basic medical skills, working with a priority to reach unevangelized populations, willingness to cooperate with other Great Commission Christians, sensitivity to national laws concerning overt evangelism, remaining apolitical and secure from state hostility, evictions, or bannings, becoming nontraditional when traditional residential missions is impossible, and becoming non- residential, as necessary, in order to reach a limited access target population.

A self-assessment of specialized qualifications may benefit the church starter by providing direction in choosing a particular type of church starting ministry. Some church starters can serve well when starting a congregation with a core group already in place but might experience stress when using the Pioneering Model. Others would fit better with the Pioneering Model and would chafe under the closer supervision in some of the other models. A well- constructed assessment should uncover these tendencies and guide prospective church starters toward the type of church starting ministry in which they would be most effective.

DISC Personality Profile

In 1928 William Moulton Marson, lecturer in Psychology at Colombia University and at New York University. published a book entitled, *Emotions of Normal People.*[196] In it, he described distinctive conscious characteristics of the following emotions: Dominance, Inducement, Submission, and Compliance.[197] Since then, a number of authors have developed personality profiles utilizing these characteristics under the rubric of "DISC."[198]

The DISC Personality Profile has been found to be an effective tool in increasing team efficiency. According to Brent Ray, "this tool helps team leaders understand themselves and their team members and helps to build 'community' and a team spirit among team members as they begin to understand one another's style."[199] He adds that: "Many teams, small group ministries, and cell churches already use the DISC extensively in leadership training and team / small group / cell development."[200]

Purpose of DISC Profile

The purpose of the DISC Personality Profile is to help team members understand their strong and their weak tendencies, to recognize their fear in a group setting, and to recognize the group settings in which they will best be able to interact constructively. There is no preferred or best personality style.

An individual style may vary from one setting to another depending on the type of leadership that is needed. One must keep in mind that even though personality types are highlighted, the purpose is not to stereotype these but rather to indicate the commonalities in each category. DISC is a tool to help one understand his/her strengths & weaknesses in group interaction. It helps us to recognize how we can minister more effectively in among a variety of personality types (1 Tim 5:14).[201]

Personality Types

"D" is dominant, determined, and direct. The "D" type person initiates action, takes charge, moves out to reach a goal, and draws upon contacts to develop projects.[202] Robert A. Rohm describes D type personalities as drivers and doers. They have a tendency to be dynamic leaders. They have a flair for the dramatic. They are very demanding. They are usually very dogmatic. They can also appear to be defiant.[203] According to Rohm, the biblical character who typifies the "D" type personality is the Apostle Paul "dogmatic, domineering, driving, demanding, doing."[204]

"I" is influencing, inspiring, and impulsive. The "I" type personality draws upon contacts to gather resources needed for the project, loves to visit with people and is talkative. In addition to these characteristics, Rohm adds "inducing, impressive, interesting, and impressionable."[205] The biblical character who, according to Rohm more nearly resembles this type of personality is the Apostle Peter who was impetuous and impatient.[206]

"S" is secure, solid, and stable. The "S" type personality ensures follow through, and offers support, Rohm adds the following characteristics: "steady, supportive, sweet, submissive, status quo, and sentimental."[207] The biblical character that Rohm feels best represents this personality type is the Apostle John.

"C" is condescending, calculative, and correct. The "C" type person ensures follow through, offers support, is excellent in carrying the day-to-day administration of the project, offers design, technical skills and excellent for quality control. This type person sees forgotten details in the strategy plans. Rohm adds the following characteristics to this type of personality: "competent, cautious, careful, critical thinker, convinced, and consistent."[208] The biblical character that Rohm suggests as the best representative of this personality type is the Apostle Thomas who needed proof of Christ's resurrection.

In addition to explaining the various personality types, Rohm categorizes these in such a way as to facilitate a greater understanding of the practical implications. Rohm first makes a circle. He then draws a horizontal line placing those above the line in the "outgoing" category and those below the line in the "reserved category." He proceeds to draw a horizontal line placing those to the right of the line as "people oriented" persons and those on the left of the line as "task oriented" persons. In this scheme, the "D" goes in the upper left hand corner indicating that these are outgoing, task oriented people. The "I" is on the upper right hand corner indicating that these are outgoing people oriented persons. The "S" is in the lower right hand corner indicating that these are reserved, people oriented persons. "C" is in the lower left hand corner indicating that these are reserved, task oriented persons.[209]

One of the values of the DISC inventory is that it can help the various team members in a church planting team have a clear idea of their personality styles which in turn can help in the selection of the various tasks that are needed to accomplish the goals. Those utilizing this tool need to keep in mind that these personality styles are present in varying degrees in individuals. For example, a person may be in the "Middle D" and "Middle I" category indicating therefore, that there is no one category that dominates completely. Looking at these categories from the perspective of a church planting team, the lead person (at times Strategy Coordinator) may be a person with D and I characteristics. A person who takes care of managing the activities may lean more toward the "C" category (consistent with the "task orientated" side of the quadrant). An "S" type person is generally better suited for bringing groups together and encouraging team members. An "I" type person may be the best one to lead out in evangelistic and discipleship efforts in the church planting team. Being "outgoing" and "people oriented" helps this person to make meaningful contacts with unbelievers and encourage them to listen to the Gospel message. As stated before, the intention of this tool is not to stereotype. Some team leaders may not necessarily have "High D" characteristics but they can enlist someone to focus on the "task oriented" and "outgoing" aspects of the ministry of a church planting team.

As was stated in the discussion on the Spiritual Gifts Inventory, this is not meant to be the final word in the determination of personality profiles. It is merely a tool that is intended to initiate careful thought and reflection. Other tools, input from other persons, actual functioning in a team setting, and concerted prayer can lead persons to a greater understanding of their personality types.[210]

Conclusion

Assessment of potential church planters is essential to the effectiveness of church planting efforts. Those who direct and sponsor church starting efforts should provide adequate assessment to those who aspire to lead such efforts. Extremely important is the insight that assessment might indicate the special type of church starting for which the candidate is fitted. Persons who might not have the qualities to allow them to serve as pioneer church starters might be able to serve effectively in team approaches. Assessment finds those who show promise in church starting efforts and also guides into the types of church starting efforts these workers who fit best. The methods discussed above can be useful in accomplishing this task.

CHAPTER 8

FINANCIAL FOUNDATION

Since the financial dimension of church starting is crucial, the preparation phase for church starting must make financial matters a primary consideration. On the one hand, the church starter does not always need to follow the model of many established churches that insist on the resources to provide for a full-time pastor and staff, spacious building facilities, generously funded programs, and abundant materials for every group in the congregation. On the other hand, certain physical demands exist and must be met.

Insisting on all equipment and materials from the beginning is comparable to a couple who wants to have their cars, house, furniture, and appliances all paid for before they get married. Such arrangements seldom happen. A new congregation needs to start with what it has and then grow to the place where it has the needed resources.

On the other hand, a church starter needs to know how to secure the resources that are needed to give the new congregation the best start possible and to lead it to attain its full potential. The first challenge the church starter faces is that of finding financial support. Several plans can help the church starter secure the funds needed to support his/her family and the new church start.

Financial Support for
the Church Starter

Financial support for the church starting effort occupies a major position in the overall needs of the mission to plant a congregation than can and will reproduce. One of the most needful and least harmful places for financial support relates to the support of the church starter and his family. This important support comes from several sources.

Denominational Support

Some denominations have support systems for church starters and their families. Some missionary agencies (e.g. denominational mission boards) appoint missionaries and provide the funding they need to care for their families and do their work on the field. Generally these missionaries have the mandate to develop self-supporting congregations in the area or areas to which they are assigned. In these instances the funding level remains fairly constant for the missionaries. The missionaries, in turn, are expected to meet the requirements of the mission board for appointment.

Some denominations and other church starting groups have support systems that are geared ultimately to lead the new congregations to self-support. Several paths can guide to this goal of self-supporting congregations.

Church Starter Developer

Some denominational national mission boards, for instance, have programs that provide funding for the church starter for three to five years. This level of support is decreased as the new congregation assumes an agreed upon portion of the funding package. This is generally done when the church starter is expected to become the permanent pastor of the new church.

Church Starter Central

Under the Church Starter Central program, the church starter is expected to go to a new area, start a church, develop it, and then utilize it to start other churches in the area. This type of program may provide for the church starter in much the same way as if he were a church-starter developer. That is to say, the level of support will decrease as the congregation assumes more of the responsibility. The mission board, however, may provide additional funding for the church starter to start additional congregations.

Church Starter Initiator

The church starter initiator is expected to start a church, develop it to a certain level, turn it over to a church developer, and then go elsewhere and start a new church. This type of arrangement works well for a person who has excellent church starting gifts but lacks the skills and attitudes to develop the new church's organizations and provide on-going maintenance and nurture. Generally this type of church starter receives on-going support in order to continue to carry out this ministry.

Church Starter Strategist

The Church Starter Strategist is usually a person with significant experience who works with an agency (urban, state,. or national). The task of the church starter strategist is to discover the places that need new congregations, enlist church starters, train them, supervise them, and provide the support systems that are needed to keep the churches going. On an international level, missionaries and regional coordinators serve as church starter strategists. These types of workers get a constant level of support and are expected to develop self-supporting churches.

Mother Church Support

Many church starters get their financial support from a mother church. Generally, these are churches that have a vision for church starting and set money aside for new congregations. As is true of denominational agencies, mother churches may have a phase-out plan which enables a church starter to have the resources that are needed at the outset and at the same time encourage the new congregation to assume financial responsibility as it grows.

In some instances, such as with the Task Force Approach and the Colony Approach, a core group from the mother church may be formed to start the new congregation. This approach makes it possible for the church starter to have not only the help of the core group in leadership positions but also their financial contribution (through tithes and offerings).

Cluster Church Support

Cluster Church Support is an approach in which two or three churches pool their resources in order to support a new congregation jointly. Many of the features of the Mother Church Support approach apply to this strategy. It is important, however, that each supporting church has a very clear idea of the amount of support that it will provide and the length of time in which this support will be provided. This does not leave the church starter without support due to lack of coordination with regard to the support plan that has been established.

Bi-vocational Church Starter

Often, when resources are limited or not available or when a church starter feels a specific type of calling, he may choose self-support through secular employment while he starts a church. This approach is limited because the church starter cannot dedicate full-time to starting a new congregation.

On the other hand, this approach has several advantages. First, the church starter can go where he feels the Lord is leading him without being bound by the financial limitations of denominational agencies or other churches. Second, often the church starter's secular employment gives him an opportunity to meet many people in the community and cultivate their friendship. A church starter, for instance, who was working as a school teacher was able to meet people on a daily basis and then invite them to the new congregation that was being started. Third, in some areas it is a definite advantage for the church starter to identify with the local community by having employment there.

Team Approach to Support

Some church starters have taken the team approach in which two couples work secularly while the third couple dedicates themselves full-time to starting the new congregation. The couples that work secularly provide financial support as well as leadership during the Bible studies and church services. This arrangement makes it possible for a group or team of people to contribute to the start of the new church and to have the type of ministries that will attract the unchurched.

Ministers of Missions

Some churches now have people on their staff who are called "Ministers of Missions." These Ministers of Missions work to involve their church members and other volunteers in starting new congregations. Like the church starter strategists, ministers of missions do the research that is necessary to pinpoint the places where new churches are needed, recruit people for the task, train them, and guide them as they start new congregations. The Minister of Missions receives on-going support.

Interested Donors

In some instances the church starter is able to enlist people with financial resources to provide the support that is needed to start a new church. This generally involves contacting potential donors personally, making a presentation that spells out the vision, challenging them to contribute to this worthy cause, and keeping them informed on a regular basis of the progress that is being made. Church starters who have been successful in obtaining substantial support stress the fact that sharing the vision is the most important step in the process. This sharing captures the imagination of donors and motivates them to give to an effort that is going to result in the conversion and discipleship of many people. A pastor who led his congregation to commit a million dollars to a nation-wide evangelistic effort was asked what motivated him to give to this and not to other denominational programs. His response was: "Previously, no one had presented to me a clear and compelling vision for winning America."

These methods of finding support for the church starting effort allow the church starter to provide for his/her family while beginning the new congregation.

Financial Support through Platforms

The use of platforms is another way in which workers can obtain funding for church planting efforts. David A. Bishop provides a definition for a platform when he states:

> Platform is a general term to describe the mission agency, charity, or business which provides a Christian worker with a valid reason to live in a country. The platform provides an identity of who you are to that foreign government and to many of the people you meet and work with. Platforms are Christian or secular organizations that provide passage for Christian workers to access their target people and live incarnationally among them.[211]

Platforms, therefore, are necessary in settings where religious workers cannot go in with a missionary visa. These are called "creative access countries." Bishop explains that "Creative access refers to situations where the 'main thing' cannot be accomplished through official Christian organizations or by those on a missionary visa due to prohibitions of governments and/or cultures."[212] He defines the "main thing" as: "Bringing about an indigenous church growth movement among a specific nation, people group or population segment."[213]

These platforms generally provided a needed service (or ministry) to the people living in the selected area and lend legitimacy for the worker to live and serve among that people group or population segment. Platform workers can be involved humanitarian efforts such as disaster relief projects, water resource development, animal husbandry, "well-baby" clinics, or agricultural methodologies involving irrigation and food production. Some workers can initially go into some countries as students (as university exchange students) interested in learning the local language. Some can teach English as a Second Language in Universities or business places. Some can set up businesses such as travel agencies, restaurants, or cultural centers. Others can be involved in sports development--e.g. Global Sports Partners--basketball, volleyball clinics; physical education training programs etc. Still others can be involved in business consulting.

Funding for platforms may come from a variety of sources. Some workers obtain funding from mission agencies. Others enlist partners in their sending country to provide the financial support that is needed. Still others support themselves from the revenue that is generated by the business platform that they have established.

Securing and obtaining funding (i.e. sending of funds) needs to take into account the political conditions of the recipient country. Giving attention to the legal aspects of the platforms is absolutely essential. Platforms provide an opportunity for people to share the gospel message in "creative access countries" that previously would have been classified as "closed countries." How this is done may determine the length as well as the effective of this strategy.

Presenting a Church Starting Proposal

One of the most productive steps in obtaining support for starting a new congregation is that of developing a written proposal. The proposal needs to present a strong case for the need to start a new church in a particular area. It is important, therefore, that a demographic analysis be done of the area and the need for a new congregation be demonstrated. A demographic analysis can also help to underscore the potential for the growth of the new congregation. If there are few or no churches in the area and many unchurched people, the potential for the establishment of a strong, growing congregation is very high.

The proposal should also be very clear regarding the overall vision and the strategy that will be employed. If the potential donors know what group is being targeted, what strategy will be employed, what specific activities are being planned and what the anticipated results are, they will become more excited about this project.

Brief information about the church starting team, their core values, their ministry approach, and their commitment will also be helpful. The written proposal should also be very specific as to the kind of financial help that is needed. Vague statements will not suffice. On the other hand a carefully written proposal can capture the imagination of those who need to become involved in this important endeavor.

PART 2

Formulate Ministry Plans

The second phase of the church starting process, the formulation phase, occupies a vitally important place. At this stage, vision is cultivated, sponsoring relationships are clarified, team members are selected, and the target group is identified. In a sense, the church starter makes the blueprints for the establishment and development of the new congregation. This blueprint will enable the church starter to determine what kind of church needs to be established, what kind of team is needed to accomplish the task, and what kind of outreach methods will be the most appropriate. Having thus formulated ministry plans, the church starter can move forward with a clearly defined strategy.

CHAPTER 9

VISION AND MISSION

The first step in the formulation phase of church starting relates to the all-important matter of establishing and sharing a vision for the new work. Without a clear and compelling vision, the church starting effort will not succeed. Church starters begin by receiving from the Lord a vision of the church that needs to be, sharing this vision with others, and clarifying the vision so that many can participate in the effort.

Developing a Vision

The Bible states categorically that "without vision, the people perish" (Prov 29:18). It is clear in Scripture that the persons who made the greatest impact for the kingdom of God were driven by a vision.[214] In the Old Testament the inspiring example of Nehemiah who led the people of God to reconstruct the wall around the city of Jerusalem demonstrated the importance of vision. First, Nehemiah became aware of the need (Neh 1:1-4). Second, he sought a vision from God (1:4) by fasting and praying (v. 5), interceding for the people (v. 6-10), and asking for God's to sacrifice to attain it (2:1-10). Fourth, he shared the vision with the people (2:18). Fifth, he developed a strategy that demanded unity and cooperation to fulfill the vision (4:15-23). Sixth, he worked blessing (v. 11). Third, he caught a vision and was willing to overcome internal and external obstacles in order to attain the vision (5:1 - 6:1-4).

In the New Testament we find evidence that Paul's life was driven by a clear and compelling vision. In 2 Tim 1:11, Paul states: "*And of this gospel I was appointed a herald and an apostle and a teacher.*" The book of Acts gives detailed accounts of the way in which Paul implemented his church starting vision. In 2 Cor 11:24-27, Paul described the struggles he encountered in fulfilling his vision. In Acts 26:19 Paul testified to the fact that he was not disobedient to the heavenly vision.

Vision is an absolutely essential element in the life and ministry of effective church starters. As we study the experiences of those who have started thriving, reproducing congregations, even in places others thought it was impossible, we invariably conclude that these church starters were motivated and guided by a clear, compelling vision of what God wanted them to do.

George Barna defines vision for ministry as: "a clear mental image of a preferable future imparted by God to His chosen servants and is based upon an accurate understanding of God, self and circumstances."[215] From this definition one can conclude that vision is clear, is preferable to the current state, concentrates on the future, is given by God, is a gift to leaders, is tailored to circumstances, reflects a realistic perspective, is dreaming the most possible dream, and is built on reality.[216]

Dale Galloway defines vision as "the ability, or God-given gift, to see those things which are not as becoming reality."[217] This definition has several implications. First, church starters must be able to form a mental picture of the end product, the church that God wants them to start. God told Abraham to "*look up in the heavens and count the stars -if indeed you can count them.*" Then he said to him, "*So shall your offspring be*" (Gen 15:5). God wanted Abraham to picture himself as the father of a mighty nation.[218] This picture would be his guiding light throughout his entire pilgrimage.

Second, church starters must have a futuristic view. The picture is not of what is but what can be with God's help. This implies that the church starter will lay aside all physical, mental, and emotional obstacles and will see the vision from the perspective of God's infinite power.

Third, it must be a compelling picture. Because God has given the vision, it carries with it the profound motivation to bring it to fruition. Church starting is not a matter of personal accomplishment but a matter of obedience to God. Church starters must be able to say with the Apostle Paul, "*I was not disobedient to the vision from heaven*" (Acts 26:19).

Significance of a Vision

Several important things happen when a church starter has a distinct vision from God. First, the vision provides a clear sense of direction. Due to the fact that initially the church starter will work in a highly unstructured setting, there can be many opinions as to what ought to be done and how it ought to be accomplished. A clear vision, however, will keep the church starter on track.

Second, a clear vision can help the church starter recruit an appropriate team of co-workers. When the church starter communicates the vision as to the target group and the type of church that is being projected, some workers will be attracted to the vision with a great deal of enthusiasm. Others, however, will indicate that this is not the type of vision that they have for a church. This selection process can be very helpful because it will prevent many future conflicts brought about by a wide divergence of views. Recruiting a team to implement a specific church starting vision harnesses an enormous amount of energy, commitment, and enthusiasm.

Third, a clear vision enhances unity. When the church starter and the team have the same vision, they have a clear concept of how their work contributes to its fulfillment. A wide variety of tasks need to be carried out in order for a church to be started. There is the potential, therefore, for a diffusion of efforts and energy. A clear vision, on the other hand, motivates people to work together and avoids the distractions of conflicting directions. Few matters provide more stability in the church starting effort than a sense of unity in the team and the proper vision, established and shared, will enhance this stability and contribute to the effort.

Attaining a Vision

A question that prospective church starters often ask is, how can I catch a clear and compelling vision? The first thing that needs to be said in response to this question is that catching a vision is the result of a process. This process involves several Important phases.

First, the church starter should spend time studying the Bible to have a clear concept of God's redemptive purpose. There must be not only an understanding of passages such as Matt 28:19-20 but a burning desire to reach people with the gospel of Jesus Christ. God will not give a vision to someone who does not have a deep commitment to implement it.

Second, the church starter should spend time in continued prayer and reflection. This prayer should seek God's will for the church starter's life, a specific commission from God, a clear understanding of the ministry focus group, discernment regarding the type of church starting team that is needed, and a clear picture of the type and size church that God wants to establish in that place. Such insights do not stem from un-aided human reflection.

Third, the church starter should gain first-hand ac-quaintance with the needs and opportunities pertaining to the ministry focus group. Personal acquaintance with the val-ues, lifestyles, needs, and attitudes of the ministry focus group can help the church starter develop a culturally rele-vant vision of the strategy that is needed to start a church among that group and the new congregation's potential for growth and reproduction.

Fourth, the church starter needs to dialogue with other vision-driven church starters to get input from them in an effort to "fine tune" the vision. Others who have devel-oped and implemented a church starting vision can contribute to the church starter's clearer concept of what the vision is and how this vision can be formulated in a culturally rele-vant manner.

Fifth, the church starter needs to articulate the vision. This articulation will involve a brainstorming type process that begins with writing down all of the ideas that come to mind and heart of the church starter. These ideas can then be organ-ized into categories for the purpose of selection and eval-uation. This process leads to the formation of a core group of ideas that can serve as the foundation for the develop-ment of a "statement of purpose, values, strategy, target group, place of ministry, and finances."[219]

The next step will be the formulation of the vision statement. In order to ensure that this statement is effec-tive in communicating the vision, the following questions need to be asked: "Is the vision clear? Is it challenging in the sense that it inspires to action? Does it create mental pictures? Is it future-oriented? Is it both realistic and stretching? Is it culturally relevant?"[220]

Sixth, the church starter needs to narrow the vision statement to a vision slogan. Malphurs suggests five steps for accomplishing a vision statement or slogan: (1) Capture the essence of the vision statement; (2) Take the essence of the vision statement or core and express it in a few words or single sentence, or as few sentences as possible; (3) Use creativity in structure and choice of words; (4) Use language that is familiar to the vision community; (5) Make a habit of collecting other vision statements and slogans.[221]

Communicating the Vision

The communication of the vision is an essential step if others are to join the church starter in its fulfillment. A vision that remains that of a single person always lacks the strengthening power of the prayers and commitment of other concerned persons. The church starter who receives from God a certain vision also receives from God a commission to share this vision with others.

Communicating with the Church Starting Team

The starting point of the communication process involves sharing the vision with the church starting team. The church starting team needs to have the same vision that the church starter has. In order for this to occur, the church starter needs to help the team to catch a vision of what God wants them to accomplish. Several activities can contribute to this.

Bible Study and Prayer

A church starting team can catch a vision as it studies the Bible and prays together. Studying the New Testament (especially the book of Acts) will help the team arrive at the conviction that the fulfillment of the Great Commission involves the establishment of churches and it is the will of God that they be involved in starting new churches. When the church of Antioch persevered in the study of the Word and in prayer it caught a vision of the will of God regarding its missionary work. The Holy Spirit said to them: *"Separate me Barnabas and Saul for the work where-unto I have called them"* (Acts 13:2). In similar fashion, as the church starting team spends time reading the Bible and praying it will have a clear sense of God's will.

Visiting the Target Community

In addition to Bible study the church starter can help a church starting team catch a vision through activities that help them to know the needs of a community. A church that has established hundreds of units (home Bible studies, ministry centers, and missions) has the practice of using the Sunday school hour to take potential team members to visit communities where churches are needed.

When team members see many children playing in the streets, adults sitting in front of their apartments just passing time, neighbors fighting, intoxicated men, and youths using drugs, they return with a new vision of what their church should be doing to reach these people with the Gospel. Jesus saw the multitude and had compassion on them because they were like sheep without a shepherd. When team members see the target group they are more likely to catch a vision of the ministry that is needed.

Communicating with Church Members

In addition to communicating the vision with the church starting team, the church starter needs to communicate the vision with potential and actual church members. Several activities can help this communication be accomplished.

First, the church starter must live the vision. When people see in the church starter a personification of the vision, they will understand it more readily and be motivated to become a part of it. Another way of stating this is that the church starter must become an incarnation of the vision. Jesus modeled his vision through everything he did and said. In a like manner, the church starter can live in such a way that there will be a natural communication of the vision.

Second, the church starter can communicate the vision through preaching and teaching. An articulation of the vision through sermons and lessons helps people know that the vision is based on biblical principles as well as a carefully designed plan to reach a specific ministry focus group. This assurance, as stated before, can provide a sense of direction, unity, and motivation for church members as they work cooperatively to fulfill the God-given vision.

Thirdly, the church starter can communicate the vision repeatedly and creatively through many media methods. These include such things as carefully designed brochures, audio and videotapes, skits, dramas, specialized classes for newcomers, testimonies, newsletters, bulletins and songs that capture the essence of the vision.[222] Repetition is absolutely necessary if the vision is to be kept alive. Creativity in presenting the vision keeps people from becoming bored and motivates them to continue their high level of commitment.

Fourthly, the church starter should communicate the vision with passion. Many causes, programs, and activities compete for the attention, time, and resources of people. It is only when church starters communicate with passion that people sit up and take notice and are motivated to participate. Vision needs to be related to a significant, eternal purpose if it is to appeal to people. In other words, people want to be a part of something that is truly significant—something that will make a difference in their lives and the lives of others. This significance must be communicated with passion if it is to elicit commitment on the part of the hearers.

In his book, *The Purpose Driven Church,* Rick Warren articulates "Saddleback's 2020 Vision for a Mature Church."[223]

> We dream of 15,000 members who have committed themselves to the Maturity Covenant...
>
> We dream of a network of 1,000 small groups...
>
> We dream of a Life Development Institute for our members...
>
> We dream our midweek believer's service involving 5,000...
>
> We dream of a faculty of 250 gifted lay teachers.

A great deal of the effectiveness of Saddleback Community Church traces precisely to the vision God gave Rick Warren and he shared with others.

Before leaving the topic of articulating a vision, it is important to distinguish between the vision and the mission of church starters. As we stated before, a vision is a mental picture of the end product that God wants to accomplish through the church starting team. A good way to address the topic of vision is to ask, what is this new church going to look like in five, ten, twenty years?

Clarifying the Mission

The God-given mission can be and should be clarified for the church starter, for those who serve with him, and for those who support the effort. This clarification is often embodied in a mission statement. The topic of a mission statement, on the other hand, answers three different questions: 1) What does God want us to accomplish? 2) Whom does God want us to reach? and 3) Why does God want us to do this? If we take the Great Commission as a model, these questions can be answered in the following manner: What? Make disciples; With whom? All nations or people groups; Why? To glorify the exalted Christ (all power is given me in heaven and on earth).[224]

There is a sense in which every mission statement of a church should be a restatement of the Great Commission. The following mission statements are examples of this requirement:[225]

> Our mission is to turn irreligious people into fully devoted followers of Jesus Christ.

> Our mission is to share the love of God with the people in mid-cities and beyond so that they can become fully devoted followers of Christ.

> We will lead our denomination to be on mission with God to bring all of the peoples of the world to saving faith in Jesus Christ.[226]

Notice that the second mission statement answers the questions mentioned above. What? - to share the love of God. With whom? - with the people of the mid-cities and beyond. Why? - so that they can become fully devoted followers of Christ. Notice also that all three mission statements are brief. Mission statements should be written in such a way that people can memorize them easily, put them on posters, letterheads, t-shirts, etc.

Also notice that all three mission statements have a biblical basis. This distinguishes them from the mission statements of secular organizations. A mission statement that is well written enables church starters to focus on the task that God wants them to accomplish, helps them to recruit team members who feel called to the same target group, and facilitates the evaluation of the ministry in future.

The Concept of "Endvisioning"

Lewis Myers and Jim Slack define "endvisioning" as: "developing a vision of the end which will serve to guide the entire planning process."[227] They explain the order of events in "endvisioning":

> In an ordinary planning process, strategists who plan from the beginning events to the final event in the process, usually follow one event with less extensive and complete plans for each successive event in the process. The aim of "endvisioning" is to give as thorough attention to the final events as to the beginning events. Endvisioning starts with a very functional description of the churches that will make up a church planting movement. The planner then backs up from the end results to the present, giving extensive explanation and description of each step of the church planting process. All discussion is in reference to the targeted people group."Endvisioning" must be functional and culture specific. Please note the description is not a description of plans but finished products at every significant stage.[228]

After defining the concept of endvisioning, Myers and Slack explain the its purpose:

> First, endvisioning serves as a check and balance between the research and multi-year plan that will be developed later in the process. One will ask of every part of the plan if what is planned will produce the end as it has been described in endvisioning. For instance, one will say: "If I follow the discipleship activities as described in the plan, will those activities produce the kind of disciple described during envisioning. Or will the training activities in the plan produce the kind of leaders described in the envisioning exercise. Second, endvisioning serves to indicate when the activities described in the mul-

ti-year plan have been completed as planned. Third, the endvisioning documents assists supervisors and prayer partners as they try to understand what the aims and completed tasks will look like. Fourth, envisioning serves the team well when success is achieved and it is time to "pass the baton" to the churches. The final "pass the baton" speech is being written during the endvisioning sessions. Thus, the endvision document serves important functions.[229]

The above mentioned authors suggest an outline according to the usual components in the entire endvisioning process:

12. A church planting movement is underway with numerous churches already in existence.

11. Believers meeting in the various outreach groups recognize that they are a New Testament church and are declaring themselves churches.

10. New Testament church characteristics begin to appear.

9. Group's identified leaders are trained.

8. A group of believers identify leaders.

7. Believers are matured into disciples.

6. Believers are baptized

5. Conversion occurs in a number of those under conviction.

4. A number of sympathizers come under spiritual conviction.

3. Individual(s) confronted with the Gospel.

2. A "willing to receive" group is gathered.

1. A large percent of the people in the "awareness" level are moved to the level of "willing to receive." [230]

As the authors explain, in actual practice, the process is the exact reverse of what is listed in this outline. As the work is done by the church planters, the first step toward a church planting movement is that a significant number of people proceed from unawareness to awareness (which is step 12 in this outline). In the endvisioning process, however, the planner starts with the end in mind which is step 12 in which a church planting movement is developing. Catching a vision from God of what the end church planting movement is going to look like in the future and inspire as well as guide the church planter to see it come to fruition.

Brent Ray while serving as a missionary to Brazil formulated a "Guidelines to Endvisioning" based on the information found in the *To The Edge* Document. He suggests:

- Describe in as great a detail as possible the various means of evangelism that will need to take place in this cultural setting to win increasing numbers of individuals to Christ to impact the lost.

- Describe the various curricula or Gospel presentation formats and items needed to carry out evangelism among the target people.

- Describe any pre-evangelism or climatization activities that will be needed to develop a more accurate awareness of Christianity and the Gospel among the target people.

- Describe in detail the characteristics of these churches that make them viable, reproducible New Testament churches in this society.

- Describe demographically in detail what the membership in the churches will be like. (Look inside the churches and describe them.)

- Describe the characteristics and functions of the kind of leader who will be able to shepherd these churches.

- Describe in detail the ways in which these churches will reproduce themselves In order to contribute to a church planting movement.

- Describe the ways in which discipled believers will have to be trained in order to shepherd these vital, reproducing churches.

- Describe the various types of curricula that will be

needed in the evangelization and training process.

- Describe how new believers will be discipled in order to be a vital member of these churches.

- Describe how new believers will have to be discipled to avoid nominalism, syncretism and their going out the "backdoor."[231]

The process of endvisioning is useful even in settings where a church planting movement is not the ultimate objective. The important thing is to envision what the ultimate goal is and to work backward in the planning process to ensure that the activities that are planned lead to its accomplishment.

CHAPTER 10

SUPPORTING RELATIONSHIPS

Church starters cannot work in isolation. Even when circumstances demand them to employ pioneering models, they require persons and resources to provide support systems for them and their work. The various church starting models each require different working relationships.

In this chapter we will discuss the church starting relationships that are necessary for the Parenting, Pioneering, Partnering, Propagating, and People Group models. Prior to discussing the implications of the various models for church starting relationships, we will focus on the general preparation necessary if sponsoring churches and groups are to be effective in carrying out their responsibilities.

General Preparation for Church Starting Support

Every group that plans to support church starting efforts, regardless of the model that the group will employ, must carefully prepare to provide for certain general matters related to this vital task. This preparation involves spiritual, emotional, sociological, philosophical, and strategic factors.

Spiritual Preparation

Spiritual preparation marks an indispensable step for any church, or other group, that desires to support a church starting effort. Plans for supporting a church starting effort must rest firmly on the conviction that God intends that the Great Commission be fulfilled by winning souls and establishing churches. This conviction should become so strong that the supporting agency (church or other group) accepts the establishment of new congregations as one of its highest priorities.

The sponsoring group should have a feeling of divine call or direction in regard to the church starting vision in general and the particular church start that they envision. No amount of physical preparation, as important as this can be, will ever take the place of genuine spiritual readiness for the task. Church starting groups will provide quality support only when the group is prepared spiritually for the task.

Needless to say, spiritual preparation for starting new churches comes only through spiritual disciplines. Prayer, Bible study, and accounts of needs for and victories in church starting can help develop the spiritual foundation for supporting the beginning new congregations. Pastors and other leaders can help the churches or other church starting groups prepare spiritually through the preaching of sermons, prayer, and training.

Emotional Preparation

The church or group needs to be willing to accept the responsibility of giving birth to and guiding this new congregation. The sponsoring group will have to be willing to sacrifice finances and personnel so that it will be able to supply the new congregation with necessary people, supplies, facilities, and funds necessary if the new congregation is to live and grow. In some cases the church will have to postpone the acquisition of some desirable but not absolutely necessary equipment or facilities in order to allow them to help the new congregation.

While giving up some of these desired church facilities and personnel may seem difficult, in the long run, the blessings of starting a new congregation will more than make up for the sacrifices. Still, the emotional preparation for church starting is a factor that every person and group must consider.

Sociological Preparation

The sponsoring church or group should also prepare itself sociologically by seeking understanding of the community and the people to be served. Deeper understanding of the demographic and psychographic characteristics of the target community creates a more intimate relationship between the sponsoring group and the community where the new congregation is envisioned. This feeling of oneness between the sponsoring group and the community forms a bond that enhances the church starting effort.

The more intimate sociological understanding of the target community also provides the sponsoring group the ability to utilize its resources more effectively. This sociological knowledge will help determine the type of congregation that is needed, the type of programs that are best suited to meet the needs of the community, and the evangelistic methods that will be most effective in winning the people to Christ.

Strategic Preparation

In order for the sponsoring church or group to understand its role and provide guidance, it is necessary for it to give attention to its church starting philosophy and strategy. The sponsoring church or group should face and answer the following questions: What is our goal for the new congregation? Is it that it remain a daughter forever or that it become a church in due time?

It will help the sponsoring church or group to study the philosophy of indigenous churches. This philosophy, which teaches that indigenous churches have (1) self-image, (2) self-function, (3) self-government, (4) self-support, (5) self-propagation, and (6) self- ministry,[232] has been discussed in greater detail in the preparation phase.

The sponsoring group might benefit from a course of study on general missionary methods. This study can supply a foundation on which to build the exact strategy for the new church start. This strategic preparation allows many decisions to be made before the actual implementation of the church starting effort. Strategic preparation is time well spent.

Organizational Preparation

In order for a church or group to be involved in the establishment of new congregations it does not only need to capture a vision and understand its role as a sponsor but it also needs to establish a missions committee, a development council, or a church starting task force. A missions committee can help the church to identify the communities that need churches.

This committee can further create an environment in the church that is conducive to the establishment of new congregations. It can coordinate the efforts of the members so that there will not be duplication of efforts. This committee can set goals with regard to the establishment of new congregations and challenge the church to reach them. Finally, The committee can be the channel of communication between the daughter congregation and the church.

By meeting regularly with the pastor of the daughter congregation this committee can be aware of its needs and seek to find resources within the church to meet them. This missions committee can help the daughter congregation resolve its problems and help the sponsoring church to continue to support the daughter congregation even if the new church is without a pastor. These and other functions of the committee of missions can help the mother church to have the greatest possible efficacy in the establishment of new congregations.

Due to the vital importance of the missions committee, the members should have the following qualities. They should be spiritual people whose lives provide an example to others in the church. They should be people with a missionary spirit that is so contagious that the church captures their enthusiasm. They should be people who are able to work with others because as a committee this group will have to relate to the church and the daughter congregation. They should be people who are willing to work.

In order to be able to challenge the church, this committee will need to do studies not only of the community but also of the human and financial resources in the church. This committee will need to be willing to receive training in order to carry out its tasks. This committee will have to work under the leadership of the pastor helping him, informing him, and collaborating with him.[233]

Relational Preparation

Another question that the church that is contemplating beginning a new congregation should consider is: "What relationship will we have with our daughter congregation?" Generally churches relate to their daughter congregations in one of the following ways: (1) as a proud grandparent, (2) as a legalistic parent, (3) as a dominant parent, and (4) as a mature parent.[234]

Proud Grandparent

Some churches relate to their daughter congregations as a proud grandparent who wants the privilege but not the responsibility. These churches are quick to boast that they have a daughter congregation but when they are called upon to help, they are not willing to do it. Consequently, the daughter congregation feels abandoned, almost as if it were an orphan. These sponsoring churches do little to enhance the health of the new churches.

Legalistic Parent

Other churches relate to their daughter congregations in a legalistic manner. Some legalistic parents have financial resources but instead of sharing these with their children, spend time talking of the difficulties they experienced when they were young and how difficult it was for them to meet their financial obligations. In like manner, these churches do little to help the new congregation. Their philosophy is: "If I had to struggle, you need to do it also."

Churches that work from this philosophy may refrain from helping their daughter congregations and expect them to struggle also. **They may purposely withhold needed aid.** Even though they have the resources to help these churches, they may be quick to criticize and slow to help.

Dominant Parent

Some churches behave like dominant parents toward their daughter congregations. They expect their daughter congregations to obey all of their dictates and even their suggestions. These churches insist on making all the decisions for their daughter congregation. They may even exert extreme financial control over the new congregation. In many cases this results in an attitude of excessive dependence. In other cases the result is a spirit of rebellion or rejection on the part of the daughter congregation.

Mature Parent

Fortunately, some churches behave like responsible parents toward their daughter congregations. These churches demonstrate an attitude of maturity. They are willing to help without creating an attitude of dependence. They allow room for their daughter congregations to develop their personalities, assume responsibilities, and reach adequate levels of maturity. These churches do not panic when the daughter congregation makes a mistake but help them to learn from their mistakes and to continue to grow.

It is important, therefore, that the churches and groups that are sponsoring daughter congregations give attention to the type of relationship that they will have with them. These general matters concerning the relationships between the sponsoring group and the new church constitute a vital phase of the church starting process.

Parenting Model Support

Certain supporting relationships take on a particular quality in Parenting Model church starting efforts. As was stated in chapter 5, the various expressions of the parenting model include: 1) Colonizing, 2) Task Force, 3) Satellite, 4) Revitalization, and 5) Reclamation approaches. Each of these models requires that specific questions be answered and particular relationships be formed and maintained.

Colonizing

Concerning relationships when using the Colonizing Model, the following questions need to be answered: 1) Who will form the core group that will go help start the new church? 2) What financial support will the sponsoring church provide and for how long? 3) Who will form the church Missions Committee? 4) What prayer support will be provided? 5) What additional materials will be provided? 6) How will the church starting leader be selected? 7) How will the sponsoring church avoid producing a replica of itself in the new congregation? 8) What will the agreement for church governance be? 9) What reporting system is established for the church starting leader?

Other necessary questions include: 10) How will the sponsoring church participate in the church starting activities: a) Surveying the community? b) Conducting a media effort? c) Conducting cultivating activities? d) Beginning home Bible studies? e) Other? 11) How will the sponsoring church assist in securing a meeting place? 12) How will the sponsoring church assist the new congregation in setting up its financial program? 13) How will the sponsoring church assist when needed in the training of new leadership? 14) How will the sponsoring church assist the new congregation to move toward incorporating (constituting)? 15) What will be the relationship of the sponsoring church to the new church after it has become autonomous?

Task Force

For the Task Force Model, the questions mentioned above will also need to be answered. Some additional questions will also need to be addressed such as: 1) How will the return of core group members to the sponsoring church be managed so as to minimize the impact on the new congregation? 2). What plan will be put in place to find, train, and utilize church leaders from the local community? Relationships in the Task Force Model can be especially difficult and lead either to most beneficial results...or to serious consequences.

Satellite Congregations

For the Satellite Congregation Model, many of the questions raised already apply. Additional questions, however, will help to focus the strategy for this model: 1) How will the sponsoring church distinguish between the satellite units that have the potential of becoming self-supporting congregations and those that will be on- going ministries? 2) For those that have the potential of becoming autonomous congregations, what criteria will the sponsoring church establish in order to move in accordance with the progress of the new congregation? 3) How will the strategy of the sponsoring church be developed in such a way as to avoid excessive dependence on the part of the new congregations?

Revitalization Project

When using the Revitalization Project Model, the sponsoring group needs to answer following questions: 1) What plan has been designed for the declining church to revert to a daughter congregation status? 2) Who will serve on the transition committee made up of members of the sponsoring church and the daughter congregation? 3) How will the members of the daughter congregation be trained? 4) Who will lead in the study of the community? 5) What will the new outreach strategies be? 6) Who will the new pastor be? 7) When will the revitalizing be launched?

Reclamation Project

The sponsoring group that follows the Reclamation Project Model must consider many of the questions utilized in the Revitalization Project Model. Additional questions, however, also will apply. 1) What date has been set for the declining church to officially go out of existence? 2) What is the procedure for the property of the declining church to be deeded to the sponsoring church or other agency (e.g. Association)? 3) How long will the church building be closed? 4) What are the plans for the renovation of the building? 5) What is the projected date for the grand opening of the new congregation?

Partnering Model Support

The Partnering Model, which consists of pooling the resources of existing churches to start new congregations, also requires definite planning for relationships between the sponsoring group and the new church. Much of what was said about sponsorship dimensions in the Parenting Models section applies to Partnering Models. The spiritual, emotional, sociological, strategic, organizational and relational preparation will simply need to be adapted to these models.

Multiple Sponsorship

The Multiple Sponsorship Model consists of several churches participating together to start a new congregation. Many of the questions raised in the Partnering Model apply to the Multiple Sponsorship Model. There are, however, some additional questions that will need to be addressed in order to ensure the effectiveness of this model. 1) How will the various sponsoring churches participate in the financial support of the new congregation? 2) How will the provision of personnel, materials, publicity, transportation, and facilities by the sponsoring congregations be coordinated? 3) How will the coordinating committee from the sponsoring churches be established? 4) To whom will the church starting leader report?

Multi-Congregational

As stated in chapter 5, the multi-congregational model is especially suited for culturally pluralistic metropolitan areas. In many cities, churches share their buildings with other congregations that conduct their worship services in other languages, in other forms, or at different times.

In order for this model to function effectively, several issues need to be addressed: 1) What covenant agreement needs to be established in order to ensure the partnership status of the various congregations that make up this model? 2) How will an Executive Council made up of leaders from each congregation be established? 3) How will the financial arrangements be handled? 4) How will the allocation of building space and other resources be made? 5) What plans can be made for the congregations to participate in common worship experiences (e.g. celebration of the Lord's Supper)? 6) What agreements are needed in order to ensure that the various congregations have the freedom to express their congregational life (e.g. leadership, worship styles) in ways that are consistent with their culture? 7) What agreements will be needed by the current and future pastors of these congregations to guarantee their commitment to this model? 8) What agreement is needed in order to ensure that congregations that grow rapidly have the freedom to branch out on their own if that becomes necessary? 9) What agreements are needed to enlist other congregations or start new ones if space is available for them?

Adoption

The Adoption Model occurs when a newly established congregation seeks affiliation with a particular denomination. In order to ensure that the adoption will result in positive, enabling relationships, some of the following questions need to be addressed: 1) What is the affinity between the newly established congregation and the church or agency with which it wishes to affiliate, doctrinally, ecclesiastically (church polity), and evangelistically? 2) Why was the new congregation formed? 3) What are the expectations of the adoptee congregation, relationally, financially? 4) How is the proposed adoptee congregation functioning? 5) What plan can be devised for a trial period prior to formal affiliation?

Key Church

The Key Church Model calls for a church to make a commitment to church starting on par with its commitment to having any other ministry such as an educational and music ministry. In light of this commitment, several questions need to be answered as a church starting strategy is developed: 1) On what date did the Key Church make a long-term commitment to make missions outreach a top priority? 2) When did the Key Church establish a Missions Committee (Missions Development Council)? 3) When did the Key Church elect a Minister of Missions to lead mission expansion? 4) How many new congregations does this Key Church commit to start every year? 5) What additional resources can the Key Church enlist to carry out its church starting program?

Pioneering Model Support

The main feature of Pioneering Models is that the church starter has to start from scratch. Due to the fact that this model may not have a sponsoring church, the church starter cannot count on a church starting team, financial resources, or hands-on guidance from a nearby community.

In light of this, there are several vital questions that the Pioneer Church Starter needs to answer: 1) What church starting role will I play: a) church starter developer? b) church starter initiator? 2) Where will I enlist financial support? a) From the outside? b) From the local community? 3) Where will I enlist a church starting team: a) from the outside? b) from the local community? 4) Where will I enlist help for church starting activities: a) from the outside? b) from the local community?

Propagating Model Support

In a certain sense, the Propagating Model has much in common with Pioneering Models. The distinctive feature of Propagating Models, however, is that workers committed to this model are also committed to maximum church multiplication. Propagating Models must give particular attention to leadership training and church starting movements.

Leadership Training

Enlisting support for Propagation Models is to some extent similar to the enlistment of support for some of the other models. One of the principal differences is that the support in not enlisted for an individual church starter but for an extensive network of new congregations. Such a network of new churches requires the establishment of a Leadership-training Program, the deployment of many church starters, and some specific relational realities.

Some of the questions that need to be answered with regard to this model are: 1) How will the leadership training director be supported? 2) What kind of leadership training program is needed to ensure that church starting is the end product? 3) How will the church starters in training be enlisted? 4) Where will the church starters in training meet? 5) What kind of bi-vocational church starting strategy needs to be established to ensure the economic viability of this program? 6) How can the church starting program be designed to follow the basic steps needed to start new churches outlined by Clay Coursey:[235] a) Select a new work committee for the church, b) Select the area for the new work, c) Prepare the sponsoring church, d) Prepare the selected area, e) Begin the infant church, f) Teach the new church about finances, g) Plan with the new church its facilities, h) Dedicate the new church."[236]

Church Starting Movements

Many of the questions for Propagation Models, which were raised concerning the Leadership Training Model, apply as well to the Church Starting Movement Model. In order to be a catalyst in initiating an ongoing church starting movement, strategy coordinators (or people with similar job descriptions) need to address additional questions: 1) With whom am I going to establish a work relationship in order to enlist support for my role in initiating a church starting movement? 2) What people group do I feel called to work with? 3) How am I going to evangelize, disciple, train, and enable members of my people group to start churches that in turn will reproduce? 4) What will be the strategy that I will use to reach my people group? 5) If my people group is pre-literate, how well versed am I with the storying strategy?

People Group Model Support

People Group (Ethnic) church starting models have much in common with the other models already discussed. This category is used primarily to underscore the cultural diversity that is found in many urban areas throughout the world and the variations with the ethnic groups themselves due to the process of assimilation.

Due to these factors, additional specialized questions need to be addressed: 1) How did they become residents of their adopted country? a) annexation,[237] b) forced migration,[238] c) voluntary migration (political refugees, documented immigration, undocumented immigration).[239] 2) What is their level of assimilation? a) total ethnic, b) median ethnic, c) marginal ethnic, d) assimilated ethnic, e) revitalized ethnic.[2409] 3) What type of church is needed to reach each of these segments? 4) How can I enlist support to start churches among these segments?

Platform Support

The utilization of platforms is yet another model to provide support for church planting efforts. David A. Bishop defines platforms when he states:

> Platform is a general term to describe the mission agency, charity, or business which provides a Christian worker with a valid reason to live in a country. Platforms are Christian or secular organizations that provide passage for Christian workers to access their target people and live incarnationally among them.[241]

In a fine PowerPoint Presentation, Bishop explains the value of utilizing platforms:

- To provide accessibility or the reason to live or travel among the population segment. Your "reason for being" in a creative access situation. Answers the question, "Why are you here?"

- To provide legitimacy or a real, viable, and logical activity or endeavor which validates your "reason for staying" in a creative access situation. Often implies some "value added" to the community or government.

- To provide facility or an opportunity to apply human and financial resources to the main objective. Builds a bridge to accomplishment of the main objective.

- To provide diversity for a team by employing more than one platform at a time. Avoids putting "all of your eggs [personnel] in one basket [platform]."May provide access to more than one strata of the target population.[242]

As can be seen from Bishop's description, platforms can serve a variety of purposes both in countries that are open to Christian workers as well as "creative access countries." Within open countries a platform can provide a bridge to reach specific people groups or population segments. A number of years ago a pharmacist went to a city in New York with the purpose of starting a church. His job not only provided the much needed financial support but a bridge to get to know people, establish friendships, and involve them in Bible studies that led to the establishment of a new congregation. Perhaps we can say that this was similar to what the apostle Paul did in Corinth. While working as a tentmaker he met Aquila and Priscilla, let them to faith in Christ, involved them in a congregation that met in a house, discipled them, and then took them with him as ministry partners to Ephesus (Acts 18).

As Bishop points out, there are many ways in which people can be involved in platforms.

- As students; Tourists; Education (CGE university exchange programs);

- Humanitarian Aid/Community Development (e.g. Global Partners (UK) includes water resource development, animal husbandry) "well-baby" clinics; Agriculture (e.g. Ethiopian Aid--irrigation and wheat production);

- Medicine (e.g. c/o GP (UK), NW China Rural Doctor Training Program);

- Art and Culture;

- Sports Development--e.g. Global Sports Partners—basketball; volleyball clinics;
- physical education training programs;
- Business--sales, consulting, tourism, can be applied to all of the above; (e.g. international representation of providers and consumers of products and/or services.)[243]

Funding for platforms can come from a variety of sources. In some instances mission agencies provide the salary and benefits (e.g., insurance). In other instances church planters are able to put a support package from churches and individual donors. Yet in other cases the funds can be generated by the platforms themselves. Church planters teaching in educational institutions, establishing businesses, or providing other needed services in the communities where they serve.

Several considerations need to be kept in mind. First, the platform must offer services that are valued in the community. Second, security conditions must be kept in mind so that the platform can continued. Third, and perhaps foremost, platforms must create the opportunity and allow the time for the good news of the Gospel to be communicated to the focus group. Platforms, therefore, can be viewed not only as a viable source of funding but as a means to have access to people who otherwise will not have an opportunity to hear the message of salvation and have the blessing of being a part of a loving and encouraging congregation of believers.

Conclusion

As clearly seen from the foregoing discussion, a wide variety of church starting models need to be considered in order to reach a wide variety of people in a wide variety of settings. The starting point is a general preparation involving the spiritual, emotional, sociological, philosophical, and strategic preparation.

Coupled with this general preparation is the imperative of understanding and articulating the various types of relationships that need to be established in particular models of church starting. In order to provide the undergirding that is necessary for each type of church starting, particular planning for relationships must relate to the definite objectives of each model. The clearer that these relationships are, the more harmonious will be the implementation of church starting strategies.

CHAPTER 11

TEAM MEMBERS

Team members constitute an indispensable ingredient in the church starting task. As Aubrey Malphurs points out:

> Paul did not attempt to carry out the Great Commission vision alone, but ministered through a team. Prior to his first church-planting journey, the team consisted of Barnabas and Paul (Acts 11:22-30). On the first church-planting trip, they added Mark to the team (Acts 13:2-3, 5), Luke (Acts 16), and others (Acts 18). On the third trip, additional people were either added to the team or used to form new teams. Acts 19 and 20 mentions Erastus, Gaius, Aristarchus, Sopater, Secundus, and Tychicus.[244]

Billy Graham attributes the effectiveness of his ministry to the marvelous teams that the Lord enabled him to assemble. He states:

> Because the name Billy Graham is usually so prominent in the media, many people cannot understand that our ministry has been a team effort. The dedicated men and women working with us have been willing to do anything and everything... In order to do whatever needed to be done, they have subordinated their personal privilege, reordered their priorities, accepted disappointments and endless changes in schedule, stretched their patience, absorbed criticism, and exhausted their energy. They were heaven-sent ones who propped me up when I was sagging and often protected me from buffetings that would have scared me or scarred me otherwise. They did not back away from correcting me when I needed it or counseling me with their wisdom when I faced decisions. I'm convinced that without them, burnout would have left me nothing but a charred cinder within five years of the 1949 Los Angeles Crusade[245].

In his book chapter entitled, *"Don't Take The Journey Alone,"*

Jeff Calloway, emphasizes the fact that teams are absolutely essential in the church planting task. He explains:

> Make no mistake, the number and quality of relationships you build during the church planting process can determine the vitality, health, and impact of your church plant in your community... A planter without the right relationships will plod along, being discouraged and not effective in the call that God has placed on his life. He will struggle with loneliness, failing to see that relationships are ingredients that lead to emotional and spiritual health. Many will get caught up in the crafting of the mission and vision of the church – with the "business end" of planting – and neglect relationship building. In fact, you may be lonely and not know where to turn. This discouragement can be multiplied many times over if you do not have others alongside you who are investing in you and you in them.[246]

A team had been defined as "a small group or people with complementary skills and abilities committed to a common purpose and a performance goal through a shared approach exercising mutual accountability."[247] It is obvious from this definition that a team is not just an assortment of people who want to be involved in activities. The compatibility of the individuals within the group as well as their commitment to work together to accomplish a task is absolutely essential.

Numerous benefits accrue to working as a team:

- Teams help strengthen lines of communication
- Teams lead to more lasting change
- Teams help capture the richness of the diversity of individuals
- Teams help improve performance in terms of quality, creativity, and cost.[248]

Teams have a number of important functions.

Among these are:

- Defining and meeting the needs of those we are ministering to / those we are trying to reach
- Studying and improving work processes

- Developing systems for evaluation
- Goal setting (the yardstick for accountability)
- Developing and implementing action plans
- Problem solving.[249]

The selection of the team members is a vital step in the church starting process. The complexity of the church starting task clearly indicates that the church starter cannot accomplish it alone. A team who undergirds and complements the work of the church starter is essential.

In most instances sufficient resources are not available to have a full-time, fully paid church-starting team. This fact demands that the church starter recruit a team of persons who can find the financial support to be full-time workers, or persons who are willing to work bi-vocationally, or persons who already have the financial resources (e.g. retired persons).

Whatever the means of support that might be available, the church starter needs to overcome the myth that there must be resources for full-time workers in order to put together a church-starting team. After much prayer, the church starter should seek persons who are both willing and able to be team members. A rule of thumb should be that the team should be made up of persons who complement the gifts and skills of the church starter rather than persons who have very similar (and perhaps competing) gifts and skills. The spiritual factors in the lives of the team members are far more important than any physical factors.

Selecting Team Members by Role

The church starting model that is chosen will obviously determine to a large extent the composition of the church starting team. A key factor in this selection process, whatever the model, concerns the role that the church starter decides to play in the starting of a new congregation.

Church Starter/Developer Role

The church starter/developer envisions starting the congregation, developing it into a full-blown church, and remaining as its pastor. This person needs a team that will help accomplish this vision. In playing this role, the church starter will need to be the key vision-caster, strategist, spiritual leader, team builder, and supervisor for the initial as well as the development phases of the new congregation.

Another way of stating this is that this person will be the senior pastor of this congregation. This church starter will need the gifts of the church developer as well as the church starter. The giftedness of the church starter and the ministry model that is envisioned will determine the composition of the team, as team members will supplement the church starter's gifts and skills.

Church Starter Initiator Role

The church starter initiator starts a congregation, develops it to a certain point, and then moves on elsewhere to start additional congregations. This person generally has strong church starting gifts but is limited in the gifts that relate to the development and maturation of congregations. This type of church starter needs a team that will not only assist in the initial stages of the congregation but also help prepare for the development stages after necessary pastoral change occurs.

In most instances the church starter initiator has strong gifts in the area of faith (vision), evangelism, and preaching but limited gifts and desire for remaining with a congregation, providing administrative leadership, and fully developing a variety of needed ministries. The church starting team, therefore, needs to possess such gifts as administration, teaching, and counseling in order to balance the ministries of the church and provide continuity after the founding church starter has left.

Propagating Church Starter Role

The propagating church starter trains and involves others in the church starting task. This type of church starting can be accomplished through extension centers or through more decentralized training strategies. In most instances this type of church starter does not start churches directly but through the leaders that have been trained.

This type of church starter obviously needs strong gifts in the areas of faith (vision), teaching, leadership, and administration. The propagating church starter needs to recruit church starters and guide them in the selection of church starting teams. Motivating these church starters becomes a major task for the propagating church starter.

The church starter that is instrumental in starting church starting movements needs to go even further. This involves not only recruiting and training persons to start churches. In addition the propagating church starter role demands training the church starters to recruit and train others to start churches. As is true in the approaches mentioned above, the church starting team will need to be selected in keeping with the gifts of the church starter and the model that is employed in light of the target group.

An additional circumstance of the Propagating Model role relates to the fact that the church starter often does not have existing churches from which to recruit church starting teams. He/she must often start from scratch leading persons to the Lord, training them, communicating the vision to them, entrusting them with the task, and undergirding them with prayer and counsel. This approach follows closely the Apostle Paul's method of approaching his church starting journeys.

People Group Church Starter's Role

The "People Group Model" discussed in the preparation section has many things in common with the Propagating Model. However, if the church starter is not a member of the target group he or she needs to have strong cross-cultural abilities (i.e. the missionary gift). The same applies to church starting team members who do not belong to the culture of the target group.

In addition to having the missionary gift, church starters utilizing this model need to establish a clearly defined program of study involving such things recommended by Tom Steffen in *Passing the Baton.* Steffen suggests training in cross-cultural studies, missiological studies, language learning, communication techniques (e.g. indigenous learning styles) and contextualized discipleship methods. These and other studies are geared toward equipping the cross-cultural church starter to design culturally relevant strategies for the pre-entry stage, pre-evangelism stage, evangelism stage, post evangelism stage, and the phase out stage.[250]

Conclusion

Clearly, the role the church starter feels led to adopt will determine the types of persons and their giftedness needed for the church starting team who will support the church-starter. Attention to this imperative step will enhance the strength of the church start and avoid many hindrances.

Steps in Selecting the Church Starting Team

Since the selection of the church starting team is one of the most crucial tasks of the church starter, the leaders of the effort must exert extreme care in recruiting the team members. Four steps guide the process of selecting church starting team members.

Determine the Gifts of Team Members

The first step is to determine the gifts of the church starter. It is expected that the church starter have a working knowledge of all of these gifts, but the primary gifts quite likely will need to be in such areas as leadership, faith, preaching, teaching, and evangelism. Most likely the church starter will not have all of these gifts and could, therefore, benefit from having team members who have such gifts as administration, evangelism, worship, small groups, children, youth, family, and pastoral care.

Obviously, some of the team members may have more than one gift and can lead in several areas of ministry such as worship and youth, small group and counseling, etc. By seeking team members with particular gifts, the church starter can assemble a team that can work together, each supplementing and enhancing the gifts of other team members. The process of team selection begins with an assessment of gifts of the prospective team members.

Determine the Needs of the Target Group

Often the needs of the target group may require certain gifts in the church starter and the church starting team and these needs will come into play in the process of selecting a church starting team. The second step in the process of assembling the church starting team, therefore, is the recruitment of a team that will complement the gifts of the church starter in light of the needs of the target group. For instance, a church that is seeking to reach young couples may not need a youth ministry immediately. It will, however, be indispensable to have an effective nursery and children's ministry. If a church is being established along traditional lines it will need to have someone who leads in the area of Sunday school for adults as well as children. A more innovative church model may call for a small-group approach. Team members whose gifts supplement those of the church starter and match the ministry model can make an invaluable contribution in the establishment of exciting, growing, and reproducing churches.

Robert Logan makes a vital distinction between team members and ministry partners.[251] Logan considers the latter to be potential staff members who make a long-term commitment to minister in the new congregation. The vision and commitment of the ministry partners need to be in harmony with those of the church starter. Their sense of calling to start that congregation is just as strong and clear as that of the church starter.

At times it may be necessary for the ministry partners to begin as bi-vocational workers due to the absence of financial resources for full-time ministry. An ideal situation is when two or three couples covenant with the church starter couple to be ministry partners. This provides the new congregation with an excellent church starting staff and a church starting team from the beginning.

Determine the Roles of Team Members

It is obvious that the different church starting models require different team members with different gifts who will fulfill different roles in the church start. As different church starter specialists look at the task, they recommend a varied composition for the teams. Malphurs advocates a variety of teams, that is, a two-person team (a leader and a manager), a three member team (leader, teacher and programmer), and even a five person team (adding a youth worker and administrator).[252] Lyle Schaller advocates a least a three-person team (pastor, evangelist, and a music specialist).[253] Robert Logan mentions seven team roles: 1) Recruiter-evangelist; 2) Worship leader-facilitator; 3) Children's ministry leader- recruiter; 4) Shepherd-care giver; 5) Organizer-implementer; 6) Recruiter-mobilizer; and 7) Financial-business administrator.[254]

A composite list of the various roles for the church starting team would need to include the following:

- Leader—the point person in the church starting endeavor

- Manager, administrator—a person who is gifted at organizing and implementing.

- Teacher—a person who leads the discipling efforts of the new congregation

- Youth worker—a person who leads the ministry to the youth and their families

- Pastor—a person who shepherds the new congregation

- Worship leader, facilitator, programmer, music specialist—a person who utilizes all the available resources to maximize the worship experience of the new congregation

- Recruiter, evangelist—a person whose entire focus is to lead in outreach efforts

- Children's ministry leader-recruiter—a person who establishes and directs the children's ministry of the new congregation

- Cell group organizer—a person who enlists, trains, deploys and enables cell group leaders

- Financial business administrator—a person who manages the finances of the new congregation

- Pastoral care—a person who organizes and maintains the pastoral care of the members.

Obviously, the selection of the church starting team will rest solidly on the needed roles foreseen by the church starter. The church starting team will include, therefore, persons with the gifts, interests, and skills to address the necessary roles in the church start. These persons will be selected and assembled with attention to how the gifts of each can relate to and supplement the gifts of the church starter and other team members.

Conclusion

Obviously, the church starting team and its selection should be based on pragmatic foundations. There are undoubtedly other gifts and roles for which team members are needed in accordance with the church starting models that are employed and the needs of the target group. The leaders of the church starting effort also will need to establish a priority list since in many situations all of the personnel and financial resources will not be available to begin with a full- fledged team. It will be important, however, to determine the types of team members that are needed and to begin working toward attracting that kind of people. As stated previously, the model that is employed and the needs of the community will undoubtedly inform the selection process.

CHAPTER 12
TARGET GROUP

A vital step in the formulation process of church starting is that of identifying and selecting the target group. The first task Paul and Barnabas undertook in their church starting missions was that of choosing where they were going to establish churches. Missiologist Roland Allen asserts that Paul, guided by the Holy Spirit, concentrated his efforts on strategic centers, such as Ephesus and then used these cities as a base for the spreading of the Gospel.[255]

In addition, the book of the Acts indicates that this team of church starters was aware of the different groups and of their receptivity. Several times in Acts the writer mentions cultural groups and the degree of their receptivity to the Gospel. Among the groups in the synagogues, for example, those who showed the greatest receptivity to the Gospel were God-fearers (Gentiles who were attracted to the Jewish religion but had not officially joined it) and the proselytes (Gentiles who had been integrated into the Jewish religion). Those who were least receptive were the traditional Jews, although a good number of them were also converted.

The Holy Spirit sometimes led Paul away from his own ideas of the target groups and pointed him to different areas. For example, Paul had planned to continue his evangelizing and church starting efforts in Bithynia. The Holy Spirit, however, intervened and led him to Macedonia (Greece) where he started churches in Philippi, Thessalonica, Berea, Athens, and Corinth (Acts 16:1- 18:22). The principle is that church starting seeks to identify and select the target group, using every resource available, especially the Holy Spirit.

Paul and his co-workers adapted the presentation of the message with the purpose of reaching the largest number of people in these groups. This team of church starters selected carefully the strategic places in which they would concentrate their efforts and paid attention to the sociocultural factors while communicating the message. The church starters in biblical times carefully identified and selected target groups and then adapted their evangelization. Church starting efforts today should note and follow this example using not only the most important source of understanding, the Holy Spirit, but also other means that are available today.

Using Syndicated Research

Choosing an appropriate place in which to establish a new congregation is not an easy task. The many needs coupled with the limited resources demand the church starter wisely employ the resources of people and finances. Several sources of syndicated research can help a church starter to make wise decisions. Do we need to say a word about the nature of syndicated research tools?

These syndicated research tools are: (1) a demographic analysis, (2) a psychographic analysis, and (3) creating a general profile. The church starter will also greatly benefit from doing the following types of research: (1) a religious survey, (2) an interview of community leaders, (3) a survey of the people in the community, (4) an analysis of awareness of the gospel, (5) a survey of decision-making processes, and (6) a survey of reasons for resistance to the gospel. These tools help determine areas where churches are most likely to thrive.

Demographic Analysis

A demographic analysis of the community can greatly assist the church starting group by providing an idea of the potential that exists in that community for a new congregation or a new kind of congregation. A complete analysis should include factors such as the number of inhabitants, the socioeconomic groups, the types of housing, the educational levels, the types of employment, and types of family structures. These facts help the church starting team focus on the needs and possibilities of the region.

The analysis of the number of inhabitants can be compared with the figures of the last decade in order to have an idea if the population is growing or decreasing. This analysis in many cases includes age groups and cultural groups. This information can help the church starter know who the prospects are in that community. In general churches grow when their communities are growing. Also, the churches grow when they reach out to age groups (e.g. youth, young couples) or cultural groups (e.g. immigrants) that other churches are not reaching.

The analysis of types of housing together with the analysis of socioeconomic levels can help the church to determine what type of ministry and leadership is needed in that community. The different socioeconomic groups have different preferences with regard to leadership, worship style, type of music, etc. The more that is known about these groups, the more appropriate will be the strategy to reach them with the Gospel.

The analysis of the types of employment and of family structures can also help the church starting team know the needs of that community. For example, if there are many single-parent families this indicates ministries to single-parent families that the new congregation can offer will be useful to these households. The presence of either working-class families or professional-class peoples will indicate directions for the new congregation or congregations.

This demographic information holds extreme importance. It can help church starters to have a better knowledge of the needs in their communities and guide them to concentrate on the groups that have the greatest needs for a church and the greatest likelihood for responding. It is important to note that generally churches grow when they are in communities that are growing. It is also important to know that in general people show more receptivity to the Gospel when they move from one place to another having left behind the social ties that sometimes prevented or hindered them from responding to the Gospel. Although it is true that demographic information is more complete and more accessible in some countries than in others, in almost all the countries of the world some information can be obtained in government offices, Chambers of Commerce, and of other societies that are interested in population information.

Some very useful tools are available to church planters that are looking for information on their target communities. These tools have evolved over the past decades and will continue to be refined to identify the most important information and method of delivery. The purpose of each is to clearly identify and logically present the statistical information for the selected location including demographics, religious trends, primary language spoken, presence of a Bible translation in the local language, and etc. Materials concerning demographic research can be purchased from persons and groups who exist to provide such information. Many church starting ventures will not, however, possess the necessary funds to purchase these services. The necessary demographic information can be gathered by the church planter from some of the following resources. The following websites make available a variety of statistical data that can be utilized in the process of identifying who the people are and what the best techniques might be for reaching them:[256]

www.PeopleGroups.info

This site includes demographics, people group data, a mapping module, and various media that highlight reaching people groups. This resource database is a joint compilation of the Center for Missional Research and the Joshua Project.

This fantastic website has been put together in conjunction with the North American Mission Board for the purposes of identifying the people groups that are represented in the United States. The searches are free and the statistics are consistently updated. Those with an interest in reaching a particular people group originating outside the United States might be interested to find that the majority of the people groups of the world are represented in the cities of the United States.

www.census.gov

The United States government does a regular census of all the people located within the borders at that time. Their work is much like a demographic snapshot, providing data for everything from taxing to infrastructure. The census is useful to the church because it provides very useful information for understanding individual communities. Many of the resources available are utilizing the U.S. Census to populate their statistics. The U.S. Census is likely the foremost provider of unique and original statistics.

These data are then distributed and interpreted by other resource providers. The site includes: the national census data, publications on economic census and population, as well as informational blogs. Church starters should not overlook this resource.

www.PerceptGroup.com

Percept is one of the oldest online demographic providers. They are well respected and give a wide variety of statistical data. Their fee, while significantly higher than some of the no cost or low cost demographic sites, has the potential to pay off in the long run because of the picture they are able to paint for the local church planter.

Many state conventions and local associations have partnered with Percept to provide packets for all of their new church plants. Their resources are known as Ministry Area Profile(s) (MAP), which seek to serve as a visual survey of the entire community. These reports can prove most beneficial in planning and beginning church starts.

You will find out standard information such as age, family structure, race, education, income levels, as well as likely religious preferences and faith involvement. Combined with Percept's Community Preference Assessment (COMPASS), you will get insight into community preferences for church programs ('how do we meet their needs?"), styles ("how do we appeal to their tastes?"), and communication ("how to we contact them?"). Both services can be had for under $400 (see site).

www.EthnicHarvest.org

Ethnic Harvest provides free demographics to help church plants in the United States reach their target communities. The site provides useful information about the particular zip code area the church starter requests. "The last ten years has seen one of the greatest migration of peoples in the history of the world. *Many of the people groups to whom we've been sending missionaries, now live right here in America.* Our site can help you learn the specifics of the people who have settled in your area."[1]

www.natdecsys.com

National Decision Systems provides online demographics.

---

1 http://www.ethnicharvest.org/regions/regionindex.htm; October 26, 2010

This type of demographic data is useful in the marketing side of church planting as the planter promotes the Launch and announces special emphases throughout the year.

The website breaks down the community into 50 different segments that are characterized by a variety of interests, patterns and behaviors. The information provided includes: "demographic, geographic, business, consumer demand, consumer behavior, industry-specific and more." 2

www.barna.org

George Barna is well known for his demographic information and surveys. His site is full of articles and useful tools for understanding segments of North America.

www.MelissaData.com

Melissa Data is helpful in a variety of ways including identifying school districts and maps.

A wise person would use these resources in much the way that he might use a prayer walk through the community; with an eye to the details he can pray toward the specific needs of the community.

Psychographic Analysis

In addition to the demographic analysis, a psychographic analysis can give additional information that will assist church starters to determine the types of churches that need to be established. This type of an analysis focuses on the socioeconomic levels and lifestyles of the residents of a given community. The CACI ACORN Profile, for instance, uses categories such as: 1) Affluent Families; 2) Upscale Households; 3) The Up and Coming Singles; 4) Retirement Styles; 5) Young Mobile Adults; 6) City Dwellers; 7) Factory and Farm Communities; 8) Downtown Residents; and 9) Non-residential Neighborhoods.

Under each of these, CACI lists sub-categories that help to narrow the focus on the various lifestyle groups. For each of these groups, CACI utilizes the Simmons Market Research Bureau, to provide such vital information as: 1) Self-Concept; 2) Buying

---

2 http://www.natdecsys.com/; October 26, 2010

Style; 3) Life Events of the Last Year; 4) Political Outlook; 5) Personal Views/ Opinions; 6) Purchasing Habits, and 7) Leisure Activities.

Understanding of these factors can guide the church starting effort to adopt the methods of evangelism, the types of advertising, the ways of worship, and the types of church leaders best adapted to the groups the effort is targeting. The next chapters will outline some of the different means of communicating with different types of audiences and suggest the means that are more effective with some groups. Whatever effort is invested in obtaining the psychographic analysis is time well spent.

The type of information mentioned above allows church starters to construct a profile of the ministry focus groups that are found in a given community and to design the most effective strategies for reaching and discipling them. Such an understanding of the target group is crucial for designing appropriate strategies. Different socioeconomic, cultural, and generational groups have different characteristics and tastes which have significant implications in determining evangelistic strategies, worship styles, preaching modes, decision making processes and leadership styles.

Some congregations have developed a profile of the target person they are trying to reach in their community. The Saddleback Community Church, for example, developed the profile of "Saddleback Sam." This profile reveals that residents of the area the church attempts to reach have the following characteristics: (1) well educated; (2) likes his job; (3) likes where he lives; (4) gives high priority to health and fitness for him and his family (5) would rather be in a large group than in small ones; (6) is skeptical of "organized religion"; (7) likes contemporary music; (8) thinks he is enjoying life more than he did five years ago; (9) is satisfied and even smug about his station in life; (10) prefers the casual and informal over the formal; and (11) is overextended in both time and money.[257]

Conducting Your Own Research

In addition to the community information that the church starter and the church starting team can secure from professional, syndicated sources, other opportunities for community understanding are available. The church starter and team can conduct their own research into the community and often unearth even more helpful materials than can be secured from the professional profiles. The direct research can ask questions and glean understandings the professional methods neither understand nor value. Below are some suggestions for conducting your own research into the community populations.

General Religious Survey

A general religious survey seeks to determine if the community being considered is the most strategic community in which to establish a church (more will be said of a specific religious survey). In a certain sense all communities need more churches. Due, however, to the fact that the church starter does not have the personnel and financial resources to establish churches in all of the needy communities simultaneously, it is often advisable to ascertain the most strategic community or communities. Prospective church starters, therefore, should seek answers to the following questions:

- How many churches are in the community?

- How many of these churches preach the message of salvation?

- What percentage of the population are these churches reaching?

- Are these churches reaching to all socioeconomic and sociocultural groups?

Generally the census taken by governmental agencies does not gather information regarding the religious affiliation of the people. This information can, however, be obtained in the following manner: (1) making a list of the churches that are in the community; (2) interviewing the leaders of each church and asking them how many active members they have, and how many of these are from the community that surrounds the church; and (3) visiting these churches to observe the groups being reached (consequently, what groups are not being reached), what style of worship the church has (how this matches the socioeconomic level of the community), what ministries the church has (comparing this with the ministries that are needed in the community). This information can help the new church sponsors to determine the potential of establishing a new congregation in that community. This information can also help the church starter to know what strategy will be needed to reach the people in this community.

The religious survey can help the church starting team understand the attitude of the people toward organized religion and churches. It can uncover certain established feelings that may impact the process of sharing the Gospel among the people and suggest ways of avoiding these hindrances. It may alert the team to past problems of previous church efforts and suggest ways of discounting problems raised by these factors. This religious survey supplies much understanding not available through the professional profiles.

Community Leadership Survey

Church starting groups can also obtain valuable information about the community and its needs by interviewing community leaders. These leaders can be school administrators, owners of local business establishments, directors of social service agencies, officers in police departments, presidents of clubs and organizations, real estate professionals, officers of home owners' associations, and pastors. In short, the church starting-team should contact people who know the inhabitants of the community and their needs.

Several questions can guide these interviews: (1) How long have you been in this community?, (2) What are some of the most urgent needs in this community?, (3) What are some things that you have learned as a result of your work in this community?, (4) What advice would you give a person who is planning some activities to help this community?, (5) What methods have you found to be effective in communicating with the people of this community? These are only examples of the type of questions that the church–starting team can utilize to learn about the characteristics and the needs of the inhabitants of a community. The experience and knowledge of key community leaders significantly provides needed information for the church starting effort. In some cases the questions will need to be modified. The important thing is to benefit from the experience of these leaders.

Community Resident Survey

Generally when a group undertakes a survey of the people in the community, many residents show little interest and sometimes even express resentment. These reactions from the residents spring partly from the fact that in many cases people have had unpleasant experiences with persons coming to their homes for religious visits or surveys. In certain communities it is almost impossible to gather information from the residents. In these cases church starters need to search for other ways to communicate with them (possibly by establishing friendship ties). In other cases, however, the problem has not been so much the resistance on the part of the community residents as it has been the defective or inadequate methods employed by previous groups.

One method of surveying community residents that has been effective in many parts of the world concentrates on discovering if the people recognize their spiritual needs and, if so, what these spiritual needs are. This method, therefore, does not try to gather a lot of information (e.g. age, educational level of each person). Instead, it simply asks the following questions: (1) What are some of the greatest needs in this community?, (2) Why do many of the people in this community not attend church?, (3) What type of activities in the church would help you and your family deal with the serious problems of life?, and (4) If we started support groups (of Bible studies) to help the families of this community, would you be interested in attending? The purpose of these questions is to know what the needs are in the community, determine what type of ministries would help the community, and who the people are that would be interested in attending a Bible study or cultivating event in the community.

These questions may need to be modified in accordance with the characteristics of the different communities. Even after utilizing them in a survey they may need to be changed. The important thing is to design an analytical tool that can help us to know the families better and to know how to adapt the programs of the church to reach these people.

"Man of Peace" Survey

Of all of the methodologies that are utilized to find people around whom to build a core for the new congregation, one of the most helpful is that of finding a "Man of peace." Some groups have utilized a method based on the concept of the man of peace found in Luke 10:6-7. This method consists of visiting the homes in a community in search of a family that is interested in hearing the Gospel. Upon finding this family, an effort is made to evangelize the parents. Then they are trained to win their children, the rest of the family, and close friends for Christ.

The church starting effort forms the group of evangelized people into a Bible Study. As these people participate in the Bible Study the church starter pays attention to persons who demonstrate abilities to serve. From this group the church starter selects a teacher, a music director, a children's leader, and a recreation leader. As these leaders perform their tasks the people are developing leadership capacities to serve in the congregation that is being established.

The "man of peace," therefore, becomes the central part of the core for the new church. This person or family holds great significance for the work. To find such a person and such a family gives great promise to the new congregation.

Community Religious Survey

Guidance for making a general religious survey of the community has already been suggested. This general survey looks at the general religious status of the area, that is, how many churches, what percentage of the people attend church, how evangelical are these churches, and what groups are being reached by the churches. The specific religious survey looks in more detail at religious factors that operate among the people in the community. This survey looks at the awareness of the Gospel among people in the community, at their decision-making patterns, and their resistance/receptivity to the Gospel.

Survey the Awareness of the Gospel

The specific religious survey begins by seeking to comprehend the awareness of the Gospel among the residents of the community. In his book, *Contemporary Christian Communications*,[258] James Engel introduces a scale to measure the amount of Gospel knowledge and receptivity that people have. This scale indicates the following stages of Awareness:

8   Awareness of a Supreme Being but no Effective Knowledge of the Gospel

7   Initial Awareness of the Gospel

6   Awareness of the Fundamentals of the Gospel

5   Grasps the Implications of the Gospel

4   Positive Attitude Toward the Gospel

3   Personal Problem Recognition

2   Decision to Act

1   Decision and Faith in Christ

*   NEW CREATURE

+1 Post Decision Evaluation

+2 Incorporates into the Body

+3 Conceptual and Behavioral Grows

Although this scale should not be used in a rigid manner, it can contribute in several ways to the evangelistic task. First, this scale helps us to understand that all people are not in the same level with regard to their knowledge of the Gospel. There are people who have grown in an evangelical environment in which they have heard the word of God from their childhood. These people have a basic knowledge of the Gospel. In the Holy Scriptures, Timothy represents this group. Paul says: "from your childhood you have known the Holy Scriptures, which makes you wise unto the salvation through faith which is in Christ Jesus" (2 Tim. 3:15). On the other hand, there are people who do not know anything about the gospel. The Greeks in the Areopagus in Athens represent this group. They did not even know the true God, Creator of heaven and earth (Acts

17:24). There are, however, people who have some religious knowledge but have lived in a tradition that makes it difficult for them to understand the Gospel. Paul says that for the Jews, Christ's cross is a "*scandalon,*" a stumbling block, something that makes their comprehension of the Gospel difficult (1 Cor. 1:23). Even Nicodemus, who was convinced that Jesus "*had come from God*" (Jn 3:2), faced difficulty in understanding Jesus' message. He asked: "*How can these things be?*" It is important, therefore, to be aware of the fact that all the people are not at the same level of understanding with regard to the Gospel.

Second, this scale helps us to understand that often the decision to receive Christ is the result of a pilgrimage in which the person gradually understands and responds to the truths of the Gospel. This is seen in the case of the Samaritan woman (John 4). Notice the way in which she saw Jesus:

1. As a Jew "*How is it that you being a Jew,*" (a member of the cultural group hated by the Samaritans).

2. As a respected person "*Sir, you have nothing to draw with.*" (Jesus earned her respect by the way in which he treated her).

3. As a prophet "*I perceive that you are a prophet.*" (a religious man from whom she could learn).

4. As the Messiah "Is this not the Christ?"

Engel's scale and the experience of the Samaritan woman helps church starters understand that there are people who learn gradually about the Gospel and come to the experience of salvation by a pilgrimage Third, one dimension is implied in this scale and needs to be emphasized more clearly—the social dimension. The positive attitude toward the Gospel (in 4) in most cases relates to a feeling of trust toward the messenger. When it comes to spiritual matters, generally people do not listen to someone whom they do not trust. There is, therefore, the conceptual dimension (that which they know) and the social dimension (the trust that they have in the messenger).

The Engel Scale shows that, in many cases (especially when the listeners do not have an evangelical background or when they have negative feelings toward evangelicals), it is absolutely necessary to give attention to the social dimension. In other words, the church starting team has to earn the trust of the listeners before they are willing to hear the Gospel. Again, we want to caution the readers that this scale should not be used in a rigid manner, but it can help us to be aware of the fact that to the extent that we earn the respect and the trust of the people they will be more receptive to the Gospel.

Survey Decision Making Patterns

The second aspect of the specific religious survey considers the decision-making patterns among peoples in the community. The diagram that traces the process of making the decision to receive Christ provides an analytic tool that can help church starters consider what evangelistic methods might be more effective in specific communities. In his book, *Communicating Christ Cross Culturally*, David Hesselgrave makes a distinction between the ways in which a decision to receive Christ is perceived: 1) as a point; or 2) as a process.[259]

Hesselgrave shows that some perceive a decision to receive Christ as a point. He diagrams this concept as shown below on the next page. In the diagram the decision viewed as a point involves three steps: (1) Discovery; (2) Determination; and (3) Discipline. In the first step, the person discovers the truth of the Gospel: "Christ died to save me from my sins." In the second step, the person makes a determination to receive Christ in his heart. In the third step, the person joins the church and follows Christ in discipleship

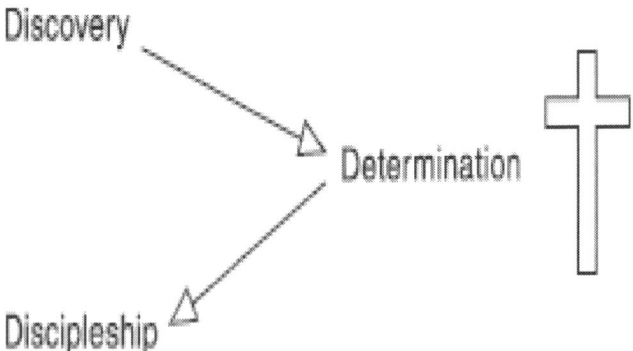

The second manner of perceiving the way in which a decision is made is as a process. This manner includes the steps mentioned already but has some intermediate steps: deliberation and dissonance. This process, therefore, includes: (1) Discovery; (2) Deliberation; (3) Determination; (4) Dissonance; and (5) Discipline. In this process the person discovers that Christ died for her. After this discovery, nevertheless, a period of deliberation follows: "Can it be true that I can attain salvation only by accepting Jesus as my Savior?" "What about the religious tradition of my family and friends that says something different?" "If I receive Christ, what will my family and friends say?"

If we continue to work with this person so that she will find answers to her questions and feel that in Christ she can find a spiritual family, very likely this person will progress toward the third step: "Determination" ("I am going to receive Jesus Christ as my Savior.") But this is not the end of the process. Often dissonance occurs: "Did I make the right decision?" In many cases dissonance is caused by pressure on the part of the relatives, friends, and neighbors. In other cases dissonance is caused by the divergence between that which they have heard in their previous religious tradition and what they are now hearing. If this dissonance is resolved in the mind and heart of the person, then he/she proceeds toward discipline (discipleship) by joining the church and living the Christian life. On the other hand, if this dissonance is not resolved, in many cases the person will stop attending the church and participating in the Bible study (or discipleship) group. This sometimes explains why, in certain sociocultural contexts, there are many "professions of faith" but very few baptisms.[260]

Decision as a process, according to Hesselgrave, can be diagramed:

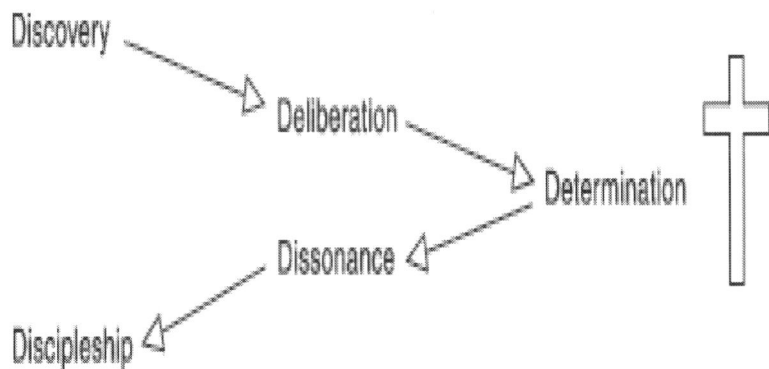

A comparative analysis of these two ways of perceiving the way in which decisions are made leads us to think that the first way (the decision as a point) perhaps describes the experience of many who have grown up in an evangelical home. From their childhood, they have heard the word of God. When they arrive at the moment in which they understand that Christ died for them, they make the decision of accepting him as Savior. Since they are surrounded by Christians (parents, Sunday School teachers, etc.) they receive significant amounts of affirmation and they do not go through extended periods of deliberation and dissonance.

The experience of those who have not grown in an evangelical home is, however, much more akin to the way of viewing decision- making as a process. This distinction has very important implications for the evangelistic methodology that the church starting team employs.

What are the implications of these two analytic tools for our church starting methodology? In the first place, if we recognize that all persons are not at the same level of understanding of the Gospel we should be willing to adapt our methodology to the socio- religious context of each person. Second, this means that there are persons who will not listen to the message of the Gospel unless they hear it from a person whom they trust. The implication of this is that in many cases, we will have to establish friendship ties through which the Gospel can be communicated. Third, this means that for many persons, due to their lack of knowledge of the Gospel message or their religious tradition, their pilgrimage toward Christ will include periods of serious deliberation and dissonance. The implication of this is that the believer will have to be patient and prepared to answer questions and help the person conquer her doubts and fears. For the church starter, knowing the type of community and the attitude toward the Gospel message of the target group can be of invaluable help in selecting the methods that will be utilized.[261]

Survey Resistance/Receptivity in the Community

One of the most crucial steps in analyzing a community through a specific religious survey involves discovering the reason why people are resistant or responsive to the gospel. Timothy C. Tennent provides help at this point when he places resistant people into four categories.[262] First, there are those who are "culturally resistant." These are the people that are resistant to change. "The truth claims of the Gospel cannot easily undermine a pre-existing cultural bias to accepting any new beliefs or practices. Although the evangelists restate the Gospel in a dozen ways, it still doesn't matter, because it represents change."[263] The church starter must seek a more culturally acceptable form for the unchanging Gospel.

Second, there are those who may be called "theologically resistant." "These groups ranging from Mormons to Muslims have been predisposed to reject certain Christian doctrines out of hand because of their own theological self-understanding which has been shaped by an explicit rejection of certain particulars of Christian theology, whether real or perceived, genuine or caricatured."[264] Church starters must seek out definite means to overcome these theological flash points if the community proves to have many in this category.

Third, some groups are "nationalistically or ethnically resistant." These people have established their national identity in connection with a particular religious entity. One example is the Protestants versus the Catholics of Ireland. Such a group's very identity, not theologically, but ethnically involves rejection of another group including their beliefs. Another example would be people in Thailand who consider that being a Thai is synonymous with being Buddhist and that any deviation from Buddhism marks one a traitor from Thailand. A local expression of Christianity is obviously imperative.

Fourth, there are those who are "politically resistant." This may include some who reject the presentation of the Gospel because it comes from a person whom the prospect considers to be a political or social rival. There are others, however, who have great difficulty gaining access to the presentation of the Gospel because their political leaders do not allow it. In each of these cases, church starters need to be trained to understand the nature of the resistance and to devise strategies to overcome the obstacles.

In every case, the path to effective evangelism among peoples who are programmed to resistance lies in achieving cultural relevance for the gospel presentation. To achieve this cultural relevance, church starters must exegete the community as well as the biblical text in order to communicate the meaning of the text to the target population in its cultural context.

Conclusion

Efforts at community analysis involve significant amounts of work. The various analyses of the community will, however, provide vital information that significantly influences the strategy that is employed to start a church in a given community. The demographic analysis will enable the church starter to know: (1) who lives in that community; (2) what racial, cultural and generational groups make up the population; (3) what their educational and socio-economic level is; (4) what the composition of the family is; (5) what types of dwellings they live in; (6) what trends are developing in the community; and (7) what the composition of the community will be like in the years to come.

The psychographic analysis provides invaluable information regarding the life styles of the people and will facilitate the development of a profile of the target person. This understanding contributes to a more specific focus on the strategies that are needed to reach the community. The general and specific religious surveys helps ascertain the number of churches that are found in the community, the approximate number of people from the community that they are reaching, and specific cultural and generational groups that are not being reached by any church.

The religious survey can help the church planter understand the peoples' awareness of the gospel, their decision making process, and the receptivity or resistance to the message. This analysis of awareness of the gospel can help church starters have a better idea of where to start in order to communicate the gospel. Assuming that they know much more than they do or that they are more receptive than they are may result in the utilization of methods that are counterproductive.

The survey of decision-making processes can enable the church starter to employ more effective strategies for evangelism and discipleship. Knowing what the prospects have to go through in their decision making process can help the church starter to be more sympathetic as well as effective in guiding people to make a decision to receive Christ as their personal Savior. Finally, the survey of reasons for resistance to the gospel can help the church starter to develop strategies that address and overcome the obstacles.

The interview of community leaders can yield valuable information on the types of people who live there, their needs, the most effective way to communicate with them, and even errors to avoid in relating to them. The survey of the people in the community can provide more specific information about the needs, preferences, and expectations of the people who live there. This survey can also assist in finding prospects for the new church and its ministries.

In general, we can affirm that the more church starters know about the communities and populations the more effective they will be in designing and implementing strategies. The investment in the process of identifying and selecting the target groups is time and money well spent. Neglect of this step in the church starting process greatly reduces effectiveness while attention to it enhances the starting of growing, effective, and reproducing congregations.

PART 3

Cultivate Community

One of the most important steps in the church starting process is that of establishing the initial core group that will help to start the new congregation. By this time the church starting team has already been put in place. It is essential, however, that others join the church starting team, share their vision, and have a willingness to participate in the activities that will contribute to the beginning and development of the new congregation. In some models the core group may be readily available. In other models, this core group will not be immediately available. It will be important, therefore, to be prepared to work with a core group that is provided, or in the case where this group is not available, to work toward the establishment of a newly formed core group.

CHAPTER 13

CORE GROUP

The core group is the nucleus of the new congregation. While the team members are a part of the core group, they are not the entire core group. The team members need to be seen as the staff of the congregation. The core group, however, is made up of the members around whom the new congregation will be built. After the church starter has enlisted the church starting team, attention will need to be given to the formation of the core group.

Enlist Core Group from Existing Churches

In discussing the Preparation Phase, we stated that core groups might be available in the Parenting and the Partnering models. In the case of the Parenting model, the sponsoring church may be willing to provide a number of people who are willing to join the church starting team in starting a new congregation. In the partnering model, several churches may be willing to encourage some of their members (perhaps those who already live in the target area) to join the church starting team. Cases may also arise in which churches that are not necessarily partnering with the church starting team may provide members who can help form a core group.

Several advantages obviously **adhere** to having a ready-made core group. These people would be mature Christians who have gifts and abilities. They also may experience in serving in leadership positions and often can contribute financially toward the budget of the emerging congregation.

Some potential disadvantages, however, exist in a ready-made core group. First, if the core group is totally different from the target group (e.g. socioeconomically) and is not willing to adapt, people from the community will not be attracted to the new fellowship. Second, if the core group and the church starting team are not compatible in such areas as worship style, church government, discipleship methodology, and leadership style, serious problems may arise in the new congregation. Another disadvantage that often arises with the core group is that of the core group assume and/or demand a place of extreme influence and almost domination in the church during the formative years.

It is of crucial importance, therefore, that the church starting team and the ready-made core group spend much time in prayer, fellowship, and dialogue in order to gain unanimity regarding their vision, goals, and methods. Unity in the new congregation is a major and significant matter.

Enlist Core Group from the Target Community

Some leaders have concluded that visitation evangelism is no longer effective under any circumstances. Perhaps this is due to the fact that they have experienced rejection while attempting to visit. This assessment does not mean, however, that visitation evangelism itself is a method that should be discarded. Different types of visitation are available. There is visitation of unknown persons, of well-known people, and of family members and close friends.

Also there are different purposes for visitation—to seek a decision; to gain acquaintance with the people and leave the open door for future visits; to offer a ministry of the church that relates to a need; and to deepen the friendship of a person that we already know with the purpose of sharing the message at an opportune time.

Obviously, if the community in general is resistant to the gospel, an evangelistic methodology, which has as its object getting a decision on the first visit, will not be successful. Such an approach might even solidify the resistance. Some people, however, may simply be resistant to the method that is being employed.

In many instances, cultivative visitation is proving to be quite productive. In this type of visitation the church starter concentrates on building relationships. This will generally require numerous informal visits to the same persons. At first the conversation can be very casual and can seek to get to know people better as well as to allow people to get better acquainted with the church starter. The church starter can take note of the receptivity of the individuals and concentrate on those who show more interest. This relationship can open the door to inviting them to a cultivative event and eventually to a church service.

As is true of other outreach efforts, cultivative visitation depends on volume. The church starter who uses the method of cultivative visitation will need to spend a significant amount of time visiting people that have already been contacted and getting to know new people. Though time consuming, this method often produces effective outreach.

In his book *Conspiracy of Kindness*[265] Steve Sjogren suggests a wide variety of ways by which church starters can contact people in their homes and minister to them in ways that open the path for the establishment of meaningful relationships. Among the activities that he lists are giving Mother's Day carnations, providing Sunday morning paper and coffee, delivering food to shut-ins, providing free house-number painting on curbs, giving light bulbs, providing blood pressure screening, organizing birthday parties, providing smoke detector batteries, giving Easter baskets, and cleaning houses.[266]

The utilization of these innovative methods stems from the conviction that "the Gospel must be spoken and shown to the watching world." This is a clear example of the fact that visitation can be a positive relation-building activity which opens the way for people to hear the message of salvation. Studies indicate a significantly larger retention rate when a personal contact has been established. Schaller explains: "If the initial invitation is delivered in person by the mission-developer pastor making a twenty-to-sixty minute visit, the vast majority of those who appear for the first worship service will become charter members."[267]

Conclusion

The core group whether enlisted from existing churches or from within the target community, holds crucial importance for the life and work of the new church. Finding and training this core group demands effort and no amount of effort and training is wasted motion. Finding and guiding the core group rests at the foundation of the new church.

By whatever method the core group is enlisted, one important factor assumes great importance. The core group should, from the beginning, be trained to eschew any proprietary feelings or attitudes toward the new church. Core groups have been known to insist on special places in and influence on the congregation. Even years after the new congregation has been started and is thriving, some core group members may expect most decisions be cleared with them. The core group needs to understand that the new church belongs to the Lord and that members of the core group are only members of the church, not the rulers of the congregation.

CHAPTER 14

COMMUNICATION METHODS

In the instances in which a ready-made core group is not available, the church starting team will need to gather a core group from the target community itself. At times, in its initial survey of the community, a church starting `team may find unchurched believers who are willing to become a part of the core group. In most instances, however, the church starting team will need to utilize methods geared at communicating with and evangelizing unbelievers.

Different peoples (and groups of people) respond differently to various communication methods. The church starting team must ascertain the most effective communication models for the people the new church is trying to reach. The demographic and psychographic information that has been gathered about the target group is, of course, most helpful in this search. Additional steps need to be taken, however, to get to know unchurched people in the community and involve them in activities that will facilitate evangelism and discipleship.

Some of the methods that are the most productive communication models include friendship evangelism, cultivative visitation, telemarketing, direct mail, and cultivative events. In each case, it is essential that the church starting team know what methods to utilize in order to communicate with and to reach people in the target community.

Select Appropriate Communication Methods

In his chapter, "Engaging Our Communities," Steve Canter emphasizes the importance of being culturally relevant. He explains:

> Being culturally relevant does not mean copying the ministries of other churches that are having great success. Instead, you should become a student of your community – learning the patterns and nuances of the community. Too often we try to do ministry in a context that is not ours, but a knockoff

of something read book or heard in a conference. Books, conferences and other forms of information-sharing are great. Use the experience of others as a creative spark, but think in ways to connect with your community.[268]

As stated earlier, differing peoples respond to differing modes of communication. The important step at this juncture of the church starting process relates to finding the communication modes most acceptable to the people to be reached. The church starter must select the most appropriate communication methods as based on the types of communities and the ways by which these communities process communication.

Types of Communities

For many church starters the most challenging (and most intimidating) task is that of contacting people and involving them in activities that will result in their becoming believers in Christ and members of the new church. Prospective church starters may have heard horror stories of rejection, indifference, and meager results. In some instances the problem may not have been resistance to the Gospel message itself but to the methods that were employed.

For instance, certain types of housing arrangements automatically insure that outsiders are not admitted. Gated communities may include such types of housing as condominiums, apartments, and cooperative subdivisions. Other housing arrangements, while not evidencing gates, have regulations that restrict access to the inhabitants. Obviously in these communities, door-to-door canvassing is not an option. Communication with outsiders, such as church starters, is limited by the physical hindrances of gates and regulations and church starting teams must find ways of effective communication with these people.

In addition to the physical arrangement of certain types of dwellings, certain social characteristics may limit communication to the residents and the church starter must take these characteristics into account when seeking to determine what communication methods to utilize. Studies done by two social workers indicate that various communities respond differently to the various communication methods.[269] For the purpose of this discussion we will classify communities under the following categories:

5. **INTEGRAL** – An integral community is cosmopolitan as well as a local center in which individuals are in close contact and share many concerns. They participate in activities of the larger community. This neighborhood has a self-identity, experiences significant interaction, and has linkages outside its own community.270

6. **PAROCHIAL** – A parochial community is a neighborhood that has a homogeneous character or ethnic identity. It is self-contained and independent of the larger community. This type of community has several ways to screen out what does not conform to its own norms. A parochial neighborhood has identity and interaction but no linkages.

7. **DIFFUSE** – A diffuse community is often a neighborhood with a homogeneous setting ranging from new subdivisions to inner-city housing projects. While the people have many things in common, there is no active internal life. It is not tied into the larger community and has little local involvement with neighbors. This neighborhood has identity but no interaction or linkages.

8. **TRANSITORY** – A transitory community is a neighborhood where population change has been occurring and may be broken down into little clusters of "old timers" and "new comers." Little collective action or organization takes place. This neighborhood may have some linkages but no identity or interaction.

9. **ANOMIC** – An anomic community is really a non-neighborhood. It is highly atomized (no cohesion, great social distance between people). It has no protective barriers to outside influences that make it responsive to some outside change. It lacks the capacity to mobilize for common action from within. There is a sense in which this type of neighborhood has no identity, interaction, or linkages.

A first step in communicating with the target community involves discovering the physical and social characteristics of the community that make the people available or unavailable, open or closed. The most effective types of communication cannot be selected until the church starter fully understands the type of community. Communication methods must be tailored to the community if effective communication is to result.

Community Communication

With these categories of types of communities in mind, we look at these communities from two perspectives: (1) information gathering, and (2) communicating information about the new church. Information gathering relates to gaining information about the community. Communicating information relates to sharing messages with the people.

When it comes to gathering information about the community, the church starter needs to answer the question as to what constitutes the most efficient way to get the needed information from the people in this community. The church starter cannot determine what type of church the community needs without this information about the people. Several methods are useful in determining which communication method for gathering information is the most appropriate for each neighborhood.

Information Gathering Methods

Church starters may use any one of four basic methods for gaining information. The door-to-door method visits each house and talks with the residents. A second method, mass media, involves advertisement through radio, television, newspaper, direct mail, and etc. The communication device known as "key local people" involves interviewing people who are leaders in the community. Random sample, a fourth communication method, calls for talking with a few selected people to get a general idea of the community.

The following chart indicates the more effective methods of gathering information in the five different types of communities. An "*" means that the method is the most effective for the community. A "No" signifies that the action is the least effective method in the community. A "+" shows the method to be somewhat effective or that this method may be effective as a follow up action.

	DOOR TO DOOR	MASS MEDIA	KEY LOCAL PEOPLE	RANDOM SAMPLE
INTEGRAL	NO	+	*	NO
PAROCHIAL	*	+	+	NO
DIFFUSE	*	+	NO	NO
TRANSITORY	*	+	NO	+
ANOMIC	*	NO	NO	+

It needs to be stated at the outset, that the purpose of this chart is primarily that of alerting the church starter to the fact that different types of methods need to be used in different types of communities. The chart provides some possible examples of ways in which people in the different communities might respond. The best procedure is to field-test a variety of methods in a given community.

Generally speaking, however, we can say that for an "Integral neighborhood," one of the most efficient ways to get information about the community is to contact "key local people." Having obtained that information, mass media such as direct mail or telephone contacts may be utilized to inform the community about the church that is being started. While door-to-door and random sampling may be acceptable in that community, these actions may not be the most efficient methods since the information may be more readily available through the key local people.

In the Parochial community a door-to-door survey, which focuses on the specific needs of that socio-cultural group, may be very helpful. Mass media can also be helpful especially if it focuses on meeting the specific needs of this community. Finding key local people who identify with and understand this neighborhood can also provide valuable information.

Due to the fact that the people in the Diffuse neighborhood have little involvement with their neighborhoods, the two more effective methods of information gathering may be door-to-door and mass media. In the Transitory neighborhood the degree of rapid change that is occurring may make it difficult to find key local people who know enough about the community to be of help. Door-to-door, mass media, and random sampling actions may be useful in this type of community.

The great heterogeneity that exists in the Anomic neighborhood may indicate that only door-to-door and random sampling actions will reveal information about the people in that community. The important feature remains that the church starter must understand the nature of the community before information about the community can be obtained.

Once information about the community is in the church starter's hands, attention can be directed to the most effective ways to communicate or share information with that type of community.

Communicating Information

In addition to obtaining information, it is necessary to communicate with people in the neighborhood about the new church that is being started. As the church starter must adapt the method of gaining information about the community to the type of community so must he/she adapt the method of dispensing information to the type of community. In some of the neighborhoods (e.g., Transitory and Anomic) the door-to-door method may be the most effective action. In others types of communities, the mass media approach (e.g., direct mail, telephone) may be the only feasible way.

Church starters may need to develop their own categories of community types and the actions most suitable for each. The following chart, which follows the same nature as the preceding, suggests the more effective communication strategies for various types of communities.

Communication Methods among Communities

	DOOR TO DOOR	MASS MEDIA	KEY LOCAL PEOPLE	RANDOM SAMPLE
INTEGRAL	+	NO	+	*

PAROCHIAL	+	*	+	+
DIFFUSE	NO	*	+	NO
TRANSITORY	NO	*	+	NO
ANOMIC	NO	*	NO	NO

This material establishes a principle that church starters must discover the type of community in which they will be working and must develop an appropriate communication strategy for that community. The information given is illustrative only. Each church starter must seek information about the community and must seek to communicate with the people in what that worker finds to be the most effective means available. The study of the community and the means of communication will guide the church starting team to select the most effective and appropriate means

Utilize Appropriate Media

Obviously, certain communication methods are more effective in certain types of communities than in others. In like manner, some types of media are more useful in some types of communities. Media utilization, if properly adjusted to the type of community, can be a powerful tool in reaching the geographical community.

Numerous types of media tools are proving effective to reach people and start new congregations. Among these are telemarketing, direct mail, radio, television, tracts, audiocassettes, films, videocassettes, and computers.

Telemarketing

In some cities the telephone is being utilized as a very effective way to find prospects for the new church. The telephone can be utilized to invite the people to cultivative events like a film series on the family, a drama (Nativity, Resurrection), a conference on money management introduced by a well-known person in the community, a musical program related to a special day celebration, etc. The church starting effort can obtain and use a conference room in a hotel for a celebration to reach those who are not related with a church and to attract to people who might not attend a church. After these unchurched persons know the believers they can more easily accept invitations for Bible studies in a home or in the church building.

Perhaps to date the most effective use of the telephone has been done in connection with the going public phase of a church starting project.[271] Norm Whan's *The Phone's for You* has been used to start over 2,500 churches in America and other countries.[272]

Following his plan, people are called, informed briefly of a new church start in their area, and asked if they would be willing to receive a brochure with information. Those who give a positive reply receive the information through the mail and a telephone call reminding them of the grand opening of this new church.

At least ten factors contribute to the effectiveness of this type of phone effort. It is mandatory that: (1) a large number of calls be made, (2) what is said over the telephone be appropriate, (3) the people be reminded of the date of the meeting, (4) the first meeting be well planned, (5) the second meeting be creatively planned, (6) a follow-up strategy be designed in advance, (7) the pastor and team be enthusiastic about this approach, (8) a large enough ministry team be assembled in advance to minister to those who respond, (9) the team be committed to use additional methods (visitation, direct mail, personalized phone calls), and (10) this effort be bathed in prayer.

The first factor requires many telephone calls. In some church starting efforts the team has made more than twenty thousand telephone calls. At first this sounds like something totally impossible but if the task is divided into four weeks this means that they will make five thousand calls per week. This procedure demands that they will make one thousand calls per day. If the one thousand calls are divided by ten, each of the ten people will make a hundred calls per day. If they enlist twenty people, each person will have to make only fifty calls which would take less than two hours per day. Again, this seems like an impossible task, but if the effort enlists a good number of people the thousands of calls can be made in the course of a month.

The second factor is that what is said over the telephone is of vital importance. The conversation, consequently, should be brief and courteous. The person who makes the telephone call should identify himself/herself immediately. In many cases it helps for those who are going to participate in this effort to come up with a name for their group that does not drive away the listeners before they have the opportunity to know this group.

After identifying himself/herself, the person who is calling can invite the people for an activity that has been planned. Those persons expressing interest can be asked if they would be willing to receive a free ticket, an invitation, or a letter with information about this activity. If the people indicate that they would be willing to receive this information, time can be taken to be sure that the name and the address are correct. In many cities this information is in the telephone directory but it is helpful to confirm that this information is correct. If a criss-cross directory can be obtained, it will be more useful in that it will list the occupants by streets instead of the alphabetical order found in the ordinary telephone directories.

The third factor is that it is important that the people who have indicated that they would be willing to receive information receive a note or a telephone call reminding them of the meeting. In some places people have reported that ten percent of the people who receive the calls are willing to receive information about the meeting. This means that if they call twenty thousand people, two thousand will be willing to receive information. It is calculated that of these two thousand people, in general, around ten percent, or about 200, will attend the first meeting. But it also means that there will be eighteen hundred people whom the church starter can consider prospects and whom he/she can follow up by inviting them to other meetings.

The fourth factor that we have mentioned is that the first meeting will have to be well planned. This means that the planners will do everything possible so that the people will have a positive experience. All that is done will need to keep the visitors in mind. This has implications for the arrangement of the meeting place, the program, and the reception of the visitors. Plans for future meetings need to be made so that information about these can be given at the first meeting.

The fifth factor is that the second meeting must be creatively planned. The telemarketing effort has succeeding in attracting the people to the meeting place for the first service, but will they return? It is generally expected that the number of those who attend the second service will drop off significantly (at times by 50 percent). Some who will not return may do so because they had different expectations of what the service would be like (e.g. too large, too small, too lively, too traditional, too impersonal, too long, too serious). The church starter may not have control over some of these factors but he may be able to do some things that will attract people to the second service.

Lyle Schaller offers excellent suggestions on how to have a successful second meeting. Among these are: (1) to make a large number of calls for the second week; (2) to invite a nationally known minister as guest preacher for that second service; (3) to make a personal phone call to every household represented at that first service and every household where one or more members were absent that first week; (4) to schedule the first Sunday on Palm Sunday on the assumption that the natural appeal of Easter will produce a larger crowd the following Sunday; (5) to prepare for a smaller crowd on succeeding Sundays and respond creatively and positively to the negative psychological implications of shrinking attendance following the first Sunday; (6) to identify, enlist and train a cadre of volunteers to design and staff a full-scale Sunday morning program that will not only make the most of those first timers who want to return but also will attract additional first time visitors; (7) to make sure that every potential first time attender is called on by a staff member or trained volunteer before the first Sunday (second meeting) so everyone will be greeted personally by someone who had met them earlier."[273]

The sixth factor is that the church-starting effort develops an effective follow-up strategy. In order to develop this follow-up strategy the church starter needs to anticipate who will respond to this telephone effort and to establish the ministry team in advance of the effort. The new church must avoid false advertising. While the church may not advertise falsely intentionally, if it does not have a well-planned follow-up program, it may give the impression that it promised more than it delivered.

According to Schaller, among those who will respond will be:

(1) dropouts and inactives who are persuaded by the friendly telephone call to return to church; (2) lonely people who seek acceptance and comfort and want to be loved; (3) venturesome people who are attracted to a new challenge; (4) newcomers to the community who have not found a church yet; (5) adults with psychological problems and who are seeking one-to-one counseling; (6) people who have felt they were rejected by other churches because of lifestyle, race, physical disabilities or their belief system; (7) church goers who are dissatisfied with their own church; (8) people on a religious pilgrimage who are attracted by the possibility that this new mission will become a destination for them.[274]

It is a reasonable assumption that people who respond to an impersonal method such as the telephone are usually people who are experiencing a deep sense of need. The implication of this is that a ministry needs to be provided for them if they are to continue relating to the new congregation. This calls for much creativity and flexibility. For example, support groups may be just as important as the Home Bible Study groups. Another implication is that new people need to be oriented as to the vision and ministry of the new church just as the original core group was. Failure to do this may result in numerous problems in the future of the church.

A seventh factor is that the pastor and the church starting team must be enthusiastic about this method. While this can be a very successful method, it is not an easy one. Many people will need to be enlisted, trained, encouraged, and guided. Some will be tempted to skip some of the vital steps. The enthusiasm of the pastor and the team will be needed to keep the people motivated and on course.

An eighth factor is that a sufficiently large ministry team is going to be needed to minister to those who respond and start attending the new church. The pastor may need to recruit many volunteers for the different ministries.

A ninth factor is that there must be a commitment to use additional methods. The initial telephone call may get the attention of the unchurched. In order to keep their attention, letters will need to be sent, visits will need to be made, brochures will need to be given, and other means of informing and staying in touch will need to be devised. No single media instrument can accomplish the job by itself. A carefully planned combination is imperative.

The tenth factor is that the telephone effort will need to be bathed in prayer. Because the telephone call invades their privacy, some recipients will be irate, rude, vulgar, and mean. It will not be easy for the callers to put up with this without getting discouraged. It must be acknowledged that reaching the unchurched involves a spiritual battle. It is important to mobilize the intercessory team to pray fervently for the recipients as well as the callers that the Lord might use this medium to reach many with the message of the gospel.

Likely, a good number of adaptations may need to be made to a telephone event. These adaptations involve the time in which the calls are made, what is said over telephone, the type of activities that are planned, the mail out that reminds the people about the meeting, etc. It is important to note, however, this or similar methods can put the church starting team in touch with thousands who are spiritually hungry. Many are skeptical of telemarking methods but they have proved effective in many areas.

Direct Mail

Some groups have utilized direct mail in much the same way as the telemarketing effort that we described above. Rick Warren and his small core group sent out 15,000 letters to their target community. On Easter Sunday, two hundred five people attended.[275] This marked the start of the public ministry of their church. The Christian and Missionary Alliance (C&MA) started 101 churches on Easter Sunday, 1987, mostly through direct mail advertising.[276] Many others have utilized direct mail in connection with their church starting efforts.

These efforts have had more success when the following factors have been considered. First, a survey of the needs in the community must be made and the activities that are planned take these needs into account. For example, if the survey reveals great concern on the part of the people in the community for the well-being of their families, the wise church starter will implement films and conferences that address this need.

Second, that which was said about the telephone survey applies to this method also. A large number of letters is needed to ensure a good number of people respond in a positive way. The C&MA budgeted the postage for 30,000 hand-addressed letters to be sent in each church start. A good number of volunteers are needed to address the letters.

Third, the letter should be written in an attractive way utilizing the vocabulary that the people understand. Fourth, letters can be sent inviting people to a wide variety of activities. Some of these can be for special celebrations such as Christmas and Easter dramas, others can be invitations to participate in special support groups, others can be for special seminars (e.g. money management, parenting, marriage enrichment), others can be to invite people to participate in special task forces relating to ministries in the church or the community. These could be precursors to the letter inviting people to the grand opening of a church. Fifth, there will need to be much preparation so that the activities create a good impression in the minds of the visitors. Sixth, as is true with all mass media, letters will need to be sent periodically to capture the attention and earn the trust of the people. Repetition can bring results.

For some church starting teams direct mail may be somewhat less threatening in that they will not have to put up with rude people. Also, this may be more effective in areas where a large percentage of the residents have unlisted telephone numbers. The results that have been obtained with this method of communication are similar to those in the telephone surveys. This means that there are communities in which this method has been more effective than in others. In designing a direct mail effort, cultural, socioeconomic, and religious factors will need to be taken into account.

Radio Spot Announcements

In addition to telemarketing and direct mail, church starters can use numerous other media in contacting prospects for the new congregation. One of these media is the radio station that allows spot announcements regarding Bible studies and other activities. The use of the radio has several advantages. It is generally available in most communities. It is widespread in that people listen to it in many different settings (home, car, work, outings). It is relatively inexpensive, especially if it is used for spot announcements. It has credence, especially if the announcement is well done.

Yet another advantage to the use of radio is that it can be targeted to specific audiences. For example, a radio station (or program) that concentrates on playing the "golden oldies" is focusing on more mature adults and not young people. The opposite may be true of stations that play rock and roll music most of the time. Knowing the target audience of the radio station (or program) can help to determine which stations to utilize.

Some limitations exist to the use of the radio, and the church starter must keep these in mind and overcome. First, the radio is impersonal which means that a way of doing follow-up needs to be established. The church starting team can accomplish this follow- up by having people call in or write to request prayer, literature, and other items offered in the radio message. A second limitation is the transient nature of the message. This means that the message needs to be presented on a continuing basis for a specific period of time and changed from time to time.

Television Spot Announcements

Television is another possible medium for both programs and spot announcements. The use of television has the following advantages. First, it is both audio and visual, and people tend to remember better what they have both seen and heard. Second, television covers a large area, which means that many people will get the message simultaneously.

Using television, however, has some limitations one of the greatest is cost. The more concentrated the area the greater the cost. This can be overcome by utilizing cable television, by using only short spot announcements, by using public service time, or by creating newsworthy events that the television station will cover on its own.

Another limitation of using television is that it requires more skills than the radio. This requirement may demand additional training on the part of the church starter or the designated person. While the use of television is more challenging, it can be a useful tool in contacting unchurched people. A Baptist group in Buffalo, New York ran thirty-second T.V. spot announcements for two weeks offering a free correspondence Bible study focusing on the family. They received around one thousand calls of people wanting to enroll. Three new congregations were started with the clusters of neighborhood Bible studies that were established. A group in Rochester, New York had a very similar experience.[277]

Audio Cassettes and CDs

Some church starters have utilized audiocassettes success-fully. Some of the advantages of using this medium are that they are inexpensive, flexible (produce many or few), and they can be played over and over. Another advantage is that cas-settes cover a wide variety of subjects, some of which may be especially suited for the needs of some of the families in the community (drug addiction, parenting, family fragmentation, etc.).

Some of the limitations are that the cassettes must be transported or mailed. In one sense, however, transporting the cassettes may be an advantage in that this provides greater opportunity for repeated contact with people being cultivated. Another limitation may be the maintenance of equipment (cassette players) if this is provided.

Tracts

Tracts can also be a very useful medium for starting the seed of the gospel in the hearts of unchurched people. Several things must be kept in mind in the use of tracts. First, they must be attractive in their presentation. This does not neces-sarily mean that they need to be very expensive but only that creativity has been utilized in preparing them. Second, tracts must be culturally relevant. This means that they need to ad-dress a subject that is of interest to the target audience and must be presented in such a way that it captures their attention. Third, tracts must have a single purpose.

Generally people will not read a tract that has too much in-formation on a wide variety of subjects. In church starting, the basic purpose is to get people to think about their relationship with God and how this new church can help them with this. Fourth, tracts need to provide a means of response. This can be a telephone number or an address that the recipients can use to obtain additional information.

Films

Films can also be used to reach people in church starting. The use of films has the following advantages. They are generally very persuasive, they cover many subjects, and they can be used in-or outdoors. Films, also have the advantage of providing an opportunity for people to respond immediately afterwards, be it to an invitation to receive Christ or to participate in a discussion group, which may lead to the formation of a Bible study.

Some of the limitations in using films are that it can be expensive to rent the film and the place in which it will be shown. Another limitation is that often there are not enough local films, which means that they may not be as culturally relevant as they should be. It must be kept in mind, however, that films (such as the *Jesus* film) are producing wonderful results in many parts of the world.

Videos

Church starters are also using videocassettes very successfully. Some of the advantages of using videos are that they create interest, especially if they focus on subjects that are of vital concern to the target community. Second, videos can lend themselves very naturally to the formation of discussion or support groups, especially if listening guides are provided and an opportunity is given for people to converse about their concerns and questions.

Yet another advantage of videocassettes is that they can be used repeatedly. Some church starters set up a library type operation allowing people to check out the various videos. This again provides additional opportunities for the church starting team to be in contact with the target audience. In a similar fashion, books and magazines can be checked out. Some use video cassettes to recruit core group members. The video will share the vision for the type of church that is being established and challenge people to become a part of this exciting endeavor.

Electronic Media

In addition to the methods that we have already discussed, the following media are gaining increasing usage in contacting unchurched people: Websites, Online Tracts, E-Mail, Discussion

Boards, Chatroom/Instant Messaging, Blogs/Vlogs, Social Networking/Microbloging, Gaming Evangelism, Pod Casting, etc.[278] These and other emerging tools are being used to communicate of the gospel to ministry focus groups locally and around the world. In each of these cases, as in those discussed above, it is important that the church starter have the following information about the target audience: lifestyles and needs, spiritual condition, decision making styles, and cultural norms and values.

Emphasize Precision Harvesting

Precision harvesting essentially is a filtering process which enables the church planter to utilize a variety of media efforts in a manner that focuses on those who show receptivity to the Gospel message. David Garrison explains:

> Precision harvesting uses "response filtering" to identify and locate individuals who have already made a positive response to the Gospel and then places longer-term workers in direct contact with them for discipleship follow-up and church planting... Working with radio broadcasters or other agents of mass evangelism, the missionary church planter is able to glean the names and addresses of respondents to another's sowing ministry then position himself in the midst of these new believers or seekers, he is able to begin to begin a discipling and church planting ministry. The ministry of precision harvesting can save years in the process of starting a church or multiple churches.[279]

A Strategy Coordinator explains the concept of precision harvesting.[280] He bases the concept on Matthew 10:16 "I am sending you out like sheep among wolves. Therefore be as shrewd as snakes and as innocent as doves." He then pointed out that:

- Jesus identified His target people (Matthew 15:24).

- *Jesus sowed the Word of God on a wide scale (Luke 9: 1-2, 6).*

- *Jesus employed a sifting tool (Matthew 13:3-17).*

- *Jesus focused his time and love on faithful disciples (John 17:4-8).*

- *Jesus committed the remaining task of evangelism to the new church leaders (Matthew 28:18-20).*

The Strategy Coordinator explains that Precision Harvesting takes place when you:

- Identify your target people,

- Sow the Word of God on a wide scale,

- Employ a sifting tool

- Focus your time and love on faithful disciples, and

- Commit the remaining task of evangelism to the new church leaders.[281]

This process involves the utilization of events and activities that attract the largest number of people possible and then filtering (sifting) those who show receptivity. An example of this is a newspaper ad for free ESL that reaches 120,000; of these 1,250 attend; then 400 watch J-film in small groups; of these 200 (in 20 groups) attend Bible study (evangelistic); then 65 attend Bible study for new converts. While the number of respondents will vary significantly from one area to another and the media as well as the activities may be different, the principle of focusing time and love on those who show receptivity is essential.

It is important to keep several things in mind in utilizing this "layered filtering" process:

- Key is feedback loop.

- Begin modeling while they are still unbelievers.

- It is more effective to group unbelievers and win them than win individuals and group them.

- Start multiple groups whenever possible.

- As much as possible, reference the available media in all other media.

- This might include: TV, videotapes, radio programs, tracts, Scripture, newspapers, audio cassettes, lectures, websites, e-mail, snail mail, personal witness, leaflets on how to start groups, etc.[282]

An example of a person who would be led through this process is someone who had limited or no knowledge of the Gospel and a negative attitude toward Christianity. This person may receive an interesting tract that catches his attention. In the tract there is information about a radio program that he can hear. The radio program provides him an opportunity to have a face to face meeting with a Christian. This leads to the person watching the Jesus Film. This may motivate the person to attend a Bible reading group. This leads to his participation in an evangelistic Bible study. This leads to his decision to receive Christ and follow him in the fellowship of a group of believers.[283]

Obviously the events and activities may vary significantly from one place to another. The process, however, of linking materials, contacts, and events in a strategic manner can contribute toward a person moving from total ignorance of and resistance to the Gospel to making an informed decision to follow Christ.

CHAPTER 15
COMMUNITY EVENTS

Cultivative events provide one of the best ways to introduce the new church to the community and to inform people of the new congregation. These gatherings allow people to get acquainted with the church starting team, to check them out, and to develop a level of trust. Conversely the church starting team can get a better idea of the needs of the guests and encourage them to become involved in the emerging congregation. The church starting team can plan cultivative activities specifically for children, youth, and adults.

Cultivative Events for Children and Youth

Certain cultivative events for children and youth can be instrumental in evangelizing them as well as their parents. In this section we will mention some of these activities and we will explain how they can be adapted especially for the establishment of new congregations. These include the Vacation Bible School, backyard Bible clubs, activities for recreational groups, voluntary tutors, special presentations, and arts and handcraft festivals.[284]

Activities with Recreational Groups

Some church starters have been successful in utilizing recreational groups to cultivate the friendship of the parents as well as of their children. This method involves the formation of teams such as soccer, baseball, basketball, and other sports. This could include table games such as ping-pong and paper and pencil games. These teams play with other teams formed by the volunteers of the church.

Social recreation such as parties, fellowships, banquets, receptions, and picnics can also be a part of these cultivative activities. Additional outdoor recreation such as hiking, backpacking, day camp, and adventure recreation can also be included. The significant thing is that they not only have these recreational activities, but rather, before these competitions they have Bible studies, dialogues, and prayer with the children. In addition to this they invite the parents to meetings in which small trophies are given to the children. In these meetings they take the opportunity to invite the parents to participate in Bible studies.

Purchasing equipment and having special days when children and young people can come and participate in recreational activities contribute to cultivating the community. Community leaders and parents appreciate a place for their children and youth that is away from the dangers and influences of exploiting adults, youth gangs, and other negative influences. These activities can provide a much- needed ministry in the community as well as an opportunity to develop friendships and share the Gospel.

Vacation Bible School

The original purpose of the Vacation Bible School was to provide additional instruction for the children of the church. Later, many churches realized that this could be a very effective method for the evangelization of children who are not a part of the family of the church. In more recent years church starters have been using this method in the process of starting new congregations. In order to employ this method for church starting the church starter must consider some necessary adaptations.

In the first place, a church starting group can have several Vacation Bible Schools. One VBS can be held in their own community and another in the community where they are projecting the establishment of a new congregation. This strategy means that the content of the lessons will have to be more basic and geared for unchurched children.

In the second place, in some extremely resistant areas the name "Vacation Bible School" may cause a reaction and will demand a change. In these instances, the church starter needs to find a name that projects a positive image so that a greater number of children will participate. Perhaps such names as "Summer Character Enrichment Conference" or "Summer Bible Course to Strengthen the Family" could communicate a positive message to the parents in the community.

In the third place, the activities of the Vacation Bible School may include special presentations to which the church starter can invite the parents, grandparents, and other family members of the children. Some, for example, have musical programs, dramas, and graduation during the worship service on Sunday. After these presentations the pastor can present a sermon explaining how the study of the Word of God can help the family to attain true peace, harmony, and happiness. The pastor can invite the parents to participate in a series of Bible studies about the family. This can be the beginning of an adult Bible study fellowship.

Bible Clubs

The Bible Club method has had significant success, and is usually held in the backyard of the homes, recreation areas, patios, or other meeting places in the community where one is planning to establish a congregation. The format of the sessions of the Bible Club is similar to that of Vacation Bible School. The primary difference is that instead of having the activities during the course of a week, they have them one day a week (e.g. Saturday mornings) for several weeks (sometimes throughout the entire summer vacation).

One advantage of this method is that it provides an opportunity to get to know the parents of the children with the possibility of involving them in activities related to the establishment of a new congregation. The Bible Club approach also allows for extended time with the children who attend. Church starters see the Bible Club approach as opening doors to the entire community—children and adults.

Afternoon Sunday Schools

One church that was interested in starting new congregations began by having afternoon Sunday schools in the recreational areas or activities rooms in multi-housing, apartment communities. These meetings generally began with recreational activities and then divided the children and young people into classes for Bible study and fellowship. The parents appreciated the Sunday schools so much that after a time classes for adults were started.

An exciting feature of the effort was that on Sunday evenings, the teachers reported the attendance of their afternoon classes to the sponsoring church and the total attendance was tabulated as part of the church's overall attendance. Within a year, the Sunday school attendance of this church went from one hundred to over five hundred. These afternoon Sunday school classes became the nucleus for the starting of three congregations in different parts of the city.

Volunteer Tutors

In some communities a program of volunteer tutors to help the children who are having problems with their studies has produced good results. In general, these classes can be held in a home, a library or other place where individual instruction to children and young people is possible. This program can help the children to complete their school assignments and to have a better understanding of the subjects they are studying.

Volunteer tutoring efforts usually increase the reputation of the new church effort in the community. This ministry also provides opportunity for the volunteer tutors to get to know the parents of the children. The tutors can invite the parents to participate in Bible studies or other cultivative events in the community.

Dramatic Arts

A church that wanted to establish a new congregation in a community sent their music director and some youths to enlist the community's children to rehearse and present a concert at the end of the summer vacation at a park adjacent to the church. Going from house-to- house, the group invited the children to rehearse for two hours each Saturday morning with the purpose of presenting the musical concert. A good number of parents who were interested in their children's cultural development gave them permission. The children became familiar with the director and his assistants and began to speak to them about their problems and challenges. The director and his assistants advised the children and shared with them their testimonies of conversion.

When the night of the concert arrived, many parents attended and were very pleased with their children's presentation. This event provided the opportunity for the director and his assistants to invite the parents to participate in a series of conferences about the family. As a result of the friendship ties that were established, a Bible study was begun around which a new congregation formed.

This same idea can be used for dramas, puppet shows, and other presentations that provide opportunities to cultivate friendships with children and young people. The presentations also provide opportunities to become acquainted with and invite their parents and extended families to these cultivative events and to the church.

Arts and Handcraft Festivals

A similar idea to the musical concert is that of an arts festival and handcrafts demonstration. This method involves enlisting the children and youth in a class every Saturday morning during the summer to learn to paint and to make other handcrafts. At the end of the summer, a festival is held in a public place to exhibit the handcrafts prepared by the children. The friendship ties that have been established with the children and their parents can be utilized to invite them to participate in other activities through which one can communicate the gospel.

Other activities that have been successful are: a mobile library with special books for the children; evening musical concerts, games, and devotionals for the children and youth; and field days for the children. Many other activities allow the church starting team to cultivate the children's friendship and that of their parents with the purpose of communicating the message of salvation.

Kite Flying Competition

Some church starters have invited large numbers of children to an open field and asked them to bring their kites. Those who do not have kites are either given the kites or helped to make one. At the appropriate time, judges are selected to decide which kites are the best in various categories. This event enables church starters establish meaningful relationships with the children and their parents.

Sports Clinics

Some church starters have invited Christian athletes, who have distinguished themselves in sports, to participate in events to help cultivate the community. These athletes spend time training children to improve their skills in their preferred sport. The parents of the children are also invited to attend. At an intermission, one of the athletes gives a personal testimony and invites the people to participate in on-going activities every week. These events often open the door to start Bible studies and other activities that can lead to the starting of a new congregation.

Church starters will seek various avenues to cultivate the area in which the new congregation will begin its services.

Cultivative Events for Adults

In addition to the cultivative events for children and young people, other activities for adults also contribute to cultivating friendships and sowing the seed of the Gospel. These activities include a Film Festival, Evening with a Purpose, Welcome Committee, and Bible Drawing.

Film (Video) Festival

The Film Festival approach involves renting a series of Christian movies that deal with topics that are related to community needs. This presentation can consist of, for example, a series of movies about the family. The movies can be presented on the night the Bible Study is being planned. After showing the movies, there can be a time of discussion in which one can give attention to questions and comments.

Some have printed a ticket that has information about the movie (e.g. title, time, and place). Additionally, the sponsoring group provides space on the ticket stub for people to write information about their names and addresses, indicate if they would like to receive a visit and/or more information on the subject of the film, and to participate in a Bible study. This ticket, then, provides the opportunity to continue cultivating the persons and encouraging them to participate in a Bible Study. At the end of the presentation of this film series an announcement can be made of the topics that will be dealt in the Bible study that will be begun the following week.

Marriage Enrichment Retreat

Often a community survey will reveal that there are many

couples that are having marital difficulties or that do not have as strong a commitment to their marriage as they should. A marriage enrichment retreat can strengthen these couples as well as provide opportunities for church starters to develop meaningful relationships with unchurched people and lead them to become a part of the fellowship of the emerging group.

Evening with a Purpose

The program "Evening with a Purpose" has been designed especially for people who need to hear a gradual presentation of the Gospel from someone whom they trust. This program consists of seven steps. The first step involves inviting and training people from the church to know how to cultivate the friendship of people who are not believers. This experience helps the church people increase their abilities to give their testimonies and to share the message of salvation by dialoging with the prospects.

The second step consists of inviting a person to share his/her testimony relating the testimony to a life experience. This testimony will have to be told in such a way that those who are not believers can understand it. In other words, they will need to leave out theological and religious words that only those who are church members can understand.

The third step involves inviting friends who are not believers to our homes for an "Evening with a Purpose" at which time the group will discuss how to find true happiness in life. When the guests arrive (it is good that there be a similar number of church members and non-believers), one can introduce the people and there can be a time of informal conversation.

The fourth step consists of introducing the person that has been invited to speak about the topic: "How I found true happiness in life." This can include a description of his life before knowing Christ; how he got to know Him; and how his life has changed since having this experience.

The fifth step consists of serving refreshments and providing an opportunity for the church members to converse informally with the guests asking them what they think about the experience that the person shared with them. This informal time, in many cases, provides an opportunity for church members to answer questions and to ascertain the degree of interest the guests hold in regard to spiritual matters. This process can be repeated in other meetings— inviting different people to share their testimonies. This effort can sow the seed of the Gospel in the hearts of people that generally would not visit an evangelical church nor participate in a Bible study.

Newcomers Welcome Team

Some groups have had good results with a program that has the purpose of welcoming the new people who are moving to the community where one is starting a congregation. This program involves preparing a packet that has information about the community. This can include things like hospitals, medical clinics, schools, libraries, and other institutions that are of importance to the community. This package can include information about the city, the climate, the principal industries, highways, etc. Sometimes this information can be obtained from the Chamber of Commerce.

This packet can also include information about the Bible study in the community and of other ministries to the community. Carrying this information to the new people of the community can open the door to cultivate friendships and involving them in Bible study. Sometimes the packet also contains some small gift of food such as cake or candy.

The church starting team can obtain information about community newcomers from newspapers, utility companies, moving companies, and real estate agencies. It is better if this service is given very soon after the people enter the community.

The first week marks the ideal time to welcome the new residents. The contact can lead to enlistment in the new church, as people who are moving are often open to new experiences and relationships. In addition to the help this method provides for the church starting team, it also helps the newcomers to feel more welcome to the community.

Free Bible Drawing

Some church starters have utilized the method of a free Bible drawing to find people who are interested in participating in a Bible study. This drawing has been promoted in the following manner. First step, buy a big and attractive Bible. Second step, obtain permission to set up a table with a sign in a place in the community where the people gather (e.g. in a market place, a shopping center, a mall, a recreation park, an apartment complex). Third step, get people from the mother church to encourage the people to fill out the card with their name and address. This action can provide the opportunity to converse with the people about a Bible study that will be held in the community. Fourth step, at the appointed date, have the drawing and deliver the Bible to the person who wins it. Fifth step, give a New Testament as a "consolation prize" to all the people that signed up for the drawing.

While delivering these New Testaments, encourage the people to participate in the Bible study in the community. Offer other biblical materials to these people. Church starters have enrolled a good number of people into Bible study through this method.

Prayer Survey

Another method to find people who are interested in a Bible study group is the prayer survey. This can be done in two ways: (1) with family and friends, or (2) by visiting the communities. This method involves conversing with the people and explaining to them that there is a group of people who is devoted to prayer and explaining that the group will be presenting to the Lord the petitions of the people. The church starting team can then ask the people if they have some need or concern for which this prayer group can pray.

In order for this method to be effective there needs to be a group of people in the church that is devoted to fervent prayer. Also there needs to be a group of people that is willing to visit the people of the community to find out what the needs are and to listen to, encourage, and pray for the people that have urgent needs. The primary purposes of this method are to know the people, earn their trust, and involve them in a Bible study.

Tent Community Outreach

Church starters in one area rented a tent that accommodated around five hundred people and erected it in a lot right in the middle of the target group they were trying to reach. After extensive advertisement, the church starting team conducted morning activities with children such as Vacation Bible School. In the afternoon they conducted activities for the youth. The evening activities targeted the adults primarily and consisted of Bible studies, testimonies, music, and evangelistic sermons.

The church starting group held activities every day and night during the summer. By the end of this period a sufficiently large core group had developed to the point that an adjacent auditorium was leased and a congregation was established. The tent outreach can obviously be held in any number of facilities all having the goal of establishing the core group for the new church.

Community Organization Events

The church starting team can promote numerous community organization events that can allow the church starters to participate in efforts to organize the community. This community organization allows the church starting team to participate in addressing specific needs and in the process become known by the community. This relationship, in turn, can enable the church to start home Bible studies as an initial church starting activity.

One church starter, for instance, noticed that there was a great deal of concern due to a rash of break-ins and burglaries in the community he was targeting for a church start. He, therefore, went to the police station and obtained the information and forms that are needed to set up a Crime Watch Program in the community. Since this type of program requires setting up a neighborhood organization, the church starter went from house-to-house inviting the people to a meeting at which the program was going to be discussed. Due to the fact that the residents saw him as a person who was trying to help the community, they welcomed him gladly. During the process of setting up the Crime Watch Program, the church starter established meaningful relationships and was able to enlist people in home Bible studies that in turn became the nucleus for a new church.

Numerous other community-centered events, similar to the Crime Watch Program, can establish relationships between the church starter and the community. Some of these programs involve setting up bicycle safety clinics, health care workshops, finger printing and photographing children for crime prevention programs, and promoting meetings with civic leaders to provide information about the various services available to the community.

Weekend Ladies' or Men' Fellowship Breakfasts

Some church starters have found it useful to invite a group of ladies or men to a fellowship breakfast generally on Saturdays. At these breakfasts a great deal of emphasis is placed on fellowship. People are given an opportunity to get acquainted with one another and to develop supportive relationships.

Often in these fellowship breakfasts persons have been contacted in advance to give a testimony of the difference that Jesus has made in their lives. This testimony time can be followed up by a time of prayer and fellowship. The events can lead to involving new comers in Bible studies and other types of fellowship that in turn can result in the formation of a church starting core group.

Acts of Kindness

In his book *Conspiracy of Kindness*,[285] Steve Sjogren lists a wide variety of cultivative activities that can put the church starting team in contact with literally thousands of prospects. The main purpose of these activities is to establish a positive initial contact with unchurched people by serving them through acts of kindness. When people ask why church starting team members are doing those acts of kindness, their response is "to show you in a practical way that God loves you. His love is free and so is ours."[286]

Sjogren's entire approach is based on "Five Discoveries That Empower Evangelism."[287] The five discoveries are: (1) People listen when I treat them like friends; (2) When I serve, hearts are touched; (3) As I serve, I redefine the perception of a Christian; (4) Doing the message precedes telling the message; (5) Focus on starting, not harvesting.

Some of these acts of kindness include: Mother's Day carnation giveaway, Sunday morning paper and coffee giveaway, soft drink giveaway at sports events, mowing lawns, free coffee at bus stops, shoe shining service, blood pressure scanning, free light bulbs, free smoke alarm batteries, door to door food collection for the poor, free carwash, and free community dinner. The acts of kindness open the way for sharing the Gospel and starting a congregation.

Special Day Events

Church starters can use specific days in the calendar for some cultivative events. Some of these specific days are national holidays. Other days have special emphases and still others are significant sports events. Taking all of these into account, a list of suggested cultivative events for each month of the year could look like this:[288]

January:	Super Bowl Sunday
February:	Valentine Banquet
March:	Block Party (in some countries, alternative to Mardi Gras)
April:	Easter Dramas
May:	Graduation Parties or Sports Award Banquets, Mother's Day Banquet
June:	Sports Clinic, Father's Day Banquet
July:	Fourth of July "Living Flag" or Block Party
August:	Children's Sports Event
September:	Back to School Parties (in some countries patriotic holidays)
October:	Hallelujah Party (instead of Halloween)
November:	Harvest Sunday or Thanksgiving Celebration
December:	Christmas dramas, living Christmas tree

Summary

These examples of activities for adults can help to cultivate the friendship of people with the purpose of involving them in Bible studies. In some cases the church starter will need to adapt these methods so that they fit in different communities. In other cases special methods will need to be designed for certain communities. Knowing the community is important so that the methods that are utilized are adequate and adapted.

Conclusion

Cultivative events hold a vital place in church starting. In many instances the cultural gap between unchurched people and the church needs to be bridged before the unchurched will become responsive to the Gospel. Many people who would not accept an invitation to attend church are willing to attend cultivative events such as the ones we have mentioned above. Once the unchurched get to know the people in a new church effort they often become more responsive and end up accepting Christ as their Savior and joining the emerging congregation.

Certainly, many of the cultivative events need to be adapted to the particular setting of the church starter. There may be other instances in which the church starter will get some initial ideas and then develop new and perhaps more contextualized approaches. It is also a good idea for the church starter to do a study of the cultivative events that are being utilized effectively in the setting where the new church is being projected. Someone has said that at times people are not resistant to the gospel; they are simply turned off by our methods. May the Lord help us to use our creativity to its maximum potential so that we can find the key to the heart of everyone we are trying to reach in our communities.

CHAPTER 16

MULTIHOUSING COMMUNITIES

Reaching people and starting churches in multihousing communities is one of the greatest challenges facing church starters in the 21st Century. By multihousing communities we mean those housing arrangements composed of apartments, condominiums, manufactured housing, and other arrangements. A majority of the multihousing communities in the world are located in urban areas. In 1970, Donald A. McGavran lamented that the Church had not done well in the task of discipling urban people[289] The situation has hardly improved since that time.

Church starting efforts must seek and find ways to reach people who reside in multihousing communities. No area of church starting thinking is more critical than considering how to evangelize and congregationalize the multihousing communities of the world. No study of church starting would be complete without consideration of the ways and means of reaching the multihousing communities of the world.

Growth in Multihousing Communities

One reason for focusing on the multihousing communities in the contemporary urban world is the simple fact that the world is becoming more urban as the years go by. In 1950, 72 percent of the world's population lived in rural areas and only 28 percent in urban areas. By 1975, 59 percent of the population lived in rural areas and 41 percent in urban areas. In the year 2000, 45 percent of the population lives in rural areas while 55 percent reside in urban areas. Obviously, a majority of the world's people live in urban areas. The trend is expected to continue to the extent that by the year 2025 there will be more than 350 cities (mega cities, super cities, and super giant cities) with populations ranging from 4 to 10 million people and beyond.

If it is true that the world is becoming more urban it is also true that much of the urban population lives in multihousing communities. This population is growing at explosive rates. In Hong Kong, Singapore, and Kuwait, 90 percent of the population is urban and the bulk of this population lives in multihousing communities.

While many other world class cities do not have such a high percentage of urban dwellers as Hong Kong and Singapore, still over half of the inhabitants who live in many urban areas reside in multihousing communities. A matter that causes deep concern for a number of denominational groups is that the percentage of their members that live in multihousing communities is extremely low.

In other words, many Christian denominations have been successful in reaching rural people and families that live in single-family homes that they own. For example, Southern Baptists in one county of Texas discovered that while 46 percent of the people in the county lived in multihousing communities, over 85 percent of the members of their churches resided in single-family houses.[290]

One of the most challenging tasks for all Christians is to reach multihousing residents with the Gospel and to involve them in establishing churches where they live. This challenge can be met; this chapter suggests ways to reach these people.

Challenges Faced by Church Starters

The task of reaching people living in multihousing communities and gathering them into congregations is a possible but not an easy task. Specific challenges face church starters who are striving to evangelize and disciple multihousing residents within their own, urban contexts. Some of these challenges are internal while the others are external.

Internal Challenges

One of the internal challenges facing church starters in multihousing communities is the fact that there is a mindset among many Christians that church buildings, full-time staff people, and traditional church programs are essential for establishing "real churches." The truth of the matter is that none of these were practices or requirements in the early church. The Bible does indicate that initially the apostles and the new believers from Pentecost met in the Temple. That, however, did not last very long due to the fact that the Christians early encountered persecution.

Numerous portions in the book of Acts and in the Epistles of Paul speak about meetings that Christians had in homes and about house churches that were established. Church buildings actually did not appear until rather late in Christian history. This challenge, which demands buildings, trained leaders, and equipment, therefore, needs to be overcome if huge segments of the population in urban areas are to be reached and discipled.

Another internal challenge stems from the fact that often there is a cultural gap between the lifestyle of the single-family homeowners and of those who reside in multihousing communities. Often this cultural gap causes single-family homeowners, who generally form the majority of the members in many churches, to resist bringing people from multihousing communities into the fellowship of their churches or at least adopt a lukewarm attitude toward reaching these people.

On the other hand, residents of multihousing communities often feel that church members are rich people who do not care for them. They also feel that they will not be either welcomed or comfortable in the churches. These attitudes, both on the part of single-family home owners and residents of multihousing communities, obviously need to be dealt with from the biblical perspective which stresses that God is no respecter of persons (Acts 10).

Many church members do not even consider ministry in multihousing communities. These church members, in a recent survey, gave six reasons for not being involved in multihousing ministries. The reasons are: (1) People will not come to my church even though I minister to them during the week and meet their needs; (2) We do not have the staff to do ministries in multihousing areas; (3) The ministry will never be a church, and, therefore, I cannot count them in my statistics; (4) Missions is a going away concept; (5) Multihousing community residents have a lifestyle that is incompatible with the church's standards; (6) Multihousing community residents have nothing to offer the church.[291]

Added to these challenges are some myths that church people generally have about those who live in multihousing communities. One of these myths is that multihousing residents live in these types of communities because they want to be left alone and not bothered by outsiders, especially church people. One must admit that there are those multihousing residents who live in expensive, gated communities. The truth of the matter is, however, that even these people can be reached if the right kinds of approaches are utilized. Many other people live in multihousing communities not because this is their first choice but because they cannot afford to purchase a home.

Another myth is that multihousing residents are too mobile; therefore, it is not worth the effort to try to reach them because they will be gone tomorrow. It is true that a segment of the multihousing community is highly mobile. Studies indicate, however, that a significantly large number of people have lived in their multihousing communities for years. There are many cities in which there are regulations regarding the raising of rents. This provides incentives for people to stay in their apartments for years instead of paying more rent elsewhere.

A third myth is that the managers of multihousing communities simply do not want religious groups around. This myth has been proven false in the vast majority of cases. As will be demonstrated later, if the right approach is used, most managers will see the well-organized, honest, and dependable church groups as allies instead of foes.

A church starter called to start churches in multihousing communities will need to deal with these challenges and myths in order to assemble the right team and enlist the support that is needed to get the response desired.

External Challenges

In addition to the internal challenges, the church starter in multihousing communities faces other challenges that are external. These challenges include such matters as geographic distance and social distances. The geographic distance between a multihousing community and an existing church meeting place will often be such a hindrance that very few of these residents will become active in these congregations.

The social distance that at times exists between single-family home owners and multi-family housing residents can militate against bringing large numbers of the latter into existing churches and often constitutes an even more serious problem than geographical distance. A survey of how multihousing residents feel about the church reveals the following perceptions: (1) The church only wants my money; (2) People all dress one way; (3) The church is unfriendly; (4) Church people do not want multihousing residents; and (5) Multihousing residents do not know how to behave properly in church.[292] Barbara Oden explains:

> "Churchiness" is a problem. The church language is not understood. The liturgy in the church service is strange. The proper conduct going to and while with-in the church is different. The dress code is unfamiliar. A church is perceived as an alien church.[293]

Especially if there is a socio-economic distance between the two, some multihousing residents may feel that "they do not have the right clothes to attend church." Others may be fearful that they will not be accepted in the established churches. As was suggested earlier, if there are attitudes in existing churches that contribute to this feeling on the part of multihousing residents, church members need to repent and make a sincere effort to relate to all types of people. A starting point is to use appropriate terminology. Terms such as "apartment dwellers" or "trailer park dwellers" may be perceived as demeaning on the part of multihousing residents. Church starters do well by listening and discovering how other groups refer to themselves.

It is helpful to look at this matter from the perspective of the multihousing resident. It is important to take these apprehensions into account along with the fact that different groups of people at different socio-economic levels have different preferences regarding styles of worship service, preaching, and leadership. The more that provision can be made for the establishment of churches in multihousing communities, the greater will be the response of these residents to the Gospel and become active in their congregations.

Types of Multihousing Communities

Different types of multihousing communities exist in different types of cities. One way to categorize these differing types of multihousing communities is by noting the styles of construction in the buildings (e.g. low-rise, high-rise, apartments, condominiums, town houses, cluster houses, manufactured homes). Another way to classify them is by styles of ownership (e.g. condominiums, cooperatives, rental).

This study utilizes the economic factor as the principal criterion for categorizing the various types of multihousing communities. A reference to types of construction will be made where applicable. The following categories are presented with the proviso that church starters need to do their own study of the types of communities that are found in their area and utilize that information in designing a strategy to start churches.[294]

High-Income Multihousing

As the name would suggest, the residents of these types of communities are generally well-off financially due to well-paying jobs (as professionals, white collar, or managerial). They usually prefer this type of housing because of the proximity to their place of employment, amenities, security, privacy, community identity, investment protection, and maintenance that are offered.

The residents of affluent multihousing can best be reached, not through the provision of material needs, but through interests, hobbies, and social interaction. Contact with them can best be established through other residents who live in the same building, friends, relationships with the manager, and direct mail. These affluent people are most likely to respond to cultural events, marriage encounter seminars, stress/time management seminars, aerobics classes, health, and fitness classes.[295]

Medium-Income Multihousing

The medium-priced multihousing communities are obviously nicer than the low rent housing communities. The medium-income multihousing residents can be categorized under middle and lower-middle socio-economic classifications. Medium income multihousing is found in several types.

Garden-Type Apartments

The more solidly middle class people generally reside in garden-type apartments. These apartments are generally buildings of two to three stories containing 50 or more units. They are not as crowded, have more amenities, and are generally closer to middle class communities. Some of the residents, usually the younger ones, prefer this type of housing because they do not need to worry about maintenance, and, therefore, have more time for their jobs and leisure.

The older adults who live in garden-type apartments are often "empty nesters" who have chosen this type of community because of security, convenience, and maintenance concerns. Some of the outreach methods mentioned in the high-income category apply to the younger residents of the middle-income multihousing communities. The older adults will respond better to activities that relate to financial freedom, travel, nutrition, medical concerns, volunteerism, dealing with loneliness, and dealing with change.

Manufactured Multihousing (Mobile Homes)

A category of multihousing, the manufactured multihousing, can be categorized as lower middle, upper-lower income, or even lower income. In one sense the mobile homes are individual homes, yet they are usually located in communities that are specifically set-aside for this purpose. Some residents rent both the mobile home and the lot, while others own the mobile home but rent the lot. Still others may own both the lot and the home.

The residents of these communities vary from singles to retired people. For the most part they are blue-collar workers. Often the best strategy is to buy or rent a mobile home in the community and utilize it to begin a new church.

Low-Income Multihousing

There are several distinct categories of low-income multihousing. Because these characteristics are so important, we will discuss them under two separate categories: Public-Multihousing and Squatter Multihousing.

Public-Multihousing

Public multihousing communities generally are made up of small apartments in which only the basic services are provided. Often these communities are crowded and not located in the better parts of the city. The apartment buildings may be just a few stories high or multiple stories. Often these buildings occupy numerous city blocks. These are generally low rent or government subsidized apartments.

The people that live in these multihousing communities, for the most part, remain in the lower socio-economic level. There is usually a higher concentration of single parents in this type of housing community. In many cases the people who live there have many material, emotional, and spiritual needs. Churches have been neither active nor successful in reaching people in the public multihousing communities.

Squatter (Favela-Type) Multihousing

In a number of countries there is a level of multihousing that represents a lower socio-economic level than public (government subsidized) housing. This is the Squatter (Favela-Type) multihousing. Often people who move to the urban cities of the world cannot afford any type of housing at all. They simply try to find unoccupied land and construct whatever types of shelters they can manage to build with whatever materials they secure.

Once these shelters are in place, it is very difficult for government authorities to evict the residents. In most cases, these types of dwellings do not have any utilities (e.g. running water, electricity, drainage). The material, social, and spiritual needs of these residents are astounding. Unlike some of the North American "inner cities" where the poor are concentrated, the squatter type dwellings in other countries are generally located on the outer fringe of city. These communities are known as "*el cinturón de miseria*" (misery belt) in some Latin American countries. The social distance between these residents and typically middle-class church members appears at times to be insurmountable. Peoples in these areas stand in great need both of the gospel and in physical matters.

Summary

As was stated at the outset of this discussion, there are a wide variety of multihousing communities who have residents with a wide variety of characteristics, needs, and interests. A study of the various types of multihousing communities and of the characteristics of the residents is absolutely crucial for the development of a relevant strategy to reach them and start churches among them.

Gaining Entrance into Multihousing Communities

Perhaps the most crucial task in starting churches in multihousing communities is gaining an entrance into them. Two types of people must be contacted to gain entrance into these communities: the managers and the owners. Generally if there has not been a multihousing ministry in that community, the starting place is the manager. An error that should be avoided at all cost is that of using a "hit and run" approach. That is to say, to sneak in, distribute tracts or speak with the people and then sneak out again. Sooner or later the manager will find out and will establish a ruling prohibiting a church presence there. Many church starters have found the best approach in multihousing church starting is that of setting up an appointment with the managers and explaining to them what services you could offer them.

Preparing to Interview the Manager

At the interview with the manager, one of the most important things you will do is offer services that help the manager to do a better job and have a better environment for the renters. Terry Willis explains:

> Management is interested in developing and maintaining a community spirit that lengthens the stay of the residents and encourages 100 percent occupancy. These are important factors in the profit scheme of management companies. Management welcomes any contribution we might make to this element of business.[296]

In light of this challenge, the church starter faces the task of enlisting a church starting team and a support group that can provide some of the services that will be offered to the manager. The starting point for the church starter, therefore, is to do a talent search around some of the basic services (ministries) that can be provided. Among these services are: (1) after school care; (2) tutoring; (3) organized recreation; (4) clothing closet; (5) crisis counseling and support; (6) financial counseling; (5) job training, (6) Bible study for adults; (7) Bible study for children. Once the church starter has completed a talent search and has trained the workers in providing some of the basic services to be offered, an appointment can be set up with the manager.

Conducting the Interview
with the Manager

The church starter must keep several things in mind when setting up an interview with the manager. First, select a time that is convenient for the manager. Managers are usually extremely busy especially at the end of the month. Second, assure the managers that you are not a sales person trying to sell them something. Third, let the manager know that your purpose is to help promote resident retention, a sense of community, and to provide beneficial services for the residents. Fourth, indicate clearly that the effort will not cost the manager anything. Fifth, be up front about your desire to have Bible studies for the children and adults who wish to participate.

Experience has taught many multihousing church starters that if they offer other services to the community, the manager will not mind if Bible studies and worship services are held on the property for those who want to participate. It helps to mention the desire to help people with material as well as spiritual needs. Bobby Wash makes the following suggestions on how to work successfully with the manager:

> On your first visit: (1) Be friendly and brief; (2) Share your desire to help; (3) Listen carefully to the manager's depth of understanding of your plans and purposes. Hear the manager's definition of the greatest needs; (4) Give the manager an outline of possible activities; (5) Discuss surveys and plans and point out the value of personal contact. Maintain an ongoing relationship with the management, which will include: (1) making regular visits, (2) being available to help in crisis situations, (3) knowing and keeping the rules of apartment management, (4) showing and giving appreciation for and giving recognition to management, (5) praying for and if possible with the managers. In

all, be led by the Spirit.[297]

Survey the Multihousing Community

After permission has been obtained, the church starter should conduct a Resident Interest Survey. This brief survey should ask for the name and address of the residents in each apartment. It should ask the residents to indicate the age group of each family member or apartment mate. It should enquire as to the residents' interest in a variety of activities and ask about other activities, not on the list, but that the resident would like to see take place. Some of these activities could be the ones listed above and others such as language classes, CPR classes, single parenting classes, cooking classes, aerobics, and etc.

This Resident Interest Survey could also ask if the resident is active in a local church. It could also query as to what they would look for in a church if they were looking for one. A more relevant outreach program can be developed on the basis of the survey. Finding the needs can provide insights into how the people can best be served.

Finding a Meeting Place

Often when managers become interested in the services offered by the church starting team they will sometimes offer the use of their activities building or an apartment if it is available. Church starters have even offered to provide an Activities Coordinator for the Multihousing Community if the manager provides an apartment for this person. This arrangement gives the Coordinator an opportunity to be there and to minister to the people on a full-time basis. The activities building could be used for Bible studies and worship services. To the extent that it is possible, the church starter should strive to obtain space within the community.

If free space is totally impossible, the church starter may consider renting an apartment and using it to initiate activities and Bible studies. When even this plan is not available, the church starting team should seek a meeting place as close as possible to the Multihousing community. Whatever the arrangement, the church starter should not allow the space to be the ruling factor in the new church's beginning. The church can begin with or without the ideal provision of space.

Starting the New Multihousing Congregation

The process of starting a new congregation in a multihousing community has much in common with the process for starting churches in other communities. Much of the help that is offered in the previous chapters of this book is applicable to multihousing church starting. Some additional characteristics related to multihousing communities must be considered. Experienced multihousing church starters such as Barbara Oden and Harvey Kenisel recommend the following steps for starting a church in a multihousing community.[298]

Step One: Enlist the Sponsoring Church

"Starting a church in a multi-housing community comes from the vision, dream, calling, and commitment of someone in the congregation who is prompted by the Holy Spirit's leadership."[299] The helping ministry of a sponsoring church is no less important for congregations in multihousing communities than for other church starts. The unique needs of these congregations may make the sponsoring church's input and support even more vital. Enlisting a supporting church should not be overlooked in the process of starting a church in a multihousing community.

Step Two: Recruit and Train Volunteer Leaders

Volunteers provide most of the leadership in multihousing church starting. The Volunteer Survey Forms provided in the workbook for this chapter can assist in locating and assigning volunteers. V olunteer leaders assume particular importance in the work and provide a Christian presence.

One of the most asked questions relates to the leadership for multihousing church starting. Some multihousing community residents have the economic base to be able to provide for a full-time pastor when the congregation reaches that stage. Others do not, and likely will not, have such resources. In these instances, a bi-vocational church starter may be the best answer.

As is the case with other church starting models discussed in this book, the strategy needs to involve finding, training, and deploying church starters. There have been many instances in which the bi-vocational church starters have emerged from the multihousing communities themselves. In these instances setting up training centers (such as the ones discussed in the Propagating Models) can ensure the continual expansion of multihousing church starting.

Step Three: Select the Multihousing Community

Several principles guide the church starter in selecting the multihousing community in which he/she will start the new congregation. At least five principles make up the list:

1. Pray and ask God to lead you.

2. Consider the proximity of the multihousing areas to the sponsoring church.

3. Approach the community where an acquaintance or church member lives.

4. Select a multihousing community in which the needs match the giftedness and skills of the sponsoring church members.

5. Visit the manager.[300]

Step Four: Establish a Process to Develop the Ministry

The church starter should establish a process that will enable the congregation to develop. The process should include such steps as: establishing credibility, doing a resident interest survey, having the first event, having other cultivative events and activities, making a calendar of events, doing the publicity, and determining the financial resources needed. This list is, of course, partial as other steps might be used and some of these may not prove necessary for the particular church start in the particular community.

Many church starters in multihousing communities have found it helpful to begin with a picnic for the entire resident membership of the multihousing community. At this picnic event the church starting team and support group provide the food, drinks, and entertainment. The main purpose is to get acquainted and to inform the residents of the services that this group will provide to them. Generally the team hands out a flyer that lists all of the activities. Provision can be made for people to sign up for the various activities.

Other church starters have tried what they call a "Kick-Off Carnival." This activity is similar to the picnic but involves setting up many more games. These games can include such things as face painting, ball tossing, darts, cake walks, golf, ring toss, moon walk, fishing, etc.

Still others have tried film festivals, choir concerts, puppet shows, sports contests and the like. Some have obtained permission to set up a tent and have recreational activities during the day and evangelistic services in the evening. Different communities will respond to the various approaches mentioned above. The church starter in the multihousing community should not be limited in the use of activities by any unnecessary constraints. So long as the activities are biblically congruent, legally approved, socially helpful, and continually effective, these activities can and should be used.

Step Five: Determine the Structure for the Church

Congregations in multihousing communities, like churches everywhere, must have structures in order to function properly. Carl Elder describes a church structure that is recommended for multihousing congregations:[301]

1. It will be small (20-50 people).

2. The leader will be a layperson or bi-vocational pastor.

3. The Bible study will be simple with few classes.

4. The worship service will be simple and in many cases shorter in length.

5. The budget will be small but members will be expected to accept responsibility for their own congregation.

6. A high priority is ministering to the needs of those in attendance, their families, and residents.

7. The congregation must be allowed to grow and develop on its own terms and in its own way.

The church starter will not allow any pre-conceived requirement to dictate the structure of the new church. The structure of the church in the multihousing community must be flexible to allow for the congregation's needs. Some congregations will need more structure than others. Adapt the structure to the congregation's needs.

Step Six: Develop a Plan to Keep it Going

Many of the activities that are essential for the growth of new congregations in other communities are also needed in multihousing congregations. In order to keep the new multihousing congregation going, however, it is essential to place special emphasis on continued prayer, to maintain good relations with the management, to maintain an accurate calendar of activities, to train and involve new participants, and to continue to network with the larger community in order to expand the resources that can be utilized in this ministry. These on-going essentials must find a place in the basic plan for the church.

Starting a New Mobile Home Church

While mobile home residents may have some characteristics in common with some of the middle class multihousing (apartment) residents, there are enough differences to warrant a specialized strategy. Joe Guerin and Don Beach suggest the following strategy:[302]

Step One: Call a Bi-Vocational Pastor

Enlist someone who is called of God to preach and who understands mobile home residents. This person does not require advanced training but should be a person who the residents can respect. The person's character and behavior is more vital than training or some special speaking ability.

Step Two: Find a Place to Meet

The new congregation can meet in the community building in the mobile home community if one exists and its use is possible. If this plan is not available, rent or buy a mobile home and place it in or near the community. The facility does not need to be made to look like a church.

Step Three: Build a Small Church-Type Building

When the church develops to the point that more formal facilities are needed, the church and the supporting congregation can erect a small, simple, church-type building near or in the community. Even the smallest building will let the residents know that you are there to stay. As usual, the church should take care that the building's cost and maintenance do not limit the church from its ministries.

Step Four: Start Bible Study and Worship

Start Bible study and worship as soon as a meeting place can be found even if you start in one of the mobile homes in the area. The church starting team will use the strategies and methods suggested for Bible study groups in other locations. The main principle calls for adjusting the studies to the needs and questions of the local people.

Step Five: Build Good Relationships

The church starter should establish a good relationship with the community manager. The church's plans and goals should be shared with the community manager. The church should inform the manager or other community leadership that the church plans to help the community in every possible way. The church and the church starter will be careful not to violate any rules or laws of the area.

Step Six: Take a Religious Survey

The church starting team should conduct a religious survey and an interest survey of the residents of the mobile home community. These two studies will give the church starter the needed information for planning cultivating events. This information can also be the start of a prospect file for the congregation.

Step Seven: Find Musicians

The new congregation will need music and music leaders for its worship times. Seek residents who can play musical instruments, especially the guitar. These persons might help with the music. Some music help might be forthcoming from the sponsoring church or from other churches in the area.

Step Eight: Start a Visitation Program

Every congregation needs a consistent and continuing visitation program to seek new persons for the church's ministry. The church starter should begin regular weekly visitation efforts from the very first week. The church starter can train people in visitation by taking them along as he/she contacts people.

Step Nine: Enlist Local Leadership

Some dependence on leadership from the sponsoring church or other groups may contribute to the new congregation in the multihousing community in the beginning of the work. Almost from the beginning, the church should seek and use people from the mobile home communities in places of leadership. This procedure gives the residents a feeling of "ownership," this is "our" church.

Step Ten: Plan Activities for Children

The new church should develop a plan to minister to children. A Vacation Bible School, a Bible Club, or a special teaching time can help children become a part of the church. Most mobile home areas are alive with children unless the community is for the retired. A plan for children's activities is essential for the new church.

Step Eleven: Schedule Evangelistic Activities

The new church should, as soon as possible, schedule a time for evangelistic services. While every service will have an evangelistic purpose, a special series dedicated to reaching the lost and unchurched can provide great blessings and contribute to the growth of the new church.

Step Twelve: Plan Social Activities

A church in a mobile home community should plan for social activities as a part of its on-going ministry. The church can plan a family type social with watermelon (in season), homemade ice cream, games, and singing. These activities can help you meet the families and learn how the church might minister to them.

Step Thirteen: Offer Training Opportunities

The church can offer training on two levels. First, the church can conduct a "job fair" to assist those residents who are out of work. This effort will let them know the church cares. Some churches have actually provided job training for persons in the community who do not have marketable skills.

A second level of training relates to helping people develop skills for ministry in and through the church. The leaders of the church in the mobile home village must be trained in order to fulfill their tasks effectively. Training is essential for the continuing development of the church.

Conclusion

Multihousing church starting is one of the greatest needs in our world today. There is a sense in which the residents of many of the multihousing communities qualify as a hidden people group category. They are all around us, yet we often fail to see them and to recognize the tremendous need for churches among these people. The residents in multihousing communities provide the potential for some of the most creative and exciting church starting endeavors of our day.

PART 4

Implement New Congregation

The launching phase of the church starting process is perhaps the most exciting and challenging. One of the reasons for this excitement is that up until this point an enormous amount of work has been done, yet the results have been neither visible nor widely known. The all-important cultivative phase has produced a core of people who have a common vision and commitment to see the new church established. This core group will need to ensure that several vital necessities are in place before the public grand opening takes place. Among these necessities are selecting a meeting place, choosing an appropriate name, beginning the small group meetings, and establishing an assimilation process.

CHAPTER 17

FINDING A MEETING PLACE

The new church must have a place to meet. Providing and preparing this meeting place constitutes a vital part of the launching phase of church starting. The place of meeting can either accelerate or hinder the development of the new congregation. The church starting team must carefully consider the matter of a meeting place for the new church.

Criteria for Selecting a Meeting Place

One of the most striking observations made by experts in the field of church starting is that new churches generally have a tendency to build too soon and too small.[303] In their desire to have a meeting place of their own, some new churches build a building in accordance with their capabilities at that time instead of waiting until they are able to build the type of building that will allow them to grow to their maximum potential. At times these churches place themselves in such debt for this building that they find they have little or no resources for those ministries that lead to further growth. The new church must guard against the tendency to build too soon, too small, and too expensive. The answer in many instances lays in the utilization of a temporary meeting place.

New congregations use many different types of facilities for their meeting places. These facilities include schools (public or private), colleges, hotel conference rooms, community activity buildings, buildings used by other congregations, portable buildings, club houses, vacant retail stores, lodges, business place conference rooms, restaurants, funeral home chapels, theaters, recreation centers, bank buildings, large homes, and stadiums. Quite often these types of meeting places are available at a reasonable price and make it possible for the new congregation to have financial resources for personnel and programs instead of tying up all of their resources in the acquisition of a building.

In selecting an appropriate meeting place, the church should keep several things in mind. First, the church starting team should consider the size of the anticipated congregation in the initial stage. If, for example, the goal is to have 200 in the grand opening as a result of telemarketing or other outreach efforts, the church starter should make inquiry concerning the availability of a meeting place that can provide for that number. While it may not hurt to be a little crowded in the initial public service, if the space is totally inadequate, many people will not return.

Second, the appearance of the building is important. A building does not have to look very expensive but must be adequate and evidence several characteristics. The meeting place, to be adequate, must be neat, well painted, well lit, and attractively decorated. It must have a spotless, well-equipped nursery, clean rest rooms, good acoustics, adequate room temperature, and clearly marked areas so people will not get lost or confused. Guests will feel comfortable and will be willing to return only if the meeting place has such characteristics.

Third, the meeting place must be accessible. Obviously it is great if the building that is rented or leased is in an area that is well known and easily found. When the meeting place is not easy to reach, some of the difficulties can be overcome with maps and signs. Some church starters put a map in their brochures, mail outs, and telephone book advertisements so that people will know how to find the meeting place. Adequate signs by the streets and on the property itself can be very helpful. While church members may be willing to go through the inconvenience of finding a meeting place, new comers may not be that persistent.

Fourth, buildings must have adequate parking space. At this point the lifestyles of the new comers need to be considered. In some metropolitan areas many people depend on public transportation (bus, subway) and do not need to have parking space provided. In other areas the ratio of attendees per car may be very low (e.g. 1.5 per car) thus making it necessary to provide more parking space.

Generally rented or leased buildings have adequate parking space available. At times it is also possible to enter into agreements with the owners of adjacent parking space (e.g., shopping malls, schools) for the church to use their space on Sundays and for their clients to have access to the church's parking space during the week. The important thing is that those who attend the new church (especially visitors) have sufficient, easily accessible parking space.

Fifth, building space must reflect the discipleship approach of the congregation. Churches, for example, that utilize the Sunday School approach for adults as well as children will need to have adequate space for the various classes to meet. Churches, on the other hand, that utilize the home-cell approach for adults and only provide Sunday School classes for children during the morning worship need less space for classes. The other programs of the church must be taken into account in determining the type of building that is needed. A congregation that is planning many weekday programs needs a building that is accessible all week long, instead of only on Sundays.

Sixth, if the new congregation is meeting in facilities that are used the rest of the week (e.g. schools, conference rooms), the church starting team must provide storage space for the equipment and a plan for setting up and taking down the chairs and other church fixtures. Storage will be much easier if the storage area is easily accessible.

Seventh, the building must have a good or at a least neutral image in the community. A bad reputation associated with a building, for whatever reason, is extremely difficult to overcome. If one of the negatives involves security risks, for example, people will be reluctant to come to that building, especially after dark.

Eighth, the church starting team needs to consider the decision related to the type of building in relationship to the target group. Generally young couples with children will feel very comfortable meeting in an elementary school. More mature adults may feel more comfortable in a setting that peoples their age visit more often such as a college auditorium, hotel conference room, or business place conference room.

Ninth, the location of the temporary meeting place is important. At least two dimensions relate to this characteristic. One is the location of the building in relation to the target group. The closer the location is to areas where the target group lives, the greater the possibility of attracting them. The second dimension is the place of the building in relation to the projected location of the permanent building. Experience has indicated that the shorter the distance between the two, the smoother the transition in the future. If the permanent building is located a long distance from the temporary location, the church may lose a significant number of members when it moves.

Use of Temporary Facilities

Temporary facilities are obviously not as convenient as meeting places owned by the new congregation. These temporary quarters are, however, an excellent means toward an end. As the church grows stronger it can develop the experience and financial resources to obtain the type of building that will enable it to continue to grow. It is helpful if the new congregation's leadership thinks in terms of following a series of stages with regard to the selection of building facilities. In the initial stage they will need to obtain the type and size building that will meet their needs yet not drain their resources to the extent that they do not have funds for personnel, programs, and advertising.

During its intermediate stage a congregation can obtain a larger building more suitable to its needs but that does not overwhelm the budget of the growing congregation. When the congregation gets to a more established stage, it can plan for the size building that will enable it to attain its potential. By this time the congregation will have the financial strength that will enable it to build for the future and avoid the mistake of having built too small and too soon.

Conclusion

Clearly, the meeting place for the new congregation holds vast importance and the church starting team must seriously consider all factors related to this facility. The major principle remains for the meeting place to be adequate for the beginning phase while not jeopardizing future growth. The team should exercise great care in providing this initial meeting place.

CHAPTER 18
APPROPRIATE NAME

Choosing an appropriate name for the new congregation is extremely important. Many believers have very positive and warm thoughts when they think of biblical names or of the names of churches they remember as they were growing up. As positive as this might seem, outsiders and new comers may have an entirely different impression of this.

Some church names have either negative or confusing implications, or, at the very least, communicate nothing to unchurched people. The principal question that we need to address is: whom are we trying to reach? If we are mainly trying to please fellow church members or ourselves then any name is acceptable. If, on the other hand, we want the name to communicate something to unchurched people so that they will feel attracted to the church, then we should take them into account when selecting an appropriate name. With this in mind we should consider the following suggestions

Errors to Avoid

Several suggestions related to selecting a name for the new church need to be made. First, do not select obscure biblical names such as "Shiloh Church," "Pisgah Church, and "Mount Moriah Church." While such names may have great meaning for some church members, they communicate very little to unchurched people and run the risk of giving them the impression that this congregation belongs to a sect or a cult.

Second, do not give your church the name of the street location in which your building is currently located. When churches move to new properties, they often experience a difficult time deciding whether to keep their name or to change it in order to keep from confusing people. The same advice applies to the utilization of the name of a small subdivision within a city. While initially it may imply identification with that community, a move in the future may necessitate a name change.

Peter Wagner points out that Robert Schuller named the church he started "Garden Grove," but later realized that the name identified the church with a relatively small community in comparison to its much broader impact. For this reason, he changed the name to the "Crystal Cathedral." He adds that Rick Warren wisely did not use "Laguna Hills," "Mission Viejo," or "El Toro" in the church name even though the church at one time met in each of these communities, but chose "Saddleback Valley," which encompasses all of these locations.[304]

Third, do not use the name of a community if it conveys a meaning that is detrimental to the name of the church. It is obvious that names like "Devil Creek Church" simply should not be used. There are other names such as "Battleground Community Church" that also convey a meaning with which the church does not want to be identified. Some names may sound somewhat humorous. A church named "Greater Harmony Baptist Church" was a split off from "Harmony Baptist Church" both of which were located in a community named "Harmony." Also names such as "Beautiful Feet Church," "Heavenly Vision Church," "Refuge King James Church," "Door of the Sheep Church," "City of Refuge Church" "Mt Zion Church," "Who Ever Will Outreach Church," "Shiloh Church," "Romans VIII Church," and "Acts Church" may have internal meaning for the congregation but create confusion in the minds of the unchurched. On the same highway a few miles apart two churches have names that might cause people to do a double take as they drive along. These signs announce "Little Hope Church" and "Midway Church." Some people may want to join churches that give them more hope and that can take them all the way. Clearly, names that reflect negatively on the church should be avoided.

Fourth, do not use a long name. Some groups want to put their entire faith statement in their names. Names such as "Bible Believing, Sanctified, Sovereign Grace Church" or "Healing Fire, Pure Heart, Walking on the Word Church" or "Love, Faith, Hope, Power, Deliverance Church," may help insiders know what they stand for, yet outsiders can either be repelled or confused by them.

Others use a long name to identify their target group. One church is listed in the telephone directory as the "Full Gospel Motorcycle Association International Church of the Highway

Ministry Services." Long names create confusion in the minds of the unchurched and are difficult to use in media efforts.

Fifth, do not give your church a name that will only have meaning for the current generation. A new congregation, for example, named its church in honor of a foreign missionary whom they greatly admired. They named the congregation the "Anderson Memorial Church." The truth of the matter is that few of the members ever knew the missionary personally and, more significantly; the people in the community had absolutely no clue as to the meaning of the church's name.

Criteria to Follow

On the positive side, several criteria can guide the church starting team in selecting an adequate name. First, make a list of possible name and field-test them. In other words, show these names to the unchurched people of your target group and ask them to tell you what comes to mind when they hear these names. Is it a name that they understand, that they have positive feelings toward, which conveys friendliness and warmth or that at the very least does not give them such negative feelings that they would never consider attending a service there?

Obviously the church starting team would not select a name that is repulsive to believers. On the other hand, knowing what names convey to unchurched people is very important. This understanding of the impression of the name can guide the group to a name that will enhance the congregation's growth.

Second, the church starter should select a name that will help people identify the church. There are some names that are so overused that people find it difficult to know which of the many churches with the same name this one happens to be. Perhaps utilizing creativity will help to come up with a name that catches the attention of the people in the target people and gives church members a feeling of satisfaction that they are identified with this church.

Third, the team should select a brief name. As noted earlier, some congregations seem to put their entire statement of beliefs in their title. While this may attract those who sense a need to express their beliefs in the exact same way, many people will either be confused or turned off by a name that appears to be more exclusive than inclusive. It is important to note that people are more prone to remember brief, attractive titles than lengthy and confusing names.

Finally, church starters should pay attention to the image that their denominational name has in the area in which they are starting a church. In some areas the denominational name has a very positive image and will encourage people from the target group to want to be a part of the new congregation. In other areas the denominational name may be necessary to assure people that the new congregation is not a part of some radical sect. In still other areas people are indifferent to the denominational name and have neither negative nor positive feelings when they hear it.

There are some areas, however, where the people either have a very negative or incorrect image of the denominational name. Using the denominational designation in the church name will actually repulse people from the church. In these areas the church starter needs to give careful consideration to using the denominational name in the church's name.

Options for Church Starters

Several options may be open to church starters as they consider the matter of the name for the new congregation and the denominational name;

- First, the church starter may do some market analysis to see just what the denominational name means to people in the target group.

- Second, the church starter may seek to improve the denominational image through publicity and cultivative events.

- Third, the church starter may omit the denominational name in the title of the church (publicity and sign on the building) but may include it in the literature that is given in the church activities and explain the denominational distinctives in the new-comers classes.

- Fourth, the church starter may use the initials of the denomination on the church sign. This conveys a positive message to those who are looking for a church of that denomination but does not say anything negative to the unchurched.

Perhaps the most important thing is that the church starter deals with this matter with integrity so that existing church members will be reassured of his loyalty and new church members will gain a new understanding and appreciation for the denomination with which the church is affiliated. Perhaps the biggest challenge that church starters face is that of selecting a name that will not turn people off before they even have a chance to hear the message of salvation and know what this congregation is all about.

CHAPTER 19
SMALL GROUPS

Small group meetings are one of the most effective methods church starters have used throughout the centuries for reaching people with the Gospel message and discipling them. This use of small groups rests on a biblical precedent related to the "oikos" concept. The following biblical texts refer to the oikos as a social unit through which the gospel was communicated:

- Luke 10:5:-7: When you enter a house *(oikos)*, first say, 'Peace to this house *(Oikos)*.' If a man of peace is there, your peace will rest on him; if not, it will return to you. Stay in that house *(oikos)*, eating and drinking whatever they give you . . . Do not move around from house *(oikos)* to house *(oikos)*.

- John 4:53: Then the father realized that this was the exact time at which Jesus had said to him, "Your son will live." So he and all his household *(oikos)* believed.

- Acts 2:46: . . . They broke bread in their homes *(oikoi)* and ate together with glad and sincere hearts . . .

- Acts 11:14: He will bring you a message through which you and all your household *(oikos)* will be saved.

- Acts 16:31: They replied, "Believe in the Lord Jesus, and you will be saved--you and your household *(oikos)*."

- Philemon 1:2: . . . to Apphia our sister, to Archippus our fellow soldier and to the church that meets in your home *(oikos)*:

- Colossians 4:15: Give my greetings to the brothers at Laodicea, and to Nympha and the church that meets in her home *(oikos)*.

- 1 Corinthians 1:11 speaks of those in Chloe's house-hold *(oikos)*.

- 1 Corinthians 16:19: The churches in the province of Asia send you greetings. Aquila and Priscilla greet you warmly in the Lord, and so does the church that meets at their house *(oikos)*.

It is evident in these Scripture references that the *oikos* (the household) was a social unit that was taken into account in communicating the gospel and gathering believers. Rad Zdero affirms this when he states:

> The gospels report that homes --- among other places--- were a natural part of Jesus' life and ministry. Christ was worshipped as a baby in a house (Mat 2:11), he healed Peter's mother-in-law at home (Mat 8:4-16), the Last Supper was held in a house (Mat 26:18), and Jesus preached to people who crowded into homes (Mark 2:1). Christ also trained his disciples during a hands-on assignment by sending them out in pairs to preach village to village. They were instructed to find a 'man of peace' in each village that was responsive to their message and build a spiritual base of operations from that home (Luke 10:1-11).
>
> Private homes also had a pivotal role in the life of the early church. Shortly after Pentecost, the apostle Peter and the Jerusalem church began a pattern of meeting daily from house to house, living a common life together which was characterized by eating meals, praying, sharing goods, and holding to the apostle's teachings (Acts 2:46, 5:42, 12:12). Peter also brought the message of Christ to the Roman officer Cornelius' friends and family who were gathered in his home (Acts 10). Sometime later, during a very severe persecution of the church in Jerusalem, Saul of Tarsus was reported to have gone from house to house searching for believers and likely barging in during the middle of church meetings (Acts 8:3). Later, as a Christian convert Saul (now known as the apostle Paul) embarked on his missionary travels across the Roman Empire, regularly clustering believers into homes and ending his letters by greeting those who hosted the gatherings (Acts 16:14-15,29-34, 20:6-8,20;

Rom 16:3-5; I Cor 16:19; Col 4:15-16; Philem
1:2). The apostle John warns readers not to welcome false teachers into their homes, referring
most probably to house church gatherings rather
than mere social occasions (2 John 10). These
house churches were spread across the empire in
cities like Jerusalem, Ephesus, Colossae, Corinth,
Laodicea, Troas, Philippi, and Rome... We do not
know for certain that all believers everywhere in the
first century met *exclusively* in homes. But what
can be said is that the early church met *primarily* in
homes for believers' meetings and even some
evangelistic efforts.[305]

The word *Oikos* is translated "household." It is viewed as the
basic building block of society. It refers to an intimate community of people. It can refer to an extended family and close as-
sociates. It is also used to refer to a cluster of *oikoi* which make
up a larger community.[306]

In their book, *Creating Communities of the Kingdom*, David
Shenk and Ervin Stutzman describe how the early church
grew:

We read that the church grew and multiplied ex-
ceedingly as neighbor told neighbor the news of Jesus Christ. We may assume that as the living rooms
became packed with people, the groups divided and
new cells were formed. Soon the original 100 or so
congregations multiplied and became hundreds of
small group fellowships throughout the whole metropolitan area. They witnessed with power and persuasion to the saving act of God.[307]

In his chapter, "Evangelization of Whole Families," Chua Wee
Han makes a strong biblical case for an *oikos* strategy:

The apostolic pattern for teaching was in and
through family units (Acts 20:20). The first acces-
sion of a Gentile grouping to the Christian church
was the family of a Roman centurion Cornelius in
Caesarea (Acts 10:7,24). At Philippi, Paul led the
families of Lydia and the jailer to faith in Christ and
incorporation into his church (Acts 16:15. 31-34).
The "first fruits" of the great missionary apostle in
Achaia were the families of Stephanas (1 Cor
16:15), Crispus and Gaius (Acts 18;8; Rom 16:23;

1 Cor 1:14). So it was clear that the early church disciple both Jewish and Gentile communities in families... It was equally clear that households were used as outposts of evangelism. Aquila and Priscilla used their home in Ephesus and Rome as a center for the proclamation of the Gospel (Room 16:35; 1 Cor 16:19). Congregations met in the homes of Onesiphorus (2 Tim 1:16; 4:19) and Nymphas (Col 4:15).[308]

In modern times the small group method is being utilized to reach literally millions of people in America as well as across the world. Two of the main strategies are the use of cell churches and house churches.

Cell Churches

A distinction can be made between a church with small groups and a church of cell groups. The former is typically a traditional program-based church with some cell groups while the latter consists exclusively or almost exclusively of small groups.

Traditional churches with cell groups typically view cell groups as appendages of their church with celebration (the Sunday morning worship service) as the main event of the life of the church. These cell groups are formed for prayer, crisis support, Bible study, and evangelistic outreach. "A good depiction of this is a bicycle wheel hub with a few spokes."[309] The hub is the congregation which meets for worship and the observance of the ordinances. The spokes are the cells in which evangelism and discipleship takes place.

In this same way of thinking, Lawrence Khong, leader of the Faith Community Baptist Church in Singapore, differentiates between the Cell Church and the church with cells. Pastor Khong declares that there is a world of difference between a church with cells and a cell group church.[310] In the cell group church, explains Khong, the cell is the church. The cell is the entrance point into the church fellowship. The cells exist to edify the participants and to evangelize as they serve through four "Ws" Welcome, Worship, Works, and Word. Pastor Khong expresses his belief in the cell group church saying,

> I believe the cell church is God's design to make His church capable of equipping and mobilizing every

member for the work of the ministry. The cell church provides the structure by which "the whole body, joined and held together by every supporting ligament, grows and builds itself up in love as each part does its work" (Ephesians 4:16).[311]

Joel Comiskey explains the difference between small groups and cell groups when he states:

> All small groups are not cell groups. One major difference between cell groups and other small groups is the cell's emphasis on evangelism, leadership development, and multiplication of each cell. Cell churches also have other types of ministries (e.g., ushering, worship, prayer, missions, and training). These ministries, however, are not called cell groups, even though the particular ministry might be small and a group. In the cell church, the cell group is the backbone, or DNA of church ministry. Cell ministry replaces the need for many traditional programs. ... Some churches have cell groups as one of their programs in the church... In the cell church, however, the lead pastor is personally involved in cell group ministry and is considered the point person and cell visionary.[312]

The two principal ways in which Christian groups are currently using small-group meetings are: 1) Cell Churches (off campus cell groups) and 2) Churches with small groups (on-church-campus meetings, principally through Sunday school classes).

Cell Churches (Off Campus Approaches)

A number of churches have their cells away from their campuses. One such church is the New Hope Community Church founded by Dale Galloway in Portland, Oregon. In his book 20/20 Vision, Galloway shares ten characteristics of what he calls Tender Loving Care Groups: 1) a close family, 2) application of the Bible to daily life, 3) sharing of life's testimony, 4) effective one-on-one pastoral care, 5) encouragement and edification, 6) unlimited opportunities for meaningful service, 7) non-threatening friendship evangelism, 8) discipling of new converts, 9) spiritual growth, and 10) development of strong leadership.[313]

The Elmbrook Church in Milwaukee, Wisconsin has established similar objectives for its Neighborhood Home Groups: 1) nurture - care and feeding of believers involves commitment to each other for mutual growth; 2) visitation - of new members, families, and friends; 3) hospitality - use of home, greeting one another, preparing/ serving refreshments; 4) follow-up - specifically new members; 5) localized projects - nursing homes, reformatories, prison ministries, resettling refugees; 6) discovery and coordination of transportation needs - for example, students, elderly, anyone in need; 7) intergroup activities- potluck dinners, picnics, and fellowship.[314]

The effectiveness of small groups in starting growing, reproducing churches cannot be questioned. Church starting teams should seriously consider the possibility that small-group methods might be the best way to begin the new congregation.

Home Cell Groups

The off-church-campus small group meeting approach has several features that allow it to contribute significantly to the growth of the new congregation. First, since people meet in places that are already available (homes, conference rooms, places of employment, etc.) these cell groups have potential for growth that is not limited by space constraints. In other words, there can be as many cell groups as there are homes (and other meeting places) in a given community. The new congregation does not have to go through the expense of providing buildings for people to meet for small group Bible study.

Second, in many instances (due to religious traditions, feelings of inadequacy, etc.) many people respond much quicker to an invitation to meet in a home or small group setting than in a church building. Third, it is generally easier to enlist leadership for home cell groups than for the more structured Bible study classes held in a church building. Fourth, the home cell approach can contribute toward the development of additional leaders since the host family is in a position to participate and learn. Fifth, the informal setting in a home generally lends itself to the type of dialogue that enables the unbeliever gradually to learn more about the message of salvation. Sixth, the fellowship that is developed in the home cell group can contribute to making the discipleship process a natural and effective one.

Seventh, the home cell group approach facilitates one-to-one care, counsel, and prayer.

Home Cell Group Structure

One of the greatest challenges that the small group meeting approach faces is that of being organized in such a way that there is continuity, leadership training, and multiplication. This challenge necessitates an organizational structure. The necessary structure for a small group must provide for and clearly point toward the following aspects of this approach.

First, the structure must include the purpose of the cell groups (evangelism and discipleship). Second, the structure provides guidance for the type of leaders that the small group needs. Third, the function expected from each type of leader (job description) must be clearly understood by all. Fourth, the structure determines the format for the cell group meetings. Fifth, the meeting reports that are expected are clearly explained. Sixth, the structure assures the accountability and discipline expectations.

New Hope Community Church has an organizational structure that includes Lay Pastors, Group Leaders, Group Leader Assistants, and Hosts or Hostesses. Lay Pastors are divided into three categories: (1) Trainee, (2) Lay Pastor, (3) Senior Lay Pastor. These serve as Group Leaders and Assistant Group Leaders. Qualifications and job descriptions for them as well as for the Hosts of Hostesses are clearly outlined.

Elmbrook Church also has a clearly defined organizational structure of leadership and authority. This involves the Senior Pastor, Pastoral Coordinator of the Neighborhood Home Groups, Regional Shepherds, Neighborhood Home Group Leaders, and Group Members.[315] The structure is clearly expressed, explained, and understood by all involved.

These two approaches are used here as examples of the fact that Home Cell Groups need to be structured and administered very carefully if they are to function effectively and reach their objectives. While they may have different titles, generally speaking the principle types of leaders that are needed to organize and operate the cell groups are: (1) Cell Group Coordinator; (2) Cell Group Leader; (3) Assistant (or Apprentice) Cell Group Leader; (4) Host or Hostess.

Cell Group Coordinator

An absolutely critical leader for cell-group methods, the cell-group coordinator, has a many sided responsibility. The principal tasks of the cell Group Coordinator are to: (1) Enlist cell group leaders; (2) Train the cell group leaders; (3) Pray for the cell group leaders and for the entire team; (4) Ensure that the cell group leaders have all the materials for their meetings; (5) Receive reports of the cell group meetings; (6) Help to enlist new hosts; (7) Plan cultivative and recruitment meetings; (8) Inform the church of the progress of the Groups (average attendance, professions of faith, plans for new cells); (9) Help to find the best materials available; (10) Ensure the support and participation of the church. The importance of the cell-group coordinator demands that the person in the position be carefully selected and thoroughly trained.

Cell Group Leader

Books such as Bob and Betty Jacks', *Your Home A Lighthouse* provide valuable information on a second level of leadership for cell groups. They include as qualifications of Cell Group Leaders the following: (1) being filled with the Holy Spirit and of good testimony; (2) cooperating with the church and its Home Cell program; (3) being responsible and persevering as they guide the group, (4) being sociable, gaining the trust of the group; and (5) being convinced of the importance of the Home Cell Groups. Some of the tasks of the Cell Group Leaders include: (1) attending the monthly planning meeting; (2) enlisting a host for the cell group meeting; (3) helping the host invite persons; (4) selecting the Bible study materials; (5) making certain that there are sufficient Bibles, materials, pencils etc., (6) leading the meeting; 7) planning for the discipleship of those who receive Christ as their Savior.[316]

Assistant (Apprentice) Group Leader

Assistant Group Leaders (or apprentices) should have similar qualifications as the Group Leaders. Their responsibilities involve: (1) helping the group leader in all of his tasks; (2) taking the place of the leader in his absence; (3) keeping an attendance roll on members and prospects; (4) maintaining a prayer list; (5) serving as the key person in the prayer ministry; 6) enlisting additional workers (for children and youth);

(7) preparing to begin a new Home Cell Group.

Many use the term "Assistant Group Leader" for this person. The term "Apprentice," however, actually better communicates both the position and the relationship of the position to the concept of reproduction. An apprentice is, therefore, one who is serving and training with the purpose of starting a new cell group, becoming its leader, and training another apprentice to follow the same cycle.

Host or Hostess

The Host or Hostess plays a vital role in the cell group approach. They are expected to: (1) invite family members and friends to the home cell group meeting; (2) provide a home for the cell group meetings; (3) create an environment of love and friendliness; (4) serve refreshments; and (5) participate in the Bible study. Only to the extent that new Hosts and Hostesses are found can the cell- group approach continue to expand.

Format for Home Cell Group Meetings

The leaders must consider several factors as plans are made for home cell group meetings. First, Bible study is the central purpose of the cell group meetings. Second, the participants need to experience genuine fellowship in the group meetings. Third, those who attend the group meetings often have overwhelming needs and find a great deal of help and encouragement as the group engages jointly in prayer. Fourth, due to family and other responsibilities, the participants need a group meeting schedule that is consistent and considerate.

The Loving Care Group format can serve as a model. This involves the following activities and time frames: 1. Opening – Introduction of guests & ice breaker (2 minutes); 2 Opening prayer (2 Min); 3. Praise – testimonies, singing, reports of answered prayer, appreciation for each other, thanks giving to God (5-10 Min); 4 Confessional prayer (10 Min); 5. Bible lesson with practical application (30 Min); Intercessory prayer to make application of lesson (5-10 Min): Closing prayer (2 Min). Total 60 minutes.

John Faulkner in Africa designed another format for cell-group meetings. When people are invited to participate in the home cell groups they are told that the purpose is that of: (1) reading and studying the Bible; (2) making new friends; (3) praying for one another; (4) helping one another; (5) and beginning other Bible studies.317

The meetings begin with a period of fellowship. In order to help people know one another better, they were asked to answer several questions. These questions have to do with their life when they were children, their present life, and that which they would desire to do in the future. One of the questions, for example, is: "Who was the person that had the most positive influence in your life?" Another question is: "What are the deepest yearnings you have with regard to your family?" Another type of question is: "What country would you like to visit if you could go on a trip?" The purpose of these questions is helping the people to know each other better and to feel free to participate in the Bible study.

After the period of fellowship, a chapter from the Gospel of John is read. At the end of the reading, an opportunity is given for people to ask questions about this chapter. This question period helps to clarify the teachings that they encounter in this chapter. In addition to this, time is given so that the people can share their prayer concerns. These requests can be regarding something they have learned in the Bible Study or some problem that they face with their families, at their work, etc. The meeting ends with a period of prayer. This method of Bible Study has the purpose not only of increasing the biblical knowledge of the people but also of providing the opportunity for fellowship and prayer.

Activities in Cell Groups

On the basis of the experience that many have had with cell groups the following suggestions may be very helpful for those planning to utilize this approach. Perhaps it is better to start with the things that should not be done. Those in cell groups should not: (1) pray long prayers (new comers do not know how to do this and will feel intimidated); (2) discuss religion or the church (focus on a relationship with Christ); (3) form small groups that exclude others; (4) ask each person to read out loud (many are intimidated by this); (5) ask new people to pray out loud; (6) try to turn the cell group into a replica of the church; and (7) have more church members than prospects in the group (this often changes the focus of the group).

In contrast with the things that should not be done, there are things that should be standard operation procedures of healthy cell groups. They should: (1) help people feel comfortable; (2) cultivate friendships by conversing about that things that are interesting to them (e.g. family, sports, work, hobbies); (3) avoid interruptions (e.g. telephone, pets, television); (4) make certain everyone is included in the conversations; (5) be considerate with those who are timid by not pressuring them; (6) provide the same material for all of the participants (e.g. if they all have the same Bibles they can refer to page numbers instead of books, chapters, and verses); (7) pay attention to the schedule so that the meetings do not habitually go overtime; (8) encourage the participants to read their Bibles at home; 9) encourage the new participants even if they have a different lifestyle; (10) concentrate on Christ and His saving work; (11) emphasize the good news of salvation and not negative attitudes or lists of things Christians should not do; (12) without pressuring them, give them an opportunity to receive Christ or to express a desire to know more about him; and (13) keep handy tracts like the Four Spiritual Laws to present the plan of salvation and give them the tract at the appropriate time.

For the church starter it may sound a bit overwhelming to think of the type of organizational structure discussed here and the number of people it takes to implement this approach. It is important, however, to note that these and other approaches started small and gradually built up to what they are today. Having an idea of the organizational structure that is needed will enable the church starter to set the foundation that will facilitate continuous growth.

Ralph Neighbor makes very specific suggestions for planting a cell church: 1. Form a leadership group; 2. Create a prayer base; 3. Select a target group; 4. Launch teams in strategic areas to develop a presence; 5. Penetrate oikoses by finding "men of peace"; 6. Make converts; 7. Form cell groups; 8. Create Sub-zones; and 9. Launch celebrations[318]

The process that Neighbor suggests begins with the formation of a leadership group that becomes instrumental in carrying out the various tasks and activities that lead to the formation of interest groups in the targeted areas. These team members initially serve as the leaders of the cell groups. However, the plan is for the converts to be disciple and trained so they will become the cell group leaders. These cell groups, at a specific time are encouraged to form into zones for the purpose of enhancing bonding between the members of the cell groups and beginning to have Sunday morning meetings. These meetings with time lead to the establishment of the Sunday Morning Worship Service (the "Celebration Time"). Neighbor cautions the group not to be too hasty in setting up the Celebration Time. He explains:

> They don't have to be on a weekly basis. Many cell churches have a monthly or 6-week celebration on Sunday morning. Be sure you have at least 10 cell groups before launching. Much work and money will go into the launching of the celebration. If you start out before you are ready, it can harm the movement. When you launch, it should be with quality worship! If you don't have a lot of quality musicians, your first celebrations could center on praise/worship teams invited to come in and help you as you start.[319]

Comiskey has outlined a carefully planned strategy for planting a cell church. The steps are: "1) recruit a team of prayer warriors; 2) develop values and vision; 3) invite people to the pilot cell group; 4) multiply the pilot group; 5) start celebration worship; 6) build the infrastructure; 7) plant new cell churches.[320]

Churches with Small Groups
(On Campus Approaches)

Some small groups employ approaches that include meetings on the church campus. These groups take the form of the traditional Sunday school. In some cases this name that is used is selected in such a way as to communicate the purpose of the group. In some settings the term "school" may communicate that this activity is primarily for children. The on-campus small group is viable method of ministry and can contribute to church starting.

Throughout the years, Sunday school has been one of the

most effective tools for reaching people with the Gospel, discipling them, and assimilating them into the fellowship and ministry of the church. Often when Sunday school is mentioned, there are those who automatically believe that this method and that of home cell groups are mutually exclusive. Nothing could be further from the truth. A church that utilizes both methods actually has greater potential for growth than one that utilizes only one.

The principal reason for the potential of a church using both home cell groups and Sunday school is that churches need to use different methods to reach and disciple different groups of unchurched people. In his book, *Revitalizing The Sunday Morning Dinosaur*, Ken Hemphill acknowledges that home cell groups have certain distinct advantages. He states:

> Cell groups cost the church less money than Sunday school because they do not require the church to construct classrooms. Cells provide more time for prayer and fellowship. Cells sometimes benefit from the intimacy provided by a home as opposed to a classroom. Many cells have to be effective for evangelistic outreach. Cells that focus on special or felt needs may be more effective at meeting that need than the traditional Sunday school class. Cells may involve more of their participants in service than the traditional Sunday school.[321]

While it is obvious that healthy cell groups that have many of the advantages mentioned above can contribute significantly toward the growth of a new congregation, it needs to be pointed out that Sunday school also has positive characteristics that can enable a church to experience continuous growth. Hemphill mentions some of the possible advantages of Sunday school:

> Sunday school is easier to organize and manage than cell groups. Sunday school tends to become less personality centered than cell groups. The Sunday school structure makes it easier to safeguard doctrinal integrity than the cell group structure. The Sunday school structure reinforces the value of the worship service by making attendance more convenient. Sunday school integrates the total family. Sunday school can be designed to incorporate all of the functions of the effective cell group. Sunday school

involves a higher portion of the church's people than
cell groups in a North American setting.[322]

As stated previously, the debate should not be whether one
or the other is a valid approach. Both are valid and each has
distinct contributions to make in the task of reaching, discipling,
and assimilating people into the life and ministry of the church.
There may be some overriding factors that may compel a new
church to concentrate on one method at least in its initial stages. One of these factors may be the availability of classrooms.
Another factor may be traditional practices in the area where
the church is being started. In some areas, new churches are
expected to have Sunday schools for both churched and unchurched people. In other areas, however, Sunday school is
perceived as being just for children. In areas where evangelical
Christians are in the minority, the home cell group may serve as
a necessary bridge between unchurched people and the
church.

In the settings where it is feasible and advantageous to have
strong, viable Sunday schools, some of the pitfalls must be
avoided. A self-centered group that meets every Sunday morning mainly to learn more about the Bible from a lecture type
teacher who provides little time for activities that relate to fellowship, support, outreach, and ministry is not going to help
the new congregation to grow. But that is not the stated purpose of Sunday school.

Many years ago Arthur Flake articulated the growth formula
for Sunday school. This formula included five basic steps: "Discover the prospects. Expand the organization. Train the workers. Provide the space. Go get the people."[323] This simple formula can help Sunday school to stay focused on the task of
reaching and discipling people.

Several things need to be done in order to accomplish this
goal. First, the Sunday school leadership needs to capture a
vision of the overall purpose of this important organization. Second, the teachers need to understand their role as disciplers
and enablers and not lecturers. Third, the classes need to be
organized in a way that enables them to fulfill their functions.
In addition to the traditional teacher and Sunday school class
officers, other key positions are needed such as Outreach
Leader, Care Leader, Prayer Coordinator, and Social Coordina-

tor. Job descriptions need to be developed for each of these. Fourth, specific goals for the establishment of new classes need to be established. Fifth, creativity needs to be exercised with regard to the utilization of classroom space. This includes such things as having multiple Sunday schools, off campus Sunday school classes, and classes that meet other days of the week.

Sunday school can be a very powerful tool to reach, disciple, and assimilate unchurched people. It can incorporate many of the features of home cell groups and at the same time capitalize on its own advantages. In areas where there is a strong tradition for adult Sunday school participation, there is already a built-in momentum and a structure that can be very advantageous in establishing a discipleship program in a new church. In other areas, unchurched people will respond better to the Home Cell approach. Whether Home Cell Groups, Sunday school or a combination of these are utilized, it is important to keep in mind that small group meetings are absolutely essential for the health and growth of new congregations.

Joel Comiskey makes a helpful observation regarding the name that is used for small groups. He states:

> I'm not married to the word cell. My conviction is that we should be flexible about what name we use to describe our groups, while standing strongly behind the meaning or definition... I do advise not to use a name that emphasizes only one characteristic of the group. For example fellowship groups, care groups, or even evangelism groups only describe one aspect of the group – thus the name itself can confuse people. I recommend choosing a name that grasps the full dynamic of the group (e.g., touch groups, life groups, heart groups, etc.).[324]

House Churches

The house church approach is yet another way to employ small groups for evangelistic outreach and church planting. The Fellowship of Church Planters defines a house church as "a group of people small enough to meet face-to-face, who have covenanted together with God and each other to be the church under the authority of Christ and the guidance of the Holy Spirit."[325] They explain that:

> The Bible describes the church as 'the family of God.' A house church is like a family. A church must have a Biblical understanding of family in order to function as one. The church family should be an extension of the household family. The same dynamics of communication, commitment, intimacy, growth, participation, caring, sharing and responsibility in our household family overflow into our church family relationships. If our household family relationships are not what they should be, our church family won't function properly. Because the house church acts like a family, it is easier to recognize and correct these problems.[326]

In his book, *Church Planting Movements*, David Garrison points out that the use of homes is one of the ten universal elements present in church planting movements.[327] In his book, *The Global House Church Movement*, Rad Zdero defines a house church in a way that differentiates it from it from traditional churches and cell churches. He explains:

> House churches are an attempt to get back to the form and function of apostolic Christianity. Stated positively, they are fully functioning churches in themselves with the freedom to partake of the Lord's Supper, baptize, marry, exercise discipline, and chart their own course. They are volunteer-led and meet in home-sized groups for participatory and interactive meetings involving prayer and worship, Bible study and discussion, mentoring and outreach, as well as food and fun. Because they are typically autonomous, they more easily adapt to persecution, growth and change, but are also more vulnerable to bad theology and behavior. So, churches become part of peer networks for health and growth, like a spider web of interlocking strands. Consequently, house churches can be explained by the principle that 'church is small groups.'[328]

The Fellowship of Church Planters has a description of a church that highlights the essential elements of body life and points out how these are taken into account in house churches:

> The New Testament depicts the church as a Christian community made up of "a chosen people, a royal priesthood, a holy nation, God's own people"

(1 Peter 2:9). An essential feature of this community is the corporate nature of its people. God chooses and covenants not with individual people but with a people collectively, who will bear his name and exist for his purposes. Although we enter the community individually by faith in Jesus Christ, it is nonetheless the corporate church that is God's concern for us in Christ. We are corporately the church, "the called out ones," joined together in common fellowship under the New Covenant, under the lordship of Christ himself, who is head of the church. Because he is head, all other parts of the body of Christ function as parts of that body, both sustained by Christ and growing up into him, as Ephesians 4:11–16 teaches. In these verses, the apostle Paul lays the foundation for body ministry. Paul states that the church has received gifts of "apostles, prophets, evangelists, pastors and teachers," who have been gifted by God to "equip the saints for the work of the ministry." As the body is equipped for service, its members in turn have the responsibility for ministering to one another. (The "one another" verses in the New Testament, noting carefully who they are written to, help us see this.)

Within this active body, we all, as members of the body, are responsible to function as ministers and priests. All members of the body are gifted to minister according to their gifts and calling. By its very nature, the house church atmosphere enables every member -- man, woman, and child -- to find his or her own niche for ministry. Each functioning member is no more important, nor less, than the next. No matter how "small" a person's gift seems to be, it is vital to the proper functioning and health of that body. As all members of that body supply their unique ministry, the body sees and experiences the fullness of being the earthly body of the living Christ. In the Christian family, each member must be kept in mind. Occasionally, each should have a special time of attention. Each member should also know that the needs of the whole family must be met, for the whole family to stay healthy, grow, and reach out to fulfill the Great Commission of our Lord. Because of the small size of a house church, it is necessary to employ everyone. Therefore, this model of church is completely participatory.

The peer network that Zdero and the Fellowship of Church Planters mention is finding expression in a number of settings. In Cuba, for example, a significant number of established traditional churches are serving as "umbrella churches" for house church networks. This makes it possible for the established churches to provide encouragement, training, and guidance to the house churches that are mainly made up of new converts. The "umbrella churches" can be individual churches, a group of churches, or even a house church that has developed leadership and has been constituted, all of which are in a position to lead a network of house churches.[329] The San Antonio Baptist Association utilizes a similar approach in training the leaders of established congregations to serve as "anchor churches" for the network of house churches that they sponsor.[330] This has enabled the house churches in Cuba and San Antonio to experience unprecedented growth while at the same time avoiding some of the potential pitfalls that Zdero mentions.

One of the things that enable house churches to reach many people who are unchurched or previously churched is the informal, friendly, and flexible setting in which activities take place. For one thing, people who belong to other religious persuasions generally find it easier to attend a meeting in the home of a relative or friend than to go to an "established church" in their community. For this reason, it is important that house churches not try to emulate the formal worship service that takes place in an established church. It is the spontaneity in which people can pray, meditate, worship in song, discuss the Word of God, enjoy a meal, celebrate the Lord's supper, and baptize believers that is attractive and refreshing to people who have never been involved in a Christian church experience or who have for a variety of reasons drifted from the church. While there is spontaneity in the life of the house church, a biblically sound pattern needs to be followed, In his book, *House Church: Simple, Strategic, Scriptural*, Steve Atkerson eloquently makes this point:

> Biblical house churches are not nearly so program or building oriented as conventional churches. Because of this, some have mistakenly concluded that biblically-based house churches are unorganized. Faithfulness to the Lord and His Word necessarily result in a church that follows God's complete pattern for His church. Home churches may not be in-

stitutional, but they are to be organized. Following the traditions laid down by the apostles means that house churches are to have definite leaders, regular and orderly meetings, solid theology proper, active church discipline, and weekly Lord's Supper celebrations.[331]

In addition to the flexibility in the worship experience of a house church there are other factors that make it more accessible to unchurched people. One of these factors is the meeting place. While the term "house church" is used, in actuality the term "simple or small church" may be more descriptive. The reason being that many of these groups, in addition to meeting in homes, meet in offices, apartments, mobile homes, conference rooms, coffee shops, car garages, carports, under trees, or whatever meeting places they can find. The fact that the group finds what is accessible to them solves several major obstacles. Among these are: 1) finances (the group finds what it can afford); 2) distance (the group meets in the place that is closest to the largest number of its members); and 3) identification (the group does not need to cross geographical, social and economic barriers to meet for worship and fellowship). The "5W" meetings that Zdero recommends are conducive to the effectiveness of house churches. He explains:

> More specifically some advocate a structured but flexible format which tries to ensure that key elements are consistently present in every meeting to ensure health, balance, and focus so that everyone has an opportunity to contribute. They use a flexible 5W format that entails Welcome (icebreaker), Worship (praise and prayer), Word (discussion Bible study), Works (mutual ministry time including prayer, prophecy, or problem solving, and Witness (engaging in, or planning for, an outreach activity). They may end by breaking up into small groups in different parts of the house for more concentrated prayer, discussion, and mutual encouragement.[332]

The participative approach to worship and Bible study encourages the utilization of the spiritual gifts of new believers and development of local leaders.[333] For example, it is easier for a new leader to learn how to sit in a circle and lead a Bible study discussion utilizing key questions than to stand before a group and preach a sermon.[334] This simple format contributes to the reproducibility of house churches.

The adaptability that characterizes house churches also contributes to their ability to reach unchurched and previously churched people. Adaptability with regard to meeting place makes it possible for people to come together in whatever circumstance they might be in. Adaptability with regard to the time in which the meetings are held makes it possible for people to meet when it is most convenient for them over against having a set time (e.g., Sunday morning at 11:00 AM). Adaptability with regard to the size of the group also contributes to the multiplication of these groups. Some groups may be able to meet in settings that make it possible for more people to attend while others need to limit the participants to a small number.

It must be kept in mind, however, that the personal interaction which attracts people to small groups must not be lost by allowing the groups to become too large. Connected with this is the desired multiplication of house churches. In a variety of ways, the DNA for multiplication needs to be inculcated in the group from the very beginning. Knowing that it is part of the genetic code of each house church to reproduce itself will keep its members from developing a consumer mentality which leads them to believe that the church exists to serve them instead of existing to serve the Lord by reaching, evangelizing, discipling and congregating people wherever there is a need.

One way to enhance reproducibility is to make sure that every house church that is started has a leader as well as an apprentice. The goal will be for either the leader or the apprentice to make plans to leave at the appropriate time to start another house church at which time each will enlist an apprentice. This process will enable the on-going training of leaders as well as the development of a mindset on the part of the members that their church is going to duplicate itself in accordance with the established strategy for the church planting movement.

Zdero shares valuable advice to those who are interested in starting new house churches:[335]

> *Deliberate*. A conscious effort should be made to plant New Testament-style house churches among unreached people group pockets... Missiological studies have concluded that church planting move-

ments are preceded by deliberate efforts to begin new disciple-making communities.[336]

Rapid House churches need to blueprint themselves with a healthy emphasis on evangelism, the goal being multiplying their house church into two and sending a team to a new one... Doing the math, in ten years there could be as many as 1,000 house churches in the region. This is a reasonable goal given that doubling a house church only means going from, say, ten to twenty people over the course of an entire year.

Small House churches should not grow too large before they decide to multiply. Otherwise the loss of intimacy, openness, and interaction will eventually compromise the group's attractiveness and plateau the numbers.

Saturation Focused Every neighborhood, apartment complex, work setting, and educational institute should be considered a potential area for a new house church. Specifically, the idea gaining attention among mission organizations and missiologists is the planting of a church for every 500 to 1,000 people so that as many people as possible will have a Christian community nearby.[337]

Volunteer Led The weight of responsibility and leadership for emerging house church movements should be placed squarely on the shoulders of grassroots volunteers... Professionals – although having a real role as coaches and strategists and mobile overseers of house church networks--- need to give way to a new wave of volunteer Christian leaders from the grassroots.[338]

The Fellowship of Church Planters affirms the fact that size is the real issue. They explain:

The church should be relational, personal, intimate, and committed. It should be like a family. The Bible uses family terms to describe our relationships to God and each other (father, mother, brothers, sisters, son, daughters, child). Size definitely affects a group's relationships. Social scientists have shown that smaller groups encourage more participation, closer interaction, more accountability, and closer relationships. This is nothing new, our Lord worked with only twelve men that he could build into a community. Spiritual growth happens best in an intimate environment. This needs face-to-face accountability, which depends on size.[339]

Reproduction is essential in all of the small group expressions of the church that we have discussed above. J. D. Payne points out that many house churches are missional in nature because they have within their very DNA a passion to take the gospel to their Jerusalem, Judea, and Samaria, and throughout the world. He further states that these congregations believe that if they cease to be intentionally and regularly involved in evangelism that they cease to be a church. These house church fellowships obey the Lord's instruction to "Go" rather than waiting for and encouraging unbelievers to come.[340]

The pattern of reproduction employed by the Fellowship of Church Planters is one that deserves serious consideration. It follows a series of three cycles: "Cycle # 1 Reproducing to form a house church fellowship; Cycle # 2 Reproducing a house church fellowship; and Cycle # 3 Developing and sending church planting teams."[341] The progression in the various forms of reproduction in wider circles facilitates the saturation of a region and even going beyond the region. Such a vision facilitates the implementation of the Great Commission.

Off-church-campus home cell groups can be an effective tool in reaching the unchurched, involving them in a small fellowship, providing the opportunity for them to hear the Gospel message, discipling them once they have made a decision for Christ and incorporating them into the life and ministry of the church. The house church method is certainly not the only means to evangelism and church starting. It is one means. While never suggesting that house churches are the only way, the evangelical Christian movement should affirm these expressions viable and fully churches. **Ebbie Smith, who prefers to call these fellowships "basic churches" states:**

> Basic churches look to the entire body of believers for service and ministry. These congregations avoid the deadening pattern of depending on paid and trained leaders who are often foreigners to the ministries in which they serve. These congregations maintain a worldwide vision as they seek to open

opportunities for loving service. They maintain a commitment to and determination for unhindered reproduction. These ministries also stimulate Christian growth and service in the lives of believers. They have every right to be called churches. The Christian movement needs to affirm these congregations as fully churches.[342]

The Church Planters Fellowship utilizes a combination of some of the methods described above. They explain:

These gathering meetings ought to run for a specified duration with a specific topic. For example: 8 studies on the Kingdom from Matthew, 6 studies on Kingdom living from the sermon on the mount, 8 studies from Acts on the growth of the Kingdom, etc... This gathering meeting is for unbelievers and thus only those believers who bring their unbelieving friends should come... Other types of topical Bible studies can be used for gathering as well. Anything that can gather unbelievers and convey the gospel should be considered. Some examples: Biblical Principles of Child Rearing, Biblical Principles for a Healthy Marriage Relationship, Principles for the Healing of Souls, How to be a Man (Women, Teenager), Financial Help in a Crumbling World. These are available through the Fellowship of Church Planters... Anything that can draw the lost and make the GOSPEL good news is fair game. We need to communicate the good news and not simply wise advice from the Bible. This requires constantly finding ways to make the Gospel relevant to the fallen world, as Jesus himself did.[343]

Obviously, off-campus small group activities are an important feature in contemporary church starting. Church starters should consider these methods as one way of reaching people and bringing them into Christian fellowships for edification and service.

Bible Study Methods in Small Groups

Whatever the approach might be to reach and congregate people, Bible studies will be an indispensable part. In some instances existing Bible studies are exactly what the group needs. In these cases it becomes a matter of ordering the printed materials and training the leaders. In other instances, however, it may be necessary to design Bible studies to meet the specific needs of the group and to start at the level they need. The following are some suggestions as to the manner in which these studies can be designed.

Chapter by Chapter

A method of studying the Bible with the purpose of evangelizing people is the chapter-by-chapter approach. The gospel of John, for example, can be studied a chapter a week. Generally people who have not studied the Bible in the past feel some apprehension in the meeting because they do not know if they are going to be asked to answer questions that they do not know how to answer. If the people, however, know ahead of time what chapter is going to be studied and what questions are going to be dealt with, they will be less apprehensive and will do a better job of preparing to participate in the Bible Study.

When the Bible Study group is formed, instructions can be given so that the participants will know to read each chapter in advance of the weekly meeting. In addition to this, they can be given a series of questions that will serve as a guide to study each chapter. The following questions can be utilized:

1. Who are the key people in this chapter?

2. What does this chapter teach about Jesus?

3. What does this chapter teach about the way in which we can relate to God?

4. Is there something in this chapter that applies to my life today?

The purpose of these questions is to help the person study the Bible, to understand it's meaning, and to apply it to their life. These questions can be used as an outline for Bible study in the homes. This method can encourage the participation of the people and can guide the discussion so that the Word of God speaks in a direct manner to their hearts. Lindsay Cofield suggests a different set of questions to guide the discussion of a biblical portion:

1. What does this verse say to me:

2. How does it guide, correct, or encourage me?

3. What is unclear to me about the meaning?

4. What will I try to do this week because of its teaching?[344]

The Parables of Jesus

Another method of evangelistic Bible Study is to select some of the parables of Jesus. Many of the parables are especially suited for evangelism. Some of these are: the prodigal son; the parable of the lost sheep; the parable of the rich man and Lazarus, and the parable of the Pharisee and the Publican.

Several questions can guide the group in the study of these parables. Some of these are: (1) what were the circumstances that led to the presentation of this parable? For example, it was the gossip of the Pharisees with regard to the practice of Jesus eating with sinners that prompted Jesus to tell the parable of the prodigal son. The younger son represents the sinners, the older son the Pharisees, and the father represents God. (2) Is an interpretation of this parable given in the Bible? If there is an interpretation (e.g. the parable of the sower) it should be taken in account in the study of the parable. (3) What is the central truth of this parable? Because the parables utilize symbolic vocabulary, sometimes people can attribute certain interpretations that are alien to the central truth. For example, there are those who say that in the parable of the Good Samaritan the oil represents the Holy Spirit, the horse represents the church, and the two denarii represent the Old and the New Testament. In order to avoid this type of interpretation one should concentrate on the principal truth of the parable. (4) Is there something in this parable that applies to my life today?

These questions can help the person find the message of Jesus Christ and to respond to His call.

Lives Transformed By Jesus

Another way of preparing evangelistic Bible studies is through the study of people whose lives were transformed by Jesus. In accordance with the needs and the characteristics of the people in the group, the leader can select Bible characters whose conversion experience can be of special meaning to the group.

Some of these can be Nicodemus (John 3:1-21); the Samaritan woman (John 4:1-42); Zaccheus (Luke 19:1-10); the Ethiopian Eunuch (Acts 8:26-40); Saul of Tarsus (Acts 9:1-22); Cornelius (Acts 10:1-42); Lydia (Acts16:11-15); and the Philippian jailer (Acts 16:23-34). Each Bible study can focus on one of these characters.

There are several questions that one can utilize while studying these characters. Some of these are:

1. What was their life like before knowing Jesus?

2. How did they get to the point of putting their faith in Jesus?

3. How did their lives change?

4. What can we learn from the experience of this person?

The purpose of these questions is to help the persons to understand that the experience of salvation that transformed the lives of these biblical characters can change their lives also. This method can be especially helpful in contexts in which people do not know the biblical concept of new birth. Just as questions were utilized in the methods suggested previously, in this case, these questions can help people to concentrate on what the Bible says about salvation.

Topical Bible Studies

Another way to organizing Bible studies is that of concentrating on felt needs. If the survey in the community has revealed that there are people who have common concerns, the church planter will design Bible studies that focus on these concerns. Some of these concerns can be with regard to the family, the children, work, society, the nation, drug addiction, and alcoholism. The people may be struggling with such emotions as anger, fear, doubt, guilt, defeatism, lack of self- confidence, etc. George Hunter declares that churches that reach unchurched people address the human struggles of anxiety, doubt, self-esteem, and out-of-control feelings at the same time they proclaim the messages of forgiveness of sins, justification by faith, and life after death.345 People may have questions about God, Jesus, the church, the Bible, etc.

Several steps can help the leader prepare Bible studies that address these concerns and questions. First, utilizing a concordance find the biblical passages that address these concerns. Second, find a key verse. Third, make an outline of the passage. Fourth, search for illustrations. Sometimes you will find these in the newspaper, in the news media, in magazines, etc. Fifth, tailor the application of this passage to the concerns that the people have.

This type of home-cell group approach can be of special value in situations in which people would not accept an invitation to participate in a "Bible Study" per se but would accept an invitation to join a group that is seeking biblical solutions to the problems they face. The fact that these groups meet off the church property helps many to attend who might otherwise be intimidated.

Conclusion

As a summary of the various methods that have been presented, we say a heartfelt AMEN! Small groups form an impressive opportunity for contemporary church starters. Small groups and house churches are not the only methods for world evangelization. They do, however, constitute one genuine and available method.

CHAPTER 20

ASSIMILATION PROCESS

In order for the new core group to increase and grow into a healthy church it must develop an on-going process for contacting, involving, and assimilating new people into its fellowship and activities. A group that does not assimilate new converts into its fellowship early in the process will most likely lose these new people.[346] J. D Payne notes as one strength of the house churches he studied was their relational means of assimilation of new people.[347] A viable and adequate assimilation process that seeks to weld the newcomer to the fellowship of the congregation occupies a vital and imperative position in every church starting effort.

Assimilation Process Examples

Over the centuries, various Christian groups have attempted to develop an assimilation process that would perform this result of welding new comers to the fellowship. John Wesley, for example, developed what he called an "order of salvation." This "order" involved four stages—a) awakening, b) enrolling in a Methodist class, c) converting (Wesley said justified), d) and growing (Wesley used the term sanctifying). Following this pattern, the Wesley groups sought to assimilate newcomers to their classes.

A more contemporary example of an assimilation process is the method of Willow Creek Community Church. Willow Creek's version of as assimilation process involves nine components. The church sees the possibility of a person traveling the stages from hostility to spiritual things to incorporation into Christian living. Between these poles, the person might well follow stages of openly considering spiritual things, activity investigating spiritual factors, committing to Christian life, learning about Christian ways, changing lifestyle, and engaging in small group service with stewardship.

Willow Creek Church sets forth a definite seven-part strategy for reaching "unchurched Harry." Some member will build a relationship with "Harry." As the Spirit provides opportunity, the member shares a verbal witness to "Harry" and then seeks to bring "Harry" to a weekend service that is designed especially for seekers.

Harry then works though the process without any pressure. The fourth step involves bringing Harry to the New Community Service for believers that meets on Wednesday or Thursday nights. Fifth, Harry is brought to a small group and as step six, he or she is incorporated into some ministry or service. The final step finds Harry working to advance the Kingdom and in turn befriends an unchurched Harry for whom the seven steps are repeated.

George Hunter offers another example of an assimilation process. He utilizes the analogy of bowling pins to outline this process of assimilation. The first bowling pin, which makes up the first row, symbolizes discovery, or what people need to discover before they can actively begin the Christian pilgrimage. The important discovery related to this row is that we matter to God. Few secular people have made this discovery and most do not realize that every person matters to God.

The second row of bowling pins, two in number, symbolizes new relationships. Hunter uses this analogy to point out that the new believer needs the relation with and support of a worshiping congregation and a small group of Christians. The new person finds stability within these new relationships.

The third row of bowling pins, consisting of three pins relates to new life. One feature of new life is doing the will of God. A second feature of the Christian life is a love for people (and God's other creations). The third feature of new life is freedom in Christ. The experience should be liberating.

The fourth row of bowling pins, consisting of four pins, represents the new lifestyle. The first of these symbolizes that believers are called to live in the world but not of it. Believers are called to live by Kingdom values, not cultural values. The second pin calls believers to a lifestyle of service and ministry. The third pin calls believers to a lifestyle of witness and mission. The fourth pin on the last row relates to the new identity. This pin symbolizes the new identity the follower of Christ discovers to begin to become the new person that God intends as the image of God is renewed within him/her. Hunter is convinced that the Gospel is congruent with our deepest aspirations for ourselves.

Rick Warren, of the Saddleback Community Church, suggests a third assimilation process. Warren views the pilgrimage of people in the following manner: 1) Community - the unchurched people in the community; 2) Crowd - the regular attenders; 3) Congregation those who have become members of the church; 4) Committed - maturing church members; 5) Core - lay ministers. The strategy of this church, therefore, involves reaching out to the community, bringing in a crowd, and building up the church by turning attenders into members, developing them into mature members, and then turning members into ministers.[348]

The discipleship strategy that helps this church accomplish these objectives utilizes the analogy of a baseball diamond. First base consists of a course of study that focuses on commitment to membership. Second base stresses commitment to maturity. Third base stresses commitment to ministry. Home plate stresses commitment to missions.[349] Warren's plan seeks to move people through these stages until the persons in the community (unbelievers), accept Christ as Savior, become part of the fellowship of Christians, mature in the Christian life and then become ministers to the community from which they have come.

Assimilation Process Design

Interestingly, each of these Christian groups that have been effective in reaching and assimilating the unchurched has had a clear concept of the trajectory that people follow from their initial contact with a Christian ministry to the point of becoming mature, ministering Christians. Having this clear understanding of the process of growing into maturing, reproducing church members enables the church to plan strategies that work toward these objectives. Certain definite qualities make up adequate assimilation processes.

Qualities of Assimilation Processes

A study of the examples of assimilation processes as well as a survey of the literature indicates that effective assimilation processes demonstrate several notable ingredients. First, effective assimilation processes rest on the conviction that Christian development and incorporation into Christian fellowship is neither automatic nor easy. The growth from the first association with the Gospel and the churches to mature, ministering members of a Christian fellowship must be closely monitored and carefully guided.

Second, the Christian group seeking to assimilate the new person must pay close attention to the conversion process. While the church will want to keep the person seeking salvation close and involved, the idea is not to incorporate unsaved people into the church. Drawing unchurched people from the community to the Gospel message, and then to their acceptance of this Gospel is the first and foremost goal. Assimilation involves bringing new believers into the life and ministry of the church.

Third, every assimilation process seeks to bring the new convert into close relationship with other believers—in worship, study, and fellowship. Should the church fail to draw the convert into these relationships, the growth of the new Christian will be severely restricted and the likelihood that this believer will incorporate with some other fellowship increases.

Fourth, the new believer will learn of and incorporate into his/her life the teachings concerning Christian living and service. The church will of necessity guide the new believer into the understanding of the demands of Christian living and service. The new member will come to see himself/herself as part of a fellowship that seeks to find and follow the will of God and serve in that will.

Fifth, the assimilation process will provide constant monitoring of the progress of the new member. This monitoring will not involve spying on the new convert but simply the loving care that includes proper and adequate discipling in Christian living.

Sixth, the assimilation process also involves providing adequate simulation toward and opportunity for Christian service. The new convert and member will be guided to discover and employ for God' glory those gifts the Spirit gives. Bringing the new convert into the fellowship of the church holds an important place in assimilation. Providing opportunity to serve in the church holds an equally important function in assimilation.

Every new church should develop an assimilation process designed to guide the unchurched through the process of interest, conversion, membership, growth, and service. An adequate assimilation process holds an importance in effective church starting equal to with any other part of the church starting model.

Selecting an Assimilation Process

Each new congregation will need to select and implement an assimilation process that best fits its personality and vision. Whatever process is developed, it is important that it includes the vital steps that a person goes through in assimilating into the fellowship and ministry of the new church. This process will include contacting new people, establishing a relationship with them, involving them in a cultivative activity, inviting them to attend a worship service, helping them to feel welcomed, encouraging them to become regular attenders, introducing them to other church members, allowing time for them to make a decision for Christ, involving them in a newcomer's class, encouraging them to join the church, enabling them to continue to grow in their Christian experience including the total stewardship of their lives (influence, talents, money), and enabling them to become a part of the outreach ministry of the church.

Church starting teams should study various assimilation processes and select from them those elements best adapted to the church they envision. Those involved in starting a new church should plan this assimilation process from the beginning. Without an adequate plan to assimilate the new people who will be reached by the church, the other plans may fail to provide the desired result. Lyle Schaller provides excellent guidance in creating and implementing these assimilation processes in his books, *Assimilating New Members* and *Growing Plans*.[350]

CHAPTER 21

PRE-PUBLIC WORSHIP SERVICES

After the church starting team has established and expanded a core group through the use of small groups and an adequate assimilation process, it is important to begin worship services that meet the spiritual needs of the core group and enable this group to begin to function as a congregation. Some church planting strategists utilize what they call "Preview Services" in their initial attempts to gather the emerging group for worship. These are generally held at long intervals to give people an opportunity to become accustomed to the idea of gathering for worship. Many church starters will then proceed toward worship activities that they call "Pre-Public Worship Services."[351]

Advantages of Pre-Public Meetings

The new church can realize several advantages by utilizing the approach of pre-public worship meetings in advance of the public gatherings. First, these activities provide an opportunity for a fellowship to develop among the leaders and the participants in the small-group meetings. At first it is quite likely that the people who make up the church starting team and the original core group do not know each other. As time goes on, however, these people begin to develop a spirit of fellowship and a common sense of identity. This important function provides the foundation for the new congregation and its fellowship.

Second, this period of pre-public worship activity gives time for leaders to be discovered and trained. People can more easily participate in activities and accept positions of responsibility when the group is still small and the activities are informal.

Third, this pre-public worship period can be a definite opportunity for the leadership to clearly communicate the vision for the new church. Further, this period allows both leaders and those who make up the core group to affirm their commitment to this vision.

Fourth, this pre-public period allows the new congregation to minister to the spiritual needs of the leaders. As they worship the Lord through hymns, communion, prayers, and preaching, the group begins to acquire the spiritual maturity that must characterize a church.

Fifth, this pre-public phase can enable the new group to gain additional experience in carrying out the vital functions of a church. Some of the functions for which the pre-public period provides are the worship service, discipleship ministry, children's ministry (including the nursery), welcoming and following up on visitors, and other activities that will enable the new congregation to maximize the response of the people who will attend the grand opening service. In a sense, implementing the pre-public worship services gives the new congregation an opportunity to practice the functions that will be necessary in the life of the new church.

Length of Pre-Public Strategy

A question that is asked frequently is: "How long should the group continue in the pre-public mode before going public?" The answer to this question involves several matters.

In the first place, the church starter should consider if the core group is sufficiently large to carry out the basic activities of a congregation—even if it is on a limited scale. These activities include, for example, worship, music, children's ministry, nursery, etc.

In the second place, the church starter should consider if there is a spirit of unity and a feeling of common purpose in the group. In most cases it takes time to develop these qualities in a group.

In the third place, the church starter should consider the doctrinal harmony that exists in the group. No one can expect everyone in the core group to understand all the doctrines in depth but it is necessary that they have a clear concept of and be in agreement with the basic doctrines of the Bible.

In the fourth place, the church starter should consider the adequacy of the financial base. One consideration concerns the sufficiency of the financial base to provide the necessary funds for the expansion of the ministry connected with the going public phase. During the pre-public stage, the core group can gain a greater understanding of the biblical teachings regarding stewardship.

Finally, the church starter should face the question concerning the strength of the group's commitment to the new church. Are the people ready to invest the time and resources that are needed to move on to the going public phase?

The rate at which the preceding characteristics develop will indicate the readiness of the core group to proceed to the next step. The answer to the question as to how long the pre-public period should last is that it should last long enough—that is, long enough for the above-mentioned characteristics to develop. No set time period will be correct for every new church.

Size of Core Group Prior to Public Phase

Another frequently asked question relates to how large the core group should become before the public phase is launched. Peter Wagner addresses this issue when he states:

> If the long-range plan for the church is to be under 200, the critical mass can be as small as 25 to 30 adults. However, if the plan is for the church to grow over 200, that is too small. The critical mass should be between 50 and 100 adults. There may well be many variables that determine the ideal nucleus size, but I am so far aware of only one study. Research by the Southern Baptist Home Mission Board has shown that Southern Baptist Churches going public with under 50 have three times the rate of failure as those that started with over 50. It would not surprise me if this applied to most other denominations as well.[352]

Joel Comiskey utilizes a standard that relates primarily to cell churches but has implications for other church planting models. He states:

> I am convinced that it's best to wait until there are 100 people in approximately ten cell groups before committing to the weekly celebration service. Until then, it's normal and acceptable for the cells to meet once a month in a celebration service or once every two weeks. Waiting for 100 people before weekly celebration assures that the same people won't be doing the same ministries over and over.

It's also essential not to depend on a few key families to show up each celebration in order to have enough people to truly celebrate. With 100 people in the cell groups, some families can miss the celebration and most likely the key celebration functions will continue as planned (e.g., children's church, worship team, and so forth).[353]

Variables for Going Public

The matter of the viable size of the core group prior to going public is, therefore, an important one. As Wagner correctly points out, numerous variables need to be considered in determining the ideal size of the core group.

One variable is the socioeconomic level of the group. The study to which Wagner refers suggests that blue-collar, working-class groups do not feel the need for as large a core group as professional, white-collar groups.[354] One reason may be that the latter group expects better facilities and more ministries and at a higher level of proficiency than the former group. This would necessitate a larger core group to provide these ministries.

Another variable, as Audrey Malphurs points out, may be geographical location. He states: "An urban church start would require a larger core, whereas a rural start might allow for fewer people."[355] The observation made above could well apply here.

There may be the additional factor of expectation. A rural church may simply not expect to have as many people as an urban congregation due to its lack of population density.

Another factor that relates to the size of the core group considers the community's receptivity. In highly receptive areas it may be easier to get 50 to 100 people to start attending home cell groups and pre-public worship services within a short period of time. In highly resistant areas (with people with non-evangelical traditions), however, this may take a long time. This factor of the core group remaining small, therefore, may become a self-fulfilling prophecy.

Church starts that have fewer than 50 prior to going public may either be in a highly resistant area or be utilizing inadequate methods. The consequence may be, therefore, that after it goes public it will continue to struggle and in some instances not survive. As a rule of thumb, a church starter should try to get the largest number possible involved in the core group within a reasonable period of time before going public. If after six months or a year the number in an urban church start continues to be very small or plateaued, a serious analysis has to be done. Conversely, if during a brief period of time the core group has grown between 50 and 100, the prospects for this new congregation are very bright.

Another factor in the consideration of the size of the group before attempting the public worship phase relates to the leader's and the group's mindset and goal. As Schaller points out:

> The decision to remain small will reinforce an approach to ministry by the church starter or mission developer and that of the initial cadre of leaders. Likewise, the decision to begin large will reinforce the pastor and the other leaders to develop an approach to ministry that is consistent with a large number of people.[356]

If all environmental factors are equal and one church begins large while another begins small, it could well be that the person projecting the large start has set goals (evangelistic contacts, organizational structure, meeting place, operational budget, advertisement, etc.) that are consistent with the vision. Conversely, those who project a small start may be establishing a self-fulfilling cycle of performance by using the methodology that leads to a small start.

The readiness of a new congregation to go public with its ministry cannot be reduced to a simple chronological formula. Instead, it should be a qualitative/quantitative formula that measures the vision and quality of commitment along with the measurable qualities that have already been established. A number of measurable and observable qualities are imperative before the new church should seek to promote public worship services.

Joel Comiskey makes very helpful observations regarding the importance of waiting for the right time before going public. He states:

> Granted, it's very hard to wait to start celebration services because church culture still expects a Sun-

day morning gathering... Launching the celebration service too early is a common problem... We started meeting on Sunday morning. I hoped to keep the home groups alive, but soon found that all my time and attention were going to the weekly celebration – just trying to get people to attend that service. It was an exhausting experience, and I don't recommend it.[357]

Ministries Needed

Before the new congregation begins the public phase it is imperative that it initiate and provide some essential ministries. These ministries influence the decisions of unchurched people regarding the new congregation.

Children's Ministry

The new church, even from the beginning of the meetings of the cell groups, must provide for the children. As stated previously, some churches have home-cell groups for adults during the week and Sunday school classes for children during the worship hour. Other churches have Sunday school classes for both adults and children and children's church during the worship service hour.

Other arrangements can of course be implemented. It is very important, however, that special provision be made for children's ministry while the adults are participating in the worship service. This must not be seen as simply "baby sitting" for the parents. Often parents make decisions regarding church membership on the basis of whether they feel that their children are being nurtured spiritually, emotionally, and socially through the children's ministries.

Parents are concerned that their children are safe and that their children will learn about the Bible and Christian living. Equally important, parents desire that their children have such a positive experience at church that they will want to return. For these reasons, the best-trained and most dedicated people in the church who have the calling and the gifts for serving children be enlisted for this ministry. Children's ministry can be one of the most valuable efforts in a church starting effort.

Youth Ministry

The age of the bulk of the visitors is often a good indicator as to the type of programs the new church needs to establish. If most of the visitors are young couples, the children's ministry should take top priority. If, on the other hand, a significant number of the visitor families have teenagers, a youth ministry is absolutely crucial from the very start of the new congregation. A demographic study can be very helpful in determining this need. Church starters must remember that in many instances the determining factor in deciding whether to be a part of a new congregation is the assurance that the new congregation has an adequate ministry for children and youth.

It goes without saying that a creative discipleship program is essential in an effective youth program. This ministry may involve discipleship classes, one-on-one discipleship, retreats, and other methods. Parents need to feel that their youth are learning something and growing as a result of the youth program and not just being entertained.

An all-important factor for young people initially is whether they are welcomed and assimilated socially into the activities of the youth. Youth leaders and the youth group must be trained to go out of their way to welcome and include visiting young people into their spiritual, social, and recreational activities. Youth leaders need to find creative ways to involve the youth in the ministries of the church.

One church sought to incorporate the youth by holding a two-hour study hall. During the first hour, tutors assisted the young people with their homework. During the second hour, the youth were led in Bible Study and recreational activities. This activity was held during the mid-week service while the parents were involved in discipleship, prayer, and other church activities.

Mission trips, recreational outings, camps, cell groups, and fund-raising projects provide opportunities for young people to grow socially, emotionally, intellectually and spiritually. The important thing is for the parents as well as the youth to know that the church deeply cares about them.

Newcomer's Class

A class for newcomers is absolutely essential in an emerging congregation. Placing unchurched people in existing Sunday school classes or cell groups often proves to be a mistake. They may feel out of place and intimidated if they are placed in a group that has considerable Bible knowledge and that has close-knit social ties.

The Newcomer's class can give these people the opportunity to meet the pastor, to meet other newcomers, to learn the basics of Christianity, to understand the vision and ministries of the church, to respond to the gospel message in a non-threatening setting, to grow in their Christian experience, to understand the process of joining the church, to become a part of the fellowship of the church, and to learn how to use their spiritual gifts in the ministry of the church. All these attainments are essential for new Christians who desire to become a part of the church.

Conclusion

The characteristics and needs of the target group should be taken into account in establishing the ministries of the new congregation. Often new congregations want to start off with all of the organizations of an established church. There are several reasons why this is a mistake. First, a multiplicity of ministries will wear out the leaders of the new congregation. Due to the fact that there is generally a limited number of leaders in a new congregation they will suffer from burnout if they have to invest large amounts of time and energy trying to carry out all of the ministries that have been assigned to them.

Second, some of the ministries of an existing church may not be appropriate in the new congregation. This situation emerges especially if the target group is different from the sponsoring church. Third, as the new congregation grows new leadership will emerge. This new leadership allows for the establishment of new ministries as the people sense the need and follow the leading of the Lord to be involved in these ministries.

It is imperative, therefore, for the new congregation to focus on the ministries that are absolutely essential at their stage of development. The new church should not engage in ever expanding efforts that dissipate their leadership and financial resources. "Do what is needed and only what is needed" should be the rallying cry of new congregations.

CHAPTER 22

PUBLIC WORSHIP SERVICES

The going public phase in the church starting process is as challenging as it is exciting. This event gives the congregation an opportunity to inform the entire community that a new church is being started there. The pre-public stage has prepared the new congregation for this new phase in its development. In order for the going public service to be a successful step, careful attention has to be given to several important matters. Someone has said: "You don't have a second chance to make a first impression." The first impression that the visitors receive will be a lasting one and will more than likely determine if they return. What is done in that first public service will either attract or repel visitors.

Selecting the Best Date

The meeting time that is selected for the first public service of the new congregation is of strategic importance. The rule of thumb is that it needs to be a Sunday (most church starts will utilize a Sunday for the first meeting) when the majority of the people are going to be in their community instead of being off on a holiday weekend. This means, therefore, that holidays that includes long weekends (including Mondays) and Sundays or when change is made to or from daylight savings time are generally the worst times for the Grand Opening. This applies also to Sundays in which major national or international sports events are scheduled.

Some have found Easter Sunday to be the best time to have the first public service. Generally more people think about going to church on this Sunday than at any other time of the year. Some have started on Palm Sunday and have sought to build up for Easter Sunday. Others have found the first Sunday of the year (provided cold weather is not a factor) to be a good time for the initial service.

Other Sundays that have proven to be effective times for the initial service have been Mother's Day or Father's Day. Perhaps on these dates, themes that relate to the family would be appropriate. A sampling of key people in the community may also provide valuable information as to the best time to have the going public service.

Whatever the date of the first meeting, the new congregation and its leader should highlight the theme of a "new beginning" for the church. The purpose and vision for the new church should be clarified for the individuals and for the community.

Publicizing the Going Public Service

Adequate publicity is imperative for a successful first public worship service. In a previous chapter, such options as cultivatative visitation, direct mail, telephone, newspaper, doorknob hangers, flyers, posters, radio, and television were noted as possible helps in publicity for the new church. In most instances a combination of these and other methods are needed to inform and attract the community.

Obviously, intense and intimate knowledge of the community allows a more intelligent decision regarding the appropriate media approaches. Studies indicate that there exists a percentage of the population in every community that is going through difficult times and are, therefore, experiencing such a spiritual hunger that they will respond regardless of the method that is used. This fact assures the church starting team that if they and the people they recruit make a concerted effort to reach people, they will find those who will respond to an invitation to attend a worship service that sounds to them as though it will meet their needs.

The fact that in every community reachable people exist does not lessen the imperative for adequate publicity for the first public service. These responsive people cannot attend if they are unaware of the service. Adequate publicity enhances the possibilities of an effective first public worship service.

Planning the Going Public Service

Careful planning should characterize the steps leading up to the first public service. Many visitors follow the pattern of first "checking out" a church service to see if they like it. If they like the service, they may continue to attend until they decide if they want to be regular attenders. This visitation process is generally followed by a decision to join the church.

Briefly put, then, if the people's first experience is positive, they may continue to attend. Producing this positive experience rests on careful attention being given to the worship service. Provision must be made for the setting in which the service is held, programs for the children, the purpose of the service, the recognition of visitors, the announcements, the length of the service, the music, the preaching, the relevance of the sermon topics, the redemptive note of the message, the vision that is communicated through the message, and the invitation[358]

Overall Tone of the Worship Service

One of the most important factors in the development of a new church is a dynamic, culturally relevant worship service. Kirk Hadaway describes this type of service when he states:

> This character is somewhat difficult to describe, but the terms that usually are employed are "exciting," "celebration," "electricity," and "spirit of revival." Whatever terms are used, anyone who has worshiped in many growing congregations will agree that the worship experience sets these churches apart.[359]

The worship service does not have to be spectacular to capture the attention of the people. There needs to be, however, something that happens in the lives of the people when they have participated fully in a worship service. That "something which happens" makes a difference in the way the person feels with relation to God, to others, to their responsibilities, and to life in general.[360] The person has worshiped when he can say like Jacob: "Truly the Lord is in this place" (Gen 28: 16). Church starters should plan the first public service so that worship can be a positive factor in the growth of the church.

Setting of the Going Public Service

The setting in which the worship service takes place either contributes toward making it an inspiring experience or hinders this experience. Some churches have the resources to acquire elegant buildings with all the amenities. Others do not have the same resources. This does not mean, however, that nothing can be done to improve the setting in which the service takes place.

A number of improvements can make the setting more suitable. In some cases so simple a matter as painting the sanctuary and improving the lighting in the sanctuary can add to the setting for the public service. Some churches can change the seating arrangement so that the people can enter and leave more easily. Often, attention to the heating or cooling can heighten the possibilities for the service.

The fundamental question that should be asked is: what impression do visitors receive when they come to our church? Sometimes the members became accustomed to seeing doors or walls that need painting but for the visitors this is a sign of negligence and perhaps low morale. While it is true that many churches have very limited resources, it is also true that in many cases the houses of the members are much more attractive than the place where they meet to worship to God.

Three areas absolutely demand attention—the nursery, the restrooms, and the parking facilities. Parents are deeply concerned that the nursery be clean and that the workers be competent. Their impression of the quality of the nursery may well determine whether they return. Good music and or preaching cannot make up for a negative impression of the nursery and childcare facilities.

A recent study by a gasoline company indicated that the one thing travelers appreciated the most at service stations is the provision of clean restrooms. Newcomers expect the same in the churches that they visit.

Adequate parking is also essential. Church members must be willing to park further away from the building in order to provide space for visitors. While church members might be more persistent, visitors may not be willing to spend a great deal of time looking for a place to park.

All these matters are extremely important in communicating to visitors that we are truly happy to see them. It is important, therefore, to pay attention to the place of worship so that everything there will contribute toward making it an uplifting experience for the members as well as for the visitors.

Purpose of the Service

One of the factors that contributes toward making the worship service a meaningful experience is defining the purpose of the service. There are so many spiritual needs that sometimes people expect each worship service to minister to the members of the church as well as the visitors simultaneously. This effort may confuse the members of the church. Sometimes, when they bring visitors, the pastor preaches doctrinal sermons and when there are no visitors the pastor preaches beautiful evangelistic sermons.

A good number of growing churches have decided that the Sunday morning worship will focus primarily on evangelism. In some cultures the Sunday evening service has the greatest number of visitors and can be designated as the visitor friendly service. The important thing is not the hour but the fact that the pastor and the members have come to an agreement on the primary purpose of each service. The members will, therefore, know when they can expect doctrinal and other sermons that contribute toward Christian maturity and when they can safely invite visitors to hear evangelistic sermons. While it is true that everyone should find every service inspiring, it is also true that when the primary purpose of each service is known, the results will be much greater.

Welcoming Visitors

Many growing churches give special attention to the way in which the visitors are welcomed. Persons who have long been evangelical Christians often think It appropriate to ask visitors to stand up, to give their names, to receive a visitor's card, and to receive a welcome to the service. Sometimes when persons who have long been members of a church visit a sister church, they feel comfortable standing up, giving a fraternal greeting, and expressing happiness for the opportunity to be there.

Some studies, however, indicate that one of the greatest fears that people have is that of speaking in public. What happens, then, when new people enter the worship services? Many times they feel uncomfortable, fearful, and intimidated when asked to stand and speak to the congregation. At the very least, they feel uncomfortable that they are being asked to stand up while everyone is looking at them. In some instances, visitors may want to come, observe, and later decide if they would feel comfortable at the church. But if we direct the attention of the entire congregation at them, it is quite unlikely that they will return.

There are perhaps two purposes that we have in mind when we ask people to stand up: (1) we want to express our joy that they are visiting us; and (2) we want to take their name and address to visit them or send them a letter. These same functions can be realized without our causing discomfort or embarrassment for our visitors.

There are several ways in which we can express our joy for their presence. First, church leaders can make a general comment simply welcoming all our visitors. Some churches have the custom of singing a hymn of welcome and of greeting members as well as visitors without requesting that the visitors stand up or say something. Some churches have people at the door of the church that greet the visitors, give them information (e.g. Sunday school class), give them a visitor's card, and help them to find a seat. Some churches reserve seats closest to the entrance for the visitors so that they will not feel embarrassed while searching for seats, especially when the service has already begun. The way in which visitors are welcomed varies from one culture to another. The rule should be, however, that visitors need to feel comfortable when they visit our church.

The church can obtain information about visitors without embarrassing the persons involved. One way is for the members that have invited the visitor to fill a card with their name and address. Another way is for the ushers at the door to welcome them and to get this information. Some churches even have people in the parking lots to greet newcomers and find names and addresses from persons as they arrive at the church building.

The church leaders should keep in mind that many unchurched persons have some apprehension when they are requested to fill a card. Some may think that they are being enrolled in the membership or some other group of the church. It will be important, therefore, to be sensitive toward these fears that the visitors have and do everything in such a way that they have a positive and uplifting experience so that they will want to visit us again.

Announcements

Many church services are harmed by the methods of making announcements. In relation to a new church, several questions need to be asked with regard to the announcements. One of these is what type of announcements should be made during the worship service? If one is speaking about a worship service designed especially to minister to the unchurched, it is recommendable that only announcements of general interest be made. The announcements that have to do with the organizations of the church (e.g. Sunday school teacher's meetings) should be placed in the bulletin or should be made during the Sunday school hour. This spares visitors from having to listen to many announcements that are not of interest to them.

Another question is, in what part of the program should the announcements be inserted? In many worship services a lengthy period of announcements squelches the spirit of worship. Some churches make the announcements before the worship service starts. Other churches make the announcements after the invitation. Each congregation will decide about the time of announcements in accordance with local customs. Church starters should be careful, however, not to allow the period of announcements to interrupt the spirit of worship that has been cultivated in the initial part of the service.

Length of the Service

The length of time of the service varies between cultures. In some cultures if the Sunday morning worship service is not over by twelve o'clock the congregation becomes restless and some may even leave. In other cultures the members feel no rush to finish the service at a certain hour. There are two factors, however, that we should consider. First, in many cities the style of life is such that the clock guides the people. If the people have become accustomed to activities that move at a rabbit's pace and the service moves at the pace of a tortoise, they will easily become bored.

Second, generally the visitors are not accustomed to lengthy worship services. We are not suggesting a particular length for worship services. What we are saying is that we should pay attention to the way in which time is utilized.

There are several things that can be done so that the service moves at a comfortable pace. First, as we have already mentioned, we can limit the announcements to only those that hold general interest. Second, one could utilize more ushers to take up the offering. If the number of ushers is doubled, the time of the offering can be cut in half. Third, one could reduce the time it takes for a person who finishes speaking or singing at the pulpit and the time it takes for another to move to the pulpit. We are not suggesting that the service should be conducted in an accelerated manner.

We are saying that in a dynamic service everything is organized in such a way that there is enough time for worship, the message of the Word, the invitation, and the other important activities. In other words, a dynamic service moves in an inspiring and sure way toward its culminating point without interrupting the spirit of worship. The people feel that one activity leads to the other and that each contributes to the glorious experience of worship.

Music in the Worship Service

Music plays a very important part in the worship service. It is especially through the music that our spirits are elevated to worship God. There are several factors that make it possible for the music to contribute in a positive way to the experience of the worship.

First, culture influences what music is utilized in the worship service. There are hymns that have been a great source of inspiration for many people throughout the years. When a group, however, depends totally on hymns that were written many decades ago (or hymns whose music represents a culture of the distant past) there is a great probability that the worship service is not going to be as dynamic and that it will not appeal to contemporary unchurched people.

Generally for most new churches, the process of writing their own hymns and music and utilizing the instruments that are representative of their own cultures takes a long period of time. Church starters should be careful that the hymns and choruses used by the congregation are sound doctrinally. There is, however, a higher degree of involvement when the congregation sings the hymns that reflect its own culture.

From time to time there are debates about the instruments that should be utilized in church. In each case, the believers, without a doubt, will use their judgment to determine what instruments contribute to the worship and are not a stumbling block because they are associated with anti-biblical practices. The study of the Old Testament reveals that a great variety of instruments was utilized in the worship of God.

Second, the participation of the congregation in the music contributes to the worship experience. Often visitors feel uncomfortable if there is an excessive amount of congregational singing of songs they do not know. Some growing churches consider this fact in the preparation of their worship service (especially in what they have designated as "seeker friendly services"). In these instances, these churches reduce the number of congregational songs and include a larger number of solos and choral groups.

Some churches also print simple hymns in the bulletin so that the visitors will not have to spend time searching for these hymns in the hymnal and trying to decipher how the stanzas are sung. Other churches project the words of the songs on a screen so that no one is embarrassed by not knowing the words. Again, the objective is that of reducing the tension on the part of the visitors so that they may have a positive experience and feel the desire to return.

Music plays an indispensable part in the worship. When the music is contextualized to the culture and to the needs of the people it becomes a valuable element in worship.

Planning the Preaching

The focal point of the worship service is the proclamation or preaching of the Word of God. Proclamation of God's Word can be effected by several means—drama, digital media, as well as the more traditional spoken word, or preaching. Though the styles of preaching are different, certain characteristics mark the styles of preaching in growing churches. Among these characteristics are: (1) the contextualization of the topics of the message, (2) the redemptive tone in which the message is presented, and (3) the communication of the vision for the church in the message.

Relevance of the Sermons

A good number of the pastors of growing churches preach messages that are relevant to the lives of the people, that is, messages that are contextualized. These pastors have taken the time and expended the effort to know and understand the problems, the anxieties, and the aspirations of the people in the communities that they are trying to reach with the gospel. These pastors have asked such questions as the following: (1) what is the worldview of these people? In other words, these pastors seek to understand what concepts they have about a supreme being, the hearers' purpose of life, and their own existence. (2) What voids exist in the souls of these people that could be fulfilled with the Gospel? (3) What challenges do these people face in their daily life in their homes, their communities, and in their jobs for which the word of God has an answer? and (4) What are the needs of these people that could serve as bridges over which the gospel can be communicated?

In an earlier chapter we mentioned the fact that Jesus adapted the presentation of the message to the needs of his listeners (e.g. Nicodemus, Zaccheus). The pastors of growing churches try to do the same. When people leave the church after the service they not only feel that they have heard a message, but they feel that they have heard God's message for them in the world in which they live. The pastors of growing churches preach messages that are relevant to the lives of the people.

Redemptive Tone of the Sermons

Another characteristic of the sermons preached by pastors of growing churches is that they have a redemptive tone. Some preachers believe that they are preaching the Gospel when they denounce sin and tell the people how sinful they are. It is true that the Bible has much to say about sin, but that is only part of the message. Roman 6: 23, for example, says, "*the wages of the sin is death*." But if we continued reading we realize that the passage also contains the promise, "*the gift of God is eternal life in Jesus Christ our Lord*." The good news Is that

God has made provision for the sin of humanity in Jesus Christ and that every person who accepts him is given abundant life in this world (John 10: 10) and the glorious hope of eternal life in Heaven. The word "gospel" in itself means good news.

The pastors of growing churches preach the good news of salvation. They not only speak about sin. They speak the glorious truth that in Jesus Christ we have liberation from the power of sin. The redemptive tone of the message not only says to human beings that they are sinners but that they can conquer sin. They not only show people their condition but also teach how they can be different. The redemptive message gives people a new vision of what they can be if Christ is in their heart.

Instead of leaving the services with a feeling of guilt and defeat for what they have done, people who hear redemptive messages leave the services with a new optimism based on the truth that with the help of the Lord their lives will be different. The text, "*I can do all things through Christ who strengthens me,*" becomes the motto of their lives. Sermons preached in growing churches proclaim this redemptive tone. The members invite their friends with confidence because they have the assurance that they also are going to hear uplifting sermons with a *redemptive note.*

Communicating the Vision through Sermons

Another characteristic of the preaching in growing churches is that it communicates and maintains alive the vision for the church. Preaching in these churches not only speaks about the individual life of the people but also presents a vision for the whole church. Through these sermons the pastors communicate the goal and the priorities of the church. The members, consequently, begin to capture the vision and feel the great satisfaction of belonging to a church that has exciting plans and goals, a church that goes forward with the full conviction that the Lord is guiding them.

The members feel a great sense of satisfaction in this type of church and invite their relatives and friends. Although at the beginning the visitors may not understand much about the vision for the church, with time, they also begin to have a positive feeling about its life and ministry. They receive the impression that this church has goals and knows where it is going. It is much easier for visitors to feel attracted to a church that is moving forward than to one that is plateaued or declining.

Studies indicate that the pastors of the growing churches may not necessarily be more eloquent or more highly trained than other pastors.[361] What has been discovered is that the sermons preached by pastors of growing churches are more contextualized, have a more redemptive tone, and are more successful in communicating the vision that God has for that church.

Inviting a Response

For many evangelical Christians, the invitation given at the end of the sermon is of great importance. Theologically the invitation is based on the fact that Jesus invited people to follow him. On many occasions this invitation was given in public. Giving the invitation, therefore, is based on the conviction that people need to make a public decision to receive Christ as savior.

Many evangelical Christians hold in their memories scenes of the moment they or a loved one responded as an invitation was given in a Billy Graham evangelistic crusade or other evangelistic service. It is an unforgettable experience, to see hundreds of people go forward in a stadium indicating their desire to receive Christ as their Savior. This type of direct invitation has been utilized effectively in many places and in different times.

There are settings, however, in which a public invitation in a church building or a stadium does not have the same results. As we have said in one of the previous chapters, there are certain contexts in which there is a need to cultivate friendships, present the message gradually, give an opportunity for people to respond to the gospel in their homes, and prepare them to share their decision in a worship service. Like the message itself, the evangelistic methods must be contextualized to the culture in which the effort is directed.

Some of the growing churches encourage people to receive Christ in their hearts but do not ask them to make their decision public immediately. A church was meeting in a school auditorium that did not have a center aisle. The pastor had to adapt his methodology for giving the invitation. His method now follows the following approach.

Upon concluding the message, the pastor asks all of the people to bow their heads and spend a moment reflecting on the message they have just heard. He then asks those who want to receive Christ in their hearts to look up and focus their attention on him. When the people follow this plan, he spends a moment speaking to them about the meaning of receiving Jesus Christ as Savior. From the pulpit, he prays for them. After this he asks that the people who have decided to follow Jesus take a card that has been included in the bulletin or that on the back of the pew in front of them. He instructs them to fill out that card and promises that during that week a minister from the church will visit them and talk in more detail about the decision that they have made.

In their homes the minister answers their questions and helps them to understand the plan of salvation. After this the minister enlists them in the new believers' class. It is not until the time of their baptism that the new converts stand before the congregation and give their testimony of salvation. In a community where response to the Gospel message had been very limited, this pastor has succeeded in winning thousands to the Lord. This method of extending the invitation has contributed significantly to this success.

The method of extending the invitation outlined above is not the only way that an invitation can be or should be used. This account simply provides an example of the contextualization of the invitation in a specific place. In order to achieve this type of contextualization we needed to distinguish between the principle and the method. The principle is that the people should have the opportunity to make the decision of receiving Christ in their heart. This decision has a dimension that goes beyond individual experience. The way by which the invitation is given in the example has to do with the method and not the principle. The pastor that we mentioned believes that it is at the baptism that the new believer makes a public profession of faith in Jesus Christ.

Others perhaps may extend invitations differently. Within this principle there is variety as to the sociocultural form that is utilized. Christ, for example, did not give the invitation while the piano was playing and the choir was singing. This method of giving an invitation is an adaptation that has arisen in more recent years. Nothing certifies that any particular method of giving the invitation is necessarily more biblical than other ways. What is important is that the church maintains the principle of calling people to a response to the voice of the Lord. The method of this calling can be adapted (the specific way of giving the invitation) to the local context so that the greatest possible number comes to have the glorious experience of receiving Christ as their Savior.

Conclusion

The worship service is an important factor that contributes to the growth of the church. In order for the worship service to be truly dynamic, attention needs to be given to the setting in which the service takes place, the definition of the purpose of the service, the way in which the visitors are welcomed, the way in which the announcements are made, the duration of the service, the music, and to the preaching. This requires much prayer, planning, and dedication. When the people leave the worship service with the firm conviction that they have been in the presence of the Lord, not only will they return, but they will also invite others with enthusiasm to participate in this spiritual feast. A dynamic worship service contributes to the growth of the church.

PART 5

Develop New Congregations

The development phase of starting a new congregation involves matters that assume a more permanent nature than the efforts of previous phases. For example, while in the launching phase, the organization remains in its formative stages. By the time a church gets to its development stage it must make decisions regarding its official status, organization, constitution, facilities, etc. At the development phase attention needs to be given to the principles that help a church to grow, the structure that it will need, and the action plans that will help it to implement its strategy.

CHAPTER 23

CHURCH INCORPORATION

Depending upon the model the church starting team utilizes the new congregation will reach the point at which it must define its official status as an incorporated church. This status has two major aspects. First, the legal aspect of incorporation is very similar to the official incorporation of a business. This step allows the church to have legal standing with the government and to carry out its financial transactions.

The second aspect of the incorporating process is the religious factor. This factor relates to the official status that the incorporated church will have with regard to its own congregation as well as other ecclesiastical bodies such as the associations and conventions of the denomination to which it belongs. In relation to both the legal and the religious incorporation process, the congregation will usually proceed through a preliminary stage and an intermediate stage, before going on to the final, necessary steps of incorporation.

The Preliminary Stage

The preliminary stage of incorporation usually is in effect during the period in which the new congregation still receives financial support, personnel assistance, and methodological guidance from a sponsoring church (or cluster of churches).

The preliminary stage of incorporation provides several advantages for the church. First, the preliminary stage can give the new congregation time to solidify its base. This can be a time when the vision is clearly communicated. The pastor, church starting team, and core group make a firm commitment to work cooperatively toward the attainment of the vision.

Second, this period can be a time when the core group develops a stronger fellowship bond. This developing fellowship will provide the base for the future relationships within the group and for the various responsibilities that they will carry out together.

Third, this period is a time when the core group is expanded and new people are assimilated. Many of the people who begin attending the new congregation, especially as a result of a media effort, will need to go through a similar process as the original core group. This process will help them develop a clear concept of the vision and the strategy that guides the activities of the new congregation.

Fourth, this is a time when new leaders are discovered. As they are given opportunity to serve in the various tasks of the new congregation, new members reach a greater understanding of the church, of their capabilities, and a refined commitment to the church.

Fifth, this can be a time when creativity is exercised regarding the use of the temporary facilities. Once the worship attendance gets to a certain number, the church can experiment with the use of multiple services. There can even be some variation in the style of worship from one service to another thus attracting people who prefer different worship styles.

This flexibility can also provide variety with regard to the time in which a service is held. For some, an early service can be very appealing while others may prefer the more traditional time. Experimentation with different approaches can help the new congregation to discover what its strengths are and which approaches are the ones that produce the greatest results.

Sixth, this can be a time when new leaders are trained and developed, especially in the areas of evangelism and discipleship. The sooner that the members of the core group are involved in evangelistic outreach the greater the potential for growth of the new congregation. During this stage the daughter congregation can take some steps toward the next stage.

Planning the Preaching

When the core group attains the characteristics that have been mentioned above, it is ready to continue on to the intermediate stage, that of becoming a functioning congregation. At this level this group begins to have the characteristics of a church. This means that this group has a worship service, a discipleship plan (Sunday School, Home-Cell Groups, or some other program), and a financial plan.

When the group arrives at this stage it is important that the new church reaches certain agreements with the sponsoring church or group. These agreements should include such things as:

1. The reception of new members in the daughter congregation

2. The handling of finances

3. Administrative matters

4. Reporting procedures

5. The procedure for calling a pastor

6. The administration of the ordinances

7. The financial backing on the part of the sponsoring church

The agreements that are reached with regard to these matters will help or hinder the development of the daughter congregation. The question that should be kept in mind in establishing these agreements is: "How will this agreement help the new congregation to continue progressing until it becomes an autonomous church?"

During this period the new church and the sponsoring church need to reach an agreement about the way in which the daughter congregation will receive new members. Technically, the members of the new congregation are members of the sponsoring church. The decision needs to be made as to whether authority will be given to the new congregation to receive members or if the names of these people will need to be presented in the business meeting of the sponsoring church for approval.

The handling of the finances of the new congregation is another very important matter. At the beginning of the new work it is expected that the sponsoring church handle the finances of the daughter congregation. Some churches, however, begin a separate bank account for the new congregation. This helps the new congregation to begin to assume responsibility for its own expenses. If the church receives the money of the new congregation but does not inform the new group as to how the finances are going, the new congregation may not develop a sense of responsibility.

Another factor that needs attention is the manner in which the new congregation will make its decisions. If the new congregation is authorized to have business meetings, parameters need to be established within which the decisions will be made and the degree to which they are binding. In the major decisions that involve the sponsoring church it is obvious that the new congregation should not make these decisions by itself. It is helpful, therefore, that agreements be reached regarding the manner in which decisions will be made.

It is important also to clarify to whom the leaders of the new congregation will report. The sponsoring church should be informed about the activities of the daughter congregation. This report can include not only the activities but also the needs of the new congregation. It helps, therefore, to clarify to whom the leader of the new congregation will report, when he should send the report, and what will be the content of the reports.

One of the most important matters with regard to the relationship of the new congregation with the sponsoring church is the procedure whereby the new congregation will choose its leader (or pastor) and other staff members. The experience of the pastor and the leaders of the sponsoring church indicate that they contribute to the process of calling a pastor for the new congregation. It is of vital importance, however, that the members of the new congregation participate in this process also.

In some cases when the members of the new congregation have not been consulted nor involved and the sponsoring church has chosen the leader (or pastor) the situation has become stressful. The leader chosen by the sponsoring entity has often experienced great difficulty in assuming leadership or having a successful ministry. The members of the new congregation do not feel that their opinions have been considered. Some sponsoring churches have established a pastor search committee composed of members from both the church and from the new congregation. This arrangement provides opportunity for both groups to participate in this process that is so important to the life of the new congregation.

At times there have been conflicts between the sponsoring church and the new congregation because the matter of the administration of the ordinances in the new congregation has not been clarified. Some churches insist that the pastor of the sponsoring church is the only one who can officiate in the ordinances. This creates problems when the new congregation is far from the sponsoring church or when the pastor is too busy to visit the new congregation. Some churches authorize the pastor and the deacons of the new congregation to officiate in the ordinances. This matter needs to be defined to avoid conflicts or delays in the observation of the ordinances.

Another matter that is of vital importance for the life of the new congregation is the financial backing. At first it is quite likely that the sponsoring church will provide most of the expenses for the new congregation so that the new congregation can grow and take on financial responsibility. Some sponsoring churches reach an agreement with the new congregation regarding their participation in the salary of the pastor. This involves a plan by means of which the financial participation of the church decreases as that of the new congregation increases until the time comes when the new congregation is self-supporting.

The clarification of these matters and the doctrinal, administrative, and financial maturity of the members of the new congregation will contribute toward its becoming an autonomous church. To the extent that the daughter congregation has a working relationship with the sponsoring church, the bylaws should reflect a spirit of cooperation.

The Incorporation Stage

As we stated earlier in this book, the ultimate goal for a new congregation is to become an autonomous, self-sustaining, and reproducing church. The incorporation event can be a marvelous time for both the sponsoring church and the daughter congregation, similar to a wedding. When both groups work cooperatively to set the target date and to make the necessary arrangements, the constitution of the church provides the type of inspiration and momentum that will help it to continue to grow and attain its potential.

What Incorporating (Constituting) Means

Incorporating a new congregation into a church brings into being a new legal status and legal identity. It means that the new church will become an autonomous spiritual unit generating its own resources for ministry. This means that it has the opportunity to establish itself as a self-supporting, self-governing, self-propagating, self-ministering, self-functioning, and self-imaging church built on the model of a New Testament church serving in its context.

When to Incorporate

Often people make the mistake of thinking only about the time element as they seek to establish a target date for constituting as a church. Should a new congregation constitute as a church after three years? The answer is rather complex. Some congregations are ready to constitute as a church even earlier than three years but others will need even more time. Several factors will guide in making this decision.

First, the church starting team, under the direction of the pastor, after much time in prayer needs to have a strong conviction that it is the will of God for them to lead the congregation to constitute into a church at that time. As they prayerfully consider the track record of the growth of the congregation and evaluate the plans that have been made for the future, they need to feel a sense of confidence that the timing is right. This step will require an even greater commitment on the part of the team. They may even be in a position of having to sacrifice more due to the fact that they will not have the financial backing of the sponsoring church. If they have strong convictions that this is what God wants for the church, they can lead the congregation with confidence.

Second, the group needs to have a clear understanding of the New Testament concept of a church. This means that the congregation needs to understand clearly the nature and mission of the church. Further, they need to understand what their mission is as a local church in relation to their ministry focus group. A church that has a clear concept of its biblical identity and mission will be able to face many pressures, trials, and difficulties and still remain firmly on course.

Third, there needs to be a strong commitment to Christ and a deep sense of fellowship with one another on the part of the congregation in order for them to have the foundation that is needed to function as a church. If they have gelled into a unit with a common vision and a strong commitment to work with one another, they have one of the characteristics that is needed to become a church.

Fourth, a congregation is ready to constitute into a church if it has the personnel, financial, and numerical resources to minister in its community. It is important, however, that this new congregation not be forced to fit the mold that some churches have of having a full-time pastor, a full-time staff, their own building, and all the programs of an established church. The congregation can be a church if it has a bi-vocational pastor and if it meets in a rented or leased building. By definition an autonomous church is a congregation that relies on its own leadership and financial resources for its activities and ministries.

Certainly, it is a great advantage when the church has enough financial resources to have a full-time pastor and its own building. These in themselves, however, do not determine if a church is autonomous. At times the congregation needs to be realistic and call a bi-vocational pastor and staff, meet in rented facilities, and provide many of the needed ministries through the work of volunteers. The crucial question that needs to be answered is, can the church provide its own resources to carry out its ministries? If the answer is yes, then it can be an autonomous church.

Fifth, the congregation needs to understand church polity sufficiently to know how it will govern itself and how it will relate to fellow churches as well as denominational agencies. The church's relationship with associations of churches should be considered at this point.

Sixth, the congregation needs to have a strong doctrinal foundation in order to function as a church. This means not only that the members understand the basic doctrines of the Bible but also that they are in harmony regarding the doctrines that they will emphasize in their new church.

Seventh, the congregation needs to have a strong leadership base in order to provide the ministries that will help it to fulfill its mission and minister to the people in its ministry focus group. This leadership foundation extends to include lay leadership. The lay leadership foundation may be even more important to the future of the new congregation than the pastoral and staff leadership.

There are, undoubtedly, other indicators of a new congregation's readiness to constitute into a church. All such matters should be considered and discussed carefully and prayerfully as the decision to constitute is considered.

The Incorporation (Constitution) Document

The incorporation (constitution) documents of churches vary from one region to another and sometimes from denomination to denomination. The committee assigned to the task of preparing an Incorporation (Constitution) document should study several examples of such documents and glean the needed factors.

Common Factors in Incorporation Documents

Most constitution documents contain several common factors that include:

1. A preamble that sets forth the purpose of the constitution.

2. The name of the church. The name that is selected becomes the official, legal title. This means that no other church can be incorporated under the same title.

3. The purpose of the church. A brief mission statement sets out what the church views as its purpose for being.

4. The doctrinal statement of the church. Some churches basically use the official doctrinal statement of the denomination with which they are affiliated. Other churches develop their own doctrinal statement.

5. The church covenant. This principally outlines the spiritual and moral principles that the church expects its members to follow.

6. The government and polity of the church. Some churches have a congregational form of government while others have more of a representative form. This needs to be stated in the constitution.

7. The denominational affiliation of the church. This section explains the relationship of the new church with its local, state, regional, and national agencies.

8. Amendment procedures. The ways by which the constitution can be amended.

Bylaws

The bylaws need to be written so that they will clearly state officially accepted procedures regarding membership, officers, committees, organizations, meetings, and other general procedural matters. These bylaws spell out the way by which the church will govern itself. The new congregation can and should establish its own bylaws. The bylaws include such things as:

1. The way in which new members will be received and dismissed. The reception of members includes those who come by baptism, letter of transfer, or statement of their conversion. The dismissal involves transfer of letter of membership to another church, deletion of inactive members from the list, and those excluded through disciplinary actions taken by the church.

2. The handling of finances. This includes such things as how the money will be collected, who will count it, the establishment of a bank account, who will sign the checks, who will give the financial reports, how a budget will be set up, who will disburse the funds salaries, bills, purchases, etc. and how an annual audit will be set up.

3. The business operation of the new congregation. This includes such things as the scheduled business meetings, who will preside, how the business will be conducted (e.g. Rules of Order). In short, this will clarify how the decisions affecting the church will be made and implemented.

4. The procedures for selecting and dismissing the pastor, the staff, and other officers of the church.

5. Procedures for the purchase and sale of property.

The bylaws should be both specific and flexible. They should be written in such a way that they are specific enough to provide guidance yet broad enough as to allow the leaders of the congregation to take action without having to call a business meeting for every activity in which they will be involved. By-laws should anticipate matters the new church will face.

The Incorporation (Constitution) Service

The incorporation (constitution) service is the meeting in which the church officially constitutes itself with the help and approval of the sponsoring group. Planning for this service should involve the appropriate officers from the sponsoring church and the officers of the new congregation. While a significant variety exists with regard to constitution services, these services generally include several items. These general items are: hymns, scripture reading, recommendation from the sponsoring church, motion formally to constitute the church, election of officers and committees, presentation of the title of property (if applicable), motion to incorporate, adoption of the constitution and bylaws, hymn, offering, sermon, invitation for new members, reception of new members, and benediction. The churches involved may of course select any combination of these or other items for the constitution service.

Generally most, if not all, of the official actions such as the recommendation from the sponsoring church, election of officers, and the adoption of the constitution have been thoroughly discussed between the sponsoring group and the new congregation prior to the constitution service. This agreement allows the actions to represent official approval for matters on which tacit approval has previously been reached. Such a procedure avoids both a lengthy constitution service and any disagreements during the service.

As a congregation goes through its stages of development (preliminary, intermediate, and incorporation), it will need to pay attention to the various legal and ecclesiastical matters that need to be defined. This will keep the new congregation from becoming entangled in confusion, controversy and conflict. Arriving at the proper agreements at the proper time will enable the new congregation to work efficiently and cooperatively as it continues to grow and achieve its potential.

CHAPTER 24

PERMANENT FACILITIES

A previous chapter discussed the utilization of temporary facilities by the new congregation. While there are several advantages to this arrangement (such as cost and flexibility) there comes a time when the constituted church needs something larger and more permanent. For one thing, if the temporary arrangement involves setting up and taking down, the people may get tired after a period of time. The time often arises when the new church does need permanent facilities and the apostolic church starter needs to prepare for this need.

Securing Permanent Facilities

Obviously congregations reach points at which they need permanent facilities. The timing for providing these facilities, however, may not be right for the new church to move toward providing its truly permanent facility. For one thing, as stated before, it is a mistake to build too soon and too small. If this happens, the congregation may be saddled with a huge debt and still not have the space it needs for future growth. It may be that at this stage the church may consider obtaining a lease on a building that is suitable for its intermediate stage needs.

Before securing permanent facilities, the congregation usually goes through at least three stages: 1) initial, 2) intermediate, and 3) permanent. When the time arrives for the new church to obtain Its permanent facility, the congregation should consider at least six all-important factors.

Size of Permanent Facilities

The size of the building is of vital importance because it will have implications on the future growth of the church as well as the indebtedness that it will incur. While it is always important to exercise faith in a church starting effort it is crucial to couple this faith with "prudent and analytical judgments.[362] The church needs to take into account several matters as it contemplates the size of the permanent facility.

First, the church should consider the growth patterns of the new church in determining the size of the new facilities. Estimates based on previous patterns can provide a very accurate picture of the expected growth of the congregation over the next five, ten, fifteen, and twenty years. The church that attempts too large a project may find itself in serious financial trouble. Robert Kilgore, a church loan expert, states:

> Enlarged building space does not necessarily result in growth of membership and attendance. People respond to ministry and programs, and these must come prior to the church building. The properly designed building will support the church ministry and program but will seldom bring them into existence.[363]

Since it is personnel, ministry, and programs that attract people, a realistic assessment of the past effectiveness of these efforts is necessary in order to project the size of the new building that is required. The provision of permanent facilities should neither interfere with nor hinder the direct ministries of the church.

Second, the growth stage in which the church finds itself is also very important. Obviously every new church goes through its initial stages. This is generally a time when the new congregation receives financial assistance from outside sources for its primary expense items such as staff salaries, rental or lease of the building, and program expenses. As a new congregation gains financial strength it assumes more and more of its financial responsibilities.

Attaining this self-support allows the new congregation to enter a period of stabilization. During this period of time the core group is solidified and expanded. Attendance becomes more regular and dependable. The financial patterns of the congregation are established and the leadership understands what they can anticipate for the annual budget. The programs of the church are also stabilized at this time and the membership exhibits a greater sense of responsibility as it carries out the ministry of the church. After the new congregation has achieved a significant degree of stability, it can move toward a period of advance in which it focuses on building plans and debt programs.[364]

Location of Permanent Facilities

The place where the building is located or will be located is also of vital importance. Several factors can function as rules of thumb in choosing a location.

Perhaps the most important factor is that the building be near the target group. It is an established fact that church members are willing to drive longer distances to church than unchurched people. While church members are willing to drive further, it is also true that generally the farther they are from the church building, the less involved they will be in the church's activities and ministries. A great distance from the target group also means that church members will have a difficult time getting their neighbors to attend their church. The building, therefore, needs to be close to the target group.

A second factor is accessibility. The building needs to be in a place that people can get to without an excessive amount of effort. The building may be near the target group yet very difficult and confusing to get to. Visitors especially may find it difficult to locate the building. There are instances where the exit ramps from freeways are so complicated that people have a difficult time reaching the church building. As has been mentioned previously, while the wise use of signs can be helpful, the selection of location for the new church building should strive to avoid the problem of poor accessibility from the beginning.

A third factor has to do with community trends. The American Society of Real Estate Appraisers has discovered that each community goes through four stages of development: growth, stabilization, transition, and renewal.[365] Depending upon the specific area, it is estimated that it takes between fifty and seventy five years to complete this cycle. In many urban areas today this type of change can occur much quicker. As a new congregation looks at a site for the location of its building it needs to ascertain the specific stage at which the community finds itself. This will help to estimate how the trend in the community will affect the future growth of the church. Kilgore observes: "A church should not create a twenty- year debt and financial program when it is evident that changes in the community within a few years will demand major adjustments in program and ministry."[366]

Land for the Permanent Building

If a church plans to build a new building, the purchase of land is an absolute essential.[367] Several things must be kept in mind when this is done. First, the topography of the land is important. The land should have sufficient level space for the building that is projected and the parking needed. Further, it should not be in an area that has problems with drainage and storm control. The church leadership should be certain that subsoil problems (e.g. lead contamination) do not exist and that the land is not close to factories that produce foul odors. The land also should not be too close to areas where there are noisy activities or near businesses that conduct activities that are offensive to the church.

Second, zoning ordinances need to be examined for several reasons. Church starters need to clearly understand that a church can be built there and that there will not be any parking restrictions that will affect the growth of the church. The leadership of the church also needs to find out if there are building requirements that will be detrimental to the building plans of the church. Some areas, for example, have restrictions on property used for religious purposes and on the number of stories a building can have.

Third, it is important to know what assessments are levied by city, county, and state governments. Some church leaders have discovered belatedly that the assessments imposed for such things as pavement, curbing, water or sewer lines, electrical lines, and the like far exceeded what they had projected in their building budget.

A fourth factor relates to future planning by city or county commissions. Generally these planners know what is being projected for that community. Some churches discovered after they had built their buildings that a highway that was going to divide the community was already planned. In other instances churches have had to relocate because of the broadening of streets that severely reduced their parking space or placed the building closer to noisy lanes of traffic. The church should anticipate and avoid changes that reflect negatively on the image and efficiency of the building.

A fifth factor relates to the future growth potential of the church. If geographical boundaries such as rivers, highways, railroad tracks, or other buildings box in a church building, it will not be able to purchase adjacent land to support its growth. The church should avoid locating in an area that will limit its future growth and expansion.

Regarding the size of the land that is to be purchased, the common wisdom is that a church should buy more land than it thinks it needs (some church-growth experts say twice as much). The rationale for this is that a church can always sell surplus land but once it is boxed in, it may be very difficult if not impossible to purchase additional land. While this is good advice if the funds are available, other possibilities should be explored if either the fund or the land is not available.

Permanent Building

The indebtedness that a new congregation incurs in connection with the purchase or construction of a building is also a very vital issue. Jack Redford explains:

> The purchase of a church site and construction of a first unit building can either kill or cure the new congregation. If the debt is prohibitive and suffocating, it will depress the spirit of the church and eliminate all joy and praise in worship. The atmosphere of strain also will prohibit new people from joining the congregation.[368]

In order to ensure that the acquisition of a building turns out to be a blessing instead of a burden, several things need to be taken into account.

First, it cannot be emphasized too strongly that most new congregations need professional advice when it comes to acquiring a building and establishing a plan to pay for it. Most denominations have experts who can advise the church on financial plans for the retirement of building debts. The church should contact these experts and seriously consider their advice.

Second, the debt that a church acquires should be examined in light of its personnel and program commitments. Kilgore advises that in most cases a church should not allocate more than a third of its budget for the retirement of the building debt. This advice is based on the conviction stated above that buildings do not attract people but rather personnel and programs.

Kilgore offers the following budget as an example:[369]

Local expenses	15% to 20%
Missions	10% to 15%
Salaries	40% to 50%
Sub-totals of programs	65% to 85%
Left for debt	35% to 15%
Total	100% to 100%

Obviously, there are a number of variables that need to be taken into account in establishing a ceiling for indebtedness. Generally as churches grow larger the percent of their budget that they spend for salaries may be smaller while the percent they give to missionary endeavors may be larger. Some churches spend more on their programs than others depending on the type of programs they have and the number of volunteers they enlist. As we stated previously, a church that utilizes a home-cell group approach for adults will spend less on educational building space than one that has Sunday School for Adults as well as children.

Other variables are the interest rates, the type of interest (e.g. simple, add-on, discount), and the length of the loan.[370] The income to debt ratio, therefore, will vary depending on the length of the loan. Kilgore strongly urges churches to keep in mind that:

> Debt should be limited to that which present income will pay. While each church expects to grow in both numbers and finances, the church should not depend on future members to pay for obligations which it previously has contracted. To state this principle in another manner, the church should endeavor to reach new people for a spiritual purpose and not for the new members to pay its debts.[371]

Architectural Design for the Permanent Building

What was said about financial matters applies just as strongly to architectural matters. Churches should seek the advice and guidance of experts in architectural church building plans. A master plan needs to be developed which maximizes the use of the land and makes it possible for the church to continue to build.

Some church leaders have made the mistake of placing their first unit in the most prominent place in the church property and then either having to tear it down or to build a larger sanctuary adjacent to it. The result is that the church property looks like a "patch up job." A master plan that calls for the construction of building units that meet the current needs of the congregation while allowing for additional units avoids the problems above and provides a more efficient church campus. Following such a master plan allows for new construction that enhances the church's ministry and provide additional space as needed.

Considering Alternative Options

Generally when the congregation thinks about providing its first permanent unit, it envisions a new building with all the amenities that are found in the buildings of long-established churches. In order to reach this plan, the new congregation would need to be large enough to have the necessary financial resources. Such a situation is seldom a reality.

The first building may not be the final place for the church. Lyle Schaller points out that in the United States, people in upper-middle and upper-income communities have the tendency to think that "the first building at the first location will be the first unit of a permanent facility at its location."[372] He adds that: "By contrast, most African American, Hispanic, Asian, and Anglo working class new missions assume their pilgrimage will take them from modest rented temporary quarters to larger rented quarters to a temporary meeting place that they will own as part of their journey to their 'permanent' church home."[373]

Unless a congregation has the number of members and the financial resources, it may need to consider other options that will lead them to the place where they have the permanent building that they desire. Schaller mentions several creative alternatives that a congregation might consider.[374]

First, a congregation may begin by constructing a one-story building with the expectation that later it will be sold for commercial uses. The expectation is that the new church will be able to sell it for more than it invested and at that time have the membership and the funds needed to build a more suitable facility.

Second, a church can design the first unit as "light construction" that resembles a residence rather than a school or a hospital. This has the advantages of lower cost per square footage (by 50%) and the utilization of volunteer workers.

Third, a church can utilize low-cost factory manufactured buildings on what is assumed to be the "permanent site." This plan has the advantages of being less expensive, providing early identification with the target location, and giving a pragmatic test of the merit of that location before it makes a long-term financial commitment.

New churches have erected lower cost metal buildings and used a brick front to give the appearance of a more permanent facility. At times this plan involves bricking the entire structure and turning it into a permanent facility. Some urban areas, however, restrict these temporary facilities.

Fourth, some churches have erected a multi-purpose building that converts from worship center to gymnasium and back. The facility can, therefore, serve both for worship and for a family life center. In time, this building becomes a family life center and the church provides a worship facility. Other churches have built an educational building with facilities for worship and used this space for both worship and education. Later, when a worship center becomes a reality, the educational building continues to be employed for educational uses.

Many churches have suffered because they attempt to provide permanent buildings too soon, or the excessive cost of these buildings left them with debt that prohibited the church from having funds for programs that relate to people yet were still too limited to satisfy growth needs. Church starters should never allow building costs to either limit the church's ministries or prohibit reproduction.

The sequences suggested above can help the church avoid the crushing responsibility of too much debt too early. Many churches have suffered because they have attempted to provide permanent buildings too soon which left them with debt that prohibited the church from spending on people yet still with facilities too small to satisfy growth needs.

Buildings on Mission Fields

The material we have shared above applies primarily to settings where the resources for purchasing land and constructing buildings are available due to the existence of sufficient church members and their economic potential. In settings where this is not the case, the employment of indigenous methodologies requires that local people utilize the resources that are available to them in obtaining meeting places. This procedure enables the rapid spread of the gospel message without having to depend on the constructions of church buildings with the utilization of external resources. In his instruction manual entitled, Village Church Planting, Bruce Bennett discusses the place of buildings in church planting movement strategies. He states:

> There are benefits in having a church building for the community to come together in and worship the Lord. The building provides protection from the elements; it is an easily recognizable symbol of faith; doubles as a school, clinic, or community hall; in a village a building can become a tool for evangelism; it can provide a shelter for communal activities that a small village hut is unable to; in an area of persecution a building can be a place or refuge and security. Rather let a church be burnt than the home and life of a pastor and his family….Village Church Planting intentionally endeavors to break the misconception that the building is a constituent part of the church organism. We recognize the value of buildings but do not provide funds or advice on how to build them. We do not allow the construction of shelters to impede the rate at which church planting takes place. We always commend the community for the erection and dedication of an indigenous structure in which they can come together and worship God. We have seen that 95% of all the initiated churches have erected an indigenous structure in which they come together for their worship meetings. Church members voluntarily contribute the land, building materials, and labor to erect the shelters. Village chiefs have often ceded land to the church when they recognize tangible benefits of the church in their community. We will encourage the

erection of suitable church training centers in strategic regions to facilitate the planting of daughter
churches and training pastors.[375]

While serving as a member of a research team of the International Mission Board in the assessment of a church planting
movement among the Kekchi people group in Guatemala, I
was impressed by the fact that every city and village we visited
had at least one church building where Evangelical believers
gathered for worship. Some of these were built with concrete
blocks while others with wood from the forest that surrounds
them. As I interviewed church members I enquired how they
were able to get the resources to construct their buildings.
Several of the interviews told me:

> When we came to know the Lord and learned about
> tithing in our discipleship meetings we started to
> gather the money that was coming in. We then
> bought a calf and when that calf grew and had a
> calf, we sold the cow and bought the land. When
> the calf we kept grew and had a calf, we sold the
> cow and bought the materials for our building. Then
> when this happened again, we bought land so that
> our pastor can plant corn and help support his fam-
> ily.[376]

It was interesting to note that at first, the new congregations
constructed their building with the lumber that was available
from the forest. Later, as the congregation grew larger and became financially stronger, they replaced the wooden structures
with concrete block buildings. Most of the labor was provided
by the church members and other people from the community.
The fact that they depended on local resources was borne out
by the response they gave to the question about outside funding. 8.9 percent (17 of 190) said "yes" they do get some kind
of help from time to time. This 8.9 percent included medical
assistance, training assistance, and volunteer help in construction type projects. 91.1 percent (173 of 190) said "no" they do
not get any kind of financial help at any time from the outside.
Jim Slack, the leader of our research team stated:

> The Kekchi look to the Lord and to their congrega-
> tions for leaders and for finances for extending the
> church among the lost. The Kekchi have become
> some of the most resourceful people in the world in

finding ways to provide for their evangelism, their training and the buildings that house their missions and churches... Attention should be given to the Kekchi concerning the historical tendencies for well-meaning Baptists and other evangelicals and para-church agencies from the outside who will likely hear of this CPM and who will come to "assist them" in ways that will rob them of their CPM foundations.[377]

Conclusion

The acquisition of church buildings can be a tremendous blessing for the new congregation. The new building can give the congregation a sense of stability and permanence. It can make a statement to the ministry focus group that the church is there to stay. A permanent building can also help the congregation to do some long-range planning knowing that it will have the building space that the new programs require.

When the right people are consulted and the right decisions are made, the acquisition of a building can provide additional momentum for the new congregation and help it to impact its community with the message of the Gospel. A church, however, should be realistic about its financial strength and make the decisions that enable it to continue to grow over against incurring such heavy indebtedness that its future is placed in jeopardy. Church planting efforts on the mission field are most helpful it they are carried out with local resources and under local leadership.

One factor that we have discussed is a pastor who has dedicated himself to the task of helping the church to grow (this Includes his personality, leadership style, the way in which he utilizes his time, and longevity in the pastorate). A second factor in the growing church, the utilization of the laity in the activities that contribute to growth, includes discovering and utilizing their gifts. Other factors for growing churches call for a balance between the expressions of the life of the church (cell, congregation, celebration), a dynamic worship service (that pays attention to the setting, the purpose, the treatment of the visitors, the announcements, the duration, the music, the preaching, and the invitation), an adequate structure for the various churches (small, medium, large), and a plan for growth (with definite goals and specific action plans).

Undoubtedly, there are other factors that contribute to the continuing growth of churches. Some of these are unique factors in certain sociocultural contexts. To find these unique factors in growth, local studies that consider the circumstances of that context are needed.

Growing churches study the factors that contribute to growth carefully. As they do this, they can concentrate their efforts and resources on the activities that help them to reach new people with the Gospel, to incorporate them in the life of the church, to help them to mature spiritually, and to guide them to be instruments that contribute to the continuous process of reproduction.

CHAPTER 25

A GROWING CONGREGATION

After a church has been established, one of the most challenging tasks is to lead the congregation to continuing growth. Many avenues are open to help the church achieve this goal of continuing growth in both numbers and health. This chapter is a brief and certainly incomplete discussion of this vital subject.

Methods Leading to Continuous Growth

Church growth is solely the result of the Holy Spirit's action. The Spirit works, however, through various strategies, circumstances, and methods. We review some of these strategies and methods that can assist in the development of a congregation.

Focus on Healthy Church Growth

Recent trends underline the need for healthy growth.[378] Concerning the importance of adding healthy to the concept of church growth, Ebbie Smith has written:

> All growth is not healthy. Malignancy and obesity are growth but not healthy growth. Is it not possible that some of what we have termed growth, while it did involve increase, has not actually been healthy either for the local church or for the cause of Christ in general? In order to be totally satisfied with any Church or any congregation we must look closely at numerical growth and be certain that the "growth" is not happening to the detriment of health.[379]

In order to start a church with the capacity for healthy growth, church starters will pay close attention to embedding into the nature of the congregations certain values and goals that pave the way toward healthy growth. The congregations will be started in such ways as to allow the development of what Stephen Macchia records as the 10 Characteristics of Healthy churches.[380] The important matter is starting churches in which such characteristics as unearthed by Macchia can naturally develop and will not in any way be impeded.

One important matter in looking toward healthy church growth relates to the types of growth sought by the congregation. Donald A. McGavran stressed the need to grow by conversion growth (winning the unchurched to Christ and the church) rather than just depending on transfer growth (members coming from other congregations) and biological growth (growth by winning children of members). The new church must be taught to concentrate evangelism on the unchurched and unsaved populations.

Also, healthy church growth demands attention on three different levels of Growth. Churches should grow bigger by adding members, primarily through conversion growth. The healthy church should also increase by becoming better, that is, move forward in its abilities to function as a Christian church. The third level of growth in healthy churches relates to growing broader, that is becoming more able to serve in missions and service ministries to others.

The church starter should pay close attention to healthy church growth and build into the new congregation the values and characteristics that allow the new congregation to grow in healthy ways.

Organizational Structure

Another factor that is important to continuing church growth calls for focusing attention on the organizational structure of the new congregation. Churches of different sizes and ages require different types of organizations. Smaller congregations need a simple structure. As the congregation moves from a small to a medium church, to a large church, it must adapt its structure to facilitate growth.[381]

The important matter about the structure of the various churches is that the structures fit the nature of the congregations and the members of the congregation. Some smaller congregations may have members who desire and need a more sophisticated structure than other smaller churches. Church planters will fit is the primary word for the structures of growing congregations.

Expressions of the Church

Another factor that contributes to the continuing growth of the church is balance in the different expressions of the life of the church. Some church growth experts have divided the expressions of the life of the church into the following categories: (1) cell, (2) congregation, (3) celebration.[382]

Cell

The cell can be described as a small group of people that have close relationships. Because they know each other well, the people in this group share their problems, their triumphs, and their aspirations. They pray for one another, visit one another, and encourage one another. Cells can operate inside and outside the church.

Cells within the church

Cells within the church are of vital importance. If people that join the church as members are not integrated into one of the cells, generally their participation in the activities of the church will be very limited.[383] Their participation in cells helps them feel that they are an integral part of the church. Cells within the church have at least three functions: (1) nurture, (2) instruction, and (3) reproduction.

Cells outside of the church

In addition to the cells that are very important inside the church, other cells function effectively outside the church. These cells can have two purposes: (1) strengthen the spiritual life of church, and (2) evangelize those who have not received Jesus Christ.

These cells, as we have mentioned in the previous chapter, can be Bible studies in homes, prayer meetings in homes, ministries to the community, etc. Cells serve as bridges so that people can get to know evangelical Christians and hear the Gospel message. Recent literature stresses the importance of cell group methods in continuing outreach.

Congregation

A vital expression of the life of the church is the congregation. Sometimes people have the idea that the church is composed of only one congregation. The truth of the matter is that churches (except for the very small ones with approximately15 people) have several congregations.

These congregations are the fellowship and service groups in the church. In many churches the departments (compound of several Sunday school classes) are congregations. The churches that make provision for this type of expression in the life of the church grow because the members feel part of a group that has similar experiences, interests, and lifestyles.

Celebration

Celebration is the worship experience of the church. In the celebration, the entire church gathers to worship God through songs, the reading of the Word, the offering, prayers, the preaching of the word, the celebration of the ordinances, etc.

In celebration there is an awareness that God is in the midst of His people who desire to worship in spirit and truth. In the celebration there is thanksgiving, repentance, petition, intercession, and dedication. In celebration, fellowship with God and with fellow believers is experienced simultaneously.

Church Growth Plans

Growing churches have well defined growth plans. In many cases, churches that are plateaued have pastors and members that concentrate all their attention on maintenance and nurture activities. These activities are important. The church that emphases maintenance will often become a self-centered organization, concerned about survival. Growing churches, on the other hand, direct their efforts to the activities that contribute to their growth. This includes setting growth goals and designing plans to reach them..

Setting Growth Goals

Setting goals is one of the most important activities of the church. A congregation without clear goals is usually a congregation that is satisfied with how things are. Schaller admonishes: "Any organization that does not have tangible, highly visible, definable, and measurable goals, directs its attention toward the maintenance of the institution as their first concern."[384] These goals should be wise. Gerber adds that goals "should be set with prayer, should be set with faith, and they should be realistic."[385]

Goals are declarations of faith in what we are willing to trust God to accomplish through us during a specific period of time. Goals should be sufficiently large so that the members are inspired to work to reach them. Goals, however, should not be so high that the members will be discouraged from the beginning.

It is very important also that the goals are measurable. This is the only way that one will know how much progress has been made toward accomplishing them. For example, if the goal is to "have a church that is better," how will we know when it has been reached? On the other hand if the goal is to evangelize and baptize 50 people next year, at the end of the year we will know how much progress we have made toward reaching it. Members need to see these goals so frequently that they never lose their vision and focus.

Designing Plans for Growth

After the church has set goals, it is necessary to design action plans for each one of them. The goals in themselves will not help the church grow. One can set very adequate and challenging goals. In order for these to be reached, the goals must include direction as to how the goals will be reached, what period of time will these activities be carried out, who will be) responsible for carrying out this activity, and how much money will be set aside for this activity.

Before leaving the topic of the establishment of goals it is necessary to make a brief comment about the contextualization of this process. Many people are accustomed to planning for the future. For others setting goals is "getting ahead of the Holy Spirit."
Church starters should lay a foundation for setting and designing growth goals in the congregation.

Adapting Church Growth Plans Socioculturally

In the process of developing church growth plans, it is wise to take the socio-economic level of the congregation into account. Some socio-cultural groups are accustomed to participating in long range plans in their places of employment as well as church. Some sociologists like Oscar Lewis assert that lower socioeconomic groups, regardless of their country of residence, have certain characteristics in common.[386] He calls these characteristics "the culture of the poverty." One of these characteristics is that they do not plan for the future. Due to their poverty they do not know if they will have resources for the following day. They only live from one day to the other. For this reason they are not accustomed to planning aggressively for the future.

It is necessary to keep two things in mind. If the members of the church are of this socioeconomic level, it is very likely that they feel a certain resistance toward making plans for the future simply because they are not accustomed to doing this in their daily lives. This mind-set can also be found in a congregation that has suffered persecution and socioeconomic marginalization. In these cases members are not accustomed to planning for the future of the church.

Pastoral Leadership

Church leaders have long realized that pastoral leadership stands as one of the most important keys in the growth of churches. The authors of this book believe that a recent study of growing Hispanic churches in Texas by Daniel Sanchez and Ebbie Smith of the Scarborough Institute for Church Growth at Southwestern Baptist Theological Seminary can contribute to the understanding of how to help a new church continue to grow.

The survey of Hispanic churches in Texas confirmed this principle in the rapidly growing Hispanic congregations. The remainder of this chapter is based on this survey that revealed that in growing congregations, the pastors have the following characteristics.

A Vision for Growth

Invariably, these Hispanic pastors gave evidence of a clear vision for the growth of the church and a willingness to pay the price for realizing this growth. The pastors' visions are clearly recognized and expressed throughout the church membership. It is imperative that the pastor's vision has been shared with the congregation and adopted by the people.

All of the pastors wanted their churches to continue to grow and were convinced that they would grow with the Lord's help. These convictions of optimism and vision were clearly stated by the pastors. One pastor stated: "We don't want to be important, but we want to have a Christian influence in our city and our state." Vision established, expressed, and shared was almost universally evidenced by the pastors of these growing churches. Pastoral vision is requisite for continuing growth in every church.

Willing to Exercise Leadership

The pastors of these growing churches shared their basic conviction that *it is the pastor's responsibility to provide strong leadership in order for the church to reach its full potential*. They see aggressive, servant leadership as the divinely intended method for leading churches. They selected "very strong and direct" over "by persuasion" or "simply following the will of the church" as their view of pastoral leadership.

These pastors do not see themselves as being autocratic and dictatorial. Instead, they see themselves as motivators. Once they have received a vision, they concentrate on communicating it to the membership, and challenging the people to become a part of this vision.

While holding to the necessity of strong pastoral leadership, these pastors insist that the church's lay leaders be involved in the decision-making process. They believe this shared leadership strategy to be the primary pattern of pastoral leadership.

Continuing growth in the new congregation only becomes a reality when the pastors are willing to assume and exercise leadership. The pastors will at the same time bring the church members into a shared leadership in which these lay workers can participate fully in both the vision and the service.

Long-Term Commitment

All of the pastors indicated that they had made a commitment to stay with the church for an extended time. They stated their commitment to stay in their churches saying: "until the Lord says," "this is the only church I plan to pastor," "until the

Lord comes," "I have no plans elsewhere." None of the pastors interviewed saw their present church as a stepping-stone for moving to larger churches.

Pastors who desire to lead their congregations in continuing growth patterns will need to commit to longer pastorates. Growth seems to go hand-in-hand with pastoral continuity. If your church is to continue to grow, you will need to commit to a long pastorate.

Managerial Skills

Another quality that was evident in these Hispanic pastors of the congregations studied was their ability to manage the work of the church. While some of them had received studies in leadership methods in connection with their theological training, most of them developed their managerial skills in connection with their secular jobs. Some have extensive experience in military service, others in the business world, and still others through individual study and personal experience.

Pastors desiring to experience continuing church growth should seek to understand and develop these managerial skills. These skills can be honed in various conferences and classes. The skills become most sharpened, however, when learned on the job. Managerial skill enhancement can be received from the secular world but will be used of the Holy Spirit as the pastor understands and uses the skills for getting the job done.

Willingness to Take Risks

In the Hispanic pastor's surveys, most of the men indicated that they were willing to take either moderate or major risks in seeking to carry out the work of the church. In the interviews with these pastors, it became evident that these pastors did not take risks for the sake of doing it. Instead, they sought the leadership of the Lord and then were willing to venture out in faith to do what they felt the Lord wanted their church to accomplish.

Some spoke of responding to risks related to their own personal lives such as quitting a part-time job and dedicating their full time to the work of the church even when it was not completely clear that the finances for their support would be available. Other risks involved leading their congregations to adopt seemingly unattainable plans for outreach and growth. Still other risks involved changing the structure and programs of the church in order to become more effective.

These risks can involve a willingness to change the style of worship or to merge with another church to strengthen the ministry of both congregations. Other risks may involve plans for buildings and other needed equipment. This willingness to venture out in faith stimulates the growth of these congregations.

Continuing church growth depends on leaders who are willing to take risks, not for the sake of the risk-taking but for the sake of the desire for growing churches. While seeking to be sensible and careful, leaders of continually growing churches will meet the needs for risk-taking.

Positive Response to Change

A second factor in the growth of these ten churches indicates that these churches have positive responses to change. Instead of feeling threatened by the social, economic, and political changes that surround them or spending all of their time trying to hold on to "the way we used to do things," these churches have found ways to accept the challenge of change and design approaches to them reach and disciple people in new ways. Changes to which these churches have responded are those of changing from surviving to thriving and from mono-cultural to multi-cultural.

Change: From Surviving to Thriving

Many Hispanics have climbed from the lower rungs of the economic ladder. Some have experienced the Great Depression. These and other experiences have caused some Hispanics to develop a survival mind-set. Some carry this survival attitude to the church. If their church building is paid for or within reach, they resist plans to assume the risk of branching out and enlarging their building, building another one, or moving to another geographical location.

Pastors who are able to challenge and guide their people to move from a surviving to a thriving mentality usually experience significant growth in the congregations. Achieving this paradigm change is, however, a major challenge. Churches that are growing, therefore, are those that have a mindset (a vision) of what the Lord wants them to do in their communities and are willing to live in this faith dimension.

As these congregations and their leaders make the necessary commitments, sacrifices, and changes to turn their vision into reality, the growth reality emerges. The same spirit is necessary for any church leader who desires to see the congregation continue to grow.

Change to Multi-cultural

All of the churches studied are aware of the sociological changes that are taking place within the Hispanic community and demonstrated a willingness to make the necessary changes to reach as many segments of this community as possible. Interviews with the pastors and church leaders revealed that these churches understand that Hispanics are now found in several stages of assimilation.

The different stages of cultural assimilation at which people find themselves and the linguistic capabilities of the pastor (and the staff) are factors that have to be taken into account in determining the approach that a particular church needs to take. The most important factor, however, is that *the pastor and the members of the church need to be committed to the fact that the primary purpose of the church is to communicate the Gospel and not to preserve the culture.* In most instances culture is an instrument for the communication of the Gospel, but churches that refuse to make changes in order to reach the various segments of the Hispanic community (especially the young people) end up being one-generation churches. In other words, these churches lose their young people.

Pastors who desire to lead their churches to continuing growth must adapt this principle to their congregations. Today's world is a multi-cultural world. Focusing on only one cultural group or sub-group will not reach the entire population.

Continuing church growth demands that pastors and churches develop plans for reaching the entire populations. Sometimes this plan will involve new services and new approaches. Sometimes it can be attained by simply reworking existing approaches. Moving from a mono-cultural to a multi-cultural vision helps churches continue to grow.

Dynamic Worship Services

A third factor in the growth of these Hispanic churches relates to the worship services involving the entire persons of the members. While significant variety exists in the format of the growing churches, one common denominator remained. *The worship services involved the total persons of members*. This is seen in the fact that these worship services are culturally relevant and leaned toward being innovative instead of traditional.

Culturally Relevant Worship Service

A factor that appears to be constant is that the services in these churches engaged the total personality of the worshipers. The services demonstrate a strong cognitive element (focusing on content) and the format is well planned. Attention is given to Bible reading and the sermons convey biblical concepts clearly.

At the same time there is a deep emotional quality in their singing, preaching, testimonies, prayers, and fellowship. In other words, people in these churches cultivate a strong sense of the presence of the Lord in the worship service and express it in a way that people feel comfortable.

Churches continue to grow as the worship services remain relevant to the lives of the members. The entire service should relate to actual problems and issues the people face every day. Well produced and presented drama can help address this need for relevance. To help your church grow, seek to make your worship services more relevant to the people.

Innovative Worship

The worship in these all these growing churches was innovative but was not all of one kind. In general the worship services took on a decided Hispanic nature that might not fit many Anglo churches. This innovation is, however, exactly the point. Worship in growing churches tends to reflect the culture of the people and does not simply conform to some traditional pattern. The nature of the worship in these growing congregations is seen in their music, instruments, praise teams, and preaching.

Music

Significant variety existed in the music in the churches. The format ranged from moderately blended (which utilizes hymns as well as choruses) to significantly innovative (which utilizes mainly choruses). One of the surprises that the survey team encountered was that the music was not necessarily typically Latin (or Mexican). While some of the songs that were sung did have a Latin flavor, by and large most of the songs (especially the choruses) were of the contemporary praise type

Instruments

In keeping with the utilization of praise music, more than half of the churches studied utilized guitars, drums, keyboards, and other instruments in addition to the piano and the organ. The volume of the music was not excessively loud as in the case of some churches. The utilization of additional instruments seems to contribute to the involvement of the people in the worship service. In most instances there was a joyful, celebrative mood during the worship service.

Praise Teams

The majority of the churches studied did not have a choir but rather used a praise team that assisted the Music Director. These praise teams usually consist of 4 to 8 persons who stand with the music leader and sing the congregational songs as well as the special music. As was true of the instruments, the praise team seemed to contribute to a greater degree of involvement on the part of the congregation.

Preaching

A wide variety of preaching styles can be found in the growing churches. Some pastors utilized an expository (verse by verse) approach to preaching. Most of them, however, utilized a more topical approach. In most cases, however, the sermons focused on the needs of the people. This was evident not only in the application of the biblical material but also in the illustrations that were used. The *sermons had a redemptive, positive note.*

Instead of focusing on what people have done wrong or how bad things are, these sermons focused on the positive ways in which people can live their Christian lives, achieve effectiveness in their work, and make a contribution to the work of the Lord. In other words, people were encouraged and inspired to keep growing in their Christian faith. One member explained, "The authoritative Word of God is being preached in a clear manner and we are being nurtured by it."

The pastor who desires to lead his church to continuing growth guides his congregation to dynamic worship. If the traditional worship methods provide this dynamic meeting with God, the pastor would be unwise to change it. If the present patterns of worship are not dynamic, that is, if the people do not leave feeling they have been in the presence of almighty God, then perhaps a change is needed. Continuing church growth depends on dynamic worship.

Perennial Programs of Evangelism

A fourth factor in the activities of these growing churches relates to sustained programs of evangelism. Even though the methods varied extensively, they had one thing in common: *The members are trained and utilized in a consistent program of evangelism.* In other words, there is a commitment to be involved in evangelism on the part of both the *pastor* and the *members.*

These growing churches engage directly in personal evangelism. All of the churches did have sustained programs of personal evangelism. These congregations use door-to-door witnessing. Friendship (relational) evangelism are at least as important in the congregations. Ministry evangelism likewise is a major part of the evangelistic efforts of these growing congregations. Ministry evangelism takes many forms. One church, for example, has a group of women on call to prepare meals for people who have lost loved ones. Other ministries include a food pantry, a clothing closet, and referrals to helping agencies. One church has a well-developed food distribution program for people who live in the immediate neighborhood of the church building.

Evangelism cannot be left to chance in continually growing churches. The church that hopes to keep on growing of necessity must place evangelism by both pastor and people in a place of highest priority. A perennial program of evangelism is a must for a growing church.

These growing churches promoted not only perennial programs of personal evangelism but also utilized various forms of public evangelism. The programs included cultivative events and revival meetings. Many of the churches utilize cultivative events as a form of public evangelism. These cultivative events feature dramas, musical presentations, and social gatherings. These churches also utilize the major Christian celebrations as outreach events. Celebrations related to Christmas, Easter, and Thanksgiving are times in which they invite many of their friends and neighbors.

Other churches also utilize some of the cultural events as a means of outreach. Special celebrations such as the 15th birthday of the young ladies are times in which family and friends are invited. One church does a banquet for all of the graduating Hispanic students in their city. These are seen as excellent outreach opportunities.

Some churches utilize recreational events such as baseball, football, and volleyball to get acquainted with new people. The pastor of one church states: "We have men that really care and are willing to serve as coaches. They spend time with the kids and young people and share the Gospel with them."

The majority of the churches also utilized revival meetings more as a time of harvest than a time for seed sowing. In other words, these churches utilize their cultivative events to establish friendships and sow the seed of the Gospel. By the time friends and neighbors are invited to a revival meeting they have already had an opportunity to hear a Christian testimony and perhaps a Gospel presentation.

An important factor in the evangelistic efforts of these churches relates to the persons evangelized. The survey team found that close to 30 percent (29.85%) of the members said their current church was their only church experience. Some 27.16 percent came from other Baptist churches and 42.98 percent had converted from another denomination. Of the members who converted, 58.87 percent were previously Catholic. This fact reinforces the idea that evangelistic efforts among our Roman Catholic friends should be emphasized.

Growing churches need to promote evangelism in every way

that is effective in their areas. These evangelistic efforts should seek every group of people in the area. Churches that continue to grow learn to find ways to witness to every group. This witness may take them out of their comfort zones but they will press on to find and implement these approaches. New approaches may be necessary for reaching some groups, but growing churches will be ready and willing to adjust to these new methods.

Provision for Small Groups

A fifth factor in the growth of these churches involves provision for small group ministries. A significant number of the churches in this survey have in one way or another promoted the use of small groups. These are groups that meet not only during Sunday school or church training but also during the week in the communities where the members live. Small groups are proving a definite factor in continuing church growth.

Small groups can be employed in evangelism and in discipleship. Small group methods continue to be important to churches as they attempt to continue a pattern of growth. Whether used for direct evangelism, for discipleship, or for training, small group approaches have become a notable part of the efforts of many growing churches. The church that desires to achieve continuing growth should seriously consider small group methodologies.

Assimilation of New Members

A sixth factor in the growth of these ten churches includes plans to welcome guests and assimilate new members. The congregations give a great deal of attention to guests from among the unchurched that attend services in these congregations. In addition to having a special place for guests' parking and greeting them in the services, members go out of their way to greet guests and encourage them to return.

In addition to making guests welcome, these churches make an effort to incorporate the newcomers into the life of the church. Some do it through the New Converts' class, others through one-on-one discipleship, still others through home-cell groups. The important thing is that they take an interest in making sure that newcomers become a part of at least one of the fellowship groups of the church. This involves not just receiving them into the fellowship of the church but finding a place of ministry for them as soon as possible.

The effectiveness of ministries to greet visitors and to disciple new people is supported by a study done by Patrick Chaffered which indicates growing churches invite strangers, make strangers feel welcome, and find ways to include outsiders in the activities of the church. He explains that churches cannot include strangers unless they recognize that the church is not their private family property "but God's house, where God is the host and we are all strangers together."[387]

Obviously, continuing church growth rests partially on the church having a strong program of attracting and incorporating new people. Churches that hope for continuing growth should develop ways and means to make guests feel comfortable and help new converts progress in their Christian lives and services. "Closing the back door" constitutes a major way to achieve continuing church growth.

A Clear Discipleship Plan

These growing churches demonstrate a strong emphasis on discipleship. One church utilizes Sunday school and church training for discipleship. They supplement existing Sunday School and Church Training quarterlies with special materials such as *Experiencing God* and *Parenting by Grace.* The strong commitment to discipleship is carried out through one-on-one discipleship, discipleship in home-cell groups, and discipleship through mid-week Bible studies.

Yet another discipleship method that is being used is that of putting new members to work immediately under the guidance of a mature Christian. A layperson commented: "It is amazing how quickly people learn when they have an opportunity to be involved in a ministry of the church." One thing was evident in the discipleship efforts of these growing churches. *They did not simply depend on an outside source to supply their discipleship materials. They determined what the needs were and set out to get the training and the materials to start an effective discipleship program.*

A clear and consistent program of discipleship helps a church maintain its record of growth. New members must be trained;

older members must be maintained. Growth and discipleship will move together.

A Workable Approach to Church Governance

The growing churches demonstrate a workable approach to church planning, organization, and governance. The study revealed some variation in the way these churches are governed. This was evident in leadership styles, organization, and frequency of business meetings.

Leadership Style

In the surveys, as well as in the interviews, it became very evident that the members of these growing churches were very convinced that *the pastor needs to provide strong leadership if the church is going to grow*. At first sight it might appear as though this meant that these pastors utilized an autocratic leadership style, but this was not necessarily the case. All of the pastors involve a group of leaders in the church (deacons, church council, or other) in developing the vision for growth and in implementing it through their participation in the various ministries of the church.

It was evident in the interviews of the church leaders that they had a *high degree of confidence in the pastor's leadership abilities*. This confidence is the result of the way in which the pastors related to the people and the manner in which they have led them. The deacons in one church told us: "There is nothing we would not do for our pastor. Another way of saying this is that *the pastors of these churches have been able to communicate their vision for growth and have involved the leadership in developing a sense of ownership of this vision and a commitment to implementing it in their communities, for the glory of God*.

Business Meetings

Several things became evident as a result of this study. *These churches have found a way of avoiding over attention to maintenance details of church governance and have focused on the activities that will help them to grow.* Patrick Chaffered points out that in non-growing churches, 35-40 percent of the time is given to governance and mediating structures while growing churches give only 10 to 20 percent of their programs to "mediating structures," that is, to committees and business meetings.[388] This was seen in several ways.

The majority of these churches have a quarterly, not a monthly, business meeting. While they keep the church members informed at all times, the pastors of these churches believe that it is too time consuming and distracting to dedicate an entire mid-week service every month to a business meeting attended by a small minority of the members of the congregation. One pastor commented, "We have such a great task discipling our people that we do not want to spend an excessive amount of time on minute details and short-term reports."

Many of these pastors meet and plan with the Church Council on a monthly basis. The Church Council, in turn, reports to the church in regular quarterly business meetings. A few of these churches have only an annual business meeting in which they give detailed reports to the church and seek a vote of confidence from the church for the following year. It appears that these churches do not focus on how all of the individual organizations are doing on a monthly basis. Instead, their focus is on their overall goals and how the organizations are contributing to the attainment of these goals.

When it comes to describing the organization of these churches, it can be stated that they are more centered on ministry than on administration. The deacons and the church council members are viewed as ministers and not as administrators.

A growing church must have a well-designed organizational life that cares for the internal matters of the church without interrupting the flow of ministry and evangelism. Churches that seek continuing growth will streamline their organization and spend less of their valuable time and energy caring for maintenance. The focus of a growing church should be on the unchurched and the spiritual development of the members.

A Vibrant Prayer Ministry

Most of the growing churches have a vibrant prayer ministry. They hold prayer meetings in homes during the week in addition to the regular prayer meeting at the church on Wednesdays. Many churches utilize prayer partners. "People pray every day." One of the churches opens its doors for prayer every morning and many members stop to pray on their way to work.

In order to enhance their prayer ministry and discipleship, several of the churches surveyed are using studies such as "*Experiencing God*" (*Mi Experiencia Con Dios*), "*Master Life*" (*El Plan Maestro*), and other materials that are helping their people to have a closer walk with the Lord.

Prayer is an indispensable part of any church that intends to keep on growing. No amount of planning or programs can take the place of prayer. Prayer speaks to the inner need of both believers and the congregations. To grow, constantly expanding churches must include a constantly enlarging prayer ministry.

Adequate Facilities

These growing congregations have ventured out in faith and have obtained, or look toward, facilities that will enable them to grow. Some have inherited buildings from other churches, bought used buildings, built their own, or in one instance, merged with an Anglo church. Somehow they have found a way to obtain adequate facilities.

A related factor is that the church buildings are easily accessible to the majority of the members. The study of the travel time shows that many of these church buildings are in locations that are easily accessible. Churches that continue to grow provide facilities that are adequate for their ministries, accessible to their people, and near the communities they desire to serve.

Commitment to Stewardship

The churches studied in this survey have secured a high degree of commitment from their members in the area of giving. Some use denominational programs while others do not. The main factor is that the members have developed a deep sense of responsibility in this area.

The giving on the part of the members appears to be directly tied with three things: (1) Their understanding of biblical principles for stewardship; (2) An understanding of and commitment to the goals that the church is trying to reach; and (3) A profound sense of confidence in the ministry and leadership of the pastor. Several pastors described instances in which the members provided large sums of money needed for specific activities. Stewardship is a necessity for a growing church.

Conclusion

Key factors contribute to the continuing growth of any church. Apostolic church starting seeks to start churches that will develop into growing and reproducing congregations. The means to achieve this continually growing congregation lies in the implementation of the factors for continuing growth as described in this chapter.

Undoubtedly, there are other factors that contribute to the continuing growth of churches. Some of these are unique factors in certain sociocultural contexts. To find these unique factors in growth, local studies that consider the circumstances of that context are needed.

Growing churches study the factors that contribute to growth carefully. As they do this, they can concentrate their efforts and resources on the activities that help them to reach new people with the Gospel, to incorporate them in the life of the church, to help them to mature spiritually, and to guide them to be instruments that contribute to the continuous process of reproduction.

PART 6

Reproduce New Congregations

The ultimate goal of 21st century church starting involves the characteristic of reproduction. In fact, any movement that fails to incorporate both the vision and the mechanisms for reproducibility cannot earn the title, "21st century church starting." To be viable for the 21st century, church starting efforts must have at their very centers the quality of reproducibility. This quality is what Mike Berg and Paul Pretiz call the quality or being "inherently expansionist."1 The question about any church planting effort must not be simply, "how large has this congregation (or Church) become?,"[389] but rather, "can this movement be infinitely reproducible?"

CHAPTER 26
KEYS TO REPRODUCTION

Church starting efforts do not just happen; they are intentional. New **congregations** come into being because someone receives a specific vision, develops a viable plan, and engages in a definite effort. Certain definite keys relate directly to these intentional efforts for starting new churches. These keys that contribute to reproducible church starting involve three factors—personnel, models, and strategies. Any church starting effort that hopes to reach effectiveness and result in **unlimited reproduction** must have personnel, models, and strategies that support and allow the starting of reproducible and reproducing churches.

Reproducible Church Starting Personnel

Enlisting and training personnel who can and will start churches that can and will reproduce constitutes a key factor in reproducing church starting. In fact, it might be said that achieving an ongoing church starting movement begins with this enlistment of personnel who will support and implement a movement to start reproducing congregations.

This study has emphasized the general spirit of church starters who start reproducible churches and also several types of church starters who function in slightly different ways to begin new congregations. To ensure reproducibility each type of church starter must first have developed in him/her the quality of apostolic temperament and also recognize and accept the goal of reproducibility. The effort to assure reproducibility is slightly different for each type of church starter.

Apostolic Temperament

Whatever type of approach the church starter employs, an apostolic temperament constitutes an absolutely essential quality. By apostolic temperament we mean that the church starter receives from the Holy Spirit a definite conviction of the imperative of new churches and a driving commitment to these new congregations. Further, this temperament drives the church starter to envision reaching all the peoples of the communities and the world. This temperament focuses the vision of the church starter on those outside the churches—on the unchurched.

No one church is an end in itself for those with apostolic temperament. The spirit of these church starters sees every church as an important step, but only a step, toward the greater goal of more new congregations. Samuel D. Faircloth in his book, *Church Planting for Reproduction*, contends that church starters should never be satisfied with "the mere birth of an infant congregation." He continues that church starters start churches that will "enthusiastically engage in planting other new churches."[390] The ultimate goal is all people in all communities, in all people groups, in the entire world.

Church starters with the apostolic temperament, then, seek to start churches that can and will reproduce. These church starters see a church that does not engage in reproduction in some way as an incomplete venture until reproduction becomes central in its vision. Every church starter should diligently seek from God's Spirit this apostolic temperament.

Starter – Developer

Readers will remember that the church starter-developer is one who feels called to a given community and is determined to remain in the community and do everything that it takes to start *and* develop a church there. This type of person must possess church starting as well as pastoral skills and be able to utilize them to start a church and to lead it to develop its full potential.

For the church starter-developer who has an apostolic temperament and who fits into a reproducible pattern, the vision does not end there. The church starter can never be satisfied with starting just the one congregation. The vision and goal of this church starter must go beyond developing the one congregation into one large church. The church starting vision of the church starter-developer who can fit into a reproducible pattern guides this new church to a vision to start other congregations that in turn are expected to reproduce themselves.[391]

The apostolic church starter must guide the church to look

beyond the one congregation to starting many congregations and to accomplish this church-multiplication ministry soon after the first church is started. The plan for such ongoing church starting must be part of the church starter-developer from the beginning. This church starter-developer will never, by teaching or example, give the idea that this one congregation is the ultimate or only goal. Only the church starter who incorporates this multiplication vision can facilitate a reproducible movement.

Starter – Initiator

A second type of church starter, the church starter-initiator, possesses the gifts that relate primarily to the area of church starting. This person generally has not received the vision or honed the skills to develop a congregation once it has been started. He might even become bored once the exciting initial phase is over and not fit into the process of development and administration. The uniqueness of the church starter-initiator lies in the gifts and abilities of this person to start new **congregations**.

Instead of fretting over the fact that this type of church starter does not possess church development gifts, the strategy should be to maximize the church starting gifts and then enable the worker to go to another field and repeat the process. Due to the fact that many people do not possess church starting gifts, those who sponsor church starting efforts should design specialized strategies and support systems to enable church starter-initiator types to continue their ministries of church starting.

Even though this approach may imply that the church starter starts just one church at a time, the commitment to reproduction can and should be built into each of the churches. The church starter-initiator should build into the DNA of the foundation of the congregation the vision and possibility of reproducing by sharing the passion for new congregations in the church that is started.

Starter – Multiplier

The church starter-multiplier works from the goal of going to an area where there are few or no churches and utilizing local leaders to start new congregations. This plan may involve starting an initial congregation and developing the leaders that emerge so that they can participate in starting new congregations. In other instances in which there are already believers in the area, the task of the starter multiplier may be that of discovering local leaders and training them to start new churches.

Even though a variety of methods may be employed, the main idea is that, in this model, church starters consider themselves multipliers over against starting a single congregation or several in succession as indicated in the two pioneer models mentioned above.

The church starter-multiplier fits directly into the concept of reproducible church starting movements. This person must possess the skills and vision to see the entire region and commit to reaching the people in the area through starting new congregations. He must have keen abilities in motivating and training others in church starting activities. He must be able to plan and share his plan with others.

Starter – Strategist

The church starter-strategist of necessity possesses viable experience in church starting. This person utilizes his skills and experience to work with a church, a group of churches, or an organization in developing and implementing a church-starting strategy, usually for a region. This work may involve doing the initial demographic and psychographic analyses of the target areas and people groups, gathering potential sponsors, sharing the information, gaining a commitment from them, enlisting and training church starters, and assisting them in the implementation of the reproducible church starting strategy.

Church starter-strategists must possess gifts of leadership and abilities in training. They must be motivators. The strategist serves as a catalyst in helping people to capture a vision of the church planning opportunities and enlisting the necessary resources to accomplish the task. This type of apostolic church starter fits perfectly the mold of one who can accomplish reproducing and reproducible church starting.

Reproducible Church Starting Models

In addition to personnel who possess the gifts and vision for reproducible church starting movements, any such endeavor must work through reproducible church starting models. All of the church starting models discussed in chapter 5 can be, and should be, designed from their inception to ensure that reproduction can and will take place. This design for an ongoing movement must, however, be intentional. The following models are especially suited for achieving reproducible church starting.

Key Church Model

The reader will remember from chapter 5 that the Key Church Model involves a well-established church and the state organization (convention) joining their resources to start new congregations.[392] The Minister of Missions leads the church to project various types of mission work in the community including ministries and evangelistic efforts. Many of these efforts will result in either church-type missions, satellite congregations, Bible Study groups, or other direct mission undertakings.

This approach starts many congregations in multi-housing areas, rest homes, and other places where churches usually do not serve. The model should seek to start some congregations that will become reproducing groups. Though these groups may be small and often not traditional, the congregations and Bible Study groups should seek to start other groups that also reach people for Christ.[393]

Obviously, reproducibility is written into the basic nature of the Key Church model of church starting. The important matter for key-church ministries would be to help each of the new congregations develop the spirit that desires to see other new congregations. Although many of the new congregations started by key-church ministries will be small and limited, they should be brought into the church starting mindset. The congregations that come into being through the key-church ministries should be taught from the beginning that they too can start other such efforts in other apartment areas or needy places. Reproduction should be written into these congregations as in all others.

Leadership Training Model

The leadership-training model, the reader will remember, reaches the goal of multiplying a network of cell groups through theological education and evangelism by extension. Designed by Honduran missionary George Peterson, this model strives for "the voluntary multiplication of a church of any size, by God's power, in daughter churches of cells that in turn start granddaughters and so forth."[394] This program integrates church starting with discipleship.

The leadership training model has at its heart those characteristics that allow for teaching and modeling the concept of reproducibility. The church starter who works through this model or some modification of this model must keep reproducibility at the forefront. As churches and training centers are established, the leader constantly seeks reproduction of these groups. Even in the Theological Education by Extension the leaders emphasize the concept of reproducing groups.

Church Starting Movement Model

God is using the Church Starting Movement Model in mighty ways in many different parts of the world. The reader will remember that David Garrison defines a church starting movement as "a rapid and exponential increase of indigenous churches starting churches within a given people group or population segment."[395] Two principle characteristics clearly exist in the model. First, the Holy Spirit plays a prominent role in calling the church starters, directing their work, and providing harvest. In most cases, the leaders are not able to keep up with the number of new congregations that are being started.

The second salient feature of this model is that the church starting leaders have the vision and employ the methodology that contributes toward the continuation of the church starting movement. These movements fulfill the Great Commission and make disciples of all peoples by providing for the unlimited reaching of disciples who will then reproduce by reaching others and the unlimited multiplication of local churches that will start other congregations.[396] The church starting movement model provides perfectly for the constant reproduction of new churches. In fact, this multiplication of churches lies at the heart of the model.[397]

The Church Starting Movement Model provides one of the better avenues for starting reproducing congregations. The concept of reproduction rests at the heart of the strategy. Those who engage in this strategy should make certain that reproducibility is maintained throughout the efforts.[398]

Reproducible Church Starting Strategies

In addition to church starting personnel and church starting models that provide for reproducibility, efforts to achieve reproducing church growth must be built on reproducible church starting strategies. Starting churches that can and will reproduce by starting still other congregations follows the basic strategy of effective Christian advance in every age. In biblical perspective, obviously starting churches that reproduced occupied a major place in world evangelism. Today, the Holy Spirit continues to utilize this strategy to spark church starting movements in many parts of the world.

Building Reproduction into the DNA of the New Church

An indispensable part of the strategy of a reproducible church start relates to building into the new church's vision of itself the quality of reproducibility. This quality and conviction must become a part of the genetic makeup of the strategy from its inception. Tom Steffen points out in *Passing the Baton,* the importance of having a clear picture of the desired outcome at the very outset of the church starting endeavor. This clearly stated vision must become integral to the overall blue print for the entire church starting effort.

The strategies for church starting, then, demand attention, from the very beginning to the incorporation of the goal of reproducibility. By building in this reproducibility concept from the beginning, the church starter can ensure that the new church will see its nature as being that of starting still other new congregations. Everything in the strategy will point in the direction of helping the new church perceive and center on this responsibility of reproducing. Charles Brock accurately says that "if the church planter is fully aware of the need for 'thinking reproducible' in everything done, he will more likely plant a church capable of reproduction."[399]

Following a Viable Process

One of the better strategies for communicating and implementing the reproducible church starting mentality calls for following a viable process in the entire effort. Samuel Faircloth suggests one such viable process as part of a reproducible church starting strategy. Faircloth's process uses insights from PERT (Program Evaluation and Review Techniques) planning and MOR (Management by Objectives and Results).[400] Without reproducing the excellent suggestions from Faircloth's presentation, we can point church starters toward the concept of having definite, observable goals and working toward the goals. The technique involves beginning with the final goal and working back to ensure every step is reached to provide a foundation for those that will follow until the final goal is attained.

The primary point in the process is that of seeing reproduction by the new congregation as the goal of the effort. Deliberate planning to help the new congregation recognize and accept the responsibility for starting new churches lies at the heart of Faircloth's process. Faircloth correctly observes that only if the church has a plan and constantly monitors its attainment of each part of the plan is this church likely to reach the goal of reproducing.[401]

Andy Anderson developed the plan for Sunday School Growth known as the growth spiral. In this plan, Anderson suggested that to build a strong Sunday School, one had to set up the final goal as to size and function and then make certain that as the particular entity grew, it continued to plan to provide the needed teachers, materials, and space for the expanding organization.[402]

Anderson adapted the same idea for starting new churches. This plan involved adopting a goal for a new church by understanding the size of congregation that would be able to thrive in the target cultural group. Having recognized this critical size, Anderson suggests that the church starter begin a number of Bible Study groups, perhaps with leaders from existing churches. When these groups progress to having enough followers to answer the need of the new church in the area, the people from all the Bible Studies can be brought together to be the core group for the new congregation. The important point is that there be a process and the church starting team follows the process.[403]

Another strategy for church starting involves a process clearly outlined and followed in this book. This process calls for guiding the sponsoring church or entity, the church starting team, the core group, and the new congregation through the process from the initial planning to the reproducing church. This process involves leading everyone involved in the effort through the six basic phases: Preparation, Formulation, Cultivation, Implementation, Development, and Reproduction. At every step, the concept of reproducibility must be included and its possibility maintained.

In the preparation phase, the church starter will employ the exercises provided in the Workbook to prepare himself/herself for the task. Secondly, those initiating the church starting effort will help the sponsoring church, the church starting team, the core group, and the new congregation to build a strong motivational, biblical, spiritual, evangelistic, leadership and financial foundation. Utilizing the materials in this book and the exercises provided in the Workbook, all who are a part of this church starting effort can go through a similar process as that which the church starter has experienced. This plan allows the entire church starting team to operate from a common base and common strategy.

By going through the formulation phase, the church starter will be able to help the team cultivate their vision, clarify church starting relationships, assess their leadership characteristics, determine their role, and identify the target group on which they are going to focus. If there is an existing church out of which the new church will be started, the vision can be communicated through a variety of ways including preaching, teaching, prayer walks, and outreach activities.

Leading the church starting team through the cultivative phase can enable them to be actively involved in enlisting a core group and reaching the community through the media, cultivative events, and contextualized evangelism. In the instances in which a church has already been established, the option exists of enlisting a core group from the church, training them, and involving them in outreach efforts. Care needs to be given to the matter of helping the new congregations to properly identify with their target communities.

One of the most exciting aspects of church starting is the implementation phase. This effort involves such activities as finding a meeting place, choosing an appropriate name, beginning small group meetings, establishing an assimilation process, beginning pre-public worship services, and starting public worship services.

The development phase of the new congregation involves such things as constituting the church and securing permanent facilities. Depending upon the church starting model that is utilized, the manner in which the church is constituted and the meeting place that is secured will vary. The goal of leading these congregations to become autonomous needs to be instilled in the leaders and ingrained in the planning from the very beginning.

The reproductive phase focuses on church-growth principles, church-growth structures, and church-growth possibilities, from the perspective of church reproduction. Reproduction needs to be an integral part of all of the church starting plans and activities described in this book and this chapter. Leading the church to grow is an absolutely essential part of the church starting endeavor. As the church grows, its potential for starting churches and additional congregations increase. It is important, therefore, that the congregation view church starting as a part of its development and reproducing processes.

Again, the important factor is a plan that the church starting team can follow. The process integral to this plan will help the church starter be certain that he/she meets all the necessities for the new church. A clearly outlined and followed process helps keep the church starting effort on course.

The Strategy of Local Resources

Still another factor in any strategy demands that the church starting team rely on local resources of customs, personnel, and finances. While some outside help can be useful in the beginning, the wise church starting effort takes care never to provide equipment or finances that the new church cannot provide for the congregations it may start. Garrison contends that calling on people to abandon their valued ethnic identities and move to a different culture in order to become believers inhibits any genuine church starting movement.

Garrison further declares that using subsidy, which so easily creates dependency, can block genuine growth toward development of the new congregations. Garrison concludes saying, "When well-intentioned outsiders prop up growth by purchasing buildings or subsidizing pastors' salaries, they limit the capacity of the movement to reproduce itself spontaneously and indigenously."[404] This insight from Garrison concerning using local resources is one of the more important teachings for reproducing church growth.

The Strategy of Withdrawal

The strategy for implementing a continuously expanding church starting movement includes as an essential part a plan for the church starter to withdraw and allow local leaders to assume leadership. This withdrawal does not mean leaving the new church on its own with no further contact or influence from the church starter. David Garrison suggests the MAWL pattern—model, assist, watch, & leave. He teaches that the period of transferring responsibility is critical for church starting efforts.[405] This same concept is central to Tom Steffen's approach in *Passing the Baton*. He contends that a smooth hand over of the leadership of the church is essential for continued and healthy growth.[406]

What is true for the church starter is also essential for the sponsoring church (or organization), the core group, and others involved in the new church. The goal is a congregation that can stand on its own feet, provide for its own ministry, and reproduce itself in other new congregations. Every effort at church starting should build into the strategies a viable and definite withdrawal of the church starter and or the sponsoring church.

Summary

Starting churches that reproduce by starting still new congregations obviously has been critical in every period— the biblical, historical, and today. The person or group desiring to see continuous outreach to the lost and unchurched should follow these examples and seek to start churches which by their very natures (their DNA, if you please) will continue the movement by starting other churches. The method of starting reproducing churches must continue if the Christian movement is to have its "God-intended" expansion. The goal of the church planter is that of bringing responsible, reproducing believers into responsible, reproducing churches.

Conclusion

Following Timothy Starr, we must say that if ever the world has needed new churches this is the hour! Starr declares that the time has come to rise up and start churches across our continent and in the rest of the world as well. No question remains as to our authority to perform this task. None can question the validity and effectiveness of the method of reproducible church starting. It was used by the apostles and continues to be employed today. Starting reproducible and reproducing churches reaches every strata of society—resulting in congregations in the slums, in middle class areas, in the suburbs, and in affluent communities.[407]

To meet the needs of our world we must start and develop congregations that reach their own people and then provide for other groups as well. The only feasible approach to this gigantic task is that of starting multitudes of churches that will multiply by themselves and start other churches. Reproducibility must, therefore, be foremost in the minds and hearts of church starters and those who sponsor them. From the beginning, reproducibility must be written into the hearts and minds of church starting personnel, be evident in the models they use, and be central to the strategies they employ.

Endnotes

[1] George G. Hunter, *How To Reach Secular People* (Nashville: Abingdon Press, 1992), 35.

[2] George G. Hunter, *Church For The Unchurched* (Nashville: Abingdon Press, 1996), 22.

[3] Loren B. Mead, *The Once And Future Church* (New York: Alban Institute, 1991), 13-22. In the Christendom Paradigm, which began with the conversion of Emperor Constantine (313 A.D.) and grew progressively as Christianity became the official religion of Europe, the separation between the world and the church disappeared. The law removed the hostility from the environment but also made the environment and the church identical. This resulted in unity of the sacred and the secular; the perception of mission as a "far off enterprise;" the identification of the church with the parish; the drive for administrative, theological, and political uniformity; the inheritance of church membership through birth; and the identification of Christian responsibility with unqualified support of the Empire.

[4] C. Peter Wagner, unpublished paper, 5.

[5] Diogenes Allen, *Christian Belief In A Postmodern World* (Louisville: Westminster/John Knox Press, 1989).

[6] Leith Anderson, *A Church For The 21st Century* (Minneapolis: Bethany House Publishing, 1992), 19.

[7] Wagner, op. cit., 6.

[8] Alan C. Klass, *In Search of the Unchurched* (Alban Institute, 1996), 2.

[9] Bjork contends that there is a sense in which many in Europe never abandoned animism. See, David E. Bjork, *Unfamiliar Paths* (Pasadena: William Carey Library, 1997).

[10] See, Gailyn Van Rheenen, *Communicating Christ in Animistic Contexts* (Grand Rapids: Baker Book House, 1991).

[11] Loren B. Mead, *The Once And Future Church*, 10

[12] Mead, 11-12

[13] George G. Hunter, *How To Reach Secular People*, 35.

[14] Some of the seminaries are Southwestern Baptist Theological Seminary in Ft Worth, Texas; Southeastern Baptist Theological Seminary in Wake Forest, North Carolina; and Southern Baptist Theological Seminary in Louisville, Kentucky.

[15] Michael Green, *Evangelism in the Early Church* (Grand Rapids: William Eerdmans, 1970), 13-28.

Endnotes Chapter 1

[16] George Eldon Ladd explains it this way: "The Kingdom is God's kingly rule which has two moments: a fulfillment of the Old Testament promises in the historical mission of Jesus and a consummation at the end of the age, inaugurating the Age to Come." *A Theology of the New Testament*. (Grand Rapids: Eerdmans, 1974), 60. James A. Brooks writes: "There are so many references in the New Testament to both the present and future aspects of God's reign that both must be embraced in any theology that is truly biblical." James A. Brooks, "The Kingdom of God in the New Testament." *Southwestern Journal of Theology* 40, 2 (Spring 1998): 35.

[17] H. D. Wendland in *The Kingdom of God and History*, edited by H. G. Wood. (Chicago: Willett, Clark & Company, 1938), 188.

[18] Charles Colson with Ellen Santilli Vaughn, *The Body* (Dallas: Word Publishing, 1992), 72.

[19] Bracketed information added. Inagrace T. Diettrich, "A Particular People: Toward a Faithful and Effective Ecclesiology," in *The Church Between Gospel and Culture: The Emerging Mission in North America* (Grand Rapids: Eerdmans, 1996), 367.

[20] Stanley J. Grenz, *Theology for the Community of God* (Grand Rapids: Eerdmans, 2001), 465.

[21] For an insightful comparison see: John R. Hendrick, "Congregations with Missions versus Missionary Congregations," in *The Church Between Gospel and Culture: The Emerging Mission in North America* (Grand Rapids: Eerdmans, 1996), 298-308. The seminal work in this area is: Darrell L. Guder, editor, *Missional Church: A Vision for the Sending of the Church in North America* (Grand Rapids: Eerdmans, 1998).

[22] Lesslie Newbigin, *Foolishness to the Greeks: The Gospel and Western Culture* (Grand Rapids: Eerdmans, 1986), 20.

[23] Gordon Fee, *The First Epistle to the Corinthians*. The New International Commentary on the New Testament (Grand Rapids: Eerdmans, 1987), 426.

[24] F. F. Bruce, *The Acts of the Apostles: Greek Text with Introduction and Commentary*, third revised and enlarged edition (Grand Rapids: Eerdmans, 1990), 55.

[25] Kirk Hadaway. "New Churches and Church Growth in the Southern Baptist Convention," *The Quarterly Review*. 49, 2, (1989): 44-45.

[26] Lyle E. Schaller, *44 Questions for Church Planters* (Nashville: Abingdon Press, 1991), 50.

[27] See Phil Jones, "An Examination of the Statistical Growth of the Southern Baptist Convention," *Understanding Church Growth and Decline 1950-1978* (New York, NY: The Pilgrim Press, 1979), 351.

[28] C. Peter Wagner, *Church Planting for a Greater Harvest* (Ventura, CA: Regal Books, 1990), 12.

[29] Ibid, 20.

[30] Gene Getz & Joe Wall, *Effective Church Growth Strategies*. Swindoll Leadership Library (Nashville: Word Publishing, 2000), 132-33.

[31] Italicized quotations in this section come from Getz & Wall. Use of the italics may be found in the original source.

[32] Lyle E. Schaller, *44 Questions for Church Planters* (Nashville: Abingdon Press, 1992), 29-30.

[33] Wagner, 11.

End Notes Chapter 2

[34] Ed Stetzer, *Planting Missional Churches* (Nashville: TN: Broadman & Holman Publishers, 2006), 14.

[35] Alexander Rattray Hay, *The New Testament Order for Church and Missionary*, (Auburn, NJ: New Testament Missionary Union, 1947, 53.

[36] Ken Hemphill, *The Antioch Effect: 8 Characteristics of Highly Effective Churches* (Nashville, TN: Broadman & Holman, 1994).

[37] John Polhill, *The American Commentary*: Acts, volume 26, Nashville: Broadman Press, 1992, 211.

[38] Martin Hengel, Anna Maria Schwemerer, *Paul Between Damascus and Antioch: The Unknown Years*, London: SMC Press, 1997, 179-80, 218.

[39] John Polhill, *The American Commentary*: Acts, volume 26, Nashville: Broadman Press, 1992, 273.

[40] Ibid., 289.

[41] William Barclay, *The Acts of the Apostles*, Philadelphia: Westminster Press, 1955, 98.

[42]. Campbell Morgan, cited in Hay, op. cit., p. 63.

[43] For a more extensive discussion of this see Roger S. Greenway, *Apostles to the City* (Grand Rapids, MI: Baker Book House, 1978), 87-95.

[44] David Hesselgrave, *Planting Churches Cross-Culturally* (Grand Rapids, MI: Baker Book House, 1980).

[45] For Southern Baptists: "A New Testament church of the Lord Jesus Christ is... an autonomous local congregation of baptized believers, associated by covenant

in the faith and fellowship of the gospel; observing the two ordinances of Christ, governed by His laws, exercising gifts, rights, and privileges invested in them by His word, and seeking to extend the gospel to the ends of the earth." June 14, 2000, www.sbc.net/bfm.

End Notes Chapter 3

[46]For a more extensive discussion on the subject see: Herbert J. Kane, *Christian Missions in Biblical Persprective* (Grand Rapids: Baker Book House, 1976), 125-26.

[47] Niel Cole, Cultivating a Life for God, Carol Stream, IL: ChurchSmart Resources, 1999, 9.

[48] Craig Van Gelder, *The Ministry of the Missional Church* (Grand Rapids: Baker Books, 2007), 19

[3] Albert von Ostertag, *Uebersichtliche Geshiehte der protesttische Missionen von der Reformation bis aur Gegenwart* (Stuttgart, 1858), 4.

[50]

[51] Nate Krupp, *God's Simple Plan for His Church—and Your Place in it* (Woodburn, Oregon: Solid Rock Books, 1993), 74-75.

[52] Roland Allen, *Missionary Methods: St. Paul's or Ours?* (Grand Rapids: Wm. B. Eerdmans, 1979), 15-17.

[53] Joe Hernandez, Spiritual Dynamics of a Rapid Multiplication of Churches, unpublished power point

[53] Craig presentation, North American Mission Board, October, 2004.

[54] Dallas Willard, *The Spirit Of The Disciplines* (New York: Harper Collins Publishers, 1988), 158.

[55] Daniel R. Sanchez, Ebbie Smith, *Starting Reproducing Congregations* (Fort Worth, TX: Church Starting Network, 2010)

[56] Clinton Arnold, *Three Crucial Questions About Spiritual Warfare* (Grand Rapids: Baker Book House, 1997), 19.

[57] Ebbie C. Smith, *Spiritual Warfare for 21st Century Christians* (Ft. Worth, Texas: Church Starting Network, 2005), 23.

[58] C. S. Lewis, *The Screwtape Letters* (New York: The Macmillan Co., 1959), 3

[59] Ibid., 33.

[60] Logan points this out in Robert E. Logan, Steven L Ogne, *The Church Planter's Tool Kit*.

[61] Thomas Wade Akins, *Pioneer Evangelism* (Rio de Janeiro: Brazilian Baptist Convention, 1995), 50-56.

[62] Avery Willis, *Master Life I, Discipleship Training* (Nashville: The Sunday School Board, 1982), 168-173. Ibid., 21.

[63] Foundations for Church Planting, North American Mission Board power point presentation.

[64] Dan R. Crawford, *Connecting With God* (Fort Worth, Texas: Scripta Publishing, 1994), 6.

[65] Logan, *Ministry Toolkit*, 2-6.

Endnotes Chapter 4

66 For a more complete discussion of this point, see, Daniel R. Sanchez, *Iglesia: Crecimiento y Cultura* (Nashville: Convention Press, 1993), 21-56.

67 For further discussion of this concept, see Michael Green, *Evangelism in the Early Church* (Grand Rapids, MI: William Eerdmans Publishing Co., 1970), 194-207.

68 Ibid., 207-208.

69 Donald A. McGavran, *Understanding Church Growth* (Grand Rapids: Eerdmans Publishing Co., 1970), 217.

70 Michael Green, Evangelism in the Early Church, 216-18.

71 Daniel R. Sanchez, Hispanic Realities Impacting America: Implications for Evangelism & Missions (Ft. Worth: Church Starting Network, 2006), 38.

72 E. Edgardo Silvoso, "In Rosario it was different — crusade converts are in churches," Evangelical Missions Quarterly, 14, No. 2 (April 1978): 83-88.

73 For an analysis of church starting as a follow up to a Billy Graham Crusade see: M. Rodney Webb, Church Planting as a Method of Assimilating New Converts from the Tampa Bay Area Billy Graham Crusade, D.Min./Missiology project, Trinity Evangelical Divinity School, 2001.

74 Malcolm R. Bradshaw, Church Growth through Evangelism in Depth (South Pasadena: William Carey Library, 1969).

75 Ralph Neighbor states that in the United States only five percent are in this category. Ralph Neighbor, Target Group Evangelism: Reaching People Where They Are (Nashville, TN: Broadman Press, 1975), 18. In some countries the percentage may even be smaller while in others it might be much greater.

76 See Carlos Mraida, La Iglesia en las Casas: Manual Para Círculos Familiares (The Church in Homes: Manual For Family Cell Groups) (Buenos Aires, Argentina: Asociación Bautista Argentina De Publicaciones, 1988).

77 Elmer L. Towns, "Evangelism: The Why And How," in Church Growth State of the Art, ed., C. Peter Wagner (Wheaton, IL: Tyndale House Publishers, 1986).

78 Lyle Schaller, Assimilating New Members (Nashville: Abingdon Press, 1978), 76.

79 W. Charles Arn, Master Plan for Making Disciples (Pasadena, CA: Church Growth Press, 1982).

80 W. Oscar Thompson, Concentric Circles of Concern (Nashville, TN: Broadman Press, 1981), 21.

81 Daniel R. Sánchez and Rudolph D. González, Sharing the Good News With Roman Catholic Friends (Ft. Worth: Church Starting Network, 2003).

Endnotes Chapter 5

82 Robert E. Logan and Steve L. Ogne, The Church Planter's Tool Kit (Alta Loma: CRM, 1991), 14-15; Paul R. Orjala, Get Ready to Grow (Kansas City: Beacon Hill, 1978), 108-115; John N. Vaughn, The Large Church (Grand Rapids: Baker Book House, 1985), 100-106.

83 See J.V. Thomas, Investing In Eternity: Indigenous Satellite Church Strategy (Dallas: J. V. Thomas, 1991).

84 Tim Ahlen and J.V. Thomas, One Church, Many Congregations (Nashville: Abingdon Press, 1990).

85 Harvey Kneisel, New Life for Declining Churches (Houston: Macedonian Call Foundation, 1995).

86 An excellent example of this is the way in which the Lord utilized Rick Warren to start and develop the Saddleback Community Church. See Rick Warren, The Purpose Driven Church (Grand Rapids: Zondervan, 1995).

87 Robert E. Logan and Steve L. Ogne, The Church Planter's Tool Kit , 4-15.

88 Information provided by Minh Ha Nguyen in an unpublished power point presentation: A Vision for Richmond, All Peoples Worshiping God, Infinity Initiative.

89 Ibid.

90 Ibid.

91 Ibid.

92 Ibid.

93 Geoff Surratt, Greg Ligon, and Warren Bird, The Multi-Site Church Revolution (Grand Rapids: Zondervan, 2009), 10.

94 Ibid., While some multi-site churches range from 2 to as many as 400 campuses, the majority of them (85%) have fewer than 3 campuses and 7 worship services.

Endnotes

[95] Warren Bird & Kristin Walters, "Multi-Site is Multiplying," Survey conducted by Leadership, 2010, 17.

[96] Warren Bird & Kristin Walters, "Multi-Site is Multiplying," Survey conducted by Leadership, 2010, 2. The authors estimate that there are 3,000 multisite churches in the United States.

[97] Ray Oldenburg, *Great Good Place: Cafes, Coffee Shops, Book Stores, Bars, Hair Salons, and Other Hangouts at the Heart of the Community,* 3rd edition (New York: Marlowe and Company, 1999).

[98] Ray Oldenburg cited in Surratt, Ligon, *The Multi-Site Church.*

[99] Ibid., 69.

[100] Warren Bird and Kristin Walters, "Multisite is Multiplying: Survey Identifies Leading Practices and Confirms New Developments in the Movement's Expansion," Leadership Network, 2010, 2.

[101] Ibid., 3.

[102] John Piper cited in Geoff Surratt, Greg Ligon, Warren Bird, *A Multi-site Church Road Trip* (Grand Rapids: Zondervan, 2009), 201.

[103] Ibid., 202.

[104] *A Multi-site Church Road Trip*, 204.

[105] The Leadership Network survey reported that 33% of the multi-site churches added a campus through a merger. Multisite is Multiplying, 5.

[106] , *A Multi-site Church Road Trip,* 206.

[107] The Leadership Network survey indicates that one in four multisites have a campus in another language. Multisite is Multiplying, 3.

[108] Multisite is Multiplying, 5.

[109] Pamphlet, "Texas Key Church Strategy."

[110] See J. Timothy Ahlen and J. V. Thomas, *One Church, Many Congregations: the Key Church Strategy* (Abingdon Press, 1999).

[111] George Patterson and Richard Scoggins, *Church Multiplication Guide* (Pasadena: William Carey Library, 1993), 12.

[112] Ibid., p. 15.

[113] Claylan Coursey, *How Churches Can Start Churches* (Nairobi: Baptist Publishing House, 1984).

[114] Ibid., 14.

[115] Paterson, 7.

[116] Ibid

[117] David Garrison, *Church Planting Movements* (Richmond, VA: International Mission Board of the Southern Baptist Convention, 2000), 7.

[118] Ibid., 2

[119] Ibid., 29-30.

[120] David L. Watson, "Inside a Strategy Coordinator-led Church Planting Movement," unpublished power point presentation.

[121] Lewis Myers, Jim Slack, To The Edge: A Planning Process for People Group Specific Strategy Development, Richmond: International Mission Board, 1998, Section 2, Page 39.

[122] Watson, Op., Cit.

[123] Joe Hernandez, un published Power Point presentation, North American Mission Board, 2004

[124] Ibid. The North American Mission Board also uses the term "Church Planter Multiplier" in a similar fashion.

[125] Ibid.

[126] Ibid.

[127] David Garrison, *Church Planting Movements.*

[128] James B. Slack, "Initiating Church Starting Movements among Peoples on the Frontiers of Lostness," paper presented at the joint meeting of EMS and ISFM, November, 1997.

[129] Ibid. 1

[130] Raymond Fung, *Households of God on China's Soil* (New York: Orbis Books, 1982), x.

[131] Clyde Meador, "Left Side of the Graph," in Church Planting Movements, Mid-America Baptist Theological Seminary Journal of Evangelism and Missions, Volume 6, Spring 2007, 60,60

[132] James Slack, "Church Planting Movement Assessment of the of Guatemala," unpublished article, 2005. The missionaries Slack mentions are Ted & Sue Lindwall – 1964, Dick & Lahoma Greenwood – 1966, and Wendell & Jane Parker – 1971.

[133] Jim Slack has a policy that the correlation level of a given characteristic within an assessed CPM should be at least 75% in order for it to be acknowledged as present in the CPM. Based upon a study of common characteristics with assessed and proven CPMs, Richmond: International Mission Board, SBC 4rd Edition: June 2009.

[134] For an extensive critique of church planting movements see, Church Planting Movements, Mid-America Baptist Theological Seminary Journal of Evangelism and Missions, Volume 6, Spring 2007.

[135] Oscar Romo, "Starting Ethnic Churches," *Missions USA*, (November-December, 1989), 37.

[136] Dr. Romo's article asserts that the 500 ethnic groups in the United States communicate in 636 different languages. Ibid. p. 37

[137] In the United States this includes Native Americans, Hispanic Americans of the Southwestern U.S. and Puerto Rico.

[138] In the United States this includes African Americans.

[139] For a discussion of these types of migration see R. A Schermerhorn, *Comparative Ethnic Relations* (New York: Random House, 1970).

[140] Schermerhorn, ibid.

[141] For a discussion of these types of migration see R. A Schermerhorn, *Comparative Ethnic Relations* (New York: Random House, 1970).

[142] Malcolm McFee, "The 150% Man: The Product Of Blackfeet Acculturation," *American Anthropologist* 70, pp. 1096-1103. McFee's "Two-Culture Matrix Model" employs the terms: "Unacculturated, Bicultural, Marginal, and Acculturated."

[143] Milton M. Gordon, *Assimilation In American Life* (New York: Oxford University Press, 1964)

[144] Greeley presents this assimilation from the perspective of the ethnic group when he describes the various stages as: Nuclear, Fellow Traveler, Marginal, and Alienated Ethnic. Greeley, op. cit., pp. 106-112. Schermerhorn outlines a similar process, the principal difference being that he views it from the perspective of the predominant society.

[145] To illustrate how ethnics might fit into these categories it could be stated that among Hispanics of Mexican ancestry, Total Ethnics have a tendency to call themselves "Mexican;" Median Ethnics may be more comfortable with the term "Mexican American;" Marginal Ethnics may be more prone to refer to themselves as "Americans of Mexican Heritage;" Alienated Ethnics may prefer the term "American;" while Revitalized Ethnics may call themselves "Chicanos." For a discussion of the various terms that Hispanics of Mexican heritage use to refer to themselves see Susan E. Keefe and Amado A. Padilla, *Chicano Ethnicity* (Albuquerque: University of New Mexico Press, 1987).

[146] Exceptions to this are generally found where existing majority culture churches have made some cultural modifications in their organizational and fellowship patterns.
[147] Nineteenth Avenue Church in San Francisco is an example of this.
[148] A helpful instrument for a sociocultural analysis is found in *New Catholic World*, op. cit., p. 143.
[149] Tom A. Steffen, *Passing The Baton* (La Habra: Center for Organizational & Ministry Development, 1993), 81-82.

Endnotes Chapter 6

[150] Donald A. McGavran, "Wrong Strategy: the Real Crisis in Mission," *International Review of Missions* 54 (1965): 451-61.
[151] David Garrison, *Church Planting Movements* (Richmond, VA: International Mission Board of the Southern Baptist Convention, 1999), 8.
[152] C. Peter Wagner, *Churchquake* (Ventura, CA: Regal, 1999), 183.
[153] Keith Eitel, "'To Be or Not to Be?': The Indigenous Church Question," in *Missiology: An Introduction to the Foundations, History, and Strategies of World Missions*, ed. John Mark Terry, Ebbie Smith, and Justice Anderson (Nashville: Broadman & Holman Publishers, 1998), 301.
[154] Joe Hernandez unpublished Power Point Presentation on Indigenous Church Planting, October 2004. For more information see, John L. Nevius, *Planting and Development of Missionary Churches*, The Presbyterian And Reformed Publishing Company, 1958., Charles Brock, *Indigenous Church Planting: A Practical Journey*, Neosho, Missouri: Church Growth International, 1994.
[155] See A. R. Tippet, *Verdict Theology in Mission Theory* (Lincoln, IL: Lincoln Christian College Press, 1969).
[156] See William A. Smalley, "Cultural Implications of an Indigenous Church," *Readings In Dynamic Indigeneity*, ed. Charles H. Kraft & Tom Wisely (Pasadena, CA: William Carey, 1979), 31-51.
[157] Joe Hernandez, unpublished Power Point Presentation on Indigenous Church Planting, October 2004.
[158] Tom Steffen, *Passing the Baton,* 13-20.
[159] Garrison, *Church Planting Movements,* 44.
[160] Steffen, *Passing the Baton*, 214.
[161] Ibid., 215.

Endnotes Chapter 7

[162] Dave Page, *Church Planting Notebook* (Loomis, CA: CPR: Church Planting Resources), 25.
[163] Aubrey Malphurs, *Planting Growing Churches for the 21st Century*, 2d ed. (Grand Rapids: Baker Books, 1992, 1998), 83.
[164] David Fisher, *The 21st Century Pastor* (Grand Rapids: Zondervan, 1996), 204.
[165] Thomas D. Lea and Hayner P. Griffin Jr., *The New American Commentary*, volume 34, *1,2 Timothy, Titus* (Nashville: Broadman Press,1992), 109.
[166] Joseph M. Stowell, *Shepherding the Church: Effective Spiritual Leadership in a Changing Culture* (Chicago: Moody Press, 1994).
[167] See Lea, 113.
[168] Joseph M. Stowell, *Shepherding the Church*, 148.
[169] Stowell, 207.
[170] Malphurs 1998, 71-73.
[171] Stowell, 207.
[172] See Reggie McNeal, 1998, 25.
[173] See Rick Warren, *The Purpose Driven Church* and David Garrison, *Church Planting Movements*.

[174] Claylan Coursey, *How Churches Can Plant Churches* (Nairobi, Kenya: Baptist Publication House, 1984).

[175] Logan, *Beyond Church Growth,* 198.

[176] Mark Terry, *Church Evangelism,* 213.

[177] Charles Brock, *Indigenous Church Planting,* 30.

[178] Tom A. Steffen, *Passing The Baton,* (La Habra: Center for Organizational & Ministry Development, 1993), 174-75.

[179] Charles Brock, *Indigenous Church Planting*, 130-33.

[180] Tom Steffen, *Passing the Baton,* 174.

[181] Ibid., 174.

[182] Garrison, *Church Planting Movements,* 51.

[183] Brock, *Indigenous Church Planting,* 128.

[184] Garrison, *Church Planting Movements,* 51.

[185] Ibid., 51.

[186] Brock, *Indigenous Church Planting,* 130.

[187] Thomas Graham, "How to Select the Best Church Planters," *Evangelical Missions Quarterly* 23 (1): 70-79. Cited in Tom A. Steffen, *Passing The Baton: Church Planting That Empowers* (La Habra: Center for Organizational and Ministry Development, 1993), 40.

[188] Joel Comiskey, *Planting Churches that Reproduce* (Moreno Valley: CA, CCS Publishing, 2009), 74-75.

[189] Charles R. Ridley, *How To Select Church Planters* (Fuller Evangelistic Association, 1988), 7-11.

[190] C. Peter Wagner, *Church Planting For A Greater Harvest* (Ventura: Regal Books, 1990), 52-56.

[191] Tom A. Steffen, *Passing The Baton,* 43-53.

[192] Dr Bill Fudge, an Area Director for the International Mission Board, SBC, has provided some information regarding the use of oral tradition. Fudge explains that Paul did not do "Bible Studies" but used oral traditions on who Jesus was. The Apostle used rote memorization techniques. In Asian contexts, people do not respond well if the emphasis is on sin, but do respond well if the emphasis is on blessing and reciprocity. Bill Fudge, "Church Planting Movements," unpublished paper.

[193] Ibid.

[194] Susan Atkinson, *Explore Pathways to Missions: Self-Assessment*, Richmond: International Mission Board, 2004, 7-20.

[195] Aubrey Malphurs, *Planting Growing Churches for the 21st Century,* 78.

[196] William Moulton Marson, Emotions of Normal People, New York: Harcourt, Brace and Company, 1928, 87-285.

[197] While he described other emotions (e.g., appetite, love, etc.) the ones mentioned above are the ones on which many writers have focused.

[198] Among these are John G. Greer and Dorothy Downey's, *Personal Profile System* and Robert R. Rohm, *Positive Personality Profiles.*

[199] Brent Ray, unpublished power point presentation.

[200] Ibid.

[201] Ibid.

[202] Brent Ray, unpublished power point presentation.

[203] Robert R. Rohm, *Positive Personality Profiles*, Atlanta, Georgia: Personality Insights Incorporated, 1998, 29-38.

[204] Ibid., 32.

[205] Ibid., 48-50.

[206] Ibid., 56, 57.

[207] Ibid., 69-76.

[208] Ibid., 91-97.

[209] Ibid., 20.

[210] The Explore Pathways to Missions workbooks designed by the International Center for Excellence in Leadership, International Mission Board, SBC, has excellent self-assessment sections that can be of significant help.

Endnotes Chapter 8

[211] David A. Bishop, Power Point Presentation prepared for the International Mission Board. He can be contacted at dab@pobox.com

[212] Ibid.

[213] Ibid.

Endnotes Chapter 9

[214] See, George Barna, *The Power of Vision* (Ventura: Regal Books, 1992).

[215] Ibid., 28.

[216] Ibid., 27.

[217] Dale E. Galloway, *20/20 Vision: How To Create A Successful Church With Lay Pastors And Cell Groups* (Portland: Scott Publishing, 1986), 29.

[218] Galloway, 30.

[219] See, George Barna, *The Power of Vision*

[220] Ibid., 239. For a more extensive discussion of this see Aubrey Malphurs, *Vision for Ministry in the 21st Century* (Grand Rapids: Baker, 1992), 31-39.

[221] Malphurs, *Planting Growing Churches*, 240.

[222] For a more extensive discussion, see Malphurs, *Planting Growing Churches*, 242-244.

[223] Rick Warren, 363.

[224] Aubrey Malphurs, *Ministry Nuts and Bolts* (Grand Rapids: Kregel Publishers, 1997), 63.

[225] These are the mission statements of Matthew Road Baptist Church and Willow Creek Community Church listed in Aubrey Malphurs, *Ministry Nuts and Bolts*, 64-5.

[226] Vision statement of the Southern Baptist Convention Foreign Mission Board adopted February 15, 1995.

[227] Lewis Myers, Jim Slack, *To The Edge: A Planning Process for People Group Specific Strategy Development* (Richmond, VA: International Mission Board of the Southern Baptist Convention, 1999), Section 4, p. 7.

[228] Ibid.

[229] Ibid., Section 4, p. 8

[230] Ibid., pp 8, 9. This is an outline of the steps described by these authors.

[231] Brent Ray, Unpublished Power Points, See, George Barna, *The Power of Vision* (Ventura: Regal Books, 1992

[231] Ibid., 28.

[231] Ibid., 27.

[231] Dale E. Galloway, *20/20 Vision*, 29.

[231] Galloway, 30.

[231] See, George Barna, *The Power of Vision.*

[231] Ibid., 239. For a more extensive discussion of this see Aubrey Malphurs, *Vision for Ministry in the 21st Century* (Grand Rapids: Baker, 1992), 31-39.

[231] Malphurs, *Planting Growing Churches*, 240.

[231] For a more extensive discussion, see Malphurs, *Planting Growing Churches*, 242-244.

[231] Rick Warren, 363.

[231] Aubrey Malphurs, *Ministry Nuts and Bolts* (Grand Rapids: Kregel Publishers, 1997), 63.

[231] Endvisioning, Beginning with the End in Mind."

Endnotes Chapter 10

[232] See A. R. Tippett, *Verdict Theology in Mission Theory* (Lincoln, IL: Lincoln Christian College Press, 1969).

[233] For a discussion on the Missions Committee, see Jack Redford, *Planting New Churches* (Nashville, TN: Broadman Press, 1978), 29-33.

[234] See Don F. Mabry, "What Kind of Sponsoring Church are You?" Louisiana Baptist Convention, Alexandria, Louisiana.

[235] Claylan Coursey, *How Churches Can Start Churches* (Nairobi: Baptist Publishing House, 1984).

[236] Ibid. p. 14

[237] In the U.S. this includes Native Americans, Southwestern U.S. Hispanic Americans, and Puerto Ricans.

[238] In the U. S. this includes African Americans.

[239] For a discussion of these types of migration see R. A. Shermerhorn, *Comparative Ethnic Relations* (New York: Random House, 1970).

[240] Greeley presents this assimilation from the perspective of the ethnic group when he describes the various stages as: nuclear, fellow traveler, marginal, and alienated ethnic. Greeley, op. cit., 106-112. Schermerhorn outlines a similar process, the principal difference being that he views it from the perspective of the predominant society.

[241] David A. Bishop, Unpublished power point presentation. For more information contact him at **dab@pobox.com**

[242] Ibid.

[243] Ibid.

Endnotes Chapter 11

[244] Aubrey Malphurs, *Planting Growing Churches* (Grand Rapids, MI: Baker Books), 248.

[245] Billy Graham, *Just As I Am: The Authorized Biography of Billy Graham* (Harper San Francisco: Zondervan, 1997), 662-63.

[246] Jeff Calloway, "Don't Take The Journey Alone," in John M Bailey, Steve Cantor, and Randy Ferguson, eds., *Ready? Preparing For The Pressure Of Church Planting* (Alpharetta, GA: North American Mission Board, 2009), 53.

[247] Brent Ray, unpublished power point presentation entitled "The Meaning of Teams."

[248] Ibid.

[249] Ibid.

[250] Tom A. Steffen, *Passing The Baton* (La Habra: Center for Organizational & Ministry Development, 1993).

[251] Robert E. Logan & Steve L. Ogne, *The Church Planter's Toolkit* (Alta Loma: CRM New Church Development, 1991), 2-15.

[252] Malphurs, *Planting Growing Churches*, 254.

[253] Lyle E. Schaller, "Southern Baptists Face Two Choices for the Future," *Biblical Recorder* (April 27, 1991): 8.

[254] *Church Planter's Toolkit*, 2-4.

Endnotes Chapter 12

[255] Roland Allen, *Missionary Methods: Saint Paul's or Ours?* (Grand Rapids, MI: Eerdmans, 1962).

[256] We are indebted to Shannon Cunningham, currently a Ph.D. student at Southwestern Baptist Theological Seminary, for researching and compiling the information in this section regarding the excellent sources where information can be attained.

[257] Rick Warren, *Purpose Driven Church*, 170.

[258] James F. Engel, *Contemporary Christian Communications* (New York: Thomas Nelson Publishers, 1979), 207.

Endnotes

[259] David J. Hesselgrave, *Communicating Christ Cross-culturally*, 444-57.

[260] C. Kirk Hadaway, *Church Growth Principles* (Nashville, TN: Broadman Press, 1991), 28-32.

[261] For an excellent discussion on this see, Viggo Sogaard, *Media In Church and Mission* (Pasadena: William Carey, 1993).

[262] Timothy C. Tennent, "Training Missionaries to Resistant Peoples," paper presented at the joint meeting of EMS and ISFM, November 22, 1997, p. 1.

[263] Ibid

[264] Ibid

Endnotes Chapter 13

[265] Steve Sjogren, *Conspiracy of Kindness* (Ann Arbor: Servant Publications, 1993).

[266] Ibid. 215-226.

[267] Lyle E. Schaller, *44 Questions for Church Planters* (Nashville: Abingdon Press, 1991), 86.

Endnotes Chapter 14

[268] Steve Canter, "Engaging Our Communities," in John M Bailey, Steve Cantor, and Randy Ferguson, eds., *Ready? Preparing For The Pressure Of Church Planting* (Alpharetta, GA: North American Mission Board, 2009), 208.

[269] Rochelle B. Warren & Donald L. Warren, *The Neighborhood Organizer's Handbook* (Notre Dame: The University of Notre Dame Press, 1977).

[270] Ibid., 96.

[271] Dawn Dwyer, *TeleReach Manual: Using the Telephone to Reach People* (Nashville: Convention Press, 1989).

[272] Norm Whan, *The Phone's For You!* Available from Church Growth Development International, 420 W. Lambert, Suite E. Brea. CA. 92621 (714-900-9551).

[273] Schaller, *44 Questions*, 92-93.

[274] Ibid., 95-96.

[275] Rick Warren, *The Purpose Driven Church*, 44.

[276] Wagner, *Church Planting for A Greater Harvest,* 106.

[277] For more information see Norman Beckam, "Home Bible Fellowship Campaign," (unpublished paper, 1983).

[278] This list of electronic-based media was provided by Dr. Matthew Queen, Professor of Evangelism, Southwestern Baptist Theological Seminary, 2010.

[279] David Garrison, *Church Planting Movements*, (Richmond, VA: International Mission Board, 2000), 42, 43.

[280] A Strategy Coordinator working in the 10/40 Window. Article provided by the International Mission Board of the Southern Baptist Convention.

[281] Ibid.

[282] Ibid.

[283] Ibid. This process is outlined as an example by the Strategy coordinator.

Endnotes Chapter 15

[284] This is an adaptation of activities discussed in Daniel Sanchez, *Iglesia: Crecimiento y Cultura* (Nashville: Convention Press, 1993), 83.

[285] Steve Sjogren, *Conspiracy of Kindness*, 212-226.

[286] Ibid., 102.

[287] Ibid., 101-126.

[288] This list has been adapted from a list provided by Thad Hamilton in a "Special Evangelistic Events" notebook produced by the Home Mission Board in 1991.

Endnotes Chapter 16

[289] Donald A. McGavran, *Understanding Church Growth* (Grand Rapids: Eerdmans, 1970), 332.

[290] Ebbie C. Smith, *A Comparison of the Socioeconomic Standing of Members of Southern Baptist Churches and the Population of Tarrant County, Texas*, MA. The-

sis, University of Texas at Arlington, 1987.

[291] David T. Bunch, Harvey J. Kneisel, Barbara Oden, *Multi-Housing Congregation* (Atlanta: Home Mission Board, 1993), 4.

[292] Ibid., 5.

[293] Barbara Oden, "Reaching People in Apartment Communities," cited in Bunch, op cit., p. 5.

[294] Bunch, Kneisel, Oden, 2.

[295] For a more complete list see Bunch, p. 84.

[296] Terry Willis, "Characteristics of Multi-Family Housing Residents," In *Strategies For Starting New Churches In Multifamily Housing Communities*, compiled by Carl Elder (Dallas: Baptist General Convention of Texas, 1985).

[297] Bobbie Wash, *The Coordinator's Handbook for Multi-Housing Communities* (Houston: Union Baptist Association, n.d.).

[298] Bunch, Kneisel, Oden, 2.

[299] Ibid., 39.

[300] Adapted from Bunch, 45.

[301] Carl Elder, cited in Bunch. 58.

[302] Joe Guerin and Don Beach, "Strategies For Starting Churches in Multi Housing," in *Strategies For Starting New Churches In Multifamily Housing Communities*, compiled by Carl Elder, 1985.

Endnotes Chapter 17

[303] Rick Warren, *The Purpose Driven Church*, 46.

Endnotes Chapter 18

[304] Wagner, *Church Planting for a Greater Harvest*, 118-19.

Endnotes Chapter 19

[305] Rad Zdero, *The Global House Church Movement* (Pasadena: William Carey Library, 2004), 21, 22.

[306] Ralph Neighbor, unpublished power points.

[307] David W. Shenk and Ervin R. Strutzman, *Creating Communities of the Kingdom: New Testament Models of Church Planting* (Scottsdale, PA: Herald Press, 1988), 94-95.

[308] Chua Wee Han, "Evangelization of Whole Families," in Ralph D. Winter, Steven C. Hawthorne, *Perspectives On The World Christian Movement*, Third Edition (Pasadena: William Carey Library, 1999), 616.

[309] Rad Zdero, The Global House Church Movement, 134.

[310] Lawrence Khong, *The Apostolic Cell Church* (Singapore: Touch Ministries International, 2000), 35.

[311] Ibid. 47 and 31.

[312] Joel Comiskey, *Planting Churches that Reproduce*, (Moreno Valley, CA: 2009), 108-109.

[313] Dale E. Galloway, *20/20 Vision* (Portland, OR: Scott Publishing Col. 1993), 142-45.

[314] C. Kirk Hadaway, Stuart A. Wright, Francis M. Dubose, *Home Cell Groups and House Churches* (Nashville: Broadman Press, 1987), 118, 119.

[315] Ibid., 124.

[316] Bob & Betty Jacks, Ron Wormer, Sr., *Your Home A Lighthouse* (Colorado Springs: NavPress, 1986).

[317] John Faulkner, unpublished paper,

[318] Ralph Neighbor, "Planting Cell Churches," unpublished power point presentation.

[319] Ibid.

[320] Joel Comiskey, *Planting Churches that Reproduce*, 115-136. I recommend a careful reading of this chapter in Comiskey's book to obtain very helpful details on how to accomplish this task.

[321] Ken Hemphill, *Revitalizing The Sunday Morning Dinosaur* (Nashville: Broadman & Holman Publishers, 1996), 87, 88.

[322] Ibid., 88-91.

[323] Arthur Flake, *Building a Standard Sunday School* (Nashville: The Southern Baptist Convention, 1922), 49, 59.

[324] Joel Comiskey, *Planting Churches that Reproduce*, 196.

[325] The Fellowship of Church Planters, *Planting House Churches in Networks, 467 Armistice Boulevard, Pawtucket, Rhode Island 02861, Email Address Farides@AOL.com*

[326] Ibid. 33.

[327] David Garrison, *Church Planting Movements*, Richmond: International Mission Board,

[328] Zdero, op. cit., 4, 5

[329] See, Daniel Gonzalez' "A Profile the Cuban Church", unpublished paper 2008.

[330] Need footnote

[331] Steve Atkerson, ed., *House Church: Simple, Strategic, Scriptural* (Atlanta: The New Testament Reformation Fellowship, 2008), 26.

[332] Zdero, op. cit., 92, 93.

[333] For an extensive discussion on participatory meetings read chapter 3 in Steve Atkerson, *House Church: Simple, Strategic, Scriptural*.

[334] For those with the gift of preaching, this skill will develop with time. Initially, however, new leaders will find it easier to sit in a circle with a group and lead a discussion session.

[335] This is a brief summary of the suggestions made by Rad Zdero, op. cit., 112-114. This is a brief summary of the suggestions made by Rad Zdero, op. cit., 112-114.

[336] David Garrison, *Church Planting Movements*, 34.

[337] Robert Fitts, *The Church in the House*, 2001, 55-60

[338] Rad Zdero, op. cit.

[339] The Fellowship of Church Planters, *Planting House Churches in Networks,* op. cit., 36.

[340] J. D. Payne, *Missional House Churches: Reaching Our Communities with the Gospel* (Colorado Springs: Paternoster, 2007), 8-9.

[341] The Fellowship of Church Planters, *Planting House Churches in Networks,* 8

[342] Ebbie C. Smith, *Basic Churches are Real Churches: Biblical Support for Simple Churches, organic Churches, House Churches, and Congregation that Grow Out of Church Multiplication Movements* (Ft. Worth, TX: Church Starting Network, 2009), 9.

[343] The Fellowship of Church Planters, *Planting House Churches in Networks,* 65.

[344] Lindsay Cofield, Semester Church, Dallas: Baptist General Convention of Texas, nd., 20, 21.

[345] George Hunter, *How to Reach Secular People*, 60-66.

[346] See Thom S. Rainer, *High Expectations: The Remarkable Secret for Keeping People in Your Church* (Nashville, TN: Broadman & Holman Publishers, 1999), 45.

[347] J. D. Payne, *Missional House Churches: Reaching Our Communities with the Gospel* (Colorado Springs: Paternoster, 2007), 85.

Endnotes Chapter 20

[348] Rick Warren, *The Purpose Driven Church*, 144.

[349] Ibid.

[350] Lyle Schaller, *Assimilating New Members* (Nashville: Abingdon Press, 1978); *Growing Plans* (Nashville: Abingdon Press, 1983).

[351] Many of the observations made in this chapter about pre-public worship services can apply to preview services as well.

Endnotes Chapter 21

[352] C. Peter Wagner, *Church Planting for a Greater Harvest,* 119, 120.

[353] Joel Comiskey, *Planting Churches that Reproduce* (Moreno Valley, CA: 2009), 130-31.

[354] Ibid.

[355] Audrey Malphurs, *Planting Growing Churches* (Grand Rapids, MI: Baker Books, 1998), 290.

[356] Lyle E. Schaller, *44 Questions for Church Planters* (Nashville: Abingdon Press, 1991), 66.

[357] Joel Comiskey, *Planting Churches that Reproduce*, 128-29.

Endnotes Chapter 22

[358] For a more extensive discussion of this subject see, Daniel R. Sanchez, *Iglesia: Crecimiento y Cultura* (Nashville, TN: Convention Press, 1993), 139-42, and Rick Warren, *The Purpose Driven Church*.

[359] Kirk Hadaway, *Church Growth Principles* (Nashville, TN: Broadman Press, 1991), 62.

[360] Anne Ortlund, *Up With Worship* (Glendale, Ca: G/L Publications, 1975).

[361] See Hadaway, 82.

Endnotes Chapter 24

[362] See, Robert H. Kilgore, *How Much A Debtor* (Atlanta: Home Mission Board, 1974), 1.

[363] Ibid., 8.

[364] For further discussion, see Kilgore, p. 6

[365] Kilgore, 22.

[366] Kilgore, 22.

[367] Malphurs has an excellent discussion of the advantages and disadvantages of purchasing used versus new buildings. Aubrey Malphurs, *Planting Growing Churches*, 337, 338.

[368] Jack Redford, *Planting New Churches* (Nashville: Broadman Press, 1978), 95.

[369] Kilgore, 12.

[370] See Kilgore, pp. 40-50.

[371] Kilgore, 13

[372] Schaller, *44 Questions*, 142.

[373] Ibid., 142.

[374] Ibid., 142,144.

[375] Bruce Bennett, *Village Church Planting: Planting a Church in Every African Village* (OMS International, Brackenhurst, South Africa), bbennett@omssa.co.za, 26.

[376] Interview conducted by Daniel R. Sanchez, in Guatemala, February, 2005.

[377] Jim Slack, Report on Ketcki Church Planting Movement, February, 2005.

Endnotes Chapter 25

[378] For example, Peter C. Wagner, Your Church Can Be Healthy 1976 (republished in 1996 as The Healthy Church, Regal, 199; Peter L. Steinke, Healthy Congregations: A Systems Approach (Alban Institute, 1996); Christian A. Schwarz, Natural Church Development A Guide to Eight Essential Qualities of Healthy Churches (ChurchSmart Resources, 1998); Stephen A. Macchia, Becoming A Healthy Church: 10 Characteristics (Baker Books, 1999) .

[379] Ebbie C. Smith, *Growing Healthy Churches: New Directions for Church Growth in the 21st Century* (Church Starting Network, 2003), 24-25.

380 Stephen A. Macchia, *Becoming a Healthy Church: 10 Characteristics* (Grand Rapids: Baker Books, 1999).14-16.

381 For a fuller discussion, see Harry H. Fowler, *Breaking Barriers of New Church Growth* (Rocky Mountain, NC: Creative Growth Dynamics, 1988), 27-61; Carl F. George, *Prepare Your Church For the Future* (Terrytown, NY: Revell, 1991); and *How to Break Growth Barriers* (Grand Rapids: Baker Book House, 1993).

382 See Pedro Larson, *Crecimiento de la Iglesia* (El Paso, TX: Casa Bautista de Publicaciones, 1989), 220-21; Peter Wagner, *Your Church Can Grow: Seven Signs of a Healthy Church* (Glendale, CA: Regal Books, 1971), 97-109.

383 See Chaney, *Design for Church Growth*.

384 Lyle Schaller, *Parish Planning* (Nashville, TN: Abingdon Press, 1971), 95.

385 Gerber, 69-70.

386 See Oscar Lewis, *Five Families: Mexican case studies in the culture of poverty* (New York, NY: Basic Books Inc., Publishers, 1959).

387 Patrick Chaffered, Church Innovations Institute, St. Paul MN., cited by Andy Lang in UCC ONE NEWS, Nov. 6, 1995

388 Ibid.

389 Mike Berg and Paul Pretiz. *Spontaneous Combustion: Grass-Roots Christianity, Latin American Style* (Pasadena, CA: William Carey Library, 1996), 63.

Endnotes Chapter 26

390 Samuel D. Faircloth, *Church Planting for Reproduction* (Grand Rapids: Baker Book House, 1991), 34.

391 An excellent example of this is the way in which the Lord utilized Rick Warren to start and develop the Saddleback Community Church. See Rick Warren, *The Purpose Driven Church* (Grand Rapids: Zondervan, 1995).

392 J. Timothy Ahlen and J. V. Thomas, *One Church, Many Congregations: The Key Church Strategy* (Nashville: Abandon Press, 1999).

393 Pamphlet, "Texas Key Church Strategy."

394 George Paterson and Richard Scoggins, *Church Multiplication Guide* (Pasadena: William Carey Library, 1993), 12.

395 Garrison, *Church Planting Movements*, 7.

396 Ebbie C. Smith, *Growing Healthy Churches: New Directions for Church Growth in the 21st Century* (Ft. Worth, TX: Church Starting Network, 2003), 76-78.

397 Ed Stetzer, *Planting Missional Churches* (Nashville, TN: Broadman & Holman Publishers, 2006), 325-33.

398 Garrison, *Church Planting Movements*.

399 Charles Brock, *The Principles and Practice of Indigenous Church Planting* (Nashville: Broadman, 1981), 55-61.

400 Faircloth, 27-35.

401 Ibid., 173-74.

402 Andy Anderson, *The Growth Spiral: The Proven Step-by-Step Method for Calculating and Predicting Growth Potential in Your Church* (Nashville: Broadman & Holman, Publishers, 1993).

403 Andy Anderson, "Using the Growth Spiral to Start New Churches." Video Cassette, Roberts Library, Southwestern Baptist Theological Seminary, Ft. Worth, Texas, 1979.

404 Garrison, 48-51.

405 Ibid, 44.

406 Ibid, 44.

[407] Timothy Starr, *Church Planting Always in Season* (Toronto, Canada: Fellowship of Evangelical Baptist Churches in Canada, 1978),193.

Made in the USA
Charleston, SC
30 August 2015